THE CAPITAL COME UNDER
BOURGEOIS
RULE AND PRESENT SCENARIO OF
POLITICAL
BUSINESS

Threads of Justice

N K S R Nantu Roy   Mr Salween Roy

BLUEROSE PUBLISHERS
India | U.K.

Copyright © N K S R Nantu Roy & Mr Salween Roy 2023

All rights reserved by author. No part of this publication may be reproduced, stored in a retrieval system or transmitted in any form or by any means, electronic, mechanical, photocopying, recording or otherwise, without the prior permission of the author. Although every precaution has been taken to verify the accuracy of the information contained herein, the publisher assumes no responsibility for any errors or omissions. No liability is assumed for damages that may result from the use of information contained within.

BlueRose Publishers takes no responsibility for any damages, losses, or liabilities that may arise from the use or misuse of the information, products, or services provided in this publication.

For permissions requests or inquiries regarding this publication, please contact:

BLUEROSE PUBLISHERS
www.BlueRoseONE.com
info@bluerosepublishers.com
+91 8882 898 898
+4407342408967

ISBN: 978-93-5819-223-0

Cover design: Shivam
Typesetting: Namrata Saini

First Edition: October 2023

Contents

World Political System 1

British India Situation and Society 64

Post Independent India and Development under Nationalist 68

The Capital Come Under Bourgeois and Political Business 187

Indian Trading Business and Commercial Strategy: 297

Saraj Party Activity: Motilal Nehru and C. R. Das 312

Present Scenario of Political Business 409

Ancient Politics and Myth 416

World Political System

Socialism

It is a populist economic and political system based on collective, common, or public ownership of the means of production. Those means of production include the machinery, tools, and factories used to produce goods that aim to directly satisfy human needs. In contrast to Capitalism whereby business owners control the means of production and pay wages to workers to use those means, socialism envisions shared ownership and control among the laboring class.

In a purely socialist system, all production and distribution decisions are made by the collective, directed by a central planner or government body. Worker cooperatives, however, are also a form of socialized production. Socialist systems tend to have robust welfare systems and social safety net so that individuals rely on the state for everything from food to healthcare. The government determines the output and pricing levels of these goods and services.

Socialists contend that shared ownership of resources and central planning provide a more equal distribution of goods and services and a more equitable society.

KEY TAKEAWAYS

Socialism is an economic and political system based on collective ownership of the means of production.

All legal production and distribution decisions are made by the government in a socialist system. The government also determines all output and pricing levels and supplies its citizens with everything from food to healthcare.

Proponents of socialism believe that it leads to a more equal distribution of goods and services and a more equitable society.

Socialist ideals include production for use, rather than for profit; an equitable distribution of wealth and material resources among all people; no more competitive buying and selling in the market; and free access to goods and services.

Capitalism, with its belief in private ownership and the goal to maximize profits, stands in contrast to socialism, but most capitalist economies today have some socialist aspects.

Socialism vs. Communism

Communism and socialism are umbrella terms referring to two left-wing schools of economic thought; both oppose capitalism, but socialism predates the "Communist Manifesto," an 1848 pamphlet by Karl Max and Friedrich Engels by a few decades. These are both economic philosophies that advocate for public ownership, particularly over the means of production and the distribution and exchange of goods in a society. Both philosophies run contrary to free market capitalism, which, they contend, exploits workers and creates a widening gap between rich and poor.

There are differences between socialism and communism, however. In fact, communism can be thought of as a strict and all-encompassing version of socialism. Under communism, all property is communally owned; private property doesn't exist. Under socialism, individuals can still own private property. Karl Marx predicted that a violent worker uprising against the middle and upper classes would bring about the communist state, whereas socialists tend to seek change and reform without overthrowing the prevailing social and political structure. And according to communist theory, workers should be given what they need, while under socialist theory, they are to be compensated for their level of contribution to the economy.

Autocracy

Autocracy is a system of government in which absolute power over a state is concentrated in the hands of one person, whose decisions are subject neither to external legal restraints nor to regularized mechanisms of popular control In earlier times, the term autocrat was coined as a favorable description of a ruler, having some connection to the concept of "lack of conflict of Interest" as well as an indication of grandeur and power. Autocracy is the most common and durable regime type since the emergency of the state.

There are several significant distinctions between closed and elected autocracies, both of which are authoritarian types of governance in which one person or group has total authority.

A closed autocracy is a form of governance whereby all parties except for one official party are prohibited, although political independents who are not overtly anti-regime may occasionally be elected - this elite group faces no accountability from the population, as the population receives no civil liberties. These people may acquire their positions of authority by inheritance, a coup, or other illegitimate methods, with no "choice" over their leader. According to the 2022 V-Dem Democracy Report, there is a growing number of closed autocracies (30 countries as of 2020), that account for 26% of the global population. In order to move a country towards liberal democracy in a closed autocracy, there needs to be an initial semi-liberal autocratic transition phase (unless they become occupied by foreign powers during a war who are willing to democratize).

On the other hand, an elected autocracy is a form of government in which the autocrat gains control through a democratic procedure, such as an election. Once in charge, an autocrat will, however, use their position to expand their authority, restrict the impact of other political figures, and attack democratic institutions like the court and the free press, manipulating contestation to make turnover unlikely or impossible. Although there may be some appearance of democracy under an elected autocracy, in reality the autocrat controls most of the authority and the public has little opportunity to hold them accountable, as with a closed autocracy. This is also referred to as a "hybrid regime that leans more towards the autocratic side". Elected autocracies are still considered to be the most common government structure globally - 44% of the world's population live under this regime. In order to move towards liberal democracy in an elected autocracy, the remaining barriers of illegitimacy and unfairness must be gradually removed.

Hypocrisy

Hypocrisy is the practice of feigning to be what one is not or to believe what one does not. The word "hypocrisy" entered the English language *c.* 1200 with the meaning "the sin of pretending to virtue or goodness".[1] Today, "hypocrisy" often refers to advocating behaviours that one does not practice. However, the term can also refer to other forms of preteens, such as engaging in pious or moral behaviours out of a desire for praise rather than out of genuinely pious or moral motivations.

Political Hypocrisy is "the conscious use of a mask to fool the public and gain political benefit". Hypocrisy has been a subject of folk wisdom that beginnings of human history.

Social psychologists have generally viewed hypocrisy as an instantiation of attitudinal and/or behavioral inconsistency. Accordingly, many social psychologists have focused on the role of dissonance in explaining individuals' aversion to hypocritical thinking and behavior. Individuals are motivated to avoid hypocritical stances in order to forestall the negative drive state of dissonance. For example, a dissonance-based study on the use of condoms among young adults showed that induced hypocrisy can lead to increased purchase and use of condoms. Alternatively, some social psychologists have suggested that individuals view hypocrisy negatively because it suggests that hypocrites are providing a false signal regarding their moral goodness.

Hypocrisy has been an intermittent topic of interest to philosophers since at least Machiavelli. Philosophical issues raised by hypocrisy can be broadly divided into two kinds: metaphysical/conceptual and ethical. Most philosophical commentary on hypocrisy is concerned with the ethical questions it raises: is hypocrisy morally wrong or bad? If it is, is there anything distinctly objectionable about it, or can it be easily subsumed under a broader category of morally objectionable conduct–for example, deceit? Is hypocrisy necessary or desirable for the sake of certain valuable activities– most notably, politics?

Recently, hypocrisy has emerged as a key focus in philosophical discussions of the ethics of blame. It seems that even if a person has violated some moral norm and is genuinely blameworthy for doing so, it is open to them to challenge the blame leveled at them on the grounds that it is hypocritical; a typical expression of this idea is the phrase, "You have no right to blame me!" Accordingly, some philosophers argue that in order to have the standing or entitlement to blame others, one's blame must not be hypocritical. Defenses of this position have usually focused on the connection between hypocrisy and fairness: the basic idea is that the hypocritical blamer in some way fails to treat the target of her blame as a moral equal. Other proposed explanations include the idea that standing in a moral community requires a reciprocal willingness to accept blame, a willingness that hypocrites lack. Patrick Todd argues that all and only those who are committed to the relevant norms possess the standing to blame, and hypocrites lack commitment in the relevant sense. Other philosophers reject the "No-hypocrisy" condition on standing altogether. Typically, these philosophers do not deny that sometimes the wrongness of hypocrisy can outweigh a would-be blamer's entitlement to blame others; but they will insist that this is not invariably the case, and some hypocrites do have standing to blame. R.A. Duff suggests that underlying the disagreement between these two views is a disagreement about the size and scope of moral community, while Kyle Fritz and Daniel Miller suggest that the rejection of the "No-hypocrisy" condition reflects a failure to distinguish between the right to blame and the value of blaming.

Socialism:

As an economic system, fascism is socialism with a capitalist veneer. The word derives from fasces, the Roman symbol of collectivism and power: a tied bundle of rods with a protruding as. In its day (the 1920s and 1930s), fascism was seen as the happy medium between boom-and-bust-prone liberal capitalism, with its alleged class conflict, wasteful competition, and profit-oriented egoism, and revolutionary Marxism, with its violent and socially divisive persecution of the bourgeoisie. Fascism substituted the particularity of nationalism and racialism "blood and soil" for the internationalism of both classical liberalism and Marxism.

Where socialism sought totalitarian control of a society's economic processes through direct state operation of the means of production, fascism sought that control indirectly, through domination of nominally private owners. Where socialism nationalized property explicitly, fascism did so implicitly, by requiring owners to use their property in the "national interest "that is, as the autocratic authority conceived it. (Nevertheless, a few industries were operated by the state.) Where socialism abolished all market relations outright, fascism left the appearance of market relations while planning all economic activities. Where socialism abolished money and prices, fascism controlled the monetary system and set all prices and wages politically. In doing all this, fascism denatured the marketplace. Entrepreneurship was abolished. State ministries, rather than consumers, determined what was produced and under what conditions.

Fascism is to be distinguished from interventionism, or the mixed economy. Interventionism seeks to guide the market process, not eliminate it, as fascism did. Minimum-wage and antitrust laws, though they regulate the Free Market, are a far cry from multi year plans from the Ministry of Economics.

Under fascism, the state, ***through an official*** cartel, controlled all aspects of manufacturing, commerce, finance, and agriculture. Planning boards set product lines, production levels, prices, wages, working conditions, and the size of firms. Licensing was ubiquitous; no economic activity could be undertaken without government permission. Levels of consumption were dictated by the state, and "excess" incomes had to be surrendered as taxes or "loans." The consequent burdening of manufacturers gave advantages to foreign firms wishing to export. But since government policy aimed at autarky, or national self-sufficiency, protection was necessary: imports were barred or strictly controlled, leaving foreign conquest as the only avenue for access to resources unavailable domestically. Fascism was thus incompatible with peace and the international division of labour—hallmarks of liberalism.

Fascism embodied corporatism, in which political representation was based on trade and industry rather than on geography. In this, fascism revealed its roots in syndicalism, a form of socialism originating on the left. The government cartelized firms of the same industry, with representatives of labour and management serving on myriad local, regional, and national boards—subject always to the final authority of the dictator's economic plan. Corporatism was intended to avert unsettling divisions within the nation, such as lockouts and union strikes. The price of such forced "harmony" was the loss of the ability to bargain and move about freely.

To maintain high employment and minimize popular discontent, fascist governments also undertook massive public-works projects financed by steep taxes, borrowing, and fiat money creation. While many of these projects were domestic—roads, buildings, stadiums—the largest project of all was militarism, with huge armies and arms production.

The fascist leaders' antagonism to Communism has been misinterpreted as an affinity for capitalism. In fact, fascists' anticommunism was motivated by a belief that in the collectivist milieu of early-twentieth-century Europe, communism was its closest rival for people's allegiance. As with communism, under fascism, every citizen was regarded as an employee and tenant of the totalitarian, party-dominated state. Consequently, it was the state's prerogative to use force, or the threat of it, to suppress even peaceful opposition.

Nazism

It was frequently referred to as **Hitlerism.** The later related term neo-Nazism" is applied to other far-right groups with similar ideas which formed *after World* war- II.

Nazism is a form of fascism with disdain for liberal democracy and the parliamentary system. It incorporates a Dictatorship fervent antisemitism, anti-communism white *supremacy and the* use of eugenics into its creed. Its originated in pan-Germanism and the ethno-emotionalist neopagan movement which had been a prominent aspect of pure Aryan German ultra-nationalism since the late 19th century, and it was strongly influenced by the Freikorps Paramilitary groups that emerged after Germany's defeat in World war-I, from which came the party's underlying "cult of violence". Nazism *subscribed to theories* of a racialism, identifying Germans as part of what the Nazis regarded as an Arian nomadic master race. It aimed to overcome social divisions and create a homogeneous German society based on racial which represented a people's community. The Nazis aimed to unite all Germans living in historically German territory, as well as gain additional lands for German expansion under the doctrine of lebensraum and exclude those whom they deemed either community alliance.

The term "National Socialism*" arose* out of attempts to create a nationalist redefinition of *socialism*, as an alternative to both Marxist international socialism and free market capitalism. Nazism rejected the Marxist concepts of class conflict and universal equality, opposed cosmopolitan internationalism, and sought to convince all parts of the new German society to subordinate their personal interests, accepting political interests as the main priority of economic *organization*,[which tended to match the general outlook of collectivism rather than economic socialism. The Nazi Party's precursor, the pan-German nationalist and antisemitic, was founded on 5 January 1919. By the early 1920s, the party was renamed the National Socialist German Workers' Party in order to appeal to left-wing workers, a renaming that Hitler initially objected to. The National Socialist Program, or "25 *Points' '*, was adopted in 1920 and called for a united greater Germany that would deny citizenship to Jews or those of Jewish descent, while also supporting land reform *and nationalization*. Hitler outlined the antisemitism and anti-communism at the heart of his political philosophy and his belief in Germany's right to territorial expansion. The Nazi Party won the greatest share of the popular vote in the two Reichstag general elections of 1932, making them the largest party in the legislature by far, albeit still short of an outright majority. Because none of the parties were willing or able to put together a coalition government, Hitler was appointed Chancellor of Germany on 30 January 1933 by President Paul von Hindenburg through the support and connivance of traditional conservative nationalists who believed that they could control him and his party. With the use of emergency presidential decrees by Hindenburg and a change in the Weimer Construction which allowed the Cabinet to rule by direct decree, bypassing both Hindenburg and the Reichstag, the Nazis soon established a *one-party* state.

The Sturmabteilung (SA) and the Schutzstaffel (SS) functioned as the paramilitary *organizations* of the Nazi Party. Using the SS for the task, Hitler purged the party's more socially and economically radical factions in the mid-1934 Night of Long Knives, including the leadership of the SA. After the death of President Hindenburg on 2 August 1934, political power was concentrated in Hitler's hands and he became Germany's head of state as well as the head of the government, "leader and Chancellor of Germany". From that point, Hitler was effectively the dictator of Nazi *Germany in which* Jews, political opponents and other "undesirable" elements were *marginalized,* imprisoned or murdered. During World War - II, many millions of people—including around two-thirds of the Jewish population of Europe—were eventually exterminated in a genocide which became known as Holocausts. Following

Germany's defeat in World War -II and the discovery of the full extent of the Holocaust, Nazi ideology became universally disgraced. It is widely regarded as immoral and evil, with only a few fringe racist groups, usually referred to as neo-Nazis, describing themselves as followers of National Socialism.

Racism

Racism, also called **racialism**, the belief that humans may be divided into separate and exclusive biological entities called "races"; that there is a causal link between inherited physical traits and traits of personality, intellect, morality and behavioral features; and that some race is innately superior to others. The term is also applied to political, economic, or legal institutions and systems that engage in or perpetuate discrimination on the basis of race or otherwise reinforce racial inequalities in wealth and income, education, health care, civil rights, and other areas. Such institutional, structural, or *systematic research became* a particular focus of scholarly investigation in the 1980s with the emergence of critical, an offshoot of the critical legal studies movement. Since the late 20th century the notion of biological race has been recognized as a cultural invention, entirely without scientific basis.

Following Germany's defeat in World War -I, that country's deeply ingrained anti- Semitism was successfully exploited by the Nazi Party, which seized power in 1933 and implemented policies of systematic discrimination, persecution, and eventual mass murder of Jews in Germany and in the territories occupied by the country during World War II.

In North America and apartheid-era South Africa, racism dictated that different races (chiefly blacks and whites) should be segregated from one another; that they should have their own distinct communities and develop their own institutions such as churches, schools, and hospitals; and that it was unnatural for members of different races to marry.

Historically, those who openly professed or practiced racism held that members of low-status races should be limited to low-status jobs and that members of the dominant race should have exclusive access to political power, economic resources, high-status jobs, and unrestricted civil *rights*. The lived experience of racism for members of low-status races includes acts of physical violence, daily insults, and frequent acts and verbal expressions of contempt and disrespect, all of which have profound effects on self-esteem and social relationships.

Racism was at the heart of North American slavery and the colonization and empire-building activities of western Europeans, especially in the 18th century. The idea of race was invented to magnify the differences between people of European origin and those of African descent whose ancestors had been involuntarily enslaved and transported to the Americas. By characterizing Africans and their African American descendants as lesser human beings, the proponents of slavery attempted to justify and maintain the system of exploitation while portraying the United States, democratic institutions, unlimited opportunities, and equality. The contradiction between slavery and the ideology of human equality, accompanying a philosophy of human freedom and dignity, seemed to demand the dehumanization of those enslaved.

Elective Dictatorship

The phrase "**elective dictatorship**" describes the state in which a typical *westminster* system in parliament dominated by the government of the day. It refers to the fact that the legislative programmed of Parliament is determined by the government, and government bills virtually always pass the legislature because of the nature of the majoritarian first past the past electoral system, which almost always produces strong government, in combination with the imposition of party discipline on the governing party's majority, which almost always ensures loyalty.

Theocracy:

The theocracy, government by divine guidance or by officials who are regarded as divinely guided. In many theocracies, government leaders are members of the clergy, and the state's legal system is based on religious law. Theocratic rule was typical of early civilizations. The enlightenment marked the end of theocracy in most Western countries. Contemporary examples of theocracies include Saudi Arabia, Iran, and the Vatican.

The word theocracy comes from the Greek words *theos* ('God, deity') and *kratia* (rule, governance) and can therefore be understood as meaning 'rule by God'. In practice, this usually means that the state's political leadership is drawn from the clergy of a particular religious group, who act in the name of God. These political leaders are believed to have some special God-given authority, or particular religious and moral insight, to make them legitimate rulers in the political sphere and qualified to rule in the name of God.

Theocracy government

While religion may occupy a prominent position in public life in many countries, this doesn't necessarily make these states theocracies. Even if politicians invoke religious ideas, teachings or texts when discussing political issues, this doesn't make them theocratic rulers. Theocratic government usually involves privileging one particular religious belief system (Christianity, Islam, etc.) or clerical group (mullahs, Shinto priests, the Roman Catholic Church) over others. This privileged position is often enshrined in the constitution, or other foundational documents of the state.

Historical Examples of theocracy

The first use of the term theocracy was by the Jewish historian Flavius Josephus, who lived from 37 CE - 100 CE, who used it to describe the governance of the Jewish people in biblical times. According to this record, Moses helped shape a new kind of government for the Jewish people that ascribed ultimate power and authority to God.

Papal supremacy is the doctrine of the Roman Catholic Church that the pope, by reason of his office as Vicar of Christ and as pastor of the entire Christian Church, has full, supreme, and universal power over the whole church, a power which he can always exercise unhindered—that, in brief, "the Pope enjoys, by divine institution, supreme, full, immediate, and universal power in the care of souls."

The doctrine had the most significance in the relationship between the church and the temporal state, in matters such as *ecclesiastical* privileges, the actions of monarchs, and even successions. The creation of the term "papal supremacy" dates back to the 6th century, at the time of the fall of the Western Roman Empire, which was the beginning of the rise of the bishops of Rome to not just the position religious authority, but the power to be the ultimate ruler of the kingdoms within the Christian community (Christendom), which it has since retained.

Theocracies Hybrid regime (Caliphateism)

Religious and *political* system assimilated that the term *theocracy* derives from the Koine Greek, "rule of God", a term used by Josephus for the kingdoms of Israel and Judah, reflecting the view that "God himself is recognized as the head" of the state. The common, generic use of the term, as defined above in terms of rule by a church or analogous religious leadership, may be more accurately described as an ecclesiocracy.

In a pure theocracy, the civil leader is believed to have a personal connection with the deity or deities of that civilization's religion or belief, such as Mohammad's leadership of the early Muslims with prophecies from Allah. In an ecclesiocracy, the religious leaders assume a leading role in the state, but do not claim that they are instruments of divine revelation

Caliphate, the political-religious state comprising the Muslim community and the lands and peoples under its dominion in the centuries following the death (632 CE) of the Prophet Mahammad. Ruled by a caliph, who held temporal and sometimes a degree of spiritual authority, the empire of the Caliphate grew rapidly through conquest during its first two centuries to include most of Southwest Asia, North Africa, and Spain. Dynastic struggles later brought about the Caliphate's decline, and it ceased to exist as a functioning political institution with the Mongol destruction of Bagdad in 1258.

The concept of the caliphate took on new significance in the 18th century as an instrument of statecraft in the declining Ottoman Empire. Facing the erosion of their military and political power and territorial losses inflicted in a series of wars with European rivals, the Ottoman sultans, who had occasionally styled themselves as caliphs since the 14th century, began to stress their claim to leadership of the Islamic community. This served both as means of retaining some degree of influence over Muslim populations in formerly Ottoman lands and as means of bolstering Ottoman legitimacy within the empire. The caliphate was abolished in 1924, following the dissolution of the Ottoman Empire and the rise of the Turkish Republic.

In the 20th century the reestablishment of the caliphate, although occasionally invoked by Islamists as a symbol of global Islamic unity, was of no practical interest for mainstream Islamist groups such as the Muslim Brotherhood in Egypt. It did, however, figure prominently in the rhetoric of violent extremist groups such as Al-Qaeda. In June 2014 an insurgent group known as the Islamic State in Iraq and Levant (ISIL; also known as the Islamic State in Iraq and Syria [ISIS] and the Islamic State [IS]), which had taken control of areas of eastern Syria and western Iraq, declared the establishment of a caliphate with the group's leader Abu Bakr Al-Baghdadi as caliph. Outside extremist circles, the group's claim was widely rejected.

An Islamic Republic is the name given to several states that are officially ruled by Islamic Laws, including the Islamic Republics of Iran, Pakistan and Mauritania. Pakistan first adopted the title under the constitution of 1956. Mauritania adopted it on 28 November 1958. Iran adopted it after the 1979 Iranian revolution that overthrew the Pahlavi dynasty. Afghanistan adopted it in 2004 after the fall of the Taliban government. Despite having similar names, the countries differ greatly in their governments and laws.

The term "Islamic republic" has come to mean several different things, at times contradictory. To some Muslim religious leaders in the Middle East and Africa who advocate it, an Islamic republic is a state under a particular Islamic form of Government. They see it as a compromise between a purely Islamic Caliphate and secular nationalism and republicanism. In their conception of the Islamic republic, the penal cord of the state is required to be compatible with some or all laws of Sharia, and the state may not be a monarchy, as many Middle Eastern states presently are

Saudi Arabia

The area of modern-day Saudi Arabia formerly consisted of mainly four distinct historical regions. The Kingdom of Saudi Arabia was founded in 1932 by King Abdelaziz. He united the four regions into a single state through a series of conquests. Beginning in 1902 the ancestral home of his family, the House of Saud. Saudi Arabia has since been an absolute Monarchy, where political decisions are made on the basis of consultation among the King, the council of ministers, and the country's traditional elites that oversee a highly authoritarian regime. In its basic laws, Saudi Arabia continues to define itself as a sovereign Arab Islamic state with Islam as its official religion, Arabic as its official language, and Riyadh as its capital.

Westernization:

Westernization describes a growing cultural influence on the non-western areas that gradually changes into one that speaks the west language, and incorporates west culture and identity. It has most prominently developed during the 18th century through the Western imperialism and colonization of the East, which spread during it the western language and culture. The terms westernization and Westernizes get linguistic origins in the west, which means the sunset direction. He becomes a westerner; he follows or uses one or more western languages and cultures in his daily life. Western and westernism are two obvious terms that mean he made his tongue western, or he is proficient in the foreign or non-Arabic language. Consequently, he gets a fluent tongue in one or more of the western languages in spite of the fact that he is not a westerner, actually he is Arab. Westernizers, he becomes similar to Westerners. Western who live in the European, Occidental, and United States of America. Therefore, he becomes Westernizers because he acquires their culture, language, traditions, and customs. Westernizers *become* an intruder in the westerns and makes himself one of them. Moreover, the Westernizers makes himself a westerner and *change* himself from a non-western Arab tongue to a western tongue, so he will be ***Westernized. He*** made himself one of the Arabs. In addition, his form and tongue become Western or Westernized, and he acquires a Western tongue.

Arabization:

Arabization *was* used in the Middle Ages, especially in the Andalusian, which termed the Christians who lived under the rule of Islam and had their arts and literature. They have played the primary role and danger in igniting revolutions and unrest against the rule of Arab in that region. Andalusia; is presently Spain, overlooking the Mediterranean Sea, in moreover the waters of the Atlantic Ocean. Also, it was overlooking the Strait of Gibraltar, while its north relates to France. Whereas they have attempted to offend the position of Prophet Mohammed, they had backed up and confirmed Islamic tolerance, and Muslims influenced them, so they hold to the Arab language and its literature. They were pushed within these movements by Fanatics Monks such as Eologiwa and Alvaro. The matter ended up when the church declared its displeasure from such as those movements which had against Arab knowledge. In the tenth century, the Arabizatists were in perfect harmony with the Muslims, who had started strongly influenced by Arab and Islam culture and spoke Arabic. Historians have used the term Arabization to describe the period when the Arab-Islamic influence came to its peak in Europe. When the Arabs were discovering the secrets of science and the arts, making miracles in civilization and literature, and overcoming the difficulties in philosophy, and religions. At the same time, the west was drenched in *ignorance, darkness* and lack of knowledge, and retardation. They were looking forward to a hand dragging them from the darkness of retardation onto the light that was emitting from the Arab knowledge Capitals, which spread east and west and clung to it with all strength. Indeed, almost this period was about 1100 to 1500 A.D. It is a period that witnessed a new civilization in Western Europe that was characterized by Islamic influences in various fields of knowledge. This period *has been known* in history as the era of European Arabization, where Europe has Arabized in its, and the Arab sciences and knowledge were the primary source of every book in Europe. This influence had begun for the first time in the early part of the eighth century AD.

Democracy

Democracy is a form of government in which the peoples have the authority to deliberate and decide legislation or to choose governing official to do so. It is considered part of "the people" and how authority is shared among or delegated by the people has changed over time and at different rates in different countries. Features of democracy often include freedom of assembly, association, property *rights*, freedom of religion and speech, inclusiveness and equality, citizenship, consent *of the governed*, voting right, freedom from unwarranted governmental deprivation of the right to life and liberty, and minority *rights*.

Parliamentary sovereignty, also called **parliamentary supremacy** or **legislative supremacy**, is a concept in the constitutional law of parliamentary democracies. It holds *that the legislative* body has absolute sovereignty and is supreme over all other government institutions, including executive or judicial bodies. It also holds that the legislative body may change or repeal any previous legislation and so it is not bound by written law or by precedent.

In some countries, parliamentary sovereignty may be contrasted with separation of powers, which limits the legislature's scope often to general law-making and makes it subject to external judicial reviews, where laws passed by the legislature may be declared invalid in certain circumstances. However, in such countries the legislative body still retains the sovereignty by the possibility to alter the constitution, which usually *requires a greater* majority, often 2/3 of votes instead of 1/2.

A **presidential democracy system**, or **single executive system**, is a form of government in which a head of government, typically with the title of president, leads an executive branch that is separate from the legislative branch in systems that use separation of power. This head of government is in most cases also the head of state. In a presidential system, the head of government is directly or indirectly elected by a group of citizens and is not responsible to the legislature, and the legislature cannot dismiss the president except in extraordinary cases. A presidential system contrasts with a parliamentary system, where the head of government comes to power by gaining the confidence of an elected legislature.

Liberal democracy or **western democracy** is the combination of a liberal political ideology that operates under a representative democratic form of government. It is characterized by elections between multiple distinct political *parties, a separation* of powers into different branches of government, the rule of law in everyday life as part of an open society, a market economy with private property, and the equal protection of human right, civil right, civil; liberties and political freedoms for all people. To define the system in practice, liberal democracies often draw upon a constitution, either codified or uncodified, to delineate the powers of government and enshrine the social contract. After a period of expansion in the second half of the 20th century, liberal democracy became a prevalent political system in the world.

Liberal democracies usually have universal suffrage, granting all adult citizens the right to vote regardless of ethnicity, sex, property ownership, race, age, sexuality, gender, income, social status, or religion. However, historically some countries regarded as liberal democracies have had a more limited franchise. Even today, some countries, considered to be liberal democracies, do not have truly universal suffrage. Many nations require positive identification before allowing people to vote. For example, in the United States 2/3 of states require their citizens to provide identification to vote, these states also provide state IDs for free. The decisions made through elections are made not by all of the citizens but rather by those who are members of the electorate and who choose to participate by voting.

The liberal democratic constitution defines the democratic character of the state. The purpose of a constitution is often seen as a limit on the authority of the government. Liberal democracy emphasizes the separation of powers, an independent judiciary and a system of checks and balances between branches of government. Multi-party systematic at least two persistent, viable political parties are characteristic of liberal democracies. In Europe, liberal democracies are likely to emphasize the importance of the state being a Rechtsstaat, i.e. a state that follows the principle of rule of law. Governmental authority is legitimately exercised only in accordance with written, publicly disclosed laws adopted and enforced in accordance with established procedure. Many democracies use federalism, also known as vertical separation of powers, in order to prevent abuse and increase public input by dividing governing powers between municipal, provincial and national governments.

Rights and freedoms

In practice, democracies do have limits on certain freedoms. There are various legal limitations such as copyright and laws against defamation. There may be limits on anti-democratic speech, on attempts to undermine human *rights* and on the promotion or justification of terrorism. In the United States more than in Europe, during the cold war such restrictions applied to communists. Now they are more commonly applied to organizations perceived as promoting terrorism or the incitement of group hatred. Examples include anti-terrorism legislation, the shutting down of Hezbollah satellite broadcasts and some laws against hate speech. Critics claim that these limitations may go too far and that there may be no due and fair judicial process. The common justification for these limits is that they are necessary to guarantee the existence of democracy, or the existence of the freedoms themselves. For example, allowing free speech for those advocating mass murder undermines the right to life and security. Opinion is divided on how far democracy can extend to include the enemies of democracy in the democratic process. If relatively small numbers of people are excluded from such freedoms for these reasons, a country may still be seen as a liberal democracy. Some argue that this is only quantitatively (not qualitatively) different from autocracies that persecute opponents, since only a small number of people are affected and the restrictions are less severe, but others emphasize that democracies are different. At least in theory, opponents of democracy are also allowed due process under the rule of law. Governments considered to be democratic may impose restrictions of free speech.

Legal systems that use politically elected court jurors, such as Sweden, view a (partly) politicized court system as a main component of accountable government. Other democracies employ trial by jury with the intent of shielding against the influence of politicians over trials.

In some cases, rights considered fundamental by some members of that country *may not* be considered fundamental by other members of that country.

The Eastern and Western Political Worlds and Classifications of World Political Systems

Public opinion research conducted by the National Democratic Institute (NDI) in 2021 across seven countries in Central and South-eastern Europe – Albania, Bosnia and Herzegovina, Kosovo, Montenegro, North Macedonia, Serbia, and Slovakia – highlighted a common trend of democratic stagnation or regression, with citizen priorities focused on improving the quality of life over democratic standards.

While strong majorities across the countries surveyed esteem democracy as the preferred system of government, they are sceptical that it can be achieved in reality. Challenges within the EU, such as Brexit, and disinformation and other foreign illiberal influences have had a deleterious impact on public attitudes regarding democratization processes.

Overall, security and law enforcement are more highly regarded than political institutions, judicial bodies, and government ministries responsible for social services like healthcare and education. The one exception was the support for the President in Slovakia and Serbia. Notably, with the exception of Slovakia, workforce emigration remains a salient political and economic issue.

After the fall of communism, and since the violent conflicts of the 1990s in the Western Balkans, countries in this region have largely focused on integration into the European Union (EU) and other Euro Atlantic structures. However, in recent years, Russia, China, and other foreign powers have increased their presence in the region, gaining public support, most visibly in Montenegro, North Macedonia, and Serbia, Russia. However, with the exception of Serbia, citizens would still prefer to follow the path toward Euro Atlantic integration, even if it meant spoiling relations with China and/or Russia. Likewise, although support for the EU or the United States (U.S.) has waned, citizens still see the U.S. and/or EU as offering the most support to their respective countries, including financial assistance, with Serbia again being the exception.

With regard to disinformation, respondents saw mainstream media outlets as key information drivers. And although the public trusts information on social media, with predominant use of Facebook, Instagram, and YouTube as preferred platforms, people generally prefer to discuss politics and news in-person

Democracy in the Middle East and North Africa

According to The Economist Group's Democracy Index 2020 study, Israel is the only democratic country in the Middle East, while Tunisia is the only democracy (also "flawed democracy") in North Africa. The level of democracy in nations throughout the world published by Freedom House and in various other freedom indices, report the Middle Eastern and North African countries with the highest scores are Israel, Tunisia, Turkey, Lebanon, Morocco, Jordan and Kuwait. Countries that have been consistently *labeled* as 'not free' by Freedom House (2017-2021) have been Iran, Iraq and Egypt. They have been increasingly becoming more and more averse to the idea of liberal democracy with their scores steadily decreasing, only Iraq out of these countries have maintained some level of internet freedom with a (partly free) score of 41/100. The remaining countries of the Middle East are *categorized* as authoritarian regimes, with the lowest scores held by Saudi Arabia and Yemen.

Freedom House categorizes Israel and Tunisia as "Free". As a result, Tunisia is the only country in North Africa classified as "Free" by the Freedom House organization. Lebanon, Kuwait and Morocco "Partly Free", and the remaining states as "Not Free" (including Western Sahara, which is largely controlled by Morocco). Events of the "Arab Spring" such as the Tunisian Revolution may indicate a move towards democracy in some countries which may not be fully captured in the democracy index. In 2015, Tunisia became the first Arab country classified as free since the beginning of Lebanon's civil war 40 years ago. Theories are diverse on the subject. "Revisionist theories" argue that democracy is slightly incompatible with Middle Eastern values. On the other hand, "post-colonial" theories for the relative absence of liberal democracy in the Middle East are diverse, from the long history of imperial rule by the Ottoman Empire, United Kingdom and France and the contemporary political and military intervention by the United States, all of which have been blamed for preferring authoritarian regimes because this ostensibly simplifies the business environment, while enriching the governing elite and the companies of the imperial countries. Other explanations include the problem that most of the states in the region are rentier states, which experience the theorized resource curse.

The decline and fall of the Ottoman Empire set the stage for nationalist movements to emerge in Southwest Asia and North Africa as the Second French Empire, the Italian Empire, and British Empire began to target and colonize the region. The century between 1820 and 1920 saw the Ottoman Empire shrink from encompassing the entirety of the Levant and Egypt, the Balkans, and significant portions of the coastal Maghreb and Arabian Peninsula, to less than half of the modern state of Turkey. During this period, nationalist movements began in reaction to both the spread of nationalism throughout Europe and to European colonial incursion prior to the Ottoman Empire's collapse.

Following the conclusion of World War I in 1918 and the fall of the Ottoman Empire in 1922, many former Ottoman territories not already under European control were colonized by European countries via League of Nations mandates. While European powers were instrumental in establishing the first independent governments that emerged from the Ottoman Empire, the mandatory period was brief, primarily spanning the interwar period and World War II. Interest in national self-determination further increased during the mandatory period, and accelerated as the process of decolonization began in the region following the end of World War II in 1948.

During decolonization, current and formerly colonized peoples of Southwest Asia, North Africa, and the horn of Africa grappled with significant political and economic upheaval, both internally and in response to neo-colonialism from Western nations. Early Arab nationalism involved transforming ethnically diverse communities coping with the effects of experiencing imperial collapse, colonization, and decolonization in under a century, into a unitary national identity. For most of these emergent countries, democratic statehood was either out of reach due to political instability, or rejected in *favor* of other forms of government.

The Cold War

The United States of America and the Soviet Union competed for allies in Southwest Asia and North Africa, and the United States has been accused of supporting dictatorships contrary to its stated democratic principles. The 1957 Eisenhower Doctrine was the beginning of a policy of American democracy promotion in the Middle East and North Africa, leading, for example, to American intervention on behalf of the democratically elected government in the 1958 Lebanon crisis.

Following the terrorist attacks of September 11, 2001, the U.S. war in Afghanistan and Iraq War represented a significant turning point for the United States' shift in foreign policy in the Muslim world. Although protests against the Iraq War in particular widely criticized American intervention as a form of neo-colonialism, American political rhetoric during the Afghanistan and Iraq wars cantered on the purpose of the wars being to bring democratization in the region, as the invasions of those countries were partly for purposes of organizing democratic governments.

Opponents of American intervention in Afghanistan and Iraq have, however, criticized that democracy cannot be imposed from outside. The two countries have since had relatively successful elections, but have also experienced serious security and development problems.

Some believe that democracy can be established "only through force" and the help of the United States. Writers such as Michele Dunne, when writing for the Carnegie Paper concurs with the rhetoric of the late Israeli prime minister Yitzhak Rabin (at that time, referring to peace and terrorism) that the foreign policy position of the US should be to 'pursue peace as though there were no democratization, and pursue democratization as though there were no peace. In other words, the U.S. government should pursue reform and democratization as policy goals in the first instance without worrying excessively about trade-offs with other goals." The U.S. pressure behind the calling of the 2006 Palestinian legislative election backfired, resulting in the democratically sound victory of Hamas, rather than the US-supported Fatah. Drawing upon the ideas of Middle East scholar Nicola Pratt it can be argued that:

Bureaucracy

It is a body of non-elected *government* officials or an administrative policy-making group. Historically, a bureaucracy was a government administration managed by departments staffed with non-elected officials. Today, bureaucracy is the administrative system governing any large institution, whether publicly owned or privately owned. The public administration in many jurisdictions and sub-jurisdictions exemplifies bureaucracy, but so does any centralized hierarchical structure of an institution, e.g. hospitals, academic entities, business firms, professional societies, social clubs, etc.

There are two key dilemmas in bureaucracy. The first dilemma revolves around whether bureaucrats should be autonomous or directly accountable to their political masters. The second dilemma revolves around bureaucrats' responsibility to follow procedure, regulation and law or the amount of latitude they may have to determine appropriate solutions for circumstances that may appear unaccounted for in advance.

Various commentators have argued for the necessity of bureaucracies in modern society. The German sociologist Max Weber (1864-1920) argued that bureaucracy constitutes the most efficient and rational way in which human activity can be organized and that systematic processes and organized hierarchies are necessary to maintain order, to maximize efficiency, and to eliminate favoritism. On the other hand, Weber also saw unfettered bureaucracy as a threat to individual freedom, with the potential of trapping individuals in an impersonal "iron cage" of rule-based, rational control.

bureaucracy, specific form of organization defined by complexity, division of labour, permanence, professional management, hierarchical coordination and control, strict chain of command, and legal authority. It is distinguished from informal and collegial organizations. In its ideal form, *bureaucracy is* impersonal and rational and based on rules rather than ties of kinship, friendship, or patrimonial or charismatic authority. Bureaucratic organization can be found in both public and private institutions.

Characteristics and paradoxes of bureaucracy

The foremost theorist of bureaucracy is the German sociologist Max Weber (1864–1920), who described the ideal characteristics of bureaucracies and offered an explanation for the historical emergence of bureaucratic institutions. According to Weber, the defining features of bureaucracy sharply distinguish it from other types of organization based on nonlegal forms of authority. Weber observed that the advantage of bureaucracy was that it was the most technically proficient form of organization, possessing specialized expertise, certainty, continuity, and unity. Bureaucracy's emergence as a preferred form of organization occurred with the rise of a money-based economy and the attendant need to ensure impersonal, rational-legal transactions. Instrumental organizations (e.g., public-stock business firms) soon arose because their bureaucratic organization equipped them to handle the various demands of capitalist production more efficiently than small-scale producers.

Contemporary stereotypes of bureaucracy tend to portray it as unresponsive, lethargic, undemocratic, and incompetent. Weber's theory of bureaucracy, however, emphasizes not only its comparative technical and proficiency advantages but also attributes its dominance as a form of organization to the diminution of caste systems and other forms of inequitable social relations based upon a person's status. In the pure form of bureaucratic organization universalized rules and procedures would dominate, rendering personal status or connections irrelevant. In this form, bureaucracy is the epitome of universalized standards under which similar cases are treated similarly as codified by law and rules, and under which the individual tastes and discretion of the administrator are constrained by due process rules. Despite the widespread derogatory stereotypes of bureaucracy, a system of government grounded in law requires bureaucracy to function.

Nevertheless, the words *bureaucracy* and *bureaucrat* are typically thought of and used pejoratively. They convey images of red tape, excessive rules and regulations, unimaginativeness, a lack of individual discretion, central control, and an absence of accountability. Far from being conceived as proficient, popular contemporary portrayals often paint bureaucracies as inefficient and lacking in adaptability. Because the characteristics that define the organizational advantages of bureaucracy also contain within them the possibilities of organizational dysfunction, both the flattering and unflattering depictions of bureaucracy can be accurate. Thus, the characteristics that make bureaucracies proficient paradoxically also may produce organizational pathologies.

Jurisdictional competency

Jurisdictional competency is a key element of bureaucratic organization, which is broken into units with defined responsibilities. Fundamentally, jurisdictional competency refers to bureaucratic specialization, with all elements of a bureaucracy possessing a defined role. The responsibilities of individuals broaden with movement upward through an organizational hierarchy. The organizational division of labour enables units and individuals within an organization to master details and skills and to turn the novel into *a* routine. Although the division of labour is highly efficient, it can lead to a number of harmful organizational pathologies; for example, units or individuals may be unable to identify and respond adequately to problems outside their competency and may approach all problems and priorities exclusively from the purview of a unit's specific capabilities. This feature of bureaucracy also can lead organizational units to shirk responsibility by allowing them to define a problem as belonging to some other unit and thereby leave the issue unattended. Alternatively, every unit within an organization is apt to put a face on a problem congenial mainly to its own interests, skills, and technologies.

Command and control

Bureaucracies have clear lines of command and control. Bureaucratic authority is organized hierarchically, with responsibility taken at the top and delegated with decreasing discretion below. Because of the risk of organizational parochialism produced by limited and specific jurisdictional competencies, the capacity to coordinate and control the multiplicity of units is essential. Authority is the glue that holds together diversity and prevents units from exercising unchecked discretion. Yet, few features of bureaucratic life have received so much adverse attention as the role of hierarchical authority as a means for achieving organizational command and control. Popular criticisms emphasize that hierarchical organization strangles creative impulses and injects hyper-cautious modes of behavior based on expectations of what superiors may desire. Command and control, which are necessary to coordinate the disparate elements of bureaucratic organization, provide for increasing responsibility upward, delegation, and decreasing discretion downward.

Democracy in the United States is a representative democracy. This means that our government is elected by citizens. Here, citizens vote for their government officials. These officials represent the citizens' ideas and concerns in government. Voting is one way to participate in our democracy. Citizens can also contact their officials when they want to support or change a law. Voting in an election and contacting our elected officials are two ways that Americans can participate in their democracy

The politics of the United States function within a framework of a constitutional federal republic and presidential system, with three distinct branches that share powers. These are: the U.S. Congress which forms the legislative branch, a bicameral legislative body comprising the House of Representatives and the Senate; the executive branch which is headed by the president of the United States, who serves as the country's head of state and government; and the judicial branch, composed of the Supreme Court and lower federal courts, and which exercises judicial power.

Each of the 50 individual state governments has the power to make laws within its jurisdiction that are not granted to the federal government nor denied to the states in the U.S. Constitution. Each state also has a constitution following the pattern of the federal constitution but differing in details. Each have three branches: an executive branch headed by a governor, a legislative body, and judicial branch. At the local level, governments are found in counties or county-equivalents, and beneath them individual municipalities, townships, school districts, and special districts.

The United States is a constitutional federal republic, in which the president , Congress, and judiciary share powers reserved to the national government, and the federal government shares sovereignty with the state governments.

The federal government is divided into three branches, as per the specific terms articulated in the U.S. Constitution:

The executive branch is headed by the president and is independent of the legislature.

Legislative power is vested in the two chambers of Congress: the Senate and the House of Representatives.

The judicial branch (or judiciary), composed of the Supreme Court and lower federal courts, exercises judicial power. The judiciary's function is to interpret the United States Constitution and federal laws and regulations. This includes resolving disputes between the executive and legislative branches.

The federal government's layout is explained in the Constitution. Two political parties, the Democratic Party and the Republican

Party, have dominated American politics since the American Civil War, although other parties have existed.

There are major differences between the political system of the United States and that of many other developed countries, including:

an upper legislative house (the Senate), with much more power than is found in equivalent bodies in most other countries;

a Supreme Court that also has a wider scope of power than is found in most countries;

a separation of powers between the legislature and the executive; and

a political landscape dominated by only two main parties. The United States is one of the world's only developed countries where all additional parties have minimal or nonexistent influence and almost no representation at the national and state level. Causes for this mainly focus on the plurality-based first-past-the-post voting system, used in most elections, which encourages strategic voting and discourages vote splitting. This also results in both major parties having multiple internal factions.

The federal entity created by the U.S. Constitution is the dominant feature of the American governmental system, as citizens are also subject to a state government and various units of local government.

State governments have the power to make laws on all subjects that are not granted to the federal government nor denied to the states in the U.S. Constitution. These include education, family law, contract law, and most crimes. Unlike the federal government, which only has those powers granted to it in the Constitution, a state government has inherent powers allowing it to act unless limited by a provision of the state or national constitution.

Like the federal government, state governments have three branches: executive, legislative, and judicial. The chief executive of a state is its popularly elected governor, who typically holds office for a four-year term (although in some states the term is two years). Except for Nebraska, which has unicameral legislature, all states have a bicameral legislature, with the upper house usually called the Senate and the lower house called the House of Representatives, the Assembly or something similar. In most states, senators serve four-year terms, and members of the lower house serve two-year terms.

The constitutions of the various states differ in some details but generally follow a pattern similar to that of the federal Constitution, including a statement of the rights of the people and a plan for organizing the government, and are generally more detailed.

At the state and local level, the process of initiatives and referendums allow citizens to place new legislation on a popular ballot, or to place legislation that has recently been passed by a legislature on a ballot for a popular vote. Initiatives and referendums, along with recall elections and popular primary elections, are signature reforms of the Progressive Era; they are written into several state constitutions, particularly in the Western states, but not found at the federal level.

Feudalism:

Feudalism and the related term feudal system are labels invented long after the period to which they were applied. They refer to what those who invented them perceived as the most significant and distinctive characteristics of the early and central Middle Ages. The expressions feudalism and feudal system were coined by the beginning of the 17th century, and the English words feudality and feudalism were in use by the end of the 18th century. They were derived from the Latin words feudum and feudalities, both of which were used during the Middle Ages and later to refer to a form of property holding. Use of the terms associated with feudum to denote the essential characteristics of the early Middle Ages has invested the fief with exaggerated prominence and placed undue emphasis on the importance of a special mode of land tenure to the detriment of other, more significant aspects of social, economic, and political life. Feudal Society

European Medieval Feudalism

European medieval feudalism has become the foremost example of an interrelationship between a social class system and an economy. Having been influenced, however, by previous cultures and their economies, especially those that combined agricultural and exchange bases, the medieval economic environment cannot be understood through exclusive examination of the feudal system. The backdrop of Greek and Roman civilization and the fundamental need for survival formed the foundation for a far more heterogeneous medieval economic culture, useful for sustenance and for social organization. To these two ends, traders, artisans, peasants, churchmen, and the nobility created an economy that enveloped Europe's contemporary medieval population. It was comprised of many different elements: trade alliances; exchange methods, both interest bearing and interest free; a manorial system combined with a monetized vassalage (nobles avoiding military service by paying their overlords); professional guilds; agriculturally self-sufficient monasteries; urban communes; and tax-based kingdoms, some of which were transformed into representational fiscal monarchies. The composite European medieval economy, derived from these many diverse elements, departed radically from economies of earlier Western cultures.

General Characteristics. No one social class system or economic form was realized for Europe over the course of the whole Middle Ages. A post medieval new economy, often identified as capitalism, was merely in formation and would not be considered all-enveloping for centuries to come. Undeniably, one element of the medieval world was the traditional economy of land and military service, leading to a feudal-based social-class system; the other was an urban society where merchants and artisans undertook trade and commerce in an economy based on money, or capital. For the urban environment, merchants, artisans, and customers formed the core of the society because towns served as centers for the individuals who lived and worked there. They saw manufacture as the most important endeavor, to provide goods for sale and purchase in the local mercantile economy. Furthermore, local manufacture was to have an impact in other areas, such as regional fairs, port cities, and eventually long-distance trade destinations.

Urban Economy: During the Middle Ages, the economy did not become fully urban. As medieval towns grew into cities and frequently dominated the abutting countryside, the agricultural economy kept itself at an independent distance, was rarely stimulated by market supply and demand, and remained relatively ignorant of means of economic progress. The late medieval nobility complained that changes in the workforce had violated its source of livelihood, virtual free labor assumed since the beginnings of the feudal economy, and set forth in many feudal codes of law which had fixed the purpose of the peasantry. The rural economy continued nonetheless to be the safer source of sustenance for many people, who saw in its connection to the soil the chance for the family to survive in good and bad years. The fact that the vast majority of the medieval population was rural overpowered some towns' premature bid for communal independence, and the urban environment was vulnerable to the vagaries of agricultural provisioning. In the later fourteenth century, the peasantry was recast as a

The bourgeoisie

The bourgeoisie in its original sense is intimately linked to the political ideology of Liberalism and its existence within cities, recognized as such by their urban charters so there was no bourgeoisie apart from the citizenry of the cities.] Rural peasants came under a different legal system.

In Communist philosophy, the bourgeoisie is the social class that came to own the means of production during modern industrialization and whose societal concerns are the value of private property and the preservation of capital to ensure the perpetuation of their economic dominance in society.

The Modern French word bourgeois BOORZH-wah. In other European languages, the etymological derivations include the Middle English burgeis, the Middle Dutch burgher, the German Bürger, the Modern English burgess, the Spanish burgués, the Portuguese burguês, and the Polish burżuazja, which occasionally is synonymous with the intelligentsia.

In the 18th century, before the French Revolution (1789–1799), in the French Ancien Régime, the masculine and feminine terms bourgeois and bourgeoisie identified the relatively rich men and women who were members of the urban and rural Third Estate – the common people of the French realm, who violently deposed the absolute monarchy of the Bourbon King Louis XVI (r. 1774–1791), his clergy, and his aristocrats in the French Revolution of 1789–1799. Hence, since the 19th century, the term "bourgeoisie" usually is politically and sociologically synonymous with the ruling upper class of a capitalist society. In English, the word "bourgeoisie", as a term referring to French history, refers to a social class oriented to economic materialism and hedonism, and to upholding the political and economic interests of the capitalist ruling-class.

Historically, the medieval French word bourgeois denoted the inhabitants of the bourgs (walled market-towns), the craftsmen, artisans, merchants, and others, who constituted "the bourgeoisie". They were the socio-economic class between the peasants and the landlords, between the workers and the owners of the means of production. As the economic managers of the (raw) materials, the goods, and the services, and thus the capital (money) produced by the feudal economy, the term "bourgeoisie" evolved to also denote the middle class – the businessmen and businesswomen who accumulated, administered, and controlled the capital that made possible the development of the bourgs into cities.

Contemporarily, the terms "bourgeoisie" and "bourgeois" (noun) identify the ruling class in capitalist societies, as a social stratum; while "bourgeois" (adjective / noun modifier) describes the Weltanschauung (worldview) of men and women whose way of thinking is socially and culturally determined by their economic materialism and philistinism, a social identity famously mocked in Molière's comedy Le Bourgeois gentilhomme (1670), which satirizes buying the trappings of a noble-birth identity as the means of climbing the social ladder. The 18th century saw a partial rehabilitation of bourgeois values in genres such as the drame bourgeois (bourgeois drama) and "bourgeois tragedy".

Emerging in the 1970s, the shortened term "bougie" became slang, referring to things or attitudes which are middle class, pretentious and suburban. In 2016, a hip-hop group Migos produced a song Bad and Boujee, featuring an intentional misspelling of the word as "boujee"[9] – a term which has particularly been used by African Americans in reference to African Americans. The term refers to a person of lower or middle class doing pretentious activities or virtue signaling as an affectation of the upper-class.

The bourgeoisie emerged as a historical and political phenomenon in the 11th century when the bourgs of Central and Western Europe developed into cities dedicated to commerce and crafts. This urban expansion was possible thanks to economic concentration due to the appearance of protective self-organization into guilds. Guilds arose when individual businessmen (such as craftsmen, artisans and merchants) conflicted with their rent-seeking feudal landlords who demanded greater rents than previously agreed.

In the event, by the end of the Middle Ages (c. AD 1500), under regimes of the early national monarchies of Western Europe, the bourgeoisie acted in self-interest, and politically supported the king or queen against legal and financial disorder caused by the greed of the feudal lords. In the late-16th and early 17th centuries, the bourgeoisies of England and the Netherlands had become the financial – thus political – forces that deposed the feudal order; economic power had vanquished military power in the realm of politics.

According to the Marxist view of history, during the 17th and 18th centuries, the bourgeoisie were the politically progressive social class who supported the principles of constitutional government and of natural right, against the Law of Privilege and the claims of rule by divine right that the nobles and prelates had autonomously exercised during the feudal order.

The English Civil War (1642–1651), the American War of Independence (1775–1783), and French Revolution (1789–1799) were partly motivated by the desire of the bourgeoisie to rid themselves of the feudal and royal encroachments on their personal liberty, commercial prospects, and the ownership of property. In the 19th century, the bourgeoisie propounded liberalism, and gained political rights, religious rights, and civil liberties for themselves and the lower social classes; thus the bourgeoisie was a progressive philosophic and political force in Western societies.

After the Industrial Revolution (1750–1850), by the mid-19th century the great expansion of the bourgeoisie social class caused its stratification – by business activity and by economic function – into the haute bourgeoisie (bankers and industrialists) and the petite bourgeoisie (tradesmen and white-collar workers). Moreover, by the end of the 19th century, the capitalists (the original bourgeoisie) had ascended to the upper class, while the developments of technology and technical occupations allowed the rise of working-class men and women to the lower strata of the bourgeoisie; yet the social progress was incidental.

According to Karl Marx, the bourgeois during the Middle Ages usually was a self-employed businessman – such as a merchant, banker, or entrepreneur – whose economic role in society was being the financial intermediary to the feudal landlord and the peasant who worked the fief, the land of the lord. Yet, by the 18th century, the time of the Industrial Revolution (1750–1850) and of industrial capitalism, the bourgeoisie had become the economic ruling class who owned the means of production (capital and land), and who controlled the means of coercion (armed forces and legal system, police forces and prison system).

In such a society, the bourgeoisie's ownership of the means of production allowed them to employ and exploit the wage-earning working class (urban and rural), people whose only economic means is labour; and the bourgeois control of the means of coercion suppressed the sociopolitical challenges by the lower classes, and so preserved the economic status quo; workers remained workers, and employers remained employers.

In the 19th century, Marx distinguished two types of bourgeois capitalist:

the functional capitalists, who are business administrators of the means of production;

rentier capitalists whose livelihoods derive either from the rent of property or from the interest-income produced by finance capital, or both.

In the course of economic relations, the working class and the bourgeoisie continually engage in class struggle, where the capitalists exploit the workers, while the workers resist their economic exploitation, which occurs because the worker owns no means of production, and, to earn a living, seeks employment from the bourgeois capitalist; the worker produces goods and services that are property of the employer, who sells them for a price.

Besides describing the social class who owns the means of production, the Marxist use of the term "bourgeois" also describes the consumerist style of life derived from the ownership of capital and real property. Marx acknowledged the bourgeois industriousness that created wealth, but criticized the moral hypocrisy of the bourgeoisie when they ignored the alleged origins of their wealth: the exploitation of the proletariat, the urban and rural workers. Further sense denotations of "bourgeois" describe ideological concepts such as "bourgeois freedom", which is thought to be opposed to substantive forms of freedom; "bourgeois independence"; "bourgeois personal individuality"; the "bourgeois family"; et cetera, all derived from owning capital and property

The "Ancient Régime", and that they belonged to the town's elite and the upper-crust of the "bourgeoisie" caste. They usually acquired high and important administrative and judicial functions, and distinguished themselves through their success, particularly in business and industry. It was through this distinction that some of these families were able to acquire titles typically associated with the nobility, a caste from which they remained nonetheless excluded.

Nazism

Nazism rejected the Marxist concept of proletarian internationalism and class struggle, and supported the "class struggle between nations", and sought to resolve internal class struggle in the nation while it identified Germany as a proletariat nation fighting against plutocratic nations. The Nazi Party had many working-class supporters and members, and a strong appeal to the middle class. The financial collapse of the white collar middle-class of the 1920s figures much in their strong support of Nazism. In the poor country that was the Weimar Republic of the early 1930s, the Nazi Party realized their social policies with food and shelter for the unemployed and the homeless—who were later recruited into the Brownshirt Sturmabteilung .

Adolf Hitler was impressed by the populist antisemitism and the anti-liberal bourgeois agitation of Karl Lueger, who as the mayor of Vienna during Hitler's time in the city, used a rabble-rousing style of oratory that appealed to the wider masses. When asked whether he supported the "bourgeois right-wing", Hitler claimed that Nazism was not exclusively for any class, and he also indicated that it favored neither the left nor the right, but preserved "pure" elements from both "camps", stating: "From the camp of bourgeois tradition, it takes national resolve, and from the materialism of the Marxist dogma, living, creative Socialism.

Hitler distrusted capitalism for being unreliable due to its egotism, and he preferred a state-directed economy that is subordinated to the interests of the Volk. Hitler told a party leader in 1934, "The economic system of our day is the creation of the Jews." Hitler said to Benito Mussolini that capitalism had "run its course". Hitler also said that the business bourgeoisie "know nothing except their profit. 'Fatherland' is only a word for them." Hitler was personally disgusted with the ruling bourgeois elites of Germany during the period of the Weimar Republic, whom he referred to as "cowardly shits

Federal System:

In federal systems, political authority is divided between two autonomous sets of governments, one national and the other subnational, both of which operate directly upon the people. Usually a constitutional division of power is established between the national government, which exercises authority over the whole national territory, and provincial governments that exercise independent authority within their own territories. Of the eight largest countries in the world by area, seven—Russia, Canada, the United States, Brazil, Australia, India, and Argentina—are organized on a federal basis. (China, the third largest, is a unitary state.) Federal countries also include Austria, Belgium, Ethiopia, Germany, Malaysia, Mexico, Nigeria, Pakistan, Switzerland, the United Arab Emirates, and Venezuela, among others.

The governmental structures and political processes found in these federal systems show great variety. One may distinguish, first, a number of systems in which federal arrangements reflect rather clear-cut cultural divisions. A classic case of this type is Switzerland, where the people speak four different languages— German, French, Italian, and Romansh—and the federal system unites 26 historically and culturally different entities, known as cantons and demicantons. The Swiss constitution of 1848, as modified in 1874, converted into the modern federal state a confederation originally formed in the 13th century by the three forest cantons of Uri, Schwyz, and Unterwalden. The principal agencies of federal government are a bicameral legislature, composed of a National Council representing the people directly and a Council of States representing the constituent members as entities; an executive branch (Bundesrat) elected by both houses of the legislature in joint session; and a supreme court that renders decisions on matters affecting cantonal and federal relations.

The Russian Federation's arrangements, although of a markedly different kind, also reflect the cultural and linguistic diversity of the country. Depending on their size and on the territories they have historically occupied, ethnic minorities may have their own autonomous republic, region, or district. These divisions provide varying degrees of autonomy in setting local policies and provide a basis for the preservation of the minorities' cultures. Some of these areas were integrated into the Russian Empire centuries ago, after the lands were taken from the Mongols of the Golden Horde, and others resisted occupation even late in the 19th century. It is not uncommon for Russians to constitute a plurality of the population in these areas. The national government consists of the executive branch, led by the nationally elected president; the parliament; and a judicial branch that resolves constitutional matters.

In other systems, federal arrangements are found in conjunction with a large measure of cultural homogeneity. The Constitution of the United States delegates to the federal government certain activities that concern the whole people, such as the conduct of foreign relations and war and the regulation of interstate commerce and foreign trade; certain other functions are shared between the federal government and the states; and the remainder are reserved for the states. Although these arrangements require two separate bodies of political officers, two judicial systems, and two systems of taxation, they also allow extensive interaction between the federal government and the states. Thus, the election of Congress and the president, the process of amending the Constitution, the levying of taxes, and innumerable other functions necessitate cooperation between the two levels of government and bring them into a tightly interlocking relationship.

Subnational political systems

Although national government is the dominant form of political organization in the modern world, an extraordinary range of political forms exists below the national level—tribal communities, the intimate political associations of villages and towns, the governments of regions and provinces, the complex array of urban and suburban governments, and the great political and administrative systems of the cities and the metropolises. These subnational entities are, in a sense, the basic political communities—the foundation on which all national political systems are built.

Tribal communities

The typical organization of humankind in its early history was the tribe. Today, in many parts of the world, the tribal community is still a major form of human political organization. Even within more formal political systems, traces can still be found of its influence. Some of the Länder of modern Germany, such as Bavaria, Saxony, or Westphalia, have maintained their identity since the days of the Germanic tribal settlements. In England, too, many county boundaries can be explained only by reference to the territorial divisions in the period after the end of the Roman occupation.

In many African countries the tribe or ethnic group is still an effective community and a vehicle of political consciousness. (Some African scholars, viewing the term tribe as pejorative and inaccurate, prefer to use ethnic groups or other similar terms to describe such communities.) Most African countries are the successors to the administrative units established by colonial regimes and owe their present boundaries to the often arbitrary decisions of imperial bureaucracies or to the territorial accommodations of rival colonial powers. The result was often the splintering of the tribal communities or their aggregation in largely artificial entities.

Tribal loyalties continue to hamper nation-building efforts in some parts of the world where tribes were once the dominant political structure. Tribes may act through formal political parties like any other interest group. In some cases, they simply act out their tribal bias through the machinery of the political system, and in others they function largely outside of formal political structures.

In its primary sense, the tribe is a community organized in terms of kinship, and its subdivisions are the intimate kindred groupings of moieties, gentes, and totem groups. Its territorial basis is rarely defined with any precision, and its institutions are typically the undifferentiated and intermittent structures of an omni functional social system. The leadership of the tribe is provided by the group of adult males, the lineage elders acting as tribal chiefs, the village headmen, or the shamans, or tribal magicians. These groups and individuals are the guardians of the tribal customs and of an oral tradition of law. Law is thus not made but rather invoked; its repository is the collective memory of the tribal council or chief men. This kind of customary law, sanctioned and hallowed by religious belief, nevertheless changes and develops, for each time it is declared something may be added or omitted to meet the needs of the occasion.

Rural communities

The village has traditionally been contrasted with the city: the village is the home of rural occupations and tied to the cycles of agricultural life, while the inhabitants of the city practice many trades, and its economy is founded on commerce and industry; the village is an intimate association of families, while the city is the locus of a mass population; the culture of the village is simple and traditional, while the city is the Centre of the arts and sciences and of a complex cultural development. The village and the city offer even sharper contrasts as political communities. Historically, the village has been ruled by the informal democracy of face-to-face discussion in the village council or by a headman whose decisions are supported by village elders or by other cooperative modes of government; urban government has never been such a simple matter, and monarchical, tyrannical, aristocratic, and oligarchic forms of rule have all flourished in the city. In the village, the boundaries among political, economic, religious, and other forms of action have not been as clearly drawn as in cities.

The origins and development of the apparatus of government can be seen most clearly in the simple political society of the rural community. The transformation of kin-bound societies with their informal, folk-sustained systems of sociopolitical organization into differentiated, hierarchical societies with complex political structures began with the enlargement of the rural community—an increase in its population, the diversification of its economy, or its interaction with other communities. The rudimentary organs of communal government were then elaborated, the communal functions received more specialized direction, and leadership roles were institutionalized. This was sometimes a process that led by gradual stages to the growth of cities. Elsewhere, however, as in the case of ancient Attica, the city was established as the result of a process of synoikismos, or the uniting of a number of tribal or village communities. This was undoubtedly the origin of Athens, and, according to its legendary history, Rome also was established as a result of the forcible unification of the tribes that dwelt on the hills surrounding the Palatine Hill.

Even in the nation-states of today's world, the contrasts between the village or the town and the city as centers of human activity are readily apparent. In the country, life is more intimate, human contact more informal, the structure of society more stable. In the city, the individual becomes anonymous, the contacts between people are mainly formal, and the standing of the individual or the family in society is subject to rapid change. In many contemporary systems, however, the differences in the forms of government of rural and urban communities appear to be growing less pronounced. In the United States, for example, rural institutions have been seriously weakened by the movement of large numbers of people to the city. The township meeting of New England and other forms of direct citizen participation in the affairs of the community have declined in importance and have often been displaced by more formal structures and the growth of local governmental bureaucracies.

The caste system in India

It is the paradigmatic ethnographic instance of social classification based on castes. It has its origins in ancient India, and was transformed by various ruling elites in medieval, early-modern, and modern India, especially the Mughal Empire and the British Raj.It is today the basis of affirmative action programs in India as enforced through its constitution. The caste system consists of two different concepts, varna and jati, which may be regarded as different levels of analysis of this system.

The caste system as it exists today is thought to be the result of developments during the collapse of the Mughal era and the rise of the British colonial government in India. The collapse of the Mughal era saw the rise of powerful men who associated themselves with kings, priests and ascetics, affirming the regal and martial form of the caste ideal, and it also reshaped many apparently casteless social groups into differentiated caste communities. The British Raj furthered this development, making rigid caste organization a central mechanism of administration. Between 1860 and 1920, the British incorporated the Indian caste system into their system of governance, granting administrative jobs and senior appointments only to Christians and people belonging to certain castes. Social unrest during the 1920s led to a change in this policy. From then on, the colonial administration began a policy of positive discrimination by reserving a certain percentage of government jobs for the lower castes. In 1948, negative discrimination on the basis of caste was banned by law and further enshrined in the Indian constitution in 1950; however, the system continues to be practiced in parts of India. There are 3,000 castes and 25,000 sub-castes in India, each related to a specific occupation.

Caste-based differences have also been practiced in other regions and religions in the Indian subcontinent, like Nepalese Buddhism,[13] Christianity, Islam, Judaism and Sikhism. It has been challenged by many reformist Hindu movements, Sikhism, Christianity, and present-day Indian Buddhism. With Indian influences, the caste system is also practiced in Bali and parts of Southeast Asia such as Cambodia, Laos and Thailand.

India after achieving independence in 1947 enacted many affirmative action policies for the upliftment of historically marginalized groups as enforced through its constitution. These policies included reserving a quota of places for these groups in higher education and government employment.

Varna literally means type, order, colour or class and was a framework for grouping people into classes, first used in Vedic Indian society. It is referred to frequently in the ancient Indian texts. The four classes were the Brahmins (priestly people), the Kshatriyas (rulers, administrators and warriors; also called Rajanyas), the Vaishyas (artisans, merchants, tradesmen and farmers), and Shudras (labouring classes). The varna categorisation implicitly had a fifth element, being those people deemed to be entirely outside its scope, such as tribal people and the untouchables (Dalits). India is home to over 200 million Dalits.

Jati, meaning birth, is mentioned much less often in ancient texts, where it is clearly distinguished from varna. There are four varnas but thousands of jatis. The jatis are complex social groups that lack universally applicable definition or characteristic, and have been more flexible and diverse than was previously often assumed. Jatis exist in India among Hindus, Muslims, Christians and tribal people, and there is no clear linear order among them.

The term caste is not originally an Indian word, though it is now widely used, both in English and in Indian languages. According to the Oxford English Dictionary, it is derived from the Portuguese casta, meaning "race, lineage, breed" and, originally, "'pure or unmixed (stock or breed)". There is no exact translation in Indian languages, but varna and jati are the two most approximate terms.

Untouchable outcastes and the varna system

The Vedic texts neither mention the concept of untouchable people nor any practice of untouchability. The rituals in the Vedas ask the noble or king to eat with the commoner from the same vessel. Later Vedic texts ridicule some professions, but the concept of untouchability is not found in them.

The post-Vedic texts, particularly Manusmriti, mentions outcasts and suggests that they be ostracised. Recent scholarship states that the discussion of outcastes in post-Vedic texts is different from the system widely discussed in colonial era Indian literature, and in Dumont's structural theory on caste system in India. Patrick Olivelle, a professor of Sanskrit and Indian Religions and credited with modern translations of Vedic literature, Dharma-sutras and Dharma-sastras, states that ancient and medieval Indian texts do not support the ritual pollution, purity-impurity premise implicit in the Dumont theory. According to Olivelle, purity-impurity is discussed in the Dharma-sastra texts, but only in the context of the individual's moral, ritual and biological pollution (eating certain kinds of food such as meat, going to the bathroom). Olivelle writes in his review of post-Vedic Sutra and Shastra texts, "we see no instance when a term of pure/impure is used with reference to a group of individuals or a varna or caste". The only mention of impurity in the Shastra texts from the 1st millennium is about people who commit grievous sins and thereby fall out of their varna. These, writes Olivelle, are called "fallen people" and considered impure in the medieval Indian texts. The texts declare that these sinful, fallen people be ostracised. Olivelle adds that the overwhelming focus in matters relating to purity/impurity in the Dharma-sastra texts concerns "individuals irrespective of their varna affiliation" and all four varnas could attain purity or impurity by the content of their character, ethical intent, actions, innocence or ignorance (acts by children), stipulations, and ritualistic behaviors.

Dumont, in his later publications, acknowledged that ancient varna hierarchy was not based on purity-impurity ranking principle, and that the Vedic literature is devoid of the untouchability concept.

During the time of the Rigveda (1500 - 1200 BCE), there were two varnas: arya varna and dasa varna. The distinction originally arose from tribal divisions. The Vedic tribes regarded themselves as arya (the noble ones) and the rival tribes were called dasa, dasyu and pani. The dasas were frequent allies of the Aryan tribes, and they were probably assimilated into the Aryan society, giving rise to a class distinction. Many dasas were, however, in a servile position, giving rise to the eventual meaning of dasa as servant or slave.[1]

The Rigvedic society was not distinguished by occupations. Many husbandmen and artisans practised a number of crafts. The chariot-maker (rathakara) and metal worker (karmara) enjoyed positions of importance and no stigma was attached to them. Similar observations hold for carpenters, tanners, weavers and others.

Towards the end of the Atharvaveda period, new class distinctions emerged. The erstwhile dasas are renamed Shudras, probably to distinguish them from the new meaning of dasa as slave. The aryas are renamed vis or Vaishya (meaning the members of the tribe) and the new elite classes of Brahmins (priests) and Kshatriyas (warriors) are designated as new varnas. The Shudras were not only the erstwhile dasas but also included the aboriginal tribes that were assimilated into the Aryan society as it expanded into Gangetic settlements. There is no evidence of restrictions regarding food and marriage during the Vedic period.

Capitalism

Capitalism is an economic system based on the private ownership of the means of production and their operation for profit. Central characteristics of capitalism include capital accumulation, competitive markets, price system, private property, property rights recognition, voluntary exchange, and wage labor. In a market economy, decision-making and investments are determined by owners of wealth, property, or ability to maneuver capital or production ability in capital and financial markets—whereas prices and the distribution of goods and services are mainly determined by competition in goods and services markets.

Economists, historians, political economists and sociologists have adopted different perspectives in their analyses of capitalism and have recognized various forms of it in practice. These include laissez-faire or free-market capitalism, anarcho-capitalism, state capitalism and welfare capitalism. Different forms of capitalism feature varying degrees of free markets, public ownership, obstacles to free competition and state-sanctioned social policies. The degree of competition in markets and the role of intervention and regulation as well as the scope of state ownership vary across different models of capitalism. The extent to which different markets are free and the rules defining private property are matters of politics and policy. Most of the existing capitalist economies are mixed economies that combine elements of free markets with state intervention and in some cases economic planning.

Market economies have existed under many forms of government and in many different times, places and cultures. Modern capitalist societies developed in Western Europe in a process that led to the Industrial Revolution. Capitalist systems with varying degrees of direct government intervention have since become dominant in the Western world and continue to spread. Economic growth is a characteristic tendency of capitalist economies.

The term "capitalist", meaning an owner of capital, appears earlier than the term "capitalism" and dates to the mid-17th century. "Capitalism" is derived from capital, which evolved from capitale, a late Latin word based on caput, meaning "head"—which is also the origin of "chattel" and "cattle" in the sense of movable property (only much later to refer only to livestock). Capitale emerged in the 12th to 13th centuries to refer to funds, stock of merchandise, sum of money or money carrying interest. By 1283, it was used in the sense of the capital assets of a trading firm and was often interchanged with other words—wealth, money, funds, goods, assets, property and so on.

Agrarianism

The economic foundations of the feudal agricultural system began to shift substantially in 16th-century England as the manorial system had broken down and land began to become concentrated in the hands of fewer landlords with increasingly large estates. Instead of a serf-based system of labor, workers were increasingly employed as part of a broader and expanding money-based economy. The system put pressure on both landlords and tenants to increase the productivity of agriculture to make profit; the weakened coercive power of the aristocracy to extract peasant surpluses encouraged them to try better methods, and the tenants also had incentive to improve their methods in order to flourish in a competitive labor market. Terms of rent for land were becoming subject to economic market forces rather than to the previous stagnant system of custom and feudal obligation.

European merchants, backed by state controls, subsidies and monopolies, made most of their profits by buying and selling goods. In the words of Francis Bacon, the purpose of mercantilism was "the opening and well-balancing of trade; the cherishing of manufacturers; the banishing of idleness; the repressing of waste and excess by sumptuary laws; the improvement and husbanding of the soil; the regulation of prices...".

After the period of the proto-industrialization, the British East India Company and the Dutch East India Company, after massive contributions from the Mughal Bengal, inaugurated an expansive era of commerce and trade. These companies were characterized by their colonial and expansionary powers given to them by nation-states. During this era, merchants, who had traded under the previous stage of mercantilism, invested capital in the East India Companies and other colonies, seeking a return on investment.

Religion Pilgrimages taxation

izya is a per capita yearly taxation historically levied in the form of financial charge on dhimmis, that is, permanent non-Muslim subjects of a state governed by Islamic law. The Quran and hadiths mention jizya without specifying its rate or amount, and the application of jizya varied in the course of Islamic history. However, scholars largely agree that early Muslim rulers adapted existing systems of taxation and tribute that were established under previous rulers of the conquered lands, such as those of the Byzantine and Sasanian empires.

Historically, the jizya tax has been understood in Islam as a fee for protection provided by the Muslim ruler to non-Muslims, for the exemption from military service for non-Muslims, for the permission to practice a non-Muslim faith with some communal autonomy in a Muslim state, and as material proof of the non-Muslims' submission to the Muslim state and its laws. Muslim jurists required adult, free, sane males among the dhimma community to pay the jizya, while exempting women, children, elders, handicapped, monks, hermits, slaves, and musta'mins.

Non-Muslim foreigners who only temporarily reside in Muslim lands. Dhimmis who chose to join military service were also exempted from payment, as were those who could not afford to pay. According to Islamic law, elders, handicapped etc., must be given pensions, and they must not go into begging.

Together with kharāj, a term that was sometimes used interchangeably with jizya, taxes levied on non-Muslim subjects were among the main sources of revenues collected by some Islamic polities, such as the Ottoman Empire and Indian Muslim Sultanates. Jizya rate was usually a fixed annual amount depending on the financial capability of the payer. Sources comparing taxes levied on Muslims and jizya differ as to their relative burden depending on time, place, specific taxes under consideration, and other factors.

The term appears in the Quran referring to a tax or tribute from People of the Book, specifically Jews and Christians. Followers of other religions like Zoroastrians and Hindus too were later integrated into the category of dhimmis and required to pay jizya. In the Indian Subcontinent the practice was eradicated by the 18th century. It almost vanished during the 20th century with the disappearance of Islamic states and spread of religious tolerance. The tax is no longer imposed by nation states in the Islamic world, although there are reported cases of organizations such as the Pakistani Taliban and ISIS attempting to revive the practice.

Conspiracy theory

Conspiracy theory, an attempt to explain harmful or tragic events as the result of the actions of a small powerful group. Such explanations reject the accepted narrative surrounding those events; indeed, the official version may be seen as further proof of the conspiracy.

Explanations of conspiracy theories

American historian Richard Hofstadter explored the emergence of conspiracy theorizing by proposing a consensus view of democracy. Competing groups would represent the interests of individuals, but they would do so within a political system that everyone agreed would frame the bounds of conflict. For Hofstadter, those who felt unable to channel their political interests into representative groups would become alienated from this system. These individuals would not accept the statements of opposition parties as representing a fair disagreement; rather, differences in views would be regarded with deep suspicion. Such alienated people would develop a paranoid fear of conspiracy, thus making them vulnerable to charismatic rather than practical and rational leadership. This would undermine democracy and lead to totalitarian rule.

Hybrid Regime

Electoral autocracy is a hybrid regime, in which democratic institutions are imitative and adhere to authoritarian methods. In these regimes, regular elections are held, but they fail to reach democratic standards of freedom and fairness

Earlier this month, in its annual report on global political rights and liberties, US-based non-profit Freedom House downgraded India from a free democracy to a "partially free democracy".

Last week, Sweden-based V-Dem Institute was harsher in its latest report on democracy. It said India had become an "electoral autocracy". And last month, India, described as a "flawed democracy", slipped two places to 53rd position in the latest Democracy Index published by The Economist Intelligence Unit.

The rankings blame Mr Modi and his Hindu nationalist BJP government for the backsliding of democracy. Under Mr Modi's watch, they say, there has been increased pressure on human rights groups, intimidation of journalists and activists, and a spate of attacks, especially against Muslims. This, they add, has led to a deterioration of political and civil liberties in the country.

Freedom House said civil liberties have been in decline since Mr Modi came to power in 2014, and that India's "fall from the upper ranks of free nations" could have a more damaging effect on the world's democratic standards.

A month after taking office in the summer of 2014, Prime Minister Narendra Modi said India's "democracy will not sustain if we can't guarantee freedom of speech and expression".

Six years on, many believe, India's democracy looks diminished, by what they say are persistent attacks on the freedom of the press.

Last year India dropped two places and was ranked 142 on the 180-country World Press Freedom Index, compiled annually by Reporters Without Borders. It's an unflattering commentary on a country that often prides itself on a vibrant and competitive media.

The latest crackdown has happened after violence during a recent rally by farmers to protest at a raft of agriculture reform laws. One protester was killed and more than 500 policemen injured in the clashes.

Now police have filed criminal charges - including sedition and making statements inimical to national integration - against eight journalists who covered the protests in Delhi.

The cause of the protester's death - at the rally on 26 January - remains disputed. While police say he died when the tractor he was driving overturned, his family alleges that he was shot. **His family's account**, which has been published by various newspapers and magazines, appears to have become the basis of these charges.

Some of the journalists were involved in reporting or publishing the story, and others only shared it on social media.

Six of them - and a prominent opposition Congress party MP who is accused of "misreporting" facts surrounding the death - are facing cases in four BJP-ruled states.

"Is it a crime *for the media* to report statements of relatives of a dead person if they question a post-mortem or police version of the cause of death?" Siddharth Varadarajan, editor-in-chief of The Wire and one of the journalists charged by police, said.

A **hybrid regime** is a type of political system often created as a result of an incomplete democratic transition from an authoritarian regime to a democratic one (or vice versa). Hybrid regimes are categorized as having a combination of autocratic features with democratic ones and can simultaneously hold political repressions and regular elections. Hybrid regimes are commonly found in developing countries with abundant natural resources such as petro-states. Although these regimes experience civil unrest, they may be relatively stable and tenacious for decades at a time There has been a rise in hybrid regimes since the end of the Cold War

The term *hybrid regime* arises from a polymorphic view of political regimes that opposes the dichotomy of autocracy or democracy Modern scholarly analysis of hybrid regimes focuses attention on the decorative nature of democratic institutions (elections do not lead to a change of power, different media broadcast government point of view and the opposition in parliament votes the same way as the ruling party, among others), from which it is concluded that democratic backsliding, a transition to authoritarianism is the most prevalent basis of hybrid regimes. Some scholars also contend that hybrid regimes may imitate a full dictatorship

Electoral authoritarianism

Electoral authoritarianism means that democratic institutions are imitative and, due to numerous systematic violations of liberal democratic norms, in fact adhere to authoritarian methods.

Electoral authoritarianism can be competitive and hegemonic, and the latter does not necessarily mean election irregularities A. Scheduler calls electoral authoritarianism a new form of authoritarian regime, not a hybrid regime or illiberal democracy. Moreover, a purely authoritarian regime does not need elections as a source of legitimacy while non-alternative elections, appointed at the request of the ruler, are not a sufficient condition for considering the regime conducting them to be hybrid.

Electoral autocracy

Electoral autocracy is a hybrid regime, in which democratic institutions are imitative and adhere to authoritarian methods. In these regimes, regular elections are held, but they fail to reach democratic standards of freedom and fairness.

Illiberal democracy

An illiberal democracy describes a governing system that hides its "nondemocratic practices behind formally democratic institutions and procedures". There is a lack of consensus among experts about the exact definition of illiberal democracy or whether it even exists.

The rulers of an illiberal democracy may ignore or bypass constitutional limits on their power. While liberal democracies protect individual rights and freedoms, illiberal democracies do not. Elections in an illiberal democracy are often manipulated or rigged, being used to legitimize and consolidate the incumbent rather than to choose the country's leaders and policies.

According to jurist András Sajó, illiberal democracy should be counted as a type of democracy because it is "democratic in a plebiscitarian sense",[91] while political scientist Ulrich Wagrandl argues that "illiberal democracy is actually more true to democracy's roots".Other theorists say that classifying illiberal democracy as democratic is overly sympathetic to the illiberal regimes and therefore prefer terms such as *electoral authoritarianism*, *competitive authoritarianism*, or *soft authoritarianism*.

Dominant-party system

A dominant-party system, or one-party dominant system, is a political occurrence in which a single political party continuously dominates election results over running opposition groups or parties. Any ruling party staying in power for more than one consecutive term may be considered a *dominant party* (also referred to as a *predominant* or *hegemonic* party). Some dominant parties were called the *natural governing party*, given their length of time in power.

Dominant-parties and their domination of a state, develop out of one-sided electoral and party constellations within a multi-party system (particularly under presidential systems of governance), and as such differ from states under a one-party system, which are intricately organized around a specific party. Sometimes the term "*de facto* one-party state" is used to describe dominant-party systems which, unlike a one-party system, allows (at least nominally) democratic multiparty elections, but the existing practices or balance of political power effectively prevent the opposition from winning power, thus resembling a one-party state.

Dominant-party systems differ from the political dynamics of other dominant multi-party constellations such as consociationalism, grand coalitions and two-party systems, which are characterized and sustained by narrow or balanced competition and cooperation.

Delegative democracy

In political science, delegative democracy is a mode of governance close to Caesarism, Bonapartism or caudillismo with a strong leader in a newly created otherwise democratic government. The concept arose from Argentinian political scientist Guillermo O'Donnell, who notes that representative democracy as it exists is usually linked solely to highly developed capitalist countries. However, newly installed democracies do not seem to be on a path of becoming fully representative democracies O'Donnell calls the former delegative democracies, for they are not fully consolidated democracies but may be enduring.

For a representative democracy to exist, there must be an important interaction effect. The successful cases have featured a decisive coalition of broadly supported political leaders who take great care in creating and strengthening democratic political institutions. By contrast, the delegative form is partially democratic, for the president has a free rein to act and justify his or her acts in the name of the people. The president can "govern as he sees fit" even if it does not resemble promises made while running for election. The president claims to represent the whole nation rather than just a political party, embodying even the Congress and the judiciary.

O'Donnell's notion of delegative democracy has been criticized as being misleading, because he renders the delegative model that is core to many current democratic governments worldwide into a negative concept.

Dictablanda

Dictablanda is a dictatorship in which civil liberties are allegedly preserved rather than destroyed. The word dictablanda is a pun on the Spanish word *dictadura* ("dictatorship"), replacing *dura*, which by itself is a word meaning "hard", with *blanda*, meaning "soft".

The term was first used in Spain in 1930 when Dámaso Berenguer replaced Miguel Primo de Rivera y Orbaneja as the head of the ruling dictatorial government and attempted to reduce tensions in the country by repealing some of the harsher measures that had been introduced by the latter. It was also used to refer to the latter years of Francisco Franco's Spanish State, and to the hegemonic 70-year rule of the Institutional Revolutionary Party (PRI) in Mexico, or by Augusto Pinochet when he was asked about his regime and the accusations about his government.

Analogously, the same pun is made in Portuguese as ditabranda or ditamole. In February 2009, the Brazilian newspaper Folha de S.Paulo ran an editorial classifying the military dictatorship in Brazil (1964–1985) as a "ditabranda", creating controversy.

Guided democracy

Guided democracy, also called managed democracy, is a formally democratic government that functions as a de facto authoritarian government or in some cases, as an autocratic government. Such hybrid regimes are legitimized by elections that are free and fair, but do not change the state's policies, motives, and goals. The concept is also related to semi-democracy or *anocracy*.

In other words, the government controls elections so that the people can exercise all their rights without truly changing public policy. While they follow basic democratic principles, there can be major deviations towards authoritarianism. Under managed democracy, the state's continuous use of propaganda techniques prevents the electorate from having a significant impact on policy.

After World War II, the term was used in Indonesia for the approach to government under the Sukarno administration from 1959 to 1966. It is today widely employed in Russia, where it was introduced into common practice by Kremlin theorists, in particular Gleb Pavlovsky.

Liberal autocracy

A liberal autocracy is a non-democratic government that follows the principles of liberalism. Until the 20th century, most countries in Western Europe were "liberal autocracies, or at best, semi-democracies".[112] One example of a "classic liberal autocracy" was the Austro-Hungarian Empire. According to Fareed Zakaria, a more recent example is Hong Kong until 1 July 1997, which was ruled by the British Crown. He says that until 1991 "it had never held a meaningful election, but its government epitomized constitutional liberalism, protecting its citizens' basic rights and administering a fair court system and bureaucracy".[

Semi-democracy

Anocracy or semi-democracy is a form of government that is loosely defined as part democracy and part dictatorship, or as a "regime that mixes democratic with autocratic features." Another definition classifies anocracy as "a regime that permits some means of participation through opposition group behavior but that has incomplete development of mechanisms to redress grievances." The term "semi-democratic" is reserved for stable regimes that combine democratic and authoritarian elements. Scholars have also distinguished anocracies from autocracies and democracies in their capability to maintain authority, political dynamics, and policy agendas. Similarly, the regimes have democratic institutions that allow for nominal amounts of competition.[

Defective democracy

Defective democracies is a concept that was proposed by the political scientists Wolfgang Merkel, Hans-Jürgen Puhle and Aurel S. Croissant at the beginning of the 21st century to subtilize the distinctions between totalitarian, authoritarian, and democratic political systems. It is based on the concept of embedded democracy. There are four forms of defective democracy, how each nation reaches the point of defectiveness varies. One recurring theme is the geographical location of the nation, which includes the effects of the influence of surrounding nations in the region. Other causes for defective democracies include their path of modernization, level of modernization, economic trends, social capital, civil society, political institutions, and education.

Embedded democracy

Embedded democracy is a form of government in which democratic governance is secured by democratic partial regimes. [125][126][127] The term "embedded democracy" was coined by political scientists Wolfgang Merkel, Hans-Jürgen Puhle, and Aurel Croissant, who identified "five interdependent partial regimes" necessary for an embedded democracy: electoral regime, political participation, civil rights, horizontal accountability, and the power of the elected representatives to govern. The five internal regimes work together to check the power of the government, while external regimes also help to secure and stabilize embedded democracies. Together, all the regimes ensure that an embedded democracy is guided by the three fundamental principles of freedom, equality, and control.

Neo Nazi Bourgeois Autocratic Hippocratic Dictatorship (hybrid regime)

BJP- RSS Compact or Joint venture rule are flower of Nazism as their Aryan racism explanation on the name of Extreme Hindus like as Arabian Religion nor formal Regime. Mythical base story and Epic base worshiping that Lord Rama *made* issued and Jai Sree Rama *made* Political Slogan as in North India common peoples worship Lord Rama and Lord Hanuman on the base of Translated Ramayana from Sanskrit to Hindi by Tulsidas. Jai Shee Rama now only *remained a political* slogan as BJP-RSS joint venture politicalized where devotional ideology ended and extreme racism of Hindiana started where Non-Hindi Peoples ignored and expiation given that if they unable to speaking or writing Hindi than left India that human right target to abolish by planning. On the Other hand, On the name of Hindu Tribal right abolishing by planning as Strong caste system *enforcement was done* where right to Horse Riding by groom *was restricted* by upper caste in BJP-RSS compact ruling. On the name of Hindi and Hindu Gujrati racism enforce to whole India as Economy draining toward Gujrat as Bourgeois groups of Business loan taken by recommendations and some parts of loan donated to BJP-RSS Fund and then Loan, Interest, tax reliefs by black hand of recommendation where loan money used for Indian National property transfer name of Gujrati business personality. Hacking Courts Judges and extended retainment to given favorite declaration for BJP RSS leaders and Enforcement Directory form by selected groups of *staff* by which misused power by dramatic ways to abolish and *demolish opposition* parties. Rapists and *criminals* given relief by recommendation or black hand or back door orders to misused power.

RSS, Bajrang Dal, Hindu Mahashava, Durga Sana violate team to *enforce* and *execute* racism of Hindiana all over India. Electoral groups remained BJP who *executed* Autocracy conspiracy Fascism. Actually, it is **hybrid regime system of Dictatorship where Lynching, mob lynching and murders done as well as rape cases increasing continuously.**

Operation Lotus that *gave* **money and** *destroyed* **democracy to hack opposition or independent candidates and** *then distributed* **or made governor or higher post offering to support BJP only. Flack Legation** *implemented* **through Enforcement Directors and then by force participation done to BJP or otherwise without bail send prison done to abolishing and demolishing life to spoiled. Illegal money transfer among leaders becomes rules and heaviest taxation** *implemented* **to every step to common peoples and rate of every commodities increases thrice or more. Petroleum rate made uncontrollable where save guard root** *established* **to Petroleum mafia on their close friend's hand.**

Lynching

It is an extrajudicial killing by a group. It is most often used to characterize informal public executions by a mob in order to punish an alleged transgressor, punish a convicted transgressor, or intimidate people. It can also be an extreme form of informal group social control, and it is often conducted with the display of a public spectacle (often in the form of a hanging) for maximum intimidation. Instances of lynchings and similar mob violence can be found in every society.

In the United States, where the word for "lynching" likely originated, lynchings of African Americans became frequent in the South during the period after the Reconstruction era, especially during the nadir of American race relations.[1]

Mob lynching refers to killing someone for an alleged offense without a legal trial. It is a form of aggression in which a mob, under the guise of administering justice without a trial, punishes and tortures a presumed offender, sometimes resulting in mass killings.

The mob believes they are punishing the victim for doing something wrong and they take the law into their own hands to punish the alleged accused without following any rules of law.

The recent lynching occurrences recorded in Amritsar and Kapurthala concerned the former chief minister of Punjab. It has again highlighted the issue of mob lynching still persisting in the country.

serial murder, also called **serial killing**, the unlawful homicide of at least two people carried out by the same person (or persons) in separate events occurring at different times. Although this definition is widely accepted, the crime is not formally recognized in any legal code, including that of the United States. Serial murder is distinguished from mass murder, in which several victims are murdered at the same time and place.

Secularity

Secularity, also **the secular** or secularness (from Latin saeculum, "worldly" or "of a generation"), is the state of being unrelated or neutral in regards to religion. Secular and religious entities were intertwined throughout the medieval period without much distinction.

Today, anything that does not have an explicit reference to religion, either negatively or positively, may be considered secular. Secularity is best understood, not as being "anti-religious", but as being "religiously neutral" since many activities in religious bodies are secular themselves, and most versions of secularity or secularization do not lead to irreligiosity. Linguistically, a process by which anything becomes secular is named *secularization*, though the term is mainly reserved for the secularization of society; and any concept *of ideology* promoting the secular may be termed secularism, a term generally applied to the ideology dictating no religious influence on the public sphere.

Most cultures around the world do not have tension or dichotomous views of religion and *secularism*. Since *religion* and *secularism* are both Western concepts that were formed under the influence of Christian theology, other cultures do not necessarily have words or concepts that resemble or are equivalent to them.

Philosopher Charles Taylor in his 2007 book A Secular Age understands and discusses the secularity of Western societies less in terms of how much of a role religion plays in public life (*secularity 1*), or how religious a society's individual members are (*secularity 2*), than as a "backdrop" or social context in which religious belief is no longer taken as a given (*secularity 3*). For Taylor, this third sense of secularity is the unique historical condition in which virtually all individuals - religious or not - have to contend with the fact that their values, morality, or sense of life's meaning are no longer underpinned by communally-accepted religious facts. All religious beliefs or irreligious philosophical positions are, in a secular society, held with an awareness that there are a wide range of other contradictory positions available to any individual; belief in general becomes a different type of experience when all particular beliefs are optional. A plethora of competing religious and irreligious worldviews open up, each rendering the other more "fragile". This condition in turn entails for Taylor that even clearly religious beliefs and practices are experienced in a qualitatively different way when they occur in a secular social context. In Taylor's sense of the term, a society could in theory be highly "secular" even if nearly all of its members believed in a deity or even subscribed to a particular religious creed; secularity here has to do with the conditions, not the prevalence, of belief, and these conditions are understood to be shared across a given society, irrespective of belief or lack thereof.

System Deformation by Planning

1. Bourgeois community develop in Illegal ways of Income as Smuggling and mafia
2. Spiritual Business and illegal business with political link
3. Power Capturing by cheating to enjoying entertainment life
4. Misuse power through Misinformation and misguide

5. Sentimental Political system development through Divide and Rule
6. Destruction Unity in Diversity
7. Planning to destruction of back bone of Farmer, Tribal and common middle-class peoples:
8. Enemy of nation and society as Anti nationalist, Anti farmer, Anti Tribal, and Anti Labour, Anti Common Peoples.
9. Acting Dress up and make up
10. Hack digital voting
11. Works as agent of Bourgeois community as criminal

British India Situation and Society

Economic impact of British imperialism

William Digby estimated that from 1870 to 1900, £900 million was transferred from India In the 17th century, India was a relatively urbanized and commercialized nation with a large export trade, devoted largely to cotton textiles, but also silk, spices, and rice. India was the world's main producer of cotton textiles and had substantial export trade to Britain as well as many other European countries, via the East India Company. According to some commentators, after the British victory over the Mughal Empire (Battle of Buxar), India was deindustrialized by the East India Company, and then the British.

In contrast, historian Niall Ferguson argues that India benefited from the British investment of £270 million in Indian infrastructure, irrigation, and industry by the 1880s (representing nearly one-fifth of all British investment overseas). That amount reached £400 million by 1914. He also writes that the British increased the area of irrigated land eight-fold, to 25% of all land. The village economy's share of total after-tax income rose under British rule from 45% to 54%. Ferguson argues that since the sector represented three quarters of the entire population, their rising share reduced income inequality in India.

Impact on trade

The British East India Company had forced open the large Indian market to British goods, which could be sold in India without tariffs or duties, compared to local Indian producers who were heavily taxed. At the same time, protectionist policies in Britain, such as bans and high tariffs, were implemented to restrict Indian textiles from being sold there. The British enforced tariffs and duties of 70-80% on textiles produced in India, making them impractical for export. In the early 1700s, India had a hold of 25% of the global textile trade.[1] Raw cotton, however, was imported without tariffs from India to British factories. The factories manufactured textiles from Indian cotton and sold them back to the Indian market. British economic policies gave them a monopoly over India's large market and cotton resources. India served as both a significant supplier of raw goods to British manufacturers and a large captive market for British manufactured goods. With the export of manufactured goods rendered unviable over the period of British rule, India's share of global manufacturing exports dropped from 27% to 2%. On the contrary, exports from Britain to India soared with duty-free goods that Indian goods could no longer compete with on quality or price.

The damage to the textile industry went beyond just a decrease in production and export. As industrial production was severely disrupted, Indian workers were forced into agriculture at levels unsustainable by the land. Rural wages were then driven down by the newly crowded market of agricultural workers. Additionally, these workers used cloth making as a backup source of income if weather affected their crops. This was no longer a viable option for them. Ultimately, poverty in rural India was catalyzed by the policies deployed by the British.

Taxation

Taxation by the British, usually 50% of income, was so burdensome on the population that they were forced to flee their lands. This form of revenue generation was a departure from the practices deployed by Indian rulers in the past, who primarily raised funds through global and regional trade networks rather than through taxing farmers. Under the zamindari revenue system deployed by the British, farmers were no longer taxed a percentage of their crops produced. Rather, they were taxed a percentage of the land rent payments, regardless of the success or failure of the crops. According to estimates by the British, agricultural taxes were two to three times higher than before British rule, and the highest in the world.

P. J. Marshall argues that the British regime did not make any sharp breaks with the traditional economy, and that control was largely left in the hands of regional rulers. The economy was sustained by general conditions of prosperity through the latter part of the 18th century, excepting the frequent famines with high fatality rates. Marshall notes the British raised revenue through local tax administrators and kept the old Mughal rates of taxation. Marshall wrote that the British managed this primarily indigenous-controlled economy through cooperation with Indian elites.

The Social and Economic Impact of British Rule in India:

Right from the beginning of their relationship with India, the British, who had come as traders and had become rulers and administrators, had influenced the economic and political systems of the country. Their impact on the cultural and social life of India was, however, gradual. Till 1813, they followed a policy of non-interference in the social and cultural life of the Indians. Yet, changes were taking place in these fields (the social life of Indians).

Education:

Initially, the East India Company did not think that it was its duty to impart education to Indians. It allowed the old system of education to continue. Pathsalas, which imparted a special type of education geared towards meeting the requirements of a rural society, were open to all. Sanskrit education was imparted in tools. Muslims attended Madrasas. Higher education was confined primarily to upper castes. This system of education was eventually changed by the British.

Around the beginning of the 19th century, the Company became aware of the need for introducing Western education in India. However, Christian missionaries, who were interested in spreading Christianity through education, had already established several educational institutions which were attached to their churches.

Drain of Wealth:

The greatest impact of British policies was the drain of wealth from India. The Indian economy, no doubt, was primarily a rural economy, but Indian artisans produced goods in bulk to meet the demands of Indian and European buyers. Several towns had flourished as centers of trade. There had been a great demand for muslin from Bengal and silk from Bengal and Banaras.

British merchants bought these Indian products in large quantities. But, at the beginning of the 18th century, Britain and other European countries passed laws prohibiting the entry of cotton and silk textiles from India although there was a demand for it. After the advent of the Industrial Revolution, India was forced to produce cotton, indigo and other products which British industries required.

Indian markets were flooded with cheap, machine-made textiles manufactured in England. Indian hand-made textiles could not compete with the cheap machine-made textiles. India was transformed into a supplier of raw materials and a market for British manufactured goods.

While British goods were exempted from duties while entering Indian markets, Indian goods entering England were burdened with heavy customs duties. Thus, the self-sufficient economy of India collapsed under the impact of British colonial policies. With the decline of the cotton industry, the towns that had flourished as centers of trade or industry also declined.

Post Independent India and Development under Nationalist

Economic Planning of Nehru – Mahalanobis Model

Base of the Mahalanobis Model

It is necessary to highlight the economic policy of India after the British colonial period. Therefore, the importance of the Mahalanobis Model and its primary objectives are necessary to be discussed. As per the study and analysis based on the entire model, it is highlighted that the model focuses on the primary objective that is efficiency to develop the economic state of the country as well as that can follow the long-term economic growth of the country. As per the second five-year plan in the economic sectors, it was necessary to construct a model that injects effectiveness in the economic sectors as well as changes the perspective of the Indian economy in the world. The Mahalanobis Model also implements several ideas that are efficient to build and maintain transparency.

The Nehru Model

Following the fundamental state of the Mahalanobis Model, it is necessary to highlight the Nehru model in contrast to the mentioned development model. As per the key area of the model, it is highlighted that the model is based on the four pillars of parliamentary democracy. Therefore, economic planning is one of the most important factors that are highlighted as one of the fundamental issues that need to develop through constructing a proper economic planning and well-fare policy.

The Essence of the Mahalanobis Model

As per the study based on the economic reforms in India, it is necessary to highlight the impact of the Mahalanobis Model as the essence follows the base of heavy industry in India. One of the primary criteria of this model is to boost up the foreign investment policy as well as invite several other industries. However, the Mahalanobis Model tries to ensure the investment of proper funds in this industry at the same time increases the potential improvement of the economic condition of the country. This modem also initiates the process of developing an internal investment policy in this industry to avoid foreign capital equipment.

Conclusion

According to the analysis of the entire Mahalanobis Model, it is clear that the models has developed following the measure of the industrial model as well as constructing a long-term model that helps in maintaining proper and sustainable growth in the financial structure of the country.

ECONOMIC ENVIRONMENT Structure 2,O Objectives 2.1 Introduction 2.2 Mixed Economy in India 2.3 Economic planning 2.4 Basic Elements of the Strategies Followed During 1956-90 (Nehru-Mahalanobis Strategy of Development) 2.5 Contemporary Economic Reforms 2.6 Let Us Sum Up 2.7 Key Words 2.8 Terminal Questions 2.0 OBJECTIVES After studying this unit you should be able to: e describe the features of mixed economy in India e . outline the structure of economic planning in India e examine the development strategies adopted in various plans an analysis the contemporary economic reforms initiated by the government,

Economic environment of business refers to the broad characteristics of the combined system in which a business firm operates. In this unit you will study the economic environment in the context of economic planning. Economic planning is supposed to give direction to the changes in the economic environment.

During the struggle for India's freedom, the leaders had committed that India would after the attainment of independence, launch a programme of planned development of the country. In pursuance of this objective., the Indian National: Congress, in 1938, appointed the National Planning ~committee with Jawaharlal Nehru the chairman to draft a plan for the development of India. The committee considered all aspects of planning and produced a series of reports. on various subjects related to economic development. The Chairman of the Committee, Jawaharlal Nehru, became the first Prime Minister of India. His ideas and policies initiated for the planned development of India reflected the consensus arrived: it in the deliberations of the National Planning Committee. The Committee rejected the Soviet model of total ownership of the means of production by the state on the one hand, the free capitalist enterprise model on the other hand; it opted for a mixed economic framework as the most suitable economic environment for India.

Introduction to Business. - Environment railways, waterways, shipping and other public utilities and, in fact, all those large scale industries which were likely to become monopolistic in character. In other words, the ~committee specified the industries which were to be owned or controlled by the public sector; (b) The remaining industries were too he in the private sector, but could be called upon to work in national interest. In case, the state at any stage felt that the monopolistic activities of private businessmen worked against national interest, it reserved the right to take over such industries; (c) The Committee should held the view that it was not possible to draw a scheme of national planning without giving a primary place to agriculture; and (d) The committee aimed at doubling the standard of living of the people in 10 years,

MIXED ECONOMY IN INDIA Soon after independence, there was a lot of confusion about the environment in which the Indian economy should function. While labor leaders wanted complete transition to socialism, the capitalists within the Congress Party spoke of a private capitalist enterprise environment. It was, therefore, necessary that the government should state clearly the type of economy which it intended to promote. The choice was either to move to a complete transformation to socialism in which all the means of production (land, factories, banks, railways, transport and communications, hospitals, educational institutions, etc.) will be owned by the state. This was popularly referred to as the Soviet model. This required total nationalization of all the spheres of economic and social activities. The other choice was to follow the capitalist model, popularly referred to as capitalism, in which the means of production are owned by the landlords and the capitalists. The nation, under the leadership of Jawaharlal Nehru, rejected the Soviet model of socialism because it led to the emergence of a totalitarian state in which democratic freedoms were denied to citizens. Indian society worked for the democratic system of government which permitted the epistemic of different schools of thought. Thus, the idea of the dictatorship of a palsy or of an individual or placing absolute power in the hands of an elite group (called as the cabinet) did not find favor in India. The command model of Soviet variety was reflected by the Indian policy in favor of democratic socialism which envisaged a mixed economy. At the same time, the Indian leaders were against the capitalist model of production. Because it helped exploration of peasants and landless workers by the landlords and of the industrial and other workers by the capitalist classes. Profit maximization could not be accepted as the supreme goal of society. The government, therefore, opted for mixed economically within the parameters laid down in the Directive Principles of the Indian Constitution. The Directive Principle stated:

The State shall, in particular, direct its policy towards securing - (a) that citizens, men and women equally, have the right to an adequate means of livelihood. (b) that the Leadership and control of the resources of the community are so distributed as best to sub serve the common good, (c) that the operation of the economic system does not result in the concentration of wealth and\ means of production to common detriment

Capture power by Bourgeois

Dress up and acting become a policy to fool common peoples. Narendra Modi Gotro, which means ancient village of his old generation, is Modh Ghanchi Tali that their old generation originated from Ghanchi village or city and Ghanchi are situated at Tajikistan. Modi originates from Modhera which means Wines that indicated his old generation also selling wines. Ghanchi Tali belongs to Muslim Tali who migrated to India in Islamic period. On the other hand, it is right that his community including the Other Backward class at his time when he remained as Chief Minister by special amendment indicated he actually did not remain in the Other Backward Class as Modi surname remained in general caste. Another case his father Adopted Abdas a Muslim Child and Islamic Eid festival also celebrated in his house as well as his childhood passing that old house of his father situated at Islamic majority locality and father of Abbas shop remained in the same place where his father has business. Abbas has so many relatives than why his father adopted a Muslim son as they also had so many brothers and that time period remained Hindu Muslim tension period when riots held around India and Hindu used to be considered untouchable to Muslim. It is also seen that in every step He is habitual to telling lies and acting to cheat with the nation and society. All of the above given evidence that he is Islamic Muslim community.

Ambani Adani and other Gujrati who suddenly became rich by any way they made an alliance by which duplicate Modi gave speech and acting by dressing up and making up as actor. Electronic media and messengers anchor of Agent media who are actually renting peoples advertising and use IT shells to brainwash innocent peoples to get votes as well as use EVM machines where hacking as Ambani Adani supply the machines mainly. Capitalist Ambani Adani getting loan by recommendation as commission paid to party funds and transfer name of national properties to their name, in foreign countries buying property by loan money also. Later loan, tax and interest were all relieved by black band that hacked the government formed under their hand as Poppet dole. Spiritual Businessmen use as agents to brainwash as well as Pilgrims temples in the name of renovation by using temple fund money and making business spots that each and every step to enter at temples or offering make heavy rate or cost where common peoples have money any right to worship directly like as before. It became a bourgeois system where sentiment for voting used to Spiritual businessman for brain washing and capitalist remained top as cheating to capture national property and monetary funds by backdoor in black hand to become richest in the quickest time period.

The Capital Come Under Criminal

Criminal become cedars and working for BJP- RSS and basically rapist getting shelter as well as mob lynches and vagabond professional murderers involving as getting shelter by BJP-RSS leadership. So many rapists get reliefs from persons of Gujarat and become members of BJP-RSS.

According to data compiled by the Amicus Curiae, a total of 4,984 criminal cases involving legislators were pending in various courts across the country as of 1st December, 2021.

The Amicus Curiae was appointed by the Supreme Court for helping the court in setting up special courts to fast-track cases against MPs and MLAs.

This trend highlights the increasing instance of criminalization of politics.

An amicus curia (literally, "friend of the court") is someone who is not a party to a case and may or may not have been solicited by a party and who assists a court by offering information, expertise, and bearing on issues of the case.

Criminalization of Politics:

The criminalization of politics means the participation of criminals in politics which includes that criminals can contest in the elections and get elected as members of the Parliament and the State legislature.

It takes place primarily due to the nexus between politicians and criminals.

Legal Aspects of Disqualification of Criminal Candidates:

In this regard, Indian Constitution does not specify as to what disqualifies a person from contesting elections for the Parliament, Legislative assembly or any other legislature.

The Representation of Peoples Act 1951 mentions the criteria for disqualifying a person for contesting an election of the legislature.

Section 8 of the act, i.e. disqualification on conviction for certain offenses, according to which an individual punished with a jail term of more than two years cannot stand in an election for six years after the jail term has ended.

The law does not bar individuals who have criminal cases pending against them from contesting elections therefore the disqualification of candidates with criminal cases depends on their conviction in these cases.

Reasons for Criminalization of Politics:

Lack of Enforcement:

Several laws and court judgments have not helped much, due to the lack of enforcement of laws and judgments.

Vested Interests:

Publishing of the entire criminal history of candidates fielded by political parties may not be very effective, as a major chunk of voters tend to vote through a narrow prism of community interests like caste or religion.

Use of Muscle and Money Power:

Candidates with serious records seem to do well despite their public image, largely due to their ability to finance their own elections and bring substantive resources to their respective parties.

Making Fool and Cheating with Nation Policy

1. Religion Sentiment peach given to attract common peoples
2. Working in favors of Bourgeois Business holder
3. Depressing to Farmers, Tribal, Laboure
4. Anti- Common people's laws implement
5. Poor making poorest and bourgeois making richest personality

Hack Government:

Bourgeois groups hack Politicians as voting money provided to fool common peoples and national property making self-property by cheating policy. Loan is the section for buying National property that the national fund uses for national property. Then Use national money and thereafter relieve loan with interest by Black Hand helping or leave the nation that money drained to foreign nation fund or sick industries mansion by Black Hand helping. Actually, black hands capturing national property and depressing common peoples as an Agent government formed.

Autocracy Fascist and Racists Antisocial and Rapist Ruled:

Anti-Nationalist, Antisocial, Gujrati and alliance peoples planning against nation and society where Rapist get shelter under BJP- RSS leaders of Gujrati leadership leading society, Economy draining to Gujrat by black hand, Thogi come back in new name Chaddi baniyan gang as in British Period stop Thogi activity who kill and antisocial activity done against common peoples, Uncontrol and most expenses for personal and political purpose national funds money used by supreme of BJP-RSS leaders, Demolishing

Opposition by ED CBI officers hack or buy by money, In black money transfer to independent candidate or Opposition competitor to get support of BJP-RSS, Judge retainment extended and court orders enforced in favor of BJP-RSS, Ordinances declare against common peoples or tribal or tribal, Heavily taxation enforces to every step to general peoples. It also makes loan sanction, national property transfer to BJP-RSS Leaders and their relatives or Capitalist Ambani Adani and then tax, loan, interest relief by black hand or recommendations as like feeling it is their parental property that means theft of national money by black hand. Caste feeling and lower caste peoples torturing are done by higher caste peoples as they execute rule in the name of Hindu Rashtra. Gujrati racism that Gujar-Jat Indo Iranian ruling executing on the name of Hindiana to executing Hindi racism where statement given if any one do not know hindi than left india that Non- Hindi state like Tamil, Telegu that all Dravidian south Indian and Assamese, Manipu that all Burmese-Tibetan group of North Eastern Regional peoples identity, languages, culture, social system demolishing and abolishing by force. The process of cheating the nation and society as antinationalist, Anti farmers, Anti Labour, Anti tribes, anti-common people's laws is implemented. It is harmful system like as-

1. Power Misused
2. Misguides nation through misinformation
3. Media hack by money
4. Military power misuse against nation
5. Courts hack by money illegal transfer to judges
6. Political Carders used to do antisocial activity
7. Doing Hepatis, hooligan, riots, mob lynching, hat speech, divide to rule, economy drain to personal name, etc.
8. BJP-RSS IT shell shooting anti national videos and spread up through What app and social media and Messengers Godi gadhar media and agent dalal anchors use and some channels used to execute bourgeois ruling spread up.

Hindiana as New form of Indo-Iranian Racism:

Hindi words are a mix of khariboli that is actually named Kharistry language with Persian, Arabian and it is sister language of Urdu. Hence grammatical contractions totally match with Urdu. In Sanskrit there have not used Auxiliary verbs and main verbs and noun changes as per Dhaturup and Sabdorup but in Hindi and Urdu main verbs dependent as per gender and added should suffix and auxiliary verbs change as per genders. But Other languages of Indo Arian/ Aryan there did not use auxiliary verbs and Afro Asian Davidian languages have no auxiliary verbs also. Hindi and Urdu were evaluated at Islamic Period where the court language remained Aramaic Persian. Where words are based on khariboli in Hindi and Persian words are based in Urdu. Marathi, Panjabi, Gujarati, Marwari languages are the base of Indo Aryan which are branch groups of Iranian Turkish sub group of languages. Sanskrit language evaluated in Sasanian rule of Iran that north Iranian language.

Ancient period Indo European sub group Indo Iranian peoples invaded Indian Peninsula where actually Austrasia and Afrasian peoples group rehabilitated from far long ago that about black peoples migrated to Indian peninsula about 60000 years ago. About 13000 to 5000 years ago Indo Iranian migrated as they invaded to black people's landmarks and made slaves to black peoples called Sutra which turn to Sudra means black peoples. Dus or Doos peoples, a branch group of Germanics, were rehabilitated at Indus who were defeated by Assyrian called Ashur, a leading group of Arabian and Iranian who arrested Dus / Doos peoples. Dus means remaining Kings but that transformed to slaves as turn to slave when arrested Dus peoples. Dus was migrated to save life and slavery they even today rehabilitate to Eastern and South India and hence in Eastern India have Dus surname to Brahmin and kayastra community and Doors remain surname in South India.

Assyrian peoples migrated to Arabian Peninsula from Caucasus and ruled to the West bank of Arabian Peninsula and genesis called their ruling ancient period. After Abraham/ Ibrahim the group divided into two branches mainly. Actually, several rulers worshiped by different groups of peoples in the Arabian Peninsula. About 99 groups of peoples assimilated who mainly worshiped and meditated on Al Salam and formed Islam and flower of Ismail. Others remained as Jews who flowed by Isaac. Guide base society form who worship and meditate on Jesus. Orthodox religion ruled and ruled the Arabian Peninsula. Non formal society formed as fabula and spread up to west Asia and North African parts as ruled theologies' hybrid regime. Central Asian Aryan who converted to Islamic believers they again invaded the Indian peninsula. Basically, Rajput and Brahmin ruled executed as agent governments in different parts of India, e.g. Mansingh and other rulers of Rajasthan and some converted to Islamic, e.g. Musid Khulikha whose original name was Surya Narayan Mishra. Afterall Aryan racism was executed as Islamic Racism in India.

Hindiana is a new form of Aryan racism by a fallacy statement of Akhanda Bharat as there had not remained single rulers which were mentioned as Akhanda Bharat. Present Bharat/ India actually British Indian Assimilated parts which were divided as India and Pakistan in 1947. Later East Pakistan became independent to form Bangladesh in 1971. As a result of Hindiana , political parties BJP, RSS, VHP, Bajarangdal, HIndumasava, etc. created an artificial political and social crisis. Lord Rama making politicization and Jay Sree Rama become political Slogan as this group's politicizations Lord Rama as North, West, Central Indian peoples habitual to worshiping and meditation to lord Rama, his family and Lord hanuman to epic base translated Hindi Ramayana from Sanskrit by Tulsi Das only. Asa result political and social crisis formed as–

1. Politicization Lord Rama transform Force Hindi racism:
2. Conflict from among Islamic Aryan with Pre-Islamic Aryan
3. Slavery system restarting as Caste felling reimplement
4. Tribal depression started by force Hindi racism
5. Hindi racism *implements Dravidian* to south India *to abolish the language*, culture and identity of Dravidians.

6. Hindi racism implements to north eastern *Indians* to abolish their language, culture and identity.
7. Rape, hooligan, riots, murder, mob lynching activity done political alliance RSS, VHP, Bajarangdal, HIndumasava, etc. as theological political hybrid regimes system implement as autocracy, conspiracy, racism, hypocrisy, Nazi system compacts system implement.

Non-Aryan Zone of India:

Actually, it is seen that India was a rehabilitation of Afro-Australasian from 50000 years but later some groups of Afros-Asian migration happened when Saharan ruled ended by Euro-Asian Germanic branch groups Jat/ Jut demolish Sino- Black peoples ruled. Egypt came under European rule. European Jut ruled in Jordan called Yden /Eden Jannha in singular meaning garden and Jannat plural number that means gardens. Basically, such peoples were worshiping Ziva, Alla and El Gods and Goddesses. God words come first and they have male and female same meaning but later Goddess mention as Feminine gender.

Sino Black peoples are called as Hindu as it means Inferior Land Mark whereas rehabilitation of Sino Black peoples remained at Lower Indus. European Slavic Branch groups migrated to Upper Hindu Kush Ranges from North Iran to Kashmir region Himalaya. Hindu Kush ranges basically Uzbekistan remains under the rule of the Indu community. But Turkish and Arabian invasions were done in two ways: one group invaded the Indian Peninsula and other groups invaded South China called Tibet. One Turkish group invaded and migrated to Siberia. Hence Tibetan is called Sino-Tibetan and hence Tibetan and Sanskrit are sister languages of each other. Tibet means Mountainous locality.

Sans means Chock and Krit means drawing that means Slate pencil use. Sanskrit language and its Script have similarity with Caucasian, Georgian and Armenian. Russian, Ukrainian, Kazak, Uralic, Check, Croatian, Lithuanian and other Baltic states languages are more or less similar.

Hindi is Aryan language where it is Avastan and South Iranian language mixed with Turkish and Arabic. We hear stories of Asur /Ashur that they were actually Sinai peoples as Ancient Arabian.

First World War and Political Change Around World:

Before 1885, there remained different political landlord organization in British India e.g. Eastern Indian Association, British Royal Indian Association, etc. The British ruled in India mainly the Agency state system where Indian rule by paying tax to British rulers. When Murder to Widow, Multi marriage, Child Marriage system Abolish and western education started for all as well as reservation to depress stating through depress commission. Hence LandLord groups started to demand Sami Independent Ruling. Hence Divide and rule as well as Economy drain out social theory given to getting support from common peoples. British rulers promised to give partial ruling rights to Indians. After the First World War, In Great Britain Democracy started and hence in Australia, New Zealand, Canada as well as India was given Sami Independency where Imperial Legislative Assembly lower members elected by voting through Election.

Indian Independent Movement for Semi-Independent India:

First stage of British Ruled from Calcutta:

East India that was called East (Asia) of the Indian Ocean Region company was executed at Calcutta and Calcutta became ruled independently when Fort William foundation was done as per permission got from England royal family and thereafter war defeated Siraj Dulha Coosipoor. Later Bengal came under rule and political power increased around India. After 1857 Company rule turned to British Rule under which England remained supreme power. When the Independent movement started under Anusilan Samiti, a Political organization and high-level movement, the British changed the capital from Calcutta to New Delhi.

Delhi Capital British Rule:

When the British ruled states from New Delhi that time the British understood the Ruling required to change its system as Maximum Britisher youth should not want to migrate to India to participate in Civil Services. Indian young's given the right to participate in Civil Services and thereafter after the First World war was held and from 1920 Election started where lower house members elected as India in Imperial Legislative Council.

Federal System Implementation:

Provincial government established by Election and different state Chief Minister deputed and about 550 remained Estate where tax payee king ruled from 1920 a mixed system started under collaboration of Indian and British

Bureaucratic and Democratic Mixed System

1. Governor General: National Supreme Authority
2. Governor: State Supreme Authority
3. Prime Minister Dominated Power
4. Chief Minister State Dominated Power
5. Chief Executive Officers District Magistrate/Officers
6. Executive Officers as Sub Division Magistrate/ Officers under Drastic Officers
7. Local Executive deputed to Village Board and Municipality

British Ruling System in India

Direct Ruling: Bureaucratic System Development

Agency Ruling: Estate System Development

Semi Independent India:

Mr. Mohandas Karamchand Gandhi and Vallabhbhai Patel who worked as Agent of British where always wanted British should rule India as they were Feudal society members of Gujarat and neither support to those people who wanted to be fully independent then decided to Hanover power to congress. Mr. Mohandas Karamchand Gandhi and Vallabhbhai Patel were working as agents of the British, so they neither supported Subash Chandra Bose nor to Bhagat Singh and other leaders who wanted to be fully independent. In the First World War Full Support to the British by Mr. Mohandas Karamchand Gandhi and Vallabhbhai Patel as well as British personality remaining alliance, e.g. Annie Besant, Charles Freer Andrews and others. Gandhi was highlighted by the British as they knew that as an agent of British Gandhi working in favor of them.

But tried to continue ruled by British as strong movement protected continued by British as they had knowledge if A political party defatted to British and started to rule in India then business of British to be abolish and demolish other British colonies by same type of movement.

When a war held then political change happened and then social and economic changes happening automatically. The colonial ruled breaking started after First World War as maximum colonizer countries royalist system ended and democratic system developed where democratic party remaining leading groups but after 20 years again Second World war hold then demolish colonial ruled as colonizer countries itself were not able to control self-country and it basic mater when self-reliance system break down then it not possible to control colonies which captured by different policy and ruled executed. Hence one after other colonies handed over to colonizer helpful political parties or to hand over ex ruler of those colonies.

General elections were held in British India in 1920 to elect members to the Imperial Legislative Council and the Provincial Councils. They were the first elections in the country's modern history.

The Central Legislative Assembly which was the lower chamber of the Imperial Legislative Council was based in Delhi had 104 elected seats, of which 66 were contested and thirty eight were reserved for Europeans elected through the Chambers of Commerce. For the upper chamber, the Council of State, 24 of the 34 seats were contested, whilst five were reserved for Muslims, three for Whites, one for Sikhs and one for the United Provinces. The Parliament was opened by the Duke of Connaught and Strathearn on 9 February 1921.

Alongside the national elections there were also elections to 637 seats in Provincial Assemblies. Of these, 440 were contested, 188 had a single candidate elected unopposed. Despite the calls by Mahatma Gandhi for a boycott of the elections, only six had no candidate Within the Provincial Assemblies 38 were reserved for White voters.

Before the Indian independence in 1947, India (also called the Indian Empire) was divided into two sets of territories, one under direct British rule (British India), and the other consisting of princely states under the suzerainty of the British Crown, with control over their internal affairs remaining in the hands of their hereditary rulers. The latter included 562 princely states which had different types of revenue-sharing arrangements with the British, often depending on their size, population and local conditions. In addition, there were several colonial enclaves controlled by France and Portugal. After independence, the political integration of these territories into an Indian Union was a declared objective of the Indian National Congress, and the Government of India pursued this over the next decade.

Every three years after election started and continued up to 1946

In July 1946, Jawaharlal Nehru pointedly observed that no princely state could prevail militarily against the army of independent India.[1] In January 1947, Nehru said that independent India would not accept the divine right of kings. In May 1947, he declared that any princely state which refused to join the Constituent Assembly would be treated as an enemy state. Vallabhbhai Patel and V. P. Menon were more conciliatory towards the princes, and as the men charged with integrating the states, were successful in the task.

Through a combination of factors, Sardar Vallabhbhai Patel and V. P. Menon coerced and coalesced the rulers of the various princely states to accede to India. Having secured their accession, they then proceeded, in a step-by-step process, to secure and extend the union government's authority over these states and transform their administrations until, by 1956, there was little difference between the territories that had been part of British India and those that had been princely states. Simultaneously, the Government of India, through a combination of military and diplomatic means, acquired de facto and de jure control over the remaining colonial enclaves, which too were integrated into India.

Although this process successfully integrated the vast majority of princely states into India, it was not as successful for a few, notably the former princely states of Jammu and Kashmir and Manipur, where active secessionist and separatist insurgencies continued to exist due to various reasons.

Provincial elections were held in British India in January 1946 to elect members of the legislative councils of the Indian provinces. The consummation of British rule in India were the 1945/1946 elections. As minor political parties were eliminated, the political scene became restricted to the Indian National Congress and the Muslim League who were more antagonized than ever. The Congress, in a repeat of the 1937 elections, won 90 percent of the general non-Muslim seats while the Muslim League won the majority of Muslim seats (87%) in the provinces. Nevertheless, the All India Muslim League verified its claim to be the sole representative of Muslim India. The election laid the path to Pakistan.

On 19 September 1945, following negotiations between Indian leaders and members of the 1946 Cabinet Mission to India from the United Kingdom, the Viceroy Lord Wavell announced that elections to the provincial and central legislatures would be held in December 1945 to January 1946. It was also announced that an executive council would be formed and a constitution-making body would be convened after these elections. These elections were important as the provincial assemblies thus formed were to then elect a new Constituent Assembly which would begin formulating a constitution for an independent India. All contesting parties began campaigning. The Congress contended that it represented the entire Indian population while the Muslim League professed to speak for the whole Muslim population. The dominant issue of the election campaign became the issue of Pakistan.

Originally, the Muslim League had been a party which received most of its support from the Muslim-minority provinces, where fear of Hindu 'domination' was greater as was the sense of 'a loss of privilege', and to showcase its argument for Muslim nationhood the League needed support from both Muslim-majority as well as Muslim-minority provinces. In the election campaign, the League resorted to establishing networks with traditional power bases, such as landowners and the religious elite, in the Muslim-majority provinces to win support. Religious slogans were utilized and the term 'Pakistan' was put forward. Some scholars state that the meaning of Pakistan was kept vague so that it meant different things to different people. On the other hand, Venkat Dhulipala observes that, rather than being vague, the proposals for Pakistan were vigorously debated in public, maps printed, economic foundations analyzed and Pakistan was envisioned as a modern Islamic state.

In contrast to earlier elections, the religious commitment was intertwined with a declaration of Muslim communal unity. Casting the vote became an Islamic act. Consequently, for the Muslim electorate, Pakistan represented both a nation-state for India's Muslims, but one which surpassed the common state structure, and an awakening of an Islamic polity where Islam would be blended with the state's functioning.

Unlike previous elections under British rule where voting was restricted by property and educational qualifications, the elections of 1946 saw the voting franchise extended to a quarter of the Indian adult population.

Names change After Independent:

Indian Civil Service (ICS) to Indian Administration Service (IAS)

Imperial Legislative Council to Parliament House/ Sanksad Bhaban

Upper House to Raja Shabha and Lower House to Lok Sabha

Central province to Madhya Pradesh

Northern Province to Uttar Pradesh

North Frontier Province to Arunachal

Bombay to Mumbai

Calcutta to Kolkata

Multi Political Party System Development in British Ruled in India:

National Congress Foundation as Platform:

Communist Party of India Formation to Flow up USSR:

Muslim Laugh formation for Recapturing Islamic Ruling to India:

Depress Laugh formation for stage of Caste and Tribal Unity:

Rastria Syangsabak Sangha & Jana Sangha Formation for Reestablishment of Indo-Iranian Racism:

Regional Political Parties Formation at Independent India

Dravida Munnatra Kaghakam

Assame Gana Parisad

Jharkhand Mukti Morcha

Talangana Mukti Morcha

Telugu Desam Party

Mr. Noranda Modi Characteristic cooperation with Tea Stall Owner:

1. Capture Vacant land and first tent establish *then start* tea stall as the same way Jami Adhigrahan system establish.

2. A tea stall owner kept a servant by whom tea stall works and home works done from morning to night as *like his* statement labour laws try to *establish*.

3. Somewhere tea stall owner thought servants are slave and physical torture also done and basically use to habit to kept child labour, in the same ways Mr. Modi have no project on child labour.

4. He should hide his personal life and his marriage life *that were* profession before he remained as CM of Gujrat. Tea stall *owners* also suddenly make *stalls* on *the roadside* and *start* tea *stalls* for common *people*.

5. Confusing and diverted the mind to other *paths* to forget basic *needs* of peoples where consuming goods cost increasing, petroleum rate increasing from Rs. 62 /- to 73/- and land cost have not any MRP which are not available without agents as housing *boards* make an inert body. At tea stall cheating and time pass discussion done at tea stall that tea may seal more and more.

BJP Leading Government always remain anti Common Peoples Policies:

1. A. B. Bajpai Government:

(i) New Pension Scheme (NPS): there *is no* option to get money from Provident fund as the NPS fund *remains in the shear* market which total should not show in pay bill that how much money deposited in fund. There *are* two *options* as phase- I which have to be every *month and* another Phase-II which is *like VPF* as extra money cutting which *has* only option to get return.

If any purpose like marriage of daughter of a Railway employee required money but on hand have not such amount of money than high interest loan require to get from any one or get loan from bank that indicate the Mahajan system should start in near future.

There *is an option to* get double money *from the fund* but only 60 % will *get it at retirement* and 40 % will remain *in the fund* which interest *will be paid* as pension. Then only *approximate deposits* will be in hand at retirement life. Whereas *in the old* pension scheme there *was* double money as added gratuity, some percent of pension money to seal and *get a large* amount, whole life family pension.

(ii) Maximum public property shear seal to *private* organization as Gazette rank *abolished* from Bank, LIC, Airport and other.

2. Noranda Modi Government:

(i) 33 years retirement or 60 years which remain first:

(a) So many employees get loan on the base of retirement time than if suddenly retirement happen at 33 years base than he should be helpless as all amount money of PF to be paid for loan and empty hand remain after retirement. The life program to be *changed* and who deposited money as LIS that premium to be pending and disturb the life.

(b) *Suddenly a large* number of *employees retire, making the* skilled worker shortage and working standard *disturbed* by the system.

As new employment recruitment will *not be* done immediately and skill works will not be available in organization.

(ii) Labor laws interfere: it is totally any *work* programmed where *only the owner is favored* by the government.

(iii) Land Bill *is an anti-ferment* program selected by the government.

(iv) Millions of money *spent* for travel and tour by Mr. Noranda Modi by the name *of* FDI by foreign companies to make India whereas infrastructure of India is not wanting to *develop* by which innovation to upgrading to be done at India and industrial development to be done. FDI *was* opposed by *him and* his party members previously where they remain in opposition *to* how he tries to do *this and that* he always tells *lies* in every step of his movement. When *the Indian* government *has* less money in *funds,* as *he explained , than* millions of *money* for *programs* of foreign traveling done by him which have not any result.

*Poor Administrative power lead by Non-Congress Parties Governments:

1. Mr. Morarji Dasia Janata Dal Government:

a. No Economical and financial proper guide and projects remain under him.

b. No industrial and communicational *development* projects remain.

c. Mr. Morarji Dasia should *not be Completed* by him and later Mr. Charon Singh became Prime Minister.

2. Mr. V. P. Singh Janata Dal Government:

a. *The Economic* system *tries* to *develop a socialist* system but *fails* quickly.

b. Mr. Davilal became Deputy Prime Minister.

c. Unstable government formed due to inter coalitions among Janata Dal members and Government fall *down at an intermediate* time and later Mr. Chandrashakher *became* Prime Minister but Midterm polling happened immediately.

3. Mr. Davagoura Janata Dal Government:

a. Not lasting 5 years and intermediate polling happened.

b. Intermediate Prime Minister Mr. I. K. Gujral Made due to Instability of Government.

c. Janata Dal Broken into Different Political parties as RJD, BJD, JDSP, etc.

4. Mr. Atal Bihari Bajpai lead *Bharatiya* Janata Party:

a. Kargil War happened due to mismanagement of Government as Military left from upper hill at winter season which were not done any time and in the meantime Pakistan Military capture the Kargil Hill area and the country force to involved war due to miss administrative power.

b. IC 814 *AirLines Airplane* High-jack by terrorist and land at *Amritsar* but Minister was to take any Action at *Amritsar* Airport but sand CRP as *special* team from New Delhi and flight flew away from Amritsher to Lahore and then Abu Dhabi and later to Kabul. Due to miss administrations chances at Amrit *she* miss and later Masood, the terrorist's leader with his group left by Mr. A. B. Bajpai Government to *save* passengers of high-jack *planes*.

c. Privatized maximum Public Autonomous organizations and *sealed* government property *at chief* rate.

d. The recruitment of public organizations stops by two years off *favoring the* new generation and students.

e. New pension system (NPS) system started *for Public* organizations *in* favor of common peoples and Pension to MLA and MPs started in favor of political persons.

f. Coffin scandal a lowest level *matter* happened to assassinated soldier motel mater.

g. Deputy Prime Minister recruited to Mr. L.K. Advani *is a poor* Administrative symbol whereas per parliament system Deputy Prime Minister post have no options.

h. Parliament House Attracted by Terrorist Group which indicated poor security of New Delhi under his ministry.

i. Narmada projects *as a half channel* and half pipe lines system to water supply from Narmada to Shipra River a Vogues system where money *expands* more but *only for single* purposes *served* by the projects. It was taken as the Madhya Pradesh ruling under

BJP lead Government but there were *no other* river projects by his Ministry.

5. Mr. Narendra Modi BJP Lead Government:

a. Miss Guide to Common Peoples -

(i) Clean India : Clean by Groom as an acting by BJP leaders and allied personality but have no any guide line and any project to clean city and village by establish proper drainage system development and sweeping by machineries under Municipalities and Village board and have not any team to establish to protects pollutions and crash the waste materials and recycles those.

(ii) Make India: Foreign companies call to investment and only make rubber stamp as make in India but have not any proper innovative and upgrading projects to make self-technological base industries and have no educational development programmed that at Universities level innovations and up gradations to done by which technological and economically county will become self-reliance's. (iii) Adopted Village: It is the policies to *restate the LandLord* system by His ministry *to give* power to rich and factory *owners* and MPs whose next generations should demand that their old generations *spend* money for Village establishment and get authority *from the government and become landlords as the old* system started.

(iv) Break the protocol miss guide to common peoples that actually he disobey the basic rules and regulation of society and administration system and supreme personality as his habit

b. Priority to Give self-importance rather than National interests:

(i) Sub PMO offices established at Gandhi Nagar and Varanasi as He is *Gujarati* and *Gujarati* Capital is Gandhi Nagar as well as His Constituency are also Varanasi.

(ii) Make *a larger* Cabinet ministry to *satisfy his* allied personality and 66 cabinet ministers recruited.

(iii) Give priority to NRI rather than common peoples who lead life to Indian land.

c. U-Turn Done which Promise to Common peoples to Do:

(i) 370 Act Abolish issues remain silent

(ii) No action taken against Pakistan to violet LOC

(iii) No Black Money Return to India from Foreign Countries.

d. Common people's mentality Diversion done:

(i) Speech giver as Hindu women required to give birth four children by his MP and Allied Political parties members but not take any action.

(ii) Religious Tension created *by the Ghar* Baposhi system started *a* controversial statement given by RSS, VHP and other parties members.

(ii) High money expenses to invited Diplomates at *Shapath* Grahan

e. Apply Rules To forget Promised at Voting:

(i) After 3 days a family *forgets an event or* death case.

(ii) After *3-months,* common *people* forget *local events and become* too busy *with their* self-works.

f. Miss Management of Administration:

(i) Adhadesh/ ordinance Implement by which break the Democratic system.

(ii) Citizenship Electronic Card system *has* not any programmed but Aadhar Card *implemented* in every field.

Future of Nation at Influence of BJP and It allied Group leading groups:

1. Communal harmony break and riot may form

2. Superstitions system increased *and the Sati* system, Bali system, Santan Bisherjan, etc. *increased* and Hindu society *entered the* Burk black age. e.g. A Sati case came *to Rajasthan* at Mr. A. B. Bajpai period, Bali case by Ram Pal at Haryana and Asharan Bapu and his son Narayan Sai rape case come at Mr. Noranda Modi period.

3. Strong Casteism may implement *an* SC, ST, OBC reservation system to be *abolished, then* even *restrictions* to learn and get education may *be implemented* like Islamic period.

Cause of death of Lal Bahadur Sassari:

USSR *arranged the same* hotel *booking* at Task hand *for the India* and Pakistan team of *the* intermediate USSR. *Lal Bahadur Sassari's death remains secret* where it *happened; they* kept both Pakistani and Indian *delicacies in the same* Hotel but why? Noranda Modi called best friend to Vladimir Putin to him but not asked *report* by Narendra Modi the investigation *report* of Russian old files to hand over to India were as telling most Close friend. As *the agent* media continued to *do* propaganda that Noranda Modi *stopped the* Russia Ukraine War but one-year pass even *today the war* continued. Actually, Noranda Modi *helping Vladimir* Putin continued as *a loan* given previously and continued business of natural oils and *other products* from Russia as Vladimir Poutine and Noranda Modi both are executing Autocracy. Actual works not done that should not *demand* death of *Lal Bahadur* Sassari investigation report that *are required to be* open to all *to the Indian* public. Hence making politics and getting *votes* to *cheat the* nation *is a basic* activity by him.

Cause of Assassination of Indira Gandhi and Rajeev Gandhi:

Conflicts are cause of assassination of *Indira* Gandhi and Rajeev Gandhi as Indira Gandhi made military operation called Blue star operation to Amritsar Golden temple from where Alkaloidal done to operation too separate different independent Punjab as Khalistan and hence conflict formed as Sikh security by planning killed to Indira Gandhi but BJP- RSS make alliance with Alkaloidal as called most close friend.

Rajiv Gandhi Killed by LTTE *members* as Jaffna when declared independent that time Indian Military operation done by order of Rajiv Gandhi and *Sri* Lanka Tamil region again came under *Sri* Lanka. Hence Conflict created and as a result Rajiv Gandhi killed by *LTTE* in Tamil Nadu Region on Voting Campaigning as *they have a social* system and language same with *Sri* Lanka and Tamil Nadu.

Cheating character of Selfish Self-Centered Narendra Modi Personality:

1. For self-rules remain difference and for other rules executed something restriction implementation
2. Tax for politician and allied business personality Exide by Narendra Modi
3. Age limit consideration to political *candidates* for other *restrictions* that not to *be above* 70 years. But he himself *crossed* 70 *years of no command*.
4. Adaptation of Villages, Public Industries and Hospital is system to theft National properties by cheating
5. Contract of lice for 80/*100 years* or selling *Public* properties with loan section and later loan with interest relief given is cheating process of BJP. E.g. like A.B Bajpai *handing* over petroleum *fields* to Ambani which *50 percent sold* out to British Companies *at double* rate and now railways units, defiance sectors production *units* hand over to Ambani, Adani, Shah, Dhamani, *that are cheating with the nation*. Hence zero-base investment kept and by cheating transfer business money and *properties to become the richest* personality. As Vijay Malia, Nirom Modi, and Dr. Subash Chandra left India after cheating with nation these root developments by A. B. Bajpai *which is an upgradation* done by Narendra Modi as it *is a habitual* character of BJP

and RSS political parties' leadership as *in the Indian independence* movement they *acted* as British Agent.

Over All Congress Ruling contribution as British left India as minor developed stage:

1. Railways converted meter gauge to *broad* gauge.

2. *Defiance* system development done.

3. Irrigation system development

4. Information System development

5. Educational system development.

6. Governmental Hospital development

7. Metro Railways development in different cities.

8. 3rd AC pass provided to Group D and C staffs in Railways.

9 Ganga Action plant and ETP plant on Factories started to control pollution and clean India.

10. Land lord and Estate system abolish to give power to common peoples.

11. Rajdhani and Satabdi Express stated to speed up connection central capital to other state capital and states capital to state capital.

12. IIT and IIM Institutions establish for Engineering and technical man power developments. 13. Postal Department economical condition developed by establishing Banking system as MIS, Requiring system development.

14. National *Highways* and Four Lens Road system developed and State Capital to Capital communication and transportation system developed.

15. Pension system started by Congress Government and bonus system started in favor of Labours and employees of public sectors.

* The condition to Left India by British Rulers:

1. Minimum Broad gauge and maximum Meter gauge railways available and mainly port city.

2. ***The British*** executed direct ruled and indirect rules under ***the estates*** of ***landlords*** in different parts ***of India*** which were off position to ***execute*** proper democracy.

3. Minimum land ***lines*** of telephone ***systems*** remain around India. Poor Communication ***systems*** remain around India.

4. Part of India as Kashmir, Hyderabad remain independent Estates and Goa, Damon Due remain under ruled of Portugal and Pondicherry remain under ruled of France.

5. Undeveloped Irrigation and Agriculture ***systems*** remain around India.

6. Educational Institutions remain minimum in Number. Only R*oor*key ***remained*** Engineering college and there ***were also*** Technical schools also.

7. Minimum Medical ***colleges*** and hospitals remain. Hospital ***remains*** under ***private*** organization.

8. Only National Highway Grant Tank Road ***remains*** which ***connects*** Calcutta to Pashober.

9. In several ***places*** Railways ***were*** not connected properly. e.g. In Malda to Mursidabad was ***required to travel*** by boat to ***cross the*** Ganga River.

** Insult to Nation, Nationality and National leaders by P.M. Noranda Modi:

1. In a top most responsible post person as national representative as Prime Minister ***he always uses*** the name ***of a country*** as Hindustan ***as an irrespective*** Nation ***whereas India is defined*** as Bharat /India ***as a secular*** country in constitution. Hindustan was not accepting by the parliament and constitution as in this nation have Shikha, Jain, Islamic, Buddhist, Christian, Persian communities also even Hindu remain majority because Kashmir and Telangana are Islamic majority, Nagaland is Christian majority, Punjab is Shikha majority and U.P. and Kerala are about 40% Islamic community. As a ***Prime*** Minister, ***the name of a***

nation and nationality should *be used* properly as per constitution only but he not *only disobeys* the nation but also *disobeys* the constitution.

2. He *insulted Netaji* Subash Chandra Bose as he is not declared as death but wanted to give Bharat Ratna Award as death. If he really interested *in respect* Mr. Subash Chandra Bose *then received the Subhash* Chandra Bose International Award to be *started* for political and social *workers under the Government* of India.

3. He insult the retired president Late Dr. Sarvopalli Radha Kishnan as His *BirthDay* 5th September *celebrated* as teacher day to encourage education in India but he declared as Guru Dibash and *gave* speech on his life only.

4. He irrespective to assassinate Mr. M. Gandhi who called as father of nation *but his birthday* 2nd October is not celebrated as national *whole* day but clean India day as clean by groom as photographic identity.

5. He irrespective *of the Assassinate* Indira Gandhi Death Anniversary as *he does not offer* garland to his memorial which is a duty of a *Prime* Minister to give respect to another late Prime Minister.

6. He *irrespective of Mr. Jawaharlal Nehru* Birth day 14th November as children celebrate Children day but *he does not encourage* any children to love *others*.

 ** Great Drama created:

1. *Parliaments are called Mother* and head down near the gate of parliament as well as call foreign Delegates.

2. Ganga called as Mother to get favor to Hindu peoples and dirty *remains* as it is as before.

3. Every time sentimental *speech is given by the nearest person*.

4. Mr. Adita Nath Yogi, Saki Maharaj saying that they are Sanashi /*monks* but in reality, they use wealths in lump *sum* and only

saffron *clothes* / garua basra are not the main point to a monk. Sannashi *means* Suno ash /zero expectation otherwise they are making drama only.

5. The BJP right hand supporter Ram Deve *Baba is nothing* But *Businessman* who *started his* business as Yoga schooling and later *entered* food *industries* and *Ayurvedic* manufacturing companies. If someone is become monk than he or she are not required any business.

6. Sentiment politics and business are main motive as Ram mandir issue created as in North and Central In

** Cheat with Common Peoples as Misguide to Nation and Society:

1. Learn some English words which used to attracted to common peoples but opposing English to use at Governmental offices where as his ministry maximum Ministers next generation and BJP Ruling States Ministry next generation like Son and Daughter or Grand Son and Grand Daughter are taking Education in English as it clear to cheating with common peoples to depress and misguide directly.

2. He *called for* Smart Cities but executing cities have not any proper drainage system and road ways and there have not any project of pollution control, garbage treatment and west land development but misguide to *execute* new cities as land capturing policies from Villagers.

3. There have not any control to Housing Board that money wastage in different projects which planning have some things fault, e.g. at Ratlam city *nearby* Shasrie Nagar several Flat House remain vacant under Housing Board but BJP leading under Mr. Sive Raj Shing Chuhan are not treating by Mr. Noranda Modi. Land Mafia and Promoter born *like husbandry*. North, West and Central Indian people *worship Lord* Ram and Lord Hanuman and hence Jai Sree Rama *politicization is done* by BJP and Alliance Political organization RSS, VHP, Bajarangdal.

4. The **pillars of Ashoka** are a series of monolithic columns dispersed throughout the Indian subcontinent, erected or at least inscribed with edicts by the 3rd Mauryan Emperor Ashoka The Great who reigned from c. 268 to 232 BCE. Ashoka used the expression *Dhaṃma thaṃbhā* (Dharma stambha), i.e. "pillars of the Dharma" to describe his own pillars.[3][4] These pillars constitute important monuments of the architecture of India, most of them exhibiting the characteristic Mauryan polish. Of the pillars erected by Ashoka, twenty still survive including those with inscriptions of his edicts. Only a few with animal capitals survive of which seven complete specimens are known. Two pillars were relocated by Firuz Shah Tughlaq to Delhi. Several pillars were relocated later by Mughal Empire rulers, the animal capitals being removed. Averaging between 12 and 15 m (40 and 50 ft) in height, and weighing up to 50 tons each, the pillars were dragged, sometimes hundreds of miles, to where they were erected.

The pillars of Ashoka are among the earliest known stone sculptural remains from India. Only another pillar fragment, the Pataliputra capital, is possibly from a slightly earlier date. It is thought that before the 3rd century BCE, wood rather than stone was used as the main material for Indian architectural constructions, and that stone may have been adopted following interaction with the Persians and the Greeks. A graphic representation of the Lion Capital of Ashoka from the column there was adopted as the official State Emblem of India in 1950.

All the pillars of Ashoka were built at Buddhist monasteries, many important sites from the life of the Buddha and places of pilgrimage. Some of the columns carry inscriptions addressed to the monks and nuns. Some were erected to commemorate visits by Ashoka. Major pillars are present in the Indian States of Bihar, Uttar Pradesh, Madhya Pradesh and some parts of Haryana.

Lion Capital of Ashoka from Sarnath, with Wheel of the Moral Law (reconstitution). 3rd century BCE.

Ashoka ascended to the throne in 269 BC inheriting the Mauryan empire founded by his grandfather Chandragupta Maurya. Ashoka was reputedly a tyrant at the outset of his reign. Eight years after his accession he campaigned in Kalinga where in his own words, "a hundred and fifty thousand people were deported, a hundred thousand were killed and as many as that perished..." As he explains in his edicts, after this event Ashoka converted to Buddhism in remorse for the loss of life. Buddhism became a state religion and with Ashoka's support it spread rapidly. The inscriptions on the pillars set out edicts about morality based on Buddhist tenets. They were added *in the 3rd* century BCE.

Highly polished Achaemenid load-bearing column with lotus capital and ashvins, Persepolis, c. 5th-4th BCE.

The traditional idea that all were originally quarried at Chunar, just south of Varanasi and taken to their sites, before or after carving, "can no longer be confidently asserted", and instead it seems that the columns were carved in two types of stone. Some were of the spotted red and white sandstone from the region of Mathura, the others of buff-colored fine grained hard sandstone usually with small black spots quarried in the Chunar near Varanasi. The uniformity of style in the pillar capitals suggests that they were all sculpted by craftsmen from the same region. It would therefore seem that stone was transported from Mathura and Chunar to the various sites where the pillars have been found, and there was cut and carved by craftsmen.

The pillars have four component parts in two pieces: the three sections of the capitals are made in a single piece, often of a different stone to that of the monolithic shaft to which they are attached by a large metal dowel. The shafts are always plain and smooth, circular in cross-section, slightly tapering upwards and always chiseled out of a single piece of stone. There is no distinct base at the bottom of the shaft. The lower parts of the capitals have the shape and appearance of a gently arched bell formed of lotus petals. The abaci are of two types: square and plain and circular and decorated and these are of different proportions. The crowning animals are masterpieces of Mauryan art, shown either seated or standing, always in the round and chiseled as a single piece with the abaci. Presumably all or most of the other columns that now lack them once had capitals and animals. They are also used to commemorate the events of the Buddha's life.

Left image: Vaishali lion of Ashoka. Right image: Assyrian relief of a lion at Nineveh (circa 640 BCE). Many stylistic elements (design of the whiskers, the eyes, the fur etc...) point to similarities.

Currently seven animal sculptures from Ashoka pillars survive. These form "the first important group of Indian stone sculpture", though it is thought they derive from an existing tradition of wooden columns topped by animal sculptures in copper, none of which have survived. It is also possible that some of the stone pillars predate Ashoka's reign.[

Western origin

There has been much discussion of the extent of influence from Achaemenid Persia,[26] where the column capitals supporting the roofs at Persepolis have similarities, and the "rather cold, hieratic style" of the Sarnath Lion Capital of Ashoka especially shows "obvious Achaemenid and Sargonid influence". India and the Achaemenid Empire had been in close contact since the Achaemenid conquest of the Indus Valley, from circa 500 BCE to 330 BCE.

Hellenistic influence has also been suggested. In particular the abaci of some of the pillars (especially the Rampurva bull, the Sankissa elephant and the Allahabad pillar capital) use bands of motifs, like the bead and reel pattern, the ovolo, the flame palmettes, lotuses, which likely originated from Greek and Near-Eastern arts Such examples can also be seen in the remains of the Mauryan capital city of Pataliputra.

It has also been suggested that 6th century Greek columns such as the Sphinx of Naxos, a 12.5m Ionic column crowned by a sited animal in the religious center of Delphi, may have been an inspiration for the pillars of Ashoka.[Many similar columns crowned by sphinxes were discovered in ancient Greece, as in

Sparta, Athens or Spata, and some were used as funerary steles.[17] The Greek sphinx, a lion with the face of a human female, was considered as having ferocious strength, and was thought of as a guardian, often flanking the entrances to temples or royal tombs.

Vikramaditya I was the third son of Pulakesin II.

He set himself the task of repelling the Pallava invasion and restoring the unity of his father's kingdom with the assistance of his maternal grandfather Bhuvikarma or Durvineet of the Western Ganga Dynasty.

He was able to put an end to Pallava's thirteen-year occupation and capture of Vatapi.

He defeated his brothers and other feudatories who sought to split the empire.

Vikramaditya I then declared himself Chalukya king in 655 AD.

He bestowed the viceroyalty of Lata in southern Gujarat on his loyal younger brother Jayasimhavarma.

He defeated Mahendravarman II (Pallava king) in AD 668 and continued his capture of Kanchi for about five to six years.

During this time, he plundered the Chola, Pandya, and Kerala kingdoms but did not annex any territory (his army remained in Thiruchirapalli).

Vikramaditya I took on the dynastic titles of Satyashraya ("refuge of truth") and Shri-prithvi-vallabha.

He was also known as Maharajadhiraja, Rajadhiraja, Parameshvara and Bhattaraka.

Vikramaditya I, in addition to the usual Chalukyan titles, assumed the title Rajamalla, implying that he became the sovereign of Mallas, i.e. the Pallavas. The word "Aulikara" in the Risthal inscription. The first letter Au is a variation in a style specific to the 6-7th century.

The Aulikaras also referred to as Aulikara dynasty or Olikara dynasty, were an ancient Indian clan from the Maurya era, that emerged into a kingdom between the 4th-century CE and 6th-century CE. They were based in the Malwa (Malawa) region of central India near Mandsaur, with their power center near what is now western Madhya Pradesh, southeastern Rajasthan and northeastern Gujarat. Two royal houses belonging to this clan ruled over the present-day western Malwa region of Madhya Pradesh state from c. 350 CE to 550 CE, much of it as feudatories of the Gupta Empire.

Several major and important inscriptions of Aulikaras are known. These inscriptions suggest that they were Hindus who built several notable temples in the Gupta-style to Shiva, Surya and Vishnu, as well as Buddhist monasteries, in western Madhya Pradesh and east Rajasthan. Among these, the notable ruins are in the region near Mandsaur and the Dara Mukundara valley passage between Kota and Jhalawar. These include the Bhim ki Chauri.

Epigraphical discoveries have brought to light two royal lines, who call themselves as the Aulikaras and ruled from Dashapura (present-day Mandsaur). The first royal house, which ruled from Dashapura comprised the following kings in the order of succession: Jayavarma, Simhavarma, Naravarma, Vishvavarma and Bandhuvarma. The Rīsthal stone slab inscription discovered in 1983 has brought to light another royal house, which comprised the following kings in the order of succession: Drumavardhana, Jayavardhana, Ajitavardhana, Vibhishanavardhana, Rajyavardhana and Prakashadharma, who defeated Toramana. In all probability, Yashodharman also belonged to this house and he was the son and successor of Prakashadharma. Yashodharma defeated Mihirakula and freed the Malwa region from the Hunas. The rule of the Aulikaras over Malwa ended with him.

Origin of the Aulikaras

Nothing is mentioned about the origin of the Aulikaras or the Olikaras (as mentioned in the Bihar Kotra inscription of

Naravarma) in their inscriptions. Based on the fact that, they used the Malava Samvat in preference to the use of Gupta era in all of their inscriptions in spite of their first royal house being a feudatory of the Guptas, historian D. C. Sircar assumed them as a clan of the Malavas. This clan settled in the Dasheraka region (present-day western Malwa) in the course of their migration from the North-West. His view was supported by K.K. Dasgupta and K.C. Jain.

First Aulikara dynasty

Earliest information regarding the first royal house is known from two inscriptions of Naravarma, the Mandsaur inscription dated Malava Samvat 461 (404 CE) and the Bihar Kotra inscription dated Malava Samvat 474 (417 CE). The founder of this house is Jayavarma. He was succeeded by his son, Simhavarma, who is mentioned as a Kshitisha (king). His son and successor Naravarma are mentioned as a Parthiva (king) and Maharaja. His epithet was Simhavikrantagami (one who moves with the stride of a lion).

Gangadhar Stone Inscription of Viśvavarman.

Naravarma was succeeded by his son Vishvavarma, who is mentioned in the Gangadhar Stone Inscription of Viśvavarman dated Malava Samvat 480 (423 CE). The Gangadhara stone inscription records construction of a Matrika temple by his minister Mayurakshaka. Mayurakshaka also constructed a temple dedicated to Vishnu. Vishvavarma was succeeded by his son Bandhuvarma, who is eulogised by poet Vatsabhatti in the Mandsaur stone inscription of the guild of silk-weavers dated Malava Samvat 529 (473 CE). This inscription informs us that he was a feudatory of the Gupta emperor Kumaragupta I. It was during his reign, a temple dedicated to Surya was constructed by the guild of silk-weavers at Dashapura in the Malava Samvat 493 (436 CE). This temple was renovated in 473 CE by the same guild.

The intermediate period

The history of Dashapura remained obscure after Bandhuvarma. The Mandsaur inscription dated Malava Samvat 524 (467 CE), written by Ravila mentions a king of Dashapura named Prabhakara, who defeated the enemies of the Guptas. Dattabhata was the commander of his army, whose donations to the Lokottara Vihara is recorded in this inscription. Soon after Prabhakara, another Aulikara royal house came to power, about which we came to know from the Risthal inscription. The exact relationship between these two royal houses is not certain.

Second Aulikara dynasty

A stone slab inscription discovered in 1983 in Risthal near Sitamau, has brought to light another royal house belonging to the Aulikara family. This inscription dated Malava Samvat 572 (515 CE) is written by poet Vasula, son of Kakka in chaste Sanskrit. The script used is the late Gupta Brahmi paleographically assignable to the 5th-6th centuries. Unlike the earlier royal house, this royal house was never a Gupta feudatory. The Risthal inscription mentions Drumavardhana as the founder of this house. He assumed the title, Senapati. He was succeeded by his son Jayavardhana, who commanded a formidable army. He was succeeded by his son Ajitavardhana. According to the Risthal inscription, he was constantly engaged in performing Soma sacrifices. Ajitavardhana was succeeded by his son Vibhishanavardhana. He was praised in the Risthal inscription for his noble qualities. Vibhishanavardhana's son and successor Rajyavardhana expanded his ancestral kingdom. Rajyavardhana was succeeded by his son Prakashadharma.

Prakashadharma

According to the Rīsthal inscription, Alchon Huns ruler Toramana (depicted) was vanquished by Prakashadharma in 515 CE.

Prakashadharma was a notable king of this dynasty, who assumed the title, Adhiraja. The Rīsthal inscription gives us information about his achievements. It records the construction of a tank and a Shiva temple at Risthal by Bhagavaddosha, a Rajasthaniya (viceroy) of Prakashadharma. This inscription mentions that Prakashadharma defeated the Huna ruler Toramana, sacked his camp and had taken away the ladies of his harem. The tank constructed at Risthal during his reign was named after his grandfather as Vibhishanasara. He also constructed a temple dedicated to Brahma at Dashapura. During the excavation at Mandsaur in 1978 by a team of Vikram University, Ujjain, led by V.S. Wakankar, his two glass seals inscribed with the legend Shri Prakashadharma were found. In all probabilities he was succeeded by his son Yashodharma Vishnuvarma.

An undated fragmentary Mandsaur inscription provides a name of a suzerain ruler Adityavardhana and his feudatory Maharaja Gauri. Adityavardhana has been recently identified with Prakashadharma by a historian Ashvini Agarwal. The Chhoti Sadri inscription dated Malava Samvat 547 (490 CE) and written by Bhramarasoma, son of Mitrasoma supplies a genealogy of Adityavardhana's feudatory ruler, Maharaja Gauri. The first ruler of this Manavayani kshatriya family was Punyasoma. He was succeeded by his son Rajyavardhana. Rashtravardhana was the son of Rajyavardhana. Rashtravardhana's son and successor was Yashogupta. The last ruler of this family, Gauri was son of Yashogupta. He excavated a tank at Dashapura for the merit of his deceased mother. This inscription also mentions the name of a prince, Gobhata but his relationship with Gauri is not known.

Yashodharma

The defeat of the Alchon Huns under Mihirakula by King Yashodharma at Sondani in 528 CE.

Main article: Yashodharman

The most prominent king of this dynasty was Yashodharma Vishnuvardhana. Yashodharma's two identical undated Mandsaur victory pillar inscriptions (found at Sondani, near present-day

Mandsaur town) and a stone inscription dated Malava Samvat 589 (532 CE) record the military achievements of him. All of these inscriptions were first published by John Faithfull Fleet in 1886. The undated pillar inscriptions, which were also written by poet Vasula, son of Kakka say that his feet were worshipped by the Huna ruler Mihirakula. These also state that his feudatories from the vicinity of the river *Lauhitya* (Brahmaputra) in the east, from the Mahendra mountains (Eastern Ghats) in the south, up to the Himalayas in the north and the *Paschima Payodhi* (Arabian Sea) in the west came to the seat of his empire to pay homage. he assumed the titles, *Rajadhiraja* and *Parameshvara.* Yashodharma's dated inscription informs us that in 532 CE, Nirdosha, his *Rajasthaniya* was governing the area between the Vindhyas and the Pariyatras (Aravalis) and his headquarters was Dashapura. Probably the rule of the Aulikaras ended with Yashodhrma.

In Line 5 of the Mandsaur pillar inscription, Yashodharman is said to have vanquished his enemies and to now control the territory from the neighbourhood of the (river) Lauhitya (Brahmaputra River) to the "Western Ocean" (Western Indian Ocean), and from the Himalayas to mountain Mahendra.

Yashodharman thus conquered vast territories from the Hunas and the Guptas, although his short-lived empire would ultimately disintegrate between 530-540 CE.

A fragmentary undated inscription of a hitherto unknown ruler Kumaravarma was found by Girija Shankar Runwal during Mandsaur excavation by the team of Vikram University, Ujjain in 1979 from the foundations of a building. This inscription, paleographically assignable to the late 5th-early 6th centuries, records a dynasty comprising four successive rulers: Yajnadeva, Virasoma, his son Bhaskaravarma and his son Kumaravarma. Wakankar claimed them as the Aulikaras[and V.V. Mirashi claimed this dynasty a separate one, which defeated and succeeded the Aulikaras. But none of these theories received support from other historians. Most probably the Kalachuris succeeded the

Aulikaras, as the Kalchuri kings Krishnaraja and his son Shankaragana are found ruling over the same region immediately after the Aulikaras. The Maitrakas too may have been successors of the Aulikaras.[

Aulikara administration

Only three offices of the Aulikaras are known from their epigraphical records: the *Senapati* (commander-in-chief), the *Amatya*s (ministers) and the *Rajasthaniya* (viceroy). The exact nature of the office of the *Rajasthaniya*, which is mentioned in several inscriptions is not clear from them. George Buhlar rendered *Rajasthaniya* as the viceroy, and his view is mostly accepted. It seems that the office of the *Rajasthaniya* of the Aulikaras became hereditary in the *Naigama* family since the days of Shashthidatta. Shashthidatta's son Varaha is identified with Varahadasa of the Chittaurgarh fragmentary inscription of his grandson by a historian D.C. Sircar. Varaha's son Ravikirti was an *amatya* under Rajyavardhana. He had three sons by his wife Bhanugutpa: Bhagavaddosha, Abhayadatta and Doshakumbha. Bhagavaddosha was a *Rajasthaniya* under Prakashadharma. His younger brother Abhayadatta was appointed a *Rajasthaniya* after him The Chiitaurgarh fragmentary inscription mentions Abhayadatta as a *Rajasthaniya* of Dashapura and *Madhyama*. The Mandsaur inscription dated Malava Samvat 589 describes Abhayadatta as the *Rajasthaniya'* between the Vindhyas and the *Pariyatra*s. His nephew and son of Doshakumbha, Nirdosha succeeded him as the *Rajasthaniya* of the same region. Nirodsha's elder brother Dharmadosha was also a high-ranking official under the Aulikaras, but his exact designation is not known.[

A victory pillar of Yashodharma at Sondani, Mandsaur district

The most significant monuments which definitely belong to the Aulikara period are two freestanding victory pillars of Yashodharma Vishnuvardhana bearing his inscriptions. These almost identical pillars, situated at Sondani, a suburb to the southeast Mandsaur, are made of sandstone. The height of the entire column is 44 ft 5 in. Its square base is 4 ft 5 in high and 3 ft 4 in wide. The bell-shaped capital is 5 ft 2 in high. Its shaft is sixteen faced rounds. Most probably there was a crowning statue, which has

The **Satavahanas,** also referred to as the **Andhras** in the Puranas, were an ancient Indian dynasty based in the Deccan region. Most modern scholars believe that the Satavahana rule began in the late second century BCE and lasted until the early third century CE, although some assign the beginning of their rule to as early as the 3rd century BCE based on the Puranas, but uncorroborated by archaeological evidence. The Satavahana kingdom mainly comprised the present-day Andhra Pradesh, Telangana, and Maharashtra. At different times, their rule extended to parts of modern Gujarat, Madhya Pradesh, and Karnataka. The dynasty had different capital cities at different times, including Pratishthana (Paithan) and Amaravati (Dharanikota).

The origin of the dynasty is uncertain, but according to the Puranas, their first king overthrew the Kanva dynasty. In the post-Maurya era, the Satavahanas established peace in the Deccan region and resisted the onslaught of foreign invaders. In particular their struggles with the Saka Western Satraps went on for a long time. The dynasty reached its zenith under the rule of Gautamiputra Satakarni and his successor Vasisthiputra Pulamavi. The kingdom had fragmented into smaller states by the early 3rd century CE.

The Satavahanas were early issuers of Indian state coinage struck with images of their rulers. They formed a cultural bridge and played a vital role in trade and the transfer of ideas and culture to and from the Indo-Gangetic Plain to the southern tip of India. They supported Hinduism as well as Buddhism and patronised Prakrit literature.

Varāhamihira's father Aditya-dasa likely trained him in jyotisha (Indian astrology and astronomy), as suggested by the *Brhaj-jataka* stanza and the opening stanza of *Pancha-siddhantika*.

Varāhamihira's commentator Utpala calls him "Magadha-dvija". According to one interpretation, this means that Varāhamihira was a Brahmin (dvija), whose ancestors belonged to the Magadha region.

According to another theory, the word "Magadha" in this context refers to the sun-worshipping Maga cult that Varāhamihira was a part of. In his Brhat-samhita, Varāhamihira mentions that the Magas were the only people suitable for consecrating an image of the Sun god, just like Bhagavatas for Vishnu, the ash-bearing Brahmanas (Pashupatas) for Shambhu, those well-versed in the mandala-krama worship for the mother goddess, the Brahmanas for Brahman, the Shakyas for the Buddha, and the Digambaras (nagnas) for Jina. The Magas, as they came to be known in India, originated from the Magi priests of the Achaemenid Empire. Historian Ajay Mitra Shastri cites a Bhavishya Purana passage according to which the term "Magadha" is a synonym of "Maga" and refers to "those who contemplate on the Maga". According to Shastri, Utpala has used the word "Magadha" to denote the Magas, who had been accepted as Shaka-dvipi (Maga) Brahmins in the Indian society.

Shastri theorizes that "Varaha-mihira" may be a Sanskritized form of the Iranian name "Varaza-Mihr", and may refer to a legend mentioned in the Mihr Yasht of the Avesta. According to this legend, the god Verethraghna, in the form of a boar (*varaza*), precedes Mihr in his march. Shastri notes that the 5th century Sassanian monarch Bahram V bore the name Mihrvaraza, which is quite similar to Varahamihira. Academic J.E. Sanjana suggests that Varāhamihira was descended from an Iranian Magi priest

Some scholars, such as M.T. Patwardhan and A.N. Upadhye, have identified Varāhamihira with Bazurjmehr, mentioned in Firishta's writings as a minister of the Sasanian king Khusraw Nushirwan (r. 531-578). However, A.M. Shastri dismisses this theory as unconvincing.

There are several historically inaccurate legends about the ancestry of Varāhamihira:

Jain writers Merutunga (14th century) and Rajashekhara-Suri claim that his original name was Varaha, and he was a brother of the Jain patriarch Bhadrabahu. He gained knowledge because of a favour by the Sun, because of which the suffix "Mihira" ("Sun") was added to his name. Jain authors seem to have fabricated this story to prove the pre-eminence of the Jain astrology over the Brahmanical astrology.

Another 20th century legend, purportedly based on "some old Gujarati text" claims that Aditya-dasa's wife was called Satya-vati alias Indu-mati: Varāhamihira was born to them in their fifties by the boon of the Sun. He was originally known as Mihira, and was given the prefix "Varaha" by King Vikramaditya when he correctly predicted that a boar (*varaha* in Sanskrit) would kill the king's son.

A tradition associates Varāhamihira with Berachampa in West Bengal, where a mound called "Varāhamihira's house" is located. This seems to be the result of an attempt to associate the locality with a famous figure. A legend from the Bengal region claims that Varaha and Mihira were a father-son duo at Vikramaditya's court, and the poet Khana was Mihira's wife. This legend is of no historical value.[1] "Varaha" and "Mihira" were alternative names for the same person - Varāhamihira, as attested by the later astronomical works.

Another legend claims that the Mimamsa teacher Shabara-svamin had four wives, one from each varna, and Varāhamihira was his son from his Brahmin wife. Some scholars, such as S.K. Dikshit, have theorized that Aditya-dasa (or Aditya-deva) was another name of Shabara-svamin, but no historical evidence supports this tradition.

Birthplace

Kapitthaka, where Varāhamihira studied, was probably his birthplace. While "Kapitthaka" is the most popular reading the place's name, several variants of this name appear in various manuscripts, including Kampilyaka, Kapilaka, Kapishthala, and Kapishkala. Utpala suggests that this village had a sun temple.

According to one theory, Kapitthaka is the modern Kayatha, an archaeological site near Ujjain. Statues of the sun deity Surya (whom Varāhamihira worshipped) dated 600-900 CE have been found there, and kapittha trees are abundant in and around Kayatha. However, no historical source suggests that Kapitthaka was another name for Kayatha. According to another theory, Kapitthaka is same as Sankissa (ancient Sankashya) in present-day Uttar Pradesh: according to the 7th-century Chinese traveler Xuanzang, this town was also known as Kah-pi-t'a. Historian Ajay Mitra Shastri notes that Kah-pi-t'a is phonetically similar to Kapittha or Kapitthaka.

Based on the term "Magadha-dvija" (see above), Sudhakara Dvivedi suggests that Varāhamihira was born and brought up in Magadha, and later migrated to Ujjain. Ajay Mitra Shastri disputes this, noting that Utpala describes him as "Avantikacharya" (Acharya of Avanti) and "Madgadha-dvija": these two terms cannot be reconciled if "Magadha-dvija" is interpreted as "Dvija (Brahmana) of Magadha"; instead "Magadha" here means Maga, as attested by the Bhavishya Purana.

Kālidāsa (*fl.* 4th–5th century CE) was a Classical Sanskrit author who is often considered ancient India's greatest poet and playwright. His plays and poetry are primarily based on the Vedas, the Rāmāyaṇa, the Mahābhārata and the Purāṇas. His surviving works consist of three plays, two epic poems and two shorter poems.

Much about his life is unknown except what can be inferred from his poetry and plays. His works cannot be dated with precision, but they were most likely authored before the 5th century CE.

Early life

Scholars have speculated that Kālidāsa may have lived near the Himalayas, in the vicinity of Ujjain, and in Kalinga. This hypothesis is based on Kālidāsa's detailed description of the Himalayas in his Kumārasambhava, the display of his love for

Ujjain in Meghadūta, and his highly eulogistic descriptions of Kalingan emperor Hemāngada in Raghuvaṃśa (sixth sarga).

Lakshmi Dhar Kalla (1891–1953), a Sanskrit scholar and a Kashmiri Pandit, wrote a book titled The birth-place of Kalidasa (1926), which tries to trace the birthplace of Kālidāsa based on his writings. He concluded that Kālidāsa was born in Kashmir, but moved southwards, and sought the patronage of local rulers to prosper. The evidence cited by him from Kālidāsa's writings includes:

Description of flora and fauna that is found in Kashmir, but not in Ujjain or Kalinga: the saffron plant, the deodar trees, musk deer etc.

Description of geographical features common to Kashmir, such as tarns and glades

Mention of some sites of minor importance that, according to Kalla, can be identified with places in Kashmir. These sites are not very famous outside Kashmir, and therefore, could not have been known to someone not in close touch with Kashmir.

Reference to certain legends of Kashmiri origin, such as that of the Nikumbha (mentioned in the Kashmiri text Nīlamata Purāṇa); mention (in Shakuntala) of the legend about Kashmir being created from a lake. This legend, mentioned in Nīlamata Purāṇa, states that a tribal leader named Ananta drained a lake to kill a demon. Ananta named the site of the former lake (now land) as "Kashmir", after his father Kaśyapa.

According to Kalla, Śakuntalā is an allegorical dramatization of Pratyabhijna philosophy (a branch of Kashmir Shaivism). Kalla further argues that this branch was not known outside of Kashmir at that time.

Another old legend recounts that Kalidasa visits Kumāradāsa, the king of Lanka and, because of treachery, is murdered there. Period

Several ancient and medieval books state that Kālidāsa was a court poet of a king named Vikramāditya. A legendary king named

Vikramāditya is said to have ruled from Ujjain around the 1st century BCE. A section of scholars believe that this legendary Vikramāditya is not a historical figure at all. There are other kings who ruled from Ujjain and adopted the title Vikramāditya, the most notable ones being Chandragupta II (r. 380 CE – 415 CE) and Yaśodharman (6th century CE).

The most popular theory is that Kālidāsa flourished during the reign of Chandragupta II, and therefore lived around the 4th-5th century CE. Several Western scholars have supported this theory, since the days of William Jones and A. B. Keith. Modern western Indologists and scholars like Stanley Wolpert also support this theory Many Indian scholars, such as Vasudev Vishnu Mirashi and Ram Gupta, also place Kālidāsa in this period. According to this theory, his career might have extended to the reign of Kumāragupta I (r. 414 – 455 CE), and possibly, to that of Skandagupta (r. 455 – 467 CE).

The earliest paleographical evidence of Kālidāsa is found in a Sanskrit inscription dated c. 473 CE, found at Mandsaur's Sun temple, with some verses that appear to imitate Meghadūta Purva, 66; and the ṛtusaṃhāra V, 2–3, although Kālidāsa is not named. His name, along with that of the poet Bhāravi, is first mentioned the 634 CE Aihole inscription found in Karnataka.

Chandragupta II (r.c. 375-415)

Chandragupta Vikramaditya, also known by his title **Vikramaditya**, as well as **Chandragupta Vikramaditya**, was the third ruler of the Gupta Empire in India, and was one of the most powerful emperors of the Gupta dynasty.

Chandragupta continued the expansionist policy of his father Samudragupta, mainly through military conquest. Historical evidence suggests that he defeated the Western Kshatrapas, and extended the Gupta Empire from the Indus River in the west to the Bengal region in the east, and from the Himalayan foothills in the north to the Narmada River in the south. His daughter Prabhavatigupta was a queen of the southern Vakataka kingdom, and he may have had influence in the Vakataka territory during her regency.

The Gupta Empire reached its zenith during the rule of Chandragupta. The Chinese pilgrim Faxian, who visited India during his reign, suggests that he ruled over a peaceful and prosperous kingdom. The legendary figure of Vikramaditya is probably based on Chandragupta II (among other kings), and the noted Sanskrit poet Kalidasa may have been his court poet.

Chandragupta II was the second ruler of the dynasty to bear the name "Chandragupta", the first being his grandfather Chandragupta I. He was also simply known as "Chandra", as attested by his coins.[5] The Sanchi inscription of his officer Amrakardava states that he was also known as Deva-raja. The records of his daughter Prabhavatigupta, issued as a Vakataka queen, call him Chandragupta as well as Deva-gupta. Deva-shri is another variation of this name. The Delhi iron pillar inscription states that king Chandra was also known as "Dhava": if this king Chandra is identified with Chandragupta (see below), it appears that "Dhava" was another name for the king. Another possibility is that "dhava" is a mistake for a common noun "bhava", although this is unlikely, as the rest of the inscription does not contain any errors.

A passage in the Vishnu Purana suggests that major parts of the eastern coast of India - Kosala, Odra, Tamralipta, and Puri - were ruled by the Devarakshitas around the same time as the Guptas. Since it seems unlikely that an obscure dynasty named Devarakshita was powerful enough to control substantial territory during the Gupta period, some scholars, such as Dasharatha Sharma, theorize that "Deva-rakshita) was another name for Chandragupta II. Others, such as D. K. Ganguly, oppose this theory, arguing that this identification is quite arbitrary, and cannot be explained satisfactorily.

Chandragupta assumed the titles *Bhattaraka* and *Maharajadhiraja*, and bore the epithet *Apratiratha* ("having no equal or antagonist").

The Supiya stone pillar inscription, issued during the reign of his descendant Skandagupta, also calls him "Vikramaditya".

Early life

Chandragupta was a son of Samudragupta and queen Dattadevi, as attested by his own inscriptions. According to the official Gupta genealogy, Chandragupta succeeded his father on the Gupta throne. The Sanskrit play Devichandraguptam, combined with other evidence suggests that he had an elder brother named Ramagupta, who preceded him on the throne. In the play, Ramagupta decides to surrender his queen Dhruvadevi to a Shaka enemy when besieged, but Chandragupta goes to the enemy camp disguised as the queen and kills the enemy. Sometime later, Chandragupta dethrones Ramagupta, and becomes the new king. The historicity of this narrative is debated among modern historians, with some believing it to be based on true historical events, while others dismissing it as a work of fiction.

Period of reign

The pillar inscribed with the Lakulisa Mathura Pillar Inscription, Mathura recording the installation of two Shiva Lingas by Udita Acharya in the "year 61 following the era of the Guptas in the reign of Chandragupta Vikramaditya, son of Samudragupta" (380 CE). Rangeshwar Temple.

The Mathura pillar inscription of Chandragupta II (as well as some other Gupta inscriptions) mention two dates: several historians have assumed that one of these dates denotes the king's regnal year, while the other date denotes the year of the Gupta calendar era. However, Indologist Harry Falk in 2004 has theorised that the date understood to be the regnal year by the earlier scholars is actually a date of the *kālānuvarttamāna* system. According to Falk, the *kālānuvarttamāna* system is a continuation of the Kushana calendar era established by emperor Kanishka, whose coronation Falk dates to 127 CE. The Kushana era restarts counting after a hundred years (e.g. the year after 100 is 1, not 101).

The date portion of the Mathura inscription reads

candragupta-sya vijarajya-saṃvatsa[re] ... kālānuvarttamāna-saṃvatsare ekaṣaṣṭhe 60 ... [pra]thame śukla-divase paṃcāmyaṃ

The letters before the words *kālānuvarttamāna-saṃvatsare* are abraded in the inscription, but historian D. R. Bhandarkar (1931–1932) reconstructed them as *gupta*, and translated the term *gupta-kālānuvarttamāna-saṃvatsare* as "year following the Gupta era". He translated the entire sentence as:[

"In the ... year of ... Chandragupta, ... on the fifth of the bright half of the first (Ashadha) of the year 61 following the Gupta era".

Historian D. C. Sircar (1942) restored the missing letters as "[paṃ]cāme" ("fifth"), and concluded that the inscription was dated to the Chandragupta's fifth regnal year. The missing letters have alternatively been read as "prathame" ("first"). According to these interpretations, the inscription is thus dated in year 61 of the Gupta era, and either the first or the fifth regnal year of Chandragupta. Assuming that the Gupta era starts around 319–320 CE, the beginning of Chandragupta's reign can be dated to either 376–377 CE or 380–381 CE.

Falk agrees that the missing letters denote a numerical year, but dismisses Sircar's reading as "mere imagination", pointing out that the missing letters are "abraded beyond recovery".In support of his Kushana era theory, Falk presents four Gupta inscriptions (in chronological order) that mention the term *kālānuvarttamāna-saṃvatsare*: Falk notes that the "dynastic year" in the table above appears to be a year of the Gupta era. The *kālānuvarttamāna* year cannot be regnal year, because Chandragupta I am not known to have ruled for as long as 61 years. If we assume "61" of the Mathura pillar inscription denotes a year of the Gupta era (as assumed by Bhandarkar, Sircar and other scholars), we must assume that "15" of the Buddhist image pedestal also denotes a year of the Gupta era: this is obviously incorrect, since Kumaragupta I ruled after Chandragupta II. Scholars K.K. Thaplyal and R.C. Sharma, who studied the Buddhist image pedestal inscription, speculated that the scribe had mistakenly interchanged the years 121 and 15, but Falk calls this assumption unnecessary.

According to Falk, the discrepancy can be explained satisfactorily, if we assume that the *kālānuvarttamāna* era denotes a system that restarts counting after a hundred years. The Yaksha figure inscription is dated to year 112 of the Gupta era (c. 432 CE), which corresponds to the *kālānuvarttamāna* year 5. Thus, the *kālānuvarttamāna* era used during Kumaragupta's time must have started in 432-5 = 427 CE. The years mentioned in the Buddhist image pedestal inscription also suggests that the epoch of this era was c. 426-427 CE. Since the *kālānuvarttamāna* system restarts counting every 100 years, the *kālānuvarttamāna* era used during the reign of Chandragupta II must have started in 327 CE. Thus, the Mathura inscription can be dated to 327+61 = c. 388 CE. While Falk's theory does not change the Gupta chronology significantly, it implies that the date of the Mathura inscription cannot be used to determine the beginning of Chandragupta's reign.

The Sanchi inscription, dated to 412-413 CE (year 93 of the Gupta era), is the last known dated inscription of Chandragupta. His son Kumaragupta was on the throne by the 415-416 CE (year 96 of the Gupta era), so Chandragupta's reign must have ended sometime during 412-415 CE.

Gupta records mention Dhruvadevi as Chandragupta's queen, and the mother of his successor Kumaragupta .The Basarh clay seal mentions Dhruva-svamini as a queen of Chandragupta, and the mother of Govindagupta. It is unlikely that Chandragupta had two different queens with similar names: it appears that Dhruvasvamini was most probably another name for Dhruvadevi, and that Govindagupta was a real brother of Kumaragupta.

Chandragupta also married Kuvera-naga (alias Kuberanaga), whose name indicates that she was a princess of the Naga dynasty, which held considerable power in central India before Samudragupta subjugated them. This matrimonial alliance may have helped Chandragupta consolidate the Gupta empire, and the

Nagas may have helped him in his war against the Western Kshatrapas.

Prabhavati-gupta, the daughter of Chandragupta and Kuvera-naga, married the Vakataka king Rudrasena II, who ruled in the Deccan region to the south of the Gupta empire. After her husband's death in c. 390, Prabhavati-gupta acted as a regent for her minor sons. In the two copper-plate inscriptions issued during her regency, the names of her Gupta ancestors with their imperial titles appear before the name of the Vakataka king with the lesser title Maharaja. This suggests that the Gupta court may have had influence in the Vakataka administration during her regency. Historians Hermann Kulke and Dietmar Rothermund believe that the Vakataka kingdom was "practically part of the Gupta empire" during her 20-year long regency. The Vakatakas may have supported Chandragupta during his conflict with the Western Kshatrapas.[

The Guptas also appear to have entered into a matrimonial alliance with the Kadamba dynasty, the southern neighbours of the Vakatakas. The Talagunda pillar inscription suggests that the daughters of the Kadamba king Kakusthavarman, married into other royal families, including that of the Guptas. While Kakusthavarman was a contemporary of Chandragupta's son Kumaragupta I, it is noteworthy that some medieval chiefs of present-day Karnataka (where the Kadambas ruled) claimed descent from Chandragupta. According to the Vikramaditya legends, emperor Vikramaditya (a character believed to be based on Chandragupta) sent his court poet Kalidasa as an ambassador to the lord of Kuntala. While the Kuntala king referred to in this legend has been identified by some scholars with a Vakataka king, it is more likely that he was a Kadamba king, because the Vakataka king did not rule over Kuntala, and was never called the lord of Kuntala.

Vannar community

Vannar community are actually Indo-European group of peoples and at Ramayana period they ruled at Kishkinda who worshiped to

Virbhadra. They spread up in South India and Sree Lanka at present south India Tamil Nadu, Kerala, Karnataka that they spread up but remained most backward. They are actually branch Jut/ Jat group of peoples and in Jat community there have several branch groups who have either surname of name of animals or subbranch (Jotra) of peoples. Lord Hanuman remained Minister of Sukhbir. Sukhbir's father named Suraya and Vali's have father named Indra. But Sukhbir and Vali remained as brothers as their mother remained same. Lord Hanuman's biological father remained Praban / Bayou where as social father remained Kasseri. All of this evidence indicated Vannar community are Indo-European. Bajrang means Lower Rank as Baja means lower and rang means ranks that Lord Hanuman remained as advisor and minister of Sukhbir.

Vannar is a Tamil caste found primarily in the Indian state of Tamil Nadu and northeastern parts of Sri Lanka. The community has traditionally been involved in laundry. also agricultural workers They are in Tamil Nadu classified as Most Backward Class.

Etymology

The word *Vannar* is thought to be derived from the Tamil word *vannam* meaning "beauty". The chief of this community uses the title *Kattadi*, meaning exorcist.

History

The Vannars traditionally occupy the Sangam landscape Marutham. The Vannars are known as the descendants of Virabhadra and are considered to be the ancient inhabitants of the state The Vannars were also involved in the practice of Ayurvedic medicine. The Vannars served as kudimakkal or domestic servants, who also gave importance as ceremonial officiators. The Vannas became the god of their clan Murugan is worshiped and all his Temples are decorated with Priests

Legacy

What is now available are the inscriptions on the famous Vannar monastery at Chidambaram, which are available in two volumes. It is also known to have been established during the reign of King Vijayanagara. It is said that the first book of the three books and the second book of the same book belong to the same period. Among these, the Shivalingam, Nandi, Sulaam, Surya, Chandra, Veeramanavalar Devi, etc. are said to have been carved in the sculptures, and it is said that the Vannarmadam was renovated during the reign of King Vijayanagara Meykirti and Krishnadevarayar and Achutharayar. Datsun, Isan's father-in-law, who was created by Isan to destroy him and the gods and goddesses who volunteered to perform the sacrifice without inviting Isan. Both destroyed the gods and goddesses in the same way. The gods and goddesses who destroyed both were then revived by the Lord and Goddess for the welfare of the world, and the blood of the wounds inflicted on them by Veerapathira and Kali was immortal on them. In order to remove that blood, Eason orders Varuna to rain, and Varuna rains in the same way. However, the blood stain remained on the clothes. So, Eason ordered the warriors to remove that stain, and he was created one of the lineages. He is named Veeran and is sent to bleach the clothes of the gods and goddesses. Those who came in the way of the heroes and the way of the hero were called Vannar. They came to earth and did the same business.

Virabhadra also rendered Veerabhadra, Veerabathira, and Veerabathiran, is a fierce form of the Hindu god Shiva. He is created by the wrath of Shiva, when the deity hurls a lock of his matted hair upon the ground, upon hearing of the self-immolation of his consort, Sati, at the Daksha yajna.

He appears in the Puranas as a vengeful being, attacking the deities who had attended the Daksha yajna with Bhadrakali. In the ensuing melee, Bhaga's eyes are plucked out, Yama's staff is broken, Pushan's teeth are knocked out, Indra is trampled, and Agni, Mitra, and ChandAgra are also accosted. The fate of Daksha himself varies from text to text: Virabhadra either decapitates him, urges him to beg forgiveness from Shiva, or is saved by Vishnu, who defeats Virabhadra.

Legend

According to Shaivism, Virabhadra's origins are described follows: Sati was the youngest daughter of Daksha. While growing up, she had her heart set on Shiva and worshipped him. During the svayamvara of Sati, Daksha invited all the devas and princes except Shiva. Sati cast her garland into the air, calling upon Shiva to receive it, and beheld him to be standing in the midst of the court, with the garland about his neck. Daksha had no choice but to accept the marriage of his daughter to Shiva.

One day, Daksha invited all the deities, as well as all of his children and grandchildren, in order to perform a ritual sacrifice, deliberately not inviting Sati and Shiva. Sati's urge to attend the event, due to her affection towards her parents, overpowered the social etiquette of not going to an uninvited ceremony. When Shiva refused to accompany her, Sati insisted on attending the ritual without him. Upon her arrival, Daksha started to humiliate her husband and she, expressing his hatred for Shiva in front of the entire assembly of people. Unable to bear the ignominy, the furious Sati leapt into the sacrificial fire, immolating herself with her yogic abilities. When Shiva heard of these tidings, he tore a clump of his matted hair, from which Virabhadra and Bhadrakali emerged. Shiva instructed Virabhadra to lay waste to the sacrifice, and destroy all of its participants.

Maheshwara replied, 'Spoil the sacrifice of Daksha'. Then the mighty Virabhadra, having heard the pleasure of his lord, bowed down his head to the feet of Shiva; and starting like a lion loosed from bonds, despoiled the sacrifice of Daksha, knowing that this had been created by the displeasure of Devi. She too in her wrath, as the fearful goddess Rudrakali, accompanied him, with all her train, to witness his deeds.

Vayu Purana

The Padma Purana identifies Virabhadra as the fierce form of Mangala (Mars). Virabhadra is born when Shiva, due to his anguish regarding the death of Sati, perspires, and his perspiration falls upon the earth. This gives birth to the fierce Virabhadra, who destroys the sacrifice. In the aftermath, Shiva calms him down and makes him Angaraka, the planet Mars.

The Skanda Purana states that ill-omens immediately started to surface when Shiva's forces started to march upon the Daksha yajna, describing a rain of blood and meteor showers. Finding these phenomena to be foreboding, Daksha sought the protection of Vishnu, who agreed to offer it, while also according blame to the former for his disrespect. The forces consisted of the Navadurga, rakshasas, yakshas, pishachas, a host of bhutas, thousands of ganas, as well as yoginis and guhyakas. These forces were commanded by the three-eyed Virabhadra, bearing a thousand arms, entwined with great serpents, with his chariot drawn by two thousand horses and a million lions. Indra and the devas were assisted by Bhrigu in routing the first wave of gana attacks. Angered, Virabhadra marshalled his forces in a counterattack, and wielding their battle-axes and iron clubs, they started to massacre the devas. The sages begged Vishnu to defend the sacrifice from the attackers, and the deity prepared to fight against Virabhadra. While Virabhadra offered his obeisance to the preserver deity, he accused him of seeking a share of the offerings of the sacrifice, and warned him against staying there. Vishnu laughed, and informed him that he had a duty to shield his devotees, and would leave after he had had his fill of Virabhadra's missiles. Indra chose to challenge Virabhadra, and struck him with his vajra. In retaliation, Virabhadra attempted to swallow Indra as well as his mount, Airavata. Vishnu intervened, saving Indra, and obstructing the assault of Virabhadra. He also summoned the Ashvins, who healed the fallen devas with their medicine. Enraged, Virabhadra confronted Vishnu. The preserver deity employed his Sudarshana Chakra against Virabhadra, which the latter swallowed whole.

After retrieving his celestial discus, satisfied that he had turned the tide of the battle, Vishnu returned to his abode. Not satisfied with the carnage, Virabhadra accosted Bhrigu, Pushan, and when he saw the terrified Daksha cowering beneath the altar, he beheaded him, offering his head to the fire as a sacrifice. The disturbed Brahma visited Shiva, and begged him to put an end to the bloodshed. Shiva arrived at the Dakha yajna, conversed with Virabhadra, and restored life to Daksha by placing the head of a deformed animal upon his neck. The resurrected Daksha offered his obeisance to Shiva, which ended the conflict.

Various scriptures, coloured by their traditions, offer variations of the conflict, and Virabhadra's role in the legend. The Kurma Purana has Virabhadra realise that Vishnu and Shiva are the same deity, and proclaim that the world was created by Narayana. In the Harivamsha, Vishnu gains the upper hand in his fight against Virabhadra.

Provisional Government of Free India

Provisional Government of Free India or, more simply, *Azad Hind*, was a short-lived Japanese-supported provisional government in India. It was established in Japanese occupied Singapore during World War II in October 1943 and has been considered a puppet state of Empire of Japan.

It was a part of the political movement originating in the 1940s outside India with the purpose of allying with the Axis powers to liberate India from British rule. It was established by Indian nationalists in exile during the latter part of the World War II in Singapore with monetary, military and political assistance from Imperial Japan.

Founded on 21 October 1943, the government was inspired by the concepts of Subhas Chandra Bose who was also the leader of the government and Head of state. The government proclaimed authority over Indian civilian and military personnel in Southeast Asian British colonial territory and prospective authority over Indian territory to fall to the Japanese forces and the Indian

National Army during the Japanese thrust towards India. The government of Azad Hind had its own currency, court and civil code, and in the eyes of some Indians, its existence gave a greater importance to the independence struggle against the British.[9][10][11] Japan also handed over nominal authority of the Japanese occupied Andaman and Nicobar Islands in 1943, though the government continued to be dependent on Japanese support. Immediately after the formation of the provisional government, Free India declared war against the Allied forces on the Indo-Burma Front. Its army, the Indian National Army (Azad Hind Fauj), went into action against the British Indian Army and the allied forces as part of the Imperial Japanese Army in the Imphal-Kohima sector. The INA had its first major engagement at the Battle of Imphal where, under the command of the Japanese Fifteenth Army, it breached the British defences in Kohima, reaching the salient of Moirang before suffering a catastrophic defeat as the Allied forces held, and Allied air dominance and compromised supply lines forced both the Japanese and the INA to retreat. The existence of Azad Hind was essentially coterminous with the existence of the Indian National Army. While the government itself continued until the civil administration of the Andaman Islands was returned to the jurisdiction of the British towards the end of the war, the limited power of Azad Hind was effectively ended with the surrender of the last major contingent of INA troops in Rangoon. The death of Bose is seen as the end of the entire Azad Hind Movement.

The legacy of Azad Hind is, however, open to judgment. After the war, the Raj observed with alarm the transformation of the perception of Azad Hind from traitors and collaborators to liberators. The British Empire, never seriously threatened by the INA, charged 300 INA officers with treason in the INA trials, but eventually backtracked in the face of opposition by the Congress.

The direct origins of Azad Hind can be linked to two conferences of Indian expatriates from across Southeast Asia, the first of which was held in Tokyo in March 1942. At this conference, convened by Rash Behari Bose, an Indian expatriate living in Japan, the

Indian Independence League was established as the first move towards an independent Indian state politically aligned with the Empire of Japan. Rash also moved to create a sort of independence army that would assist in driving the British from India – this force would later become the Indian National Army. The second conference, held later that year in Bangkok, invited Subhas Chandra Bose to participate in the leadership of the League. Bose was living in Germany at the time and made the trip to Japan via submarine.

Rash Behari Bose, who was already ageing by the time the League was founded, struggled to keep the League organized and failed to secure resources for the establishment of the Indian National Army. He was replaced as president of the Indian Independence League by Subhas Chandra Bose; there is some controversy as to whether he stepped down of his own volition or by pressure from the Japanese who needed a more energetic and focused presence leading the Indian nationalists.

Bose arrived in Tokyo on 13 June 1943 and declared his intent to make an assault against the eastern provinces of India in an attempt to oust the British from control of the subcontinent. Bose arrived in Singapore on 2 July, and in October 1943 formally announced the establishment of the Provisional Government of Free India at the Cathay Cinema Hall. In defining the tasks of this new political establishment, Subhas declared: "It will be the task of the Provisional Government to launch and conduct the struggle that will bring about the expulsion of the British and their allies from the soil of India." Bose, taking formal command of the demoralized and undermanned Indian National Army from Rash Bose, turned it into a professional army with the help of the Japanese. He recruited Indian civilians living in Japanese-occupied territories of Southeast Asia and incorporated vast numbers of Indian POWs from British forces in Singapore, Malaya and Hong Kong to man the brigades of the INA.

Ministers

The Provisional Government of Free India consisted of a Cabinet headed by Subhas Chandra Bose as the Head of the State, The Prime Minister and the Minister for War and Foreign Affairs.

Captain Dr. Lakshmi Swaminadhan (later married as Lakshmi Sahgal) was the Minister in Charge of Women's Organization. She held this position over and above her command of the Rani Jhansi Regiment, a brigade of women soldiers fighting for the Indian National Army. For a regular Asian army, this women's regiment was quite visionary; it was the first of its kind established on the continent. Lakshmi was one of the most popular and prosperous gynaecologists in Singapore before she gave up her practice to lead the troops of the Rani of Jhansi Regiment.

Other public administration ministers of the Provisional Government of Free India included:

Lakshmi Swaminadhan – The Minister in Charge of Women's Organization

S. A. Ayer – The Minister of Broadcasting and Publicity

Lt. Col. A. C. Chatterji – The Minister of Finance

The Indian National Army was represented by Armed Forces ministers, including:

Lt. Col. Aziz Ahmed

Lt. Col. N. S. Bhagat

Lt. Col. J. K. Bhonsle

Lt. Col. Guizara Singh

Lt. Col. M.Z. Kiani

Lt. Col. A. D. Loganathan

Lt. Col. Ehsan Qadir

Lt. Col. Shahnawaz Khan

The Provisional Government was also constituted and administered by a number of Secretaries and Advisors to Subhas Chandra Bose, including:

Capt. Dilip Singh Siwach

M. Sahay – Secretary

Sardar Ishar Singh Narula

A. N. Sarkar – the government's official Legal Advisor

All of these Secretaries and Advisory officials held Ministerial rank in the Provisional Government. The extent of the Provisional Government's day-to-day management of affairs for Azad Hind is not entirely well-documented, so their specific functions as government officials for the state outside their positions as support ministers for Subhas Chandra Bose is not entirely certain.

RecognitGreater East Asia Conference in November 1943, participants left to right: Ba Maw, Zhang Jinghui, Wang Jingwei, Hideki Tojo, Wan Waithayakon, José P. Laurel, Subhas Chandra Bose.

Azad Hind was recognised as a legitimate state by only a small number of countries limited solely to Axis powers and their allies.[26] Azad Hind had diplomatic relations with nine countries: Nazi Germany, the Empire of Japan, Italian Social Republic, Independent State of Croatia and Wang Jingwei Government, Thailand, the State of Burma, Manchukuo and the Second Philippine Republic. On the declaration of its formation in occupied Singapore the Taoiseach of Ireland, Éamon de Valera, sent a note of congratulations to Bose. Vichy France, however, although being an Axis collaborator, never gave formal political recognition to Azad Hind. This government participated as an observer in the Greater East Asia Conference in November 1943

Government administration and World War II

Main articles: Indian National Army, India during World War II, and Invasion and Occupation of the Andaman Islands during World War II

The same night that Bose declared the existence of Azad Hind, the government took action to declare war against the United States and Britain. The government consisted of a Cabinet ministry acting as an advisory board to Subhas Bose, who was given the title "Netaji" (translating roughly to "leader") and was no doubt the dominant figure in the Provisional Government. He exercised virtual authoritarian control over the government and the army. With regards to the government's first issuances of war declarations, the "Cabinet had not been unanimous about the inclusion of the U.S.A. Bose had shown impatience and displeasure – there was never any question then or later of his absolute authority: the Cabinet had no responsibility and could only tender advice..."

Azad Hind Bank

Azad Hind Bank was established on 5 April 1944, at Rangoon, the then headquarters of the Provisional Azad Hind Indian government supported by Imperial Japan.

Establishment

On 21 October 1943 Subhash Chandra Bose formed provisional government of Azad Hind and early after it Bose declared war against British Raj and its allies on 23 October 1943.

Bose established the Azad Hind bank to manage funds donated by the Indian community from across the world for the liberation of India from the British Raj, while utilizing the bank's services for the operations of the Azad Hind Fauj. The bank maintained its branches throughout Japan occupied countries. The currency notes were issued in the form of Promissory note, and these notes were usually printed on one side. The money collected by the Azad Hind government was kept in the Bank. Initially the bank had an authorized capital of ₹ 5 million and paid-up capital of ₹ 2.5 million.

At the end of October 1943, Bose flew to Tokyo to participate in the Greater East Asia Conference as an observer to Japan's Greater East Asia Co-Prosperity Sphere; it could not function as a delegate because India had technically fallen outside the jurisdiction of Japan's definition of "Greater East Asia", but Bose gave speeches in opposition to Western colonialism and imperialism at the conference. By the end of the conference, Azad Hind had been given a limited form of governmental jurisdiction over the Andaman and Nicobar Islands, which had been captured by the Imperial Japanese Navy early on in the war.

Unreleased postage stamps of the Azad Hind government.

Once under the jurisdiction of Azad Hind, the islands formed the government's first claims to territory. The islands themselves were renamed "Shaheed" and "Swaraj", meaning "martyr" and "self-rule" respectively. Bose placed the islands under the governorship of Lt Col A. D Loganathan, and had limited involvement with the official governorship of the territory, instead involving himself in plans to expand the Indian National Army, ensure adequate men and materiel, and formulate its course of actions and the administrations and relations of the Indian population in southeast Asia and determining Japanese designs in India and his provisional government. In theory, the government itself had the power to levy taxes on the local populace, and to make and enforce laws: in practice, they were enforced by the police force under Japanese control. Indians were willing to pay these taxes at first but became less inclined to do so towards the end of the war when the Provisional Government enacted legislation for higher war-time taxes to fund the INA. During his interrogation after the war, Loganathan admitted that he had only had full control over the islands' vestigial education department, as the Japanese had retained full control over the police force, and in protest, he had refused to accept responsibility for any other areas of Government.

He was powerless to prevent the Homfreyganj massacre of 30 January 1944, where forty-four Indian civilians were shot by the Japanese on suspicion of spying. Many of them were members of the Indian Independence League, whose leader in Port Blair, Diwan Singh, had already been tortured to death in the Cellular Jail after doing his best to protect the islanders from Japanese atrocities during the first two years of the occupation.

Azad Hind's military forces in the form of the INA saw some successes against the British and moved with the Japanese army to lay siege to the town of Imphal in eastern India. Plans to march towards Delhi, gaining support and fresh recruits along the way, stalled both with the onset of monsoon season and the failure to capture Imphal. British bombing seriously reduced morale, and the Japanese along with the INA forces began their withdrawal from India.

In addition to these setbacks, the INA was faced with a formidable challenge when the troops were left to defend Rangoon without the assistance of the Japanese in the winter of 1944–1945. Loganathan was relocated from the Andaman Islands to act as field commander. With the INA garrison about 6,000 strong, he manned the Burmese capital in the absence of any other police force or troops during the period between the departure of the Japanese and the arrival of the British. He was successful in maintaining law and order to the extent that there was not a single reported case of dacoity or of looting during the period from 24 April to 4 May 1945.

Indian areas under the administration of the Provisional Government

Almost all of the territory of the Provisional Government lay in the Andaman Islands, although the Provisional Government was allowed some authority over Indian enclaves in Japanese-occupied territories. Provisional Government civil authority was never enacted in areas occupied by the INA; instead, Japanese military authority prevailed and responsibility for administration of occupied areas of India was shared between the Japanese and the Indian forces.

INA defeat and Provisional Government collapse

Left to defend Rangoon from the British advance without support from the Japanese, the INA was soundly defeated. Bose was suggested to leave Burma to continue his struggle for Indian independence and returned to Singapore before the fall of Rangoon; the government Azad Hind had established on the Andaman and Nicobar Islands collapsed when the island garrisons of Japanese and Indian troops were defeated by British troops and the islands themselves retaken. Allegedly Bose himself was killed in a plane crash departing from Taiwan attempting to escape to the Soviet Union. The Provisional Government of Free India ceased to exist with the deaths of the Axis, the INA, and the disappearance of Bose in 1945.

Two Annas Token currency, minted in August 1947, in remembrance of the Azad Hind.

The troops who manned the brigades of the Indian National Army were taken as prisoners of war by the British. A number of these prisoners were brought to India and tried by British courts for treason, including a number of high-ranking officers such as Colonel Gurbaksh Singh Dhillon. The defence of these individuals from prosecution by the British became a central point of contention between the British Raj and the Indian Independence Movement in the post-war years.

Relations with the Axis Powers

Collaboration with the Axis Powers and Collaboration with Imperial Japan, Bose with Heinrich Himmler, the Nazi Minister of Interior, head of the SS, and the Gestapo, 1942; Subhas Bose shaking hands with Adolf Hitler.

Since Subhas Chandra Bose aligned with Empire of Japan and the Axis Powers, which also included Nazi Germany and Fascist Italy,

Britain portrayed him as a controversial figure for his official stance against imperialism which would run in opposition against Japanese imperialism in Asia during World War II. Bose himself claimed to oppose all manner of colonial practices but claimed Britain as hypocritical in "fighting a war for democracy" while refusing to extend the same respect for democracy and equal rights to their colonial subjects in India. Bose opposed British racial policy and declared working for the abolition of racial discrimination with Burmese, Japanese and other Asians.

Britain accused him of fascism, citing his control over the Provisional Government as strict as evidence of this; and pointed to him wanting to establish a totalitarian state in India with the blessings of the Axis powers. Bose believed that parliamentary democracy was unsuitable for India immediately after independence and that a centrally organized, self-sufficient, semi-socialist India under the firm control of a single party was the best course for Indian government. Some of his ideas would help shape Indian governmental policy in the aftermath of the country's independence from Britain.

It has been argued that the fact that Azad Hind was aligned politically with Japan and the Axis Powers may have had more to do with what Bose saw as a pragmatic approach to Indian independence. Disillusioned with Congress's non-violent movement, Bose was clearly of the camp that supported exploiting British weakness to gain Indian independence. Throughout the existence of Azad Hind, Bose sought to distance himself from Japanese collaboration and become more self-sufficient but found this difficult since the existence of Azad Hind as a governmental entity had only come about with the support of the Japanese, on whom the government and army of Azad Hind were entirely dependent. Bose, however, is considered a hero by some in present-day India and is remembered as a man who fought fiercely for Indian independence. However, Subhas Chandra Bose had supported Fascism and Nazism before the start of WWII, declaring that India needed "a synthesis of what modern Europe calls socialism and fascism" in a speech in made in Calcutta in 1930.

Although Japanese troops saw much of the combat in India against the British, the INA was certainly by itself an effective combat force, having faced British and allied troops and making their mark in the Battle of Imphal. On 18 April 1944 the suicide squad led by Col. Shaukat Malik broke through the British defence and captured Moirang in Manipur. The Azad Hind administration took control of this independent Indian territory. Following Moirang, the advancing INA breached the Kohima road, posing a threat to the British positions in both Silchar and Kohima. Col. Gulzara Singh's column had penetrated 250 miles into India. The Azad Brigade advanced, by outflanking the Anglo-American positions.

However, INA's most serious, and ultimately fatal, limitations were the reliance on Japanese logistics and supplies and the total air-dominance of the allies, which, along with a supply line deluged by torrential rain, frustrated the INA's and the Japanese bid to take Imphal.

With the siege of Imphal failing, the Japanese began to shift priority for resource allocation from South Asia to the Pacific, where they were fighting United States troops advancing from island to island against Japanese holdings there. When it had become clear that Bose's plans to advance to Delhi from the borders of Burma would never materialize due to the defeat of the INA at Imphal and the halt of Japanese armies by British aerial and later naval superiority in the region, Japanese support for Azad Hind declined.

The Indian National Army (INA) was a collaborationist armed unit of Indian collaborators that fought under the command of the Japanese Empire. It was founded on 1 September 1942 in Southeast Asia during World War II.

It fought under the command of the Japanese military in the British campaign in the Southeast Asian theatre of WWII, with its aim to secure Indian independence from British rule. The army was first formed in 1942 under Rash Behari Bose by Indian POWs of the British Indian Army captured by Japan in the Malayan campaign and at Singapore. This first INA, which had been handed over to

Rash Behari Bose, collapsed and was disbanded in December that year after differences between the INA leadership and the Japanese military over its role in Japan's war in Asia. Rash Behari Bose handed over INA to Subhas Chandra Bose. It was revived under the leadership of Subhas Chandra Bose after his arrival in Southeast Asia in 1943. The army was declared to be the army of Bose's Arzi Hukumat-e-Azad Hind (the Provisional Government of Free India). The INA came to be known as the puppet army of the Japanese empire.

Under Bose's leadership, the INA drew ex-prisoners and thousands of civilian volunteers from the Indian expatriate population in Malaya (present-day Malaysia) and Burma. This second INA fought under the Imperial Japanese Army against the British and Commonwealth forces in the campaigns in Burma: at Imphal and Kohima, and later against the Allied retaking of Burma.

After the INA's initial formation in 1942, there was concern in the British Indian Army that further Indian troops would defect. This led to a reporting ban and a propaganda campaign called "Jiffs" to preserve the loyalty of the Sepoy.[11] Historians consider the INA not to have had significant influence on the war.

The British Raj, never seriously threatened by the INA, charged 300 INA officers with treason in the INA trials, but eventually backtracked in the face of opposition by the Congress. These trials became a galvanising point in the Indian Independence movement for the Indian National Congress. A number of people associated with the INA during the war later went on to hold important roles in public life in India as well as in other countries in Southeast Asia, most notably Lakshmi Sehgal in India, and John Thivy and Janaki Athinahappan in Malaya.

The military unit was associated with Imperial Japan and the other Axis powers, and accusations were levelled against INA troops of being involved and complicit in Japanese war crimes. The INA's members were viewed as Axis collaborators and traitors by British soldiers and Indian PoWs who did not join the army,[1] but after the war they were seen as patriots by many Indians. Although they were widely commemorated by the Indian National Congress in the immediate aftermath of Indian independence, some of the members of the INA were denied freedom fighter status by the Government of India.

Emilie Schenkl (26 December 1910 – 13 March 1996) was an Austrian stenographer, secretary and trunk exchange operator. She was the wife or the companion of Subhas Chandra Bose, an Indian nationalist leader.

Schenkl met Bose in 1934, and the two formed a romantic relationship while she worked for him as a secretary. She later became the mother of their daughter Anita Bose Pfaff during Bose's stay in Germany from 3 April 1941 until 8 February 1943. Following his departure from wartime Europe for Southeast Asia, Schenkl and her baby daughter were left without economic support. Bose, who thereafter tried to oppose British rule in India militarily with Japanese patronage, died in a plane crash soon after the Japanese surrender in August 1945.

In 1948, Schenkl and her daughter were met by Bose's brother Sarat Chandra Bose and his family in an emotional meeting in Vienna. In the post-war years, Schenkl worked shifts in the trunk exchange and was the main breadwinner of her family, which included her daughter and her mother.

Early life

Emilie Schenkl was born in Vienna on 26 December 1910 in an Austrian Catholic family. Paternal granddaughter of a shoemaker and the daughter of a veterinarian, she started primary school late—towards the end of the Great War—on account of her father's reluctance for her to have formal schooling. Her father, moreover, became unhappy with her progress in secondary school and enrolled her in a nunnery for four years. Schenkl decided against becoming a nun and went back to school, finishing when she was 20. The Great Depression had begun in Europe; consequently, for a few years she was unemployed..She was a member of the Bund Deutscher Mädel.

She was introduced to Bose in June 1934, or sometime thereafter, through a mutual friend, Dr. Mathur, an Indian physician living in Vienna; Bose, nearly 13 years her senior, had arrived there with a contract from a British publisher for writing a book on Indian politics. As Schenkl could take shorthand and her English and typing skills were good, she was hired by Bose; the book would become The Indian Struggle. They soon fell in love and were married on 26 December 1937 in Bad Gastein during another visit by Bose in a secret Hindu ceremony, but without a Hindu priest, witnesses, or civil record. Bose went back to India and reappeared in Nazi Germany, living in Berlin during the period April 1941 – February 1943.

Berlin during the war

Sometime after Bose had arrived in Berlin, according to historian Romain Hayes, "the (German) Foreign Office procured a luxurious residence for him along with a butler, cook, gardener, and an SS-chauffeured car. Emilie Schenkl moved in openly with him. The Germans, aware of the nature of the relationship, refrained from any involvement." However, most of the staff in the Special Bureau for India, which had been set up to aid Bose, did not get along with Emilie. In particular Adam von Trott, Alexander Werth and Freda Kretschemer, according to historian Leonard A. Gordon, "appear to have disliked her intensely. They believed that she and Bose were not married and that she was using her liaison with Bose to live an especially comfortable life during the hard times of war" and that differences were compounded by issues of class In November 1942, Schenkl gave birth to their daughter. In February 1943, Bose left Schenkl and their baby daughter and boarded a German submarine to travel, via transfer to a Japanese submarine, to Japanese-occupied Southeast Asia; with Japanese support, he formed a Provisional Government of Free India and revamped an army, the Indian National Army, whose goal was to gain India's independence militarily with Japanese help. Bose's effort was unsuccessful, and he died in a plane crash in Taihoku (now Taipei), Japanese-held Formosa (now Taiwan), on 18 August 1945, while attempting to escape to the Japanese-held town of Dairen (now Dalian) on the Manchurian peninsula.

Later life

Schenkl and her daughter survived the war with no support or communication from Bose. During their seven years and eight months of marriage, Schenkl and Bose spent less than three years together, putting strains on Schenkl Bose never publicly acknowledged the fact of his marriage and privately did so only in a letter to his brother Sarat written in Bengali and given to Emilie before he left Europe, with instructions for it to be posted to him in the event of his death. In the post-war years, Schenkl worked shifts in i and was the main breadwinner of her family, which included her daughter and her mother. Although some family members from Bose's extended family, including his brother Sarat Chandra Bose, welcomed Schenkl and her daughter and met with her in Austria in 1948, Schenkl never visited India. According to her daughter, Schenkl was a very private woman and tight-lipped about her relationship with Bose. Emiie Schenkl died in 1996.

Indian National Army

Bose fled to Japan in 1915, under the alias of Priyanath Thakur, a relative of Rabindranath Thakur a famous Indian poet. There, Bose found shelter with various Pan-Asian groups. From 1915 to 1918, he changed residences and identities numerous times, as the British kept pressing the Japanese government for his extradition. He married the daughter of Aizō Sōma and Kokkō Sōma, the owners of Nakamuraya bakery in Tokyo and noted Pan-Asian supporters in 1918, and became a Japanese citizen in 1923, living as a journalist and writer. It is also significant that he was instrumental in introducing Indian-style curry in Japan. Though more expensive than the usual "British-style" curry, it became quite popular, with Rash Bihari becoming known as "Bose of Nakamuraya".

Bose along with A M Nair was instrumental in persuading the Japanese authorities to stand by the Indian patriots and ultimately to officially actively support the Indian independence struggle abroad. Bose convened a conference in Tokyo on 28–30 March 1942, which decided to establish the Indian Independence League. At the conference, he moved a motion to raise an army for Indian independence. He convened the second conference of the League at Bangkok on 22 June 1942. It was at this conference that a resolution was adopted to invite Subhas Chandra Bose to join the League and take its command as its president.

The Indian prisoners of war captured by the Japanese in the Malaya and Burma fronts were encouraged to join the Indian Independence League and become the soldiers of the Indian National Army (INA), formed on 1 September 1942 as the military wing of Rash Behari Bose's Indian National League. He selected the flag for the Azad Hind movement and handed over the flag to Subhas Chandra Bose. But although he handed over the power, his organizational structure remained, and it was on the organizational spadework of Rash Behari Bose. Rash Behari Bose built the Indian National Army (also called 'Azad Hind Fauj'). Prior to his death caused by tuberculosis, the Japanese Government honoured him with the Order of the Rising Sun (2nd grade).

Japanese invasion of China

The Second Sino-Japanese War (1937–1945) was a military conflict that was primarily waged between the Republic of China and the Empire of Japan. The war made up the Chinese theater of the wider Pacific Theater of the Second World War. The beginning of the war is conventionally dated to the Marco Polo Bridge Incident on 7 July 1937, when a dispute between Japanese and Chinese troops in Peking escalated into a full-scale invasion. This full-scale war between the Chinese and the Empire of Japan is often regarded as the beginning of World War II in Asia. (However, according to the Chinese Ministry of Education, it marked only a phase in a 14-year war that began with the 1931 invasion of Manchuria.)

As part of its operations against China, on 22 September 1940 Japan invaded French Indochina. On 27 September it signed the Tripartite Pact with Germany and Italy. War with the U.S. and other Western allies of World War II began with the attack on Pearl Harbor on 7 December 1941. Over the course of seven hours there were coordinated Japanese attacks on the U.S.-held Philippines, Guam and Wake Island, the Dutch Empire in the Dutch East Indies, Thailand and on the British Empire in Borneo, Malaya and Hong Kong. The strategic goals of the offensive were to destroy the U.S. Pacific fleet, capture oil fields in the Dutch East Indies, and maintain their sphere of influence in East Asia. It was also to expand the outer reaches of the Japanese Empire to create a formidable defensive perimeter around newly acquired territory.

China fought Japan with aid from the Soviet Union and the United States. After the Japanese attacks on Malaya and Pearl Harbor in 1941, the war merged with other conflicts which are generally categorized under those conflicts of World War II as a major sector known as the China Burma India Theater. Some scholars consider the European War and the Pacific War to be entirely separate, albeit concurrent wars. Other scholars consider the start of the full-scale Second Sino-Japanese War in 1937 to have been the beginning of World War II. The Second Sino-Japanese War was the largest Asian war in the 20th century.[5] It accounted for the majority of civilian and military casualties in the Pacific War, with between 10 and 25 million Chinese civilians and over 4 million Chinese and Japanese military personnel missing or dying from war-related violence, famine, and other causes. The war has been called "the Asian holocaust".

Decision process by Japanese leaders

Political map of the Asia-Pacific region, 1939

The decision by Japan to attack the United States remains controversial. Study groups in Japan had predicted ultimate disaster in a war between Japan and the U.S., and the Japanese economy was already straining to keep up with the demands of the war with China. However, the U.S. had placed an oil embargo on Japan and Japan felt that the United States' demands of unconditional withdrawal from China and non-aggression pacts with other Pacific powers were unacceptable. Facing an oil embargo by the United States as well as dwindling domestic reserves, the Japanese government decided to execute a plan developed by the military branch largely led by Osami Nagano and Isoroku Yamamoto to bomb the United States naval base in Hawaii, thereby bringing the United States to World War II on the side of the Allies. On 4 September 1941, the Japanese Third Konoe Cabinet (Prime Minister Fumimaro Konoe) met to consider the war plans prepared by Imperial General Headquarters, and decided:

Our Empire, for the purpose of self-defense and self-preservation, will complete preparations for war ... [and is] ... resolved to go to war with the United States, Great Britain, and the Netherlands if necessary. Our Empire will concurrently take all possible diplomatic measures vis-a-vis the United States and Great Britain, and thereby endeavor to obtain our objectives ... In the event that there is no prospect of our demands being met by the first ten days of October through the diplomatic negotiations mentioned above, we will immediately decide to commence hostilities against the United States, Britain and the Netherlands.

Vice Admiral Isoroku Yamamoto, the chief architect of the attack on Pearl Harbor, had strong misgivings about war with the United States. Yamamoto had spent time in the United States during his youth when he studied as a language student at Harvard University (1919–1921) and later served as assistant naval attaché in Washington, D.C. Understanding the inherent dangers of war with the United States, Yamamoto warned his fellow countrymen: "We can run wild for six months or maybe a year, but after that, I have utterly no confidence".

Origin of conflict

The USS Arizona was a total loss in the Japanese surprise air attack on the American Pacific Fleet at Pearl Harbor, Sunday 7 December 1941.

Propaganda illustration

Since early 1941 the United States and Japan had been engaged in negotiations in an attempt to improve their strained relations and end the war in China. During these negotiations, Japan advanced a number of proposals which were dismissed by the Americans as inadequate. At the same time the United States, the United Kingdom, and the Netherlands engaged in secret discussions for the joint defense of their territories, in the event of a Japanese attack against any of them. Roosevelt reinforced the Philippines (an American protectorate scheduled for independence in 1946) and warned Japan that the United States would react to Japanese attacks against any "neighboring countries".

Frustrated at the lack of progress and feeling the pinch of the American–British–Dutch sanctions, Japan prepared for war. On 20 November, a new government under Hideki Tojo presented an interim proposal as its final offer. It called for the end of American aid to China and for lifting the embargo on the supply of oil and other resources to Japan. In exchange, Japan promised not to launch any attacks in Southeast Asia and to withdraw its forces from southern Indochina. The American counter-proposal of 26 November required that Japan evacuate all of China without conditions and conclude non-aggression pacts with all Pacific powers. That meant Japan was essentially forced to choose between abandoning its ambitions in China, or seizing the natural resources it needed in the Dutch East Indies by force; the Japanese military did not consider the former an option, and many officers considered the oil embargo an unspoken declaration of war.

Japan planned to rapidly seize European colonies in Asia to create a large defensive perimeter stretching into the Central Pacific. The Japanese would then be free to exploit the resources of Southeast

Asia while exhausting the over-stretched Allies by fighting a defensive war. To prevent American intervention while securing the perimeter, it was further planned to neutralize the United States Pacific Fleet and the American military presence in the Philippines from the outset.

Japanese offensives (1941–1942)

On 7 December 1941 (8 December in Asian time zones), Japan attacked British and American holdings with near-simultaneous offensives against Southeast Asia and the Central Pacific. These included an attack on the American fleets at Pearl Harbor and the Philippines, Guam, Wake Island, landings in Malaya, Thailand and the Battle of Hong Kong.

The Imperial Japanese Navy made its surprise attack on Pearl Harbor, Oahu, Hawaii Territory, on Sunday morning, 7 December 1941. The Pacific Fleet of the United States Navy and its defending Army Air Forces and Marine air forces sustained significant losses. The primary objective of the attack was to incapacitate the United States long enough for Japan to establish its long-planned Southeast Asian empire and defensible buffer zones. However, as Admiral Yamamoto feared, the attack produced little lasting damage to the US Navy with priority targets like the Pacific Fleet's three aircraft carriers out at sea and vital shore facilities, whose destruction could have destroyed the fleet on their own, were ignored. Of more serious consequences, the U.S. public saw the attack as a barbaric and treacherous act and rallied against the Empire of Japan.

The Japanese invasion of Thailand led to Thailand's decision to ally itself with Japan and the other Japanese attacks led the United States, United Kingdom, China, Australia, and several other states to formally declare war on Japan, whereas the Soviet Union, being heavily involved in large-scale hostilities with European Axis countries, maintained its neutrality agreement with Japan. Germany, followed by the other Axis states, declared war on the United States[23] in solidarity with Japan, citing as justification the

American attacks on German war vessels that had been ordered by Roosevelt.

The United States entered the European Theater and Pacific Theater in full force. Four days later, Adolf Hitler of Germany, and Benito Mussolini of Italy declared war on the United States, merging the separate conflicts. Following the attack on Pearl Harbor, the Japanese launched offensives against Allied forces in East and Southeast Asia, with simultaneous attacks on British Hong Kong, Thailand, British Malaya, Dutch East Indies, Guam, Wake Island, Gilbert Islands, Borneo and the Philippines.

By 1942, the Japanese Empire had launched offensives in Dutch East Indies, New Guinea, Singapore, Burma, Yunnan and India, the Solomons, Timor, Aleutian Islands, Christmas Island and the Andaman Islands.

By the time World War II was in full swing, Japan had the most interest in using biological warfare. Japan's Air Force dropped massive amounts of ceramic bombs filled with bubonic plague-infested fleas in Ningbo, China. These attacks would eventually lead to thousands of deaths years after the war would end. In Japan's relentless and indiscriminate research methods on biological warfare, they poisoned more than 1,000 Chinese village wells to study cholera and typhus outbreaks. These diseases are caused by bacteria that with today's technology could potentially be weaponized.

Battle of Hong Kong, 8 December 1941, Downtown British Hong Kong under Japanese air raid

A map of the Canterbury in New Zealand prepared by the Japanese Military following the attack on Pearl Harbor

Battle of Singapore, February 1942. Victorious Japanese troops march through the city center. (Photo from Imperial War Museum)

The South-East Asian campaign was preceded by years of propaganda and espionage activities carried out in the region by the Japanese Empire. The Japanese espoused their vision of a

Greater Asian Co-Prosperity Sphere, and an Asia for Asians to the people of Southeast Asia, who had lived under European rule for generations. As a result, many inhabitants in some of the colonies (particularly Indonesia) actually sided with the Japanese invaders for anti-colonial reasons. However, the ethnic Chinese, who had witnessed the effects of Japanese occupation in their homeland, did not side with the Japanese.

Hong Kong surrendered to the Japanese on December 25. In Malaya the Japanese overwhelmed an Allied army composed of British, Indian, Australian and Malay forces. The Japanese were quickly able to advance down the Malay Peninsula, forcing the Allied forces to retreat towards Singapore. The Allies lacked air cover and tanks; the Japanese had air supremacy. The sinking of HMS Prince of Wales and HMS Repulse on December 10, 1941, led to the east coast of Malaya being exposed to Japanese landings and the elimination of British naval power in the area. By the end of January 1942, the last Allied forces crossed the strait of Johore and into Singapore. In the Philippines, the Japanese pushed the combined Filipino-American force towards the Bataan Peninsula and later the island of Corregidor. By January 1942, General Douglas MacArthur and President Manuel L. Quezon were forced to flee in the face of Japanese advance. This marked one of the worst defeats suffered by the Americans, leaving over 70,000 American and Filipino prisoners of war in the custody of the Japanese.

On February 15, 1942, Singapore, due to the overwhelming superiority of Japanese forces and encirclement tactics, fell to the Japanese, causing the largest surrender of British-led military personnel in history. An estimated 80,000 Indian, Australian and British troops were taken as prisoners of war, joining 50,000 taken in the Japanese invasion of Malaya (modern day Malaysia). Many were later used as forced labour constructing the Burma Railway, the site of the infamous The Bridge on the River Kwai. Immediately following their invasion of British Malaya, the Japanese military carried out a purge of the Chinese population in Malaya and Singapore.

The Japanese then seized the key oil production zones of Borneo, Central Java, Malang, Cepu, Sumatra, and Dutch New Guinea of the late Dutch East Indies, defeating the Dutch forces. However, Allied sabotage had made it difficult for the Japanese to restore oil production to its pre-war peak. The Japanese then consolidated their lines of supply through capturing key islands of the Pacific, including Guadalcanal.

Tide turns (1942–1945)

Battle of Midway. The attack by dive bombers from USS Yorktown and USS Enterprise on the Japanese aircraft carriers Soryu, Akagi and Kaga in the morning of 4 June 1942.

Japanese military strategists were keenly aware of the unfavorable discrepancy between the industrial potential of the Japanese Empire and that of the United States. Because of this they reasoned that Japanese success hinged on their ability to extend the strategic advantage gained at Pearl Harbor with additional rapid strategic victories. The Japanese Command reasoned that only decisive destruction of the United States' Pacific Fleet and conquest of its remote outposts would ensure that the Japanese Empire would not be overwhelmed by America's industrial might. In April 1942, Japan was bombed for the first time in the Doolittle Raid. In May 1942, failure to decisively defeat the Allies at the Battle of the Coral Sea, in spite of Japanese numerical superiority, equated to a strategic defeat for Imperial Japan. This setback was followed in June 1942 by the catastrophic loss of four fleet carriers at the Battle of Midway, the first decisive defeat for the Imperial Japanese Navy. It proved to be the turning point of the war as the Navy lost its offensive strategic capability and never managed to reconstruct the "'critical mass' of both large numbers of carriers and well-trained air groups".

Australian land forces defeated Japanese Marines in New Guinea at the Battle of Milne Bay in September 1942, which was the first land defeat suffered by the Japanese in the Pacific. Further victories by the Allies at Guadalcanal in September 1942, and New

Guinea in 1943 put the Empire of Japan on the defensive for the remainder of the war, with Guadalcanal in particular sapping their already-limited oil supplies. During 1943 and 1944, Allied forces, backed by the industrial might and vast raw material resources of the United States, advanced steadily towards Japan. The Sixth United States Army, led by General MacArthur, landed on Leyte on October 20, 1944. In the subsequent months, during the Philippines Campaign (1944–45), the combined United States forces, together with the native guerrilla units, liberated the Philippines. By 1944, the Allies had seized or bypassed and neutralized many of Japan's strategic bases through amphibious landings and bombardment. This, coupled with the losses inflicted by Allied submarines on Japanese shipping routes began to strangle Japan's economy and undermine its ability to supply its army. By early 1945, the U.S. Marines had wrested control of the Ogasawara Islands in several hard-fought battles such as the Battle of Iwo Jima, marking the beginning of the fall of the islands of Japan.

Air raids on Japan

The atomic bombing of Nagasaki on August 9, 1945

After securing airfields in Saipan and Guam in the summer of 1944, the United States Army Air Forces undertook an intense strategic bombing campaign, using incendiary bombs, burning Japanese cities in an effort to pulverize Japan's industry and shatter its morale. The Operation Meetinghouse raid on Tokyo on the night of March 9–10, 1945, led to the deaths of approximately 100,000 civilians. Approximately 350,000–500,000 civilians died in 66 other Japanese cities as a result of the incendiary bombing campaign on Japan. Concurrent to these attacks, Japan's vital coastal shipping operations were severely hampered with extensive aerial mining by the U.S.'s Operation Starvation. Regardless, these efforts did not succeed in persuading the Japanese military to surrender. In mid-August 1945, the United States dropped nuclear weapons on the Japanese cities of Hiroshima and Nagasaki. These atomic bombings were the first and only such weapons used against another nation in warfare. These two bombs killed approximately 120,000 to 140,000 people in a matter of minutes, and as many as a result of nuclear radiation in the following weeks, months and years. The bombs killed as many as 140,000 people in Hiroshima and 80,000 in Nagasaki by the end of 1945.

Re-entry of the Soviet Union

In spite of Soviet–Japanese Neutrality Pact, at the Yalta agreement in February 1945, the US, the UK, and the USSR had agreed that the USSR would enter the war on Japan within three months of the defeat of Germany in Europe. This Soviet–Japanese War led to the fall of Japan's Manchurian occupation, Soviet occupation of South Sakhalin island, and a real, imminent threat of Soviet invasion of the home islands of Japan. This was a significant factor for some internal parties in the Japanese decision to surrender to the US and gain some protection, rather than face simultaneous Soviet invasion as well as defeat by the US. Likewise, the superior numbers of the armies of the Soviet Union in Europe was a factor in the US decision to demonstrate the use of atomic weapons to the USSR, just as the Allied victory in Europe was evolving into division of Germany and Berlin, the division of Europe with the Iron Curtain and the subsequent Cold War.

Surrender and occupation of Japan

A drawing depicting a speech in the Imperial Japanese Diet on 1 November 1945, the end of the Second World War. In the foreground there are several Allied soldiers watching the proceedings from the back of the balcony.

Having ignored (mokusatsu) the Potsdam Declaration, the Empire of Japan surrendered and ended World War II, after the atomic bombings of Hiroshima and Nagasaki and the declaration of war by the Soviet Union. In a national radio address on August 15, Emperor Hirohito announced the surrender to the Japanese people by Gyokuon-hōsō. A period known as Occupied Japan followed after the war, largely spearheaded by United States General of the

Army Douglas MacArthur to revise the Japanese constitution and de-militarize Japan. The Allied occupation, with economic and political assistance, continued well into the 1950s. Allied forces ordered Japan to abolish the Meiji Constitution and enforce the Constitution of Japan, then rename the Empire of Japan as Japan on May 3, 1947. Japan adopted a parliamentary-based political system, while the Emperor changed to symbolic status.

American General of the Army Douglas MacArthur later commended the new Japanese government that he helped establish and the new Japanese period when he was about to send the American forces to the Korean War:

The Japanese people, since the war, have undergone the greatest reformation recorded in modern history. With a commendable will, eagerness to learn, and marked capacity to understand, they have, from the ashes left in war's wake, erected in Japan an edifice dedicated to the supremacy of individual liberty and personal dignity; and in the ensuing process there has been created a truly representative government committed to the advance of political morality, freedom of economic enterprise, and social justice. Politically, economically, and socially Japan is now abreast of many free nations of the earth and will not again fail the universal trust. ... I sent all four of our occupation divisions to the Korean battlefront without the slightest qualms as to the effect of the resulting power vacuum upon Japan. The results fully justified my faith. I know of no nation more serene, orderly, and industrious, nor in which higher hopes can be entertained for future constructive service in the advance of the human race.

In retrospect, apart from the military officer corps, the purge of alleged militarists and ultranationalists that was conducted under the Occupation had relatively small impact on the long-term composition of men of influence in the public and private sectors. The purge initially brought new blood into the political parties, but this was offset by the return of huge numbers of formerly purged conservative politicians to national as well as local politics in the early 1950s. In the bureaucracy, the purge was negligible from the outset. ... In the economic sector, the purge similarly was only mildly disruptive, affecting less than sixteen hundred individuals spread among some four hundred companies. Everywhere one looks, the corridors of power in postwar Japan are crowded with men whose talents had already been recognized during the war years, and who found the same talents highly prized in the 'new' Japan.

The criminalization of politics

The criminalization of politics means the participation of criminals in politics. Means that persons with criminal background contest in the election and get selected as a member of parliament or state legislature. It is said that the politics had reached a stage where the lawmakers became the lawbreakers. In a democratic country like India, the increasing nexus between criminals and politics threatens the survival of true democracy. It is now becoming a trend, people with criminal backgrounds have more influence in politics than people without criminal backgrounds.

The reason behind the criminalization of politics:

One of the most important reasons for the criminalization of politics is the increasing nexus between politicians and bureaucracy.

The increasing interference of politicians in administration may be regarded as another reason for the criminalisation of politics.

At the time of the election, political parties spend a huge sum of money buying the votes for another illegitimate purpose. The people don't pay attention to the people to whom they are going to cast their vote, whether he has any criminal background or not.

The poor governance of the country also plays an important role in increasing the criminalization of politics. It doesn't have the proper laws and rules for governing the procedure of the election.

Suggested measures:

There should be an amendment in the RP act to debar those persons from contesting elections against whom any serious Nature of crimes is pending.

A kind of awareness program should be started for voters to make them aware of their right to know the criminal background of the person to whom they are going to cast their votes.

The election commission should be given more rights to prevent the criminalization of politics. A penalty should be inflicted on those political parties who give tickets to those persons who have a criminal background.

Decolonization of Asia and Africa, 1945–1960

Between 1945 and 1960, three dozen new states in Asia and Africa achieved autonomy or outright independence from their European colonial rulers.

Harold MacMillan, British Prime Minister, helped begin decolonization

There was no one process of decolonization. In some areas, it was peaceful, and orderly. In many others, independence was achieved only after a protracted revolution. A few newly independent countries acquired stable governments almost immediately; others were ruled by dictators or military juntas for decades, or endured long civil wars. Some European governments welcomed a new relationship with their former colonies; others contested decolonization militarily. The process of decolonization coincided with the new Cold War between the Soviet Union and the United States, and with the early development of the new United Nations. Decolonization was often affected by superpower competition, and had a definite impact on the evolution of that competition. It also significantly changed the pattern of international relations in a more general sense.

The creation of so many new countries, some of which occupied strategic locations, others of which possessed significant natural resources, and most of which were desperately poor, altered the composition of the United Nations and political complexity of every region of the globe. In the mid to late 19th century, the European powers colonized much of Africa and Southeast Asia. During the decades of imperialism, the industrializing powers of Europe viewed the African and Asian continents as reservoirs of raw materials, labor, and territory for future settlement. In most cases, however, significant development and European settlement in these colonies was sporadic. However, the colonies were exploited, sometimes brutally, for natural and labor resources, and sometimes even for military conscripts. In addition, the introduction of colonial rule drew arbitrary natural boundaries where none had existed before, dividing ethnic and linguistic groups and natural features, and laying the foundation for the creation of numerous states lacking geographic, linguistic, ethnic, or political affinity.

During World War II Japan, itself a significant imperial power, drove the European powers out of Asia. After the Japanese surrender in 1945, local nationalist movements in the former Asian colonies campaigned for independence rather than a return to European colonial rule. In many cases, as in Indonesia and French Indochina, these nationalists had been guerrillas fighting the Japanese after European surrenders, or were former members of colonial military establishments. These independence movements often appealed to the United States Government for support.

While the United States generally supported the concept of national self-determination, it also had strong ties to its European allies, who had imperial claims on their former colonies. The Cold War only served to complicate the U.S. position, as U.S. support for decolonization was offset by American concern over communist expansion and Soviet strategic ambitions in Europe. Several of the NATO allies asserted that their colonial possessions provided them with economic and military strength that would otherwise be lost to the alliance. Nearly all of the United States' European allies believed that after their recovery from World War II their colonies would finally provide the combination of raw materials and protected markets for finished goods that would cement the colonies to Europe. Whether or not this was the case, the alternative of allowing the colonies to slip away, perhaps into the United States' economic sphere or that of another power, was unappealing to every European government interested in postwar stability. Although the U.S. Government did not force the issue, it encouraged the European imperial powers to negotiate an early withdrawal from their overseas colonies. The United States granted independence to the Philippines in 1946.

However, as the Cold War competition with the Soviet Union came to dominate U.S. foreign policy concerns in the late 1940s and 1950s, the Truman and Eisenhower Administrations grew increasingly concerned that as the European powers lost their colonies or granted them independence, Soviet-supported communist parties might achieve power in the new states. This might serve to shift the international balance of power in favor of the Soviet Union and remove access to economic resources from U.S. allies. Events such as the Indonesian struggle for independence from the Netherlands (1945–50), the Vietnamese war against France (1945–54), and the nationalist and professed socialist takeovers of Egypt (1952) and Iran (1951) served to reinforce such fears, even if new governments did not directly link themselves to the Soviet Union. Thus, the United States used aid packages, technical assistance and sometimes even military intervention to encourage newly independent nations in the Third World to adopt governments that aligned with the West. The Soviet Union deployed similar tactics in an effort to encourage new nations to join the communist bloc, and attempted to convince newly decolonized countries that communism was an intrinsically non-imperialist economic and political ideology. Many of the new nations resisted the pressure to be drawn into the Cold War, joined in the "nonaligned movement," which formed after the Bandung conference of 1955, and focused on internal development.

The newly independent nations that emerged in the 1950s and the 1960s became an important factor in changing the balance of power within the United Nations. In 1946, there were 35 member states in the United Nations; as the newly independent nations of the "third world" joined the organization, by 1970 membership had swelled to 127. These new member states had a few characteristics in common; they were non-white, with developing economies, facing internal problems that were the result of their colonial past, which sometimes put them at odds with European countries and made them suspicious of European-style governmental structures, political ideas, and economic institutions. These countries also became vocal advocates of continuing decolonization, with the result that the UN Assembly was often ahead of the Security Council on issues of self-governance and decolonization. The new nations pushed the UN toward accepting resolutions for independence for colonial states and creating a special committee on colonialism, demonstrating that even though some nations continued to struggle for independence, in the eyes of the international community, the colonial era was ending.

Decolonization is the process by which western overseas empires are broken up and replaced with independent governments in the Americas, Asia, and Africa.

Politically (achieving independence, self-government, union with the metropole, or joining another state), culturally, or both (removal of pernicious colonial effects).

The term mostly alludes to the global colonial empires that had been built prior to World War I being destroyed in the years after that conflict.

The dissolution of the Spanish Empire in the 19th century, the collapse of the German, Austro-Hungarian, Ottoman, and Russian Empires after World War I, the collapse of the British, French, Japanese, Portuguese, Belgian, and Italian colonial empires after World War II, and the collapse of the Soviet Union (the successor to the Russian Empire) after the Cold War are a few examples.

Studies have demonstrated that decolonization refers to the capacity to observe and analyse non-Western civilizations from a neutral, non-Western perspective.

There are many different ways that decolonization might take place.

The dependency most frequently develops into a new independent state, a political organization acknowledged in the international community as independent of other states and as having final control over a certain territory and population.

Less frequently, decolonization might take place when a dependency is fully assimilated into an existing state and ceases to be independent and subordinate.

The relationship between Puerto Rico and the United States can be categorized as either one of colonial dependence or free association. Portugal asserted in the 1960s that it had no colonies and that only foreign areas had been constitutionally merged into a single Portuguese state.

And where political ties are not strained, it is difficult to determine whether independence has been attained because there is no overt fighting.

Important Factors in the decolonization process

Three main factors were extremely important in this decolonization process.

First and foremost, the desire for independence among colonized peoples, followed by the Second World War's demonstration of the vulnerability of colonial powers, and finally, the United Nations' renewed emphasis on anti-colonialism.

The release of Britain's thirteen continental colonies under the name United States of America marked the beginning of the first wave of decolonization.

The French colony of Saint Domingue became Haiti after a slave insurrection that was sparked by the French Revolution. After the Napoleonic Wars, which had cut off Latin America from the Iberian Peninsula, Portuguese Brazil and Spanish Central and South America gained independence.

While the initial phase of decolonization was only applicable to the Americas. Decolonization took place worldwide in the 20th century.

Most of the Indian subcontinent, Southeast Asia, Australasia, the Middle East, Africa, and the Caribbean were all included in its scope, as well as independence. Between the two world wars, a few of Britain's colonial outposts and a few loosely governed protectorates attained full independence.

Major Asian colonies including India, Indonesia, Indochina, and the Philippines attained independence following World War II. During the 1960s, when roughly all of Africa was decolonized, this transition accelerated quickly.

Nearly every Western colony had achieved self-government or had been entirely assimilated into sovereign states by the 1980s.

Who desired independence throughout each of the two stages of decolonization was a key distinction? Creole revolutions marked the early stages of American decolonization as the descendants of European settlers sought political independence from their motherland.

Political revolutions, as opposed to social revolutions, were the American Revolution and the Spanish Wars for Independence. The only exception to the disgust of loyalists and creole nationalists abroad was the slave uprising in Haiti.

Contrarily, as decolonization came to signify freedom from ethnically foreign domination, it was deeply based on aboriginal rather than creole campaigns for independence.

After World War II, settler factions resisted decolonization because it would remove their privileged social, political, and economic status. A racialist minority administration only managed to survive decolonization in South Africa.

The degree of violence engaged also differed significantly between the first and second effects of decolonization. Early American decolonization was achieved by armed conflict between colonial and imperial troops. In the thirteen continental colonies of Great Britain, in Spanish Central and South America, and in Haiti, wars for independence raged.

Due to Brazil's greater wealth and population than Portugal's, only Portuguese Brazil was able to achieve independence without a fight.

Protracted battles for independence were fought in Algeria, Angola, Indochina, and Indonesia during the 20th century. But these were rare instances.

Without organized conflict between the imperial state and colonial nationalists, the majority of colonies achieved independence.

The Cold War

The **Cold War** was a period of geopolitical tension between the United States and the Soviet Union and their respective allies, the Western Bloc and the Eastern Bloc. The term cold war is used because there was no large-scale fighting directly between the two superpowers, but they each supported opposing sides in major regional conflicts known as proxy wars. The conflict was based on the ideological and geopolitical struggle for global influence by these two superpowers, following their temporary alliance and victory against Nazi Germany and Imperial Japan in 1945. Aside from the nuclear arsenal development and conventional military deployment, the struggle for dominance was expressed via indirect means such as psychological warfare, propaganda campaigns, espionage, far-reaching embargoes, rivalry at sports events, and technological competitions such as the Space Race.

The Western Bloc was led by the United States as well as a number of other First World nations that were generally liberal democratic but tied to a network of often Third World authoritarian states, most of which were the European powers' former colonies. The Eastern Bloc was led by the Soviet Union and its Communist Party, which had an influence across the Second World and was also tied to a network of authoritarian states. The Soviet Union had a command economy and installed similarly totalitarian regimes in its satellite states. The US government supported anti-communist and right-wing governments and uprisings across the world, while the Soviet government funded left-wing parties and revolutions around the world. As nearly all the colonial states achieved independence in the period from 1945 to 1960, many became Third World battlefields in the Cold War.

The first phase of the Cold War began shortly after the end of World War II in 1945. The United States and its Western European allies sought to strengthen their bonds and used the policy of containment against Soviet influence; they accomplished this most notably through the formation of NATO which was essentially a defensive agreement in 1949. The Soviet Union countered with the Warsaw Pact in 1955, which had similar results with the Eastern Bloc. As by 1955 the Soviet Union already had an armed presence and political domination all over its eastern satellite states, the pact has been long considered "superfluous". Although nominally a "defensive" alliance, the Pact's primary function was to safeguard the Soviet Union's hegemony over its Eastern European satellites, with the Pact's only direct military actions having been the invasions of its own member states to keep them from breaking away.[6] In 1961, Soviet-dominated East Germany constructed the Berlin Wall to prevent the citizens of East Berlin from fleeing to free and prosperous West Berlin (part of US-allied West Germany).[7] Major crises of this phase included the 1948–1949 Berlin Blockade, the 1945–1949 Chinese Communist Revolution, the 1950–1953 Korean War, the 1956 Hungarian Revolution, the 1956 Suez Crisis, the 1961 Berlin Crisis, the 1962 Cuban Missile Crisis, and the 1964–1975 Vietnam War. The US and the USSR competed for influence in Latin America, the Middle East, and the decolonizing states of Africa, Asia, and Oceania.

Following the Cuban Missile Crisis, a new phase began that saw the Sino-Soviet split between China and the Soviet Union complicate relations within the communist sphere, leading to a series of border confrontations, while France, a Western Bloc state, began to demand greater autonomy of action. The USSR invaded

Czechoslovakia to suppress the 1968 Prague Spring, while the US experienced internal turmoil from the civil rights movement and opposition to the Vietnam War. In the 1960s–1970s, an international peace movement took root among citizens around the world. Movements against nuclear weapons testing and for nuclear disarmament took place, with large anti-war protests. By the 1970s, both sides had started making allowances for peace and security, ushering in a period of détente that saw the Strategic Arms Limitation Talks and the US opening relations with the People's Republic of China as a strategic counterweight to the USSR. A number of self-proclaimed Marxist–Leninist governments were formed in the second half of the 1970s in developing countries, including Angola, Mozambique, Ethiopia, Cambodia, Afghanistan, and Nicaragua.

Détente collapsed at the end of the decade with the beginning of the Soviet–Afghan War in 1979. The early 1980s was another period of elevated tension. The United States increased diplomatic, military, and economic pressures on the Soviet Union, at a time when it was already suffering from economic stagnation. In the mid-1980s, the new Soviet leader Mikhail Gorbachev introduced the liberalizing reforms of glasnost ("openness", c. 1985) and perestroika ("reorganization", 1987) and ended Soviet involvement in Afghanistan in 1989. Pressures for national sovereignty grew stronger in Eastern Europe, and Gorbachev refused to militarily support the communist governments any longer.

In 1989, the fall of the Iron Curtain after the Pan-European Picnic and a peaceful wave of revolutions (with the exception of Romania and Afghanistan) overthrew almost all of the Marxist-Leninist regimes of the Eastern Bloc. The Communist Party of the Soviet Union itself lost control in the country and was banned following an abortive coup attempt in August 1991. This in turn led to the formal dissolution of the Soviet Union in December 1991 and the collapse of communist governments across much of Africa and Asia. The Russian Federation became the Soviet Union's successor state, while all of the other republics emerged from the USSR's collapse as fully independent post-Soviet states. The United States was left as the world's sole superpower.

The Cold War and its events have left a significant legacy. It is often referred to in popular culture, especially with themes of espionage and the threat of nuclear warfare. For subsequent history, see international relations since 1989.

Ukraine War:

Ukraine's forces are concluding their preparations for a long-expected spring counteroffensive against invading Russian troops, the country's defiance minister has said, and are, broadly speaking, ready. Oleksii Reznikov told an online briefing on Friday: "As soon as there is God's will, the weather and a decision by commanders, we will do it." He gave no date for when the counteroffensive would start but said: "Globally speaking, we are to a high percentage ready. Kyiv has been preparing a counterattack for several months aimed at repelling Russian forces from the east and south.

Russia on Friday launched a **wave of missile attacks across many of Ukraine's biggest cities**, killing a mother and young child in the port city of Dnipro, and 14 people at a high-rise apartment building in the central city of Uman. Air raid alarms were active across the country in the early hours of Friday morning, while **explosions were heard in Kyiv, and southern Mykolaiv was targeted again**.

The New York Times has reported that Amnesty International has been sitting on an independent review criticising its controversial allegation that Ukrainian forces were illegally endangering civilians. Amnesty's accusation that Ukrainian troops were illegally putting "civilians in harm's way" by basing themselves nearby and launching attacks from populated areas caused widespread anger when it was published last August. Russia claimed it as vindication but critics – including the Ukrainian president, Volodymyr Zelenskiy – said it was poorly researched, ignored wartime realities and drew a moral equivalence between Russia, the aggressor, and Ukraine, the victim.

Reports are emerging that the Russian colonel general Mikhail Mizintsev, known as the "butcher of Mariupol", has been removed as deputy defence minister in charge of logistics and supplies. Reuters cites a military blogger, Alexander Sladkov, and the news website RBC as saying Mizintsev, who orchestrated the siege of the devastated city of Mariupol last year, was no longer in the role he was appointed to last September.

The Kremlin has said Russian military units that have fought in Ukraine **will be represented in a parade in Moscow on 9 May to mark the anniversary of the Soviet victory in the second world war, Reuters reports.** The holiday is one of the most important in the Russian calendar, usually featuring a huge show of military hardware on Red Square and a speech from President Vladimir Putin.

At least seven civilians were killed and 33 injured between Wednesday and Thursday, Ukraine's presidential office said, including one person killed and 23 wounded when four Kalibr cruise missiles hit the southern city of Mykolaiv.

The parliamentary assembly of the Council of Europe has voted that the **forced detention and deportation of children from Russian occupied territories of Ukraine is genocide**.

Russia said its patience should not be tested over nuclear weapons in another repeat of hardline rhetoric. Russian foreign ministry spokesperson Maria Zakharova said that Russia will do "everything to prevent the development of events according to the worst scenario ... but not at the cost of infringing on our vital interests".

The Biden administration is sanctioning Russia's Federal Security Service for wrongfully detaining Americans. The sanctions are largely symbolic, since the organization is already under sweeping existing sanctions for the invasion of Ukraine.

Bourgeois system implement by Norendra Modi

Anti-Farmer Bill

Antifarmer Bill input by Ordinance that to making enforcement land mafia by laws. Capitalist Ambani, Adani and others becoming highly richest by black hand as hang government form by Noranda Modi and his alliance.

Citizenship Bill

Mohandas Karamchand Gandhi and Balave Bhai Patel ways Agent of British:

In First World War full supported to British Government of India

It was demanded that under British Semi Independent remaining India where Upper house member remaining British and Lower house member to be remaining Indian in Imperial Legislative House(Now Called Parliament)

In Second World War at first stage full support to British Government of India

After decided to end of colonial ruled by British then acting as nationalist to execute Civil Disobedience and Quite India movement to take credit.

They Should not supporting to Lokemanna Tilak, Subhash Chandra Bosh, Bhagat Singh and Lala Rajpat Rai as Mohandas Karamchad Gandhi and Blavbhai Patel wanted Semi Independent ruling where as other wanted to full independent.

hours working days want to started as well as different allowances demines to labour and government staffs as anti-labour mentality

Temple organization and Spiritual Business organization become under RSS and Bajarandal control that BJP alliance Political Party.

As agent of Capitalist Laws implement and national properties and fund transfer to capitalist that quick richest become his friends. Given loan and then relief loan with interests also as well as tax relief continued as hack government and hack hand helping to capitalist only.

The effect of BJP leading and allied parties to pressurized to implement Hindi to Non-Hindi state and all office of central government than have possibilities may divided country as-

1. Independent Kashmir as national and official languages will be Urdu.
2. Independent Punjab as National and official languages will be Panjabi.
3. Independent Hindustan as National and official languages will be Hindi
4. Independent Liberal United Republic Bharat with official language English at central state official Department and language to be state recognized languages as per state language.

If such situation comes in near future than Mr. Noranda Modi and Mr. Rajnath Singh remain most responsible person whom create and pressurized to implement Hindi to Non-Hindi peoples.

Jawaharlal Nehru Ideology:

Worldly Concept Population of India:

Secular means actually Worldly and his works in literature that discovery of India description given relationship of Iran and India mainly and link with world peoples where different religion remaining from long time and different language cultured remain in India hence Secular word used by him which deform by common peoples of India and later opposition political parties that they used Secular as used to link with religions where minority to

Economic Development:

Industrial Development was main purpose to development to nation as farming and industrial development is base of national economy. Prasanta Mahalanovish called for this purpose and made his as member of five years plans. Target to establish high industries and production unites to nation like Coach factory, Locomotive factory, Steel factory, Mineral refinery, Infostructure organization development. For economic development it required to developed Farming and industrial development and hence alliance made with USSR as cold War hold on Where USSR remained Against Britain and Allied group of nation. USSR enforces to implement Socialistic system but he kept nation economy as Mixed Public Privet system to national development.

Establishment and Publics Development:

Scientific Education given enlightens to development nation and hence different technical education and general educational institution kept under government body and mixed system remained to establish Education institution to development of nation. Technical education institution development done and IIT, IIM, and other schooling system development done.

Empiricism Concept:

Hyderabad captured by arm forces as it not participating in India, Goa Daman Due assimilated with India by force to supported evolutionary parties and Pondicherry assimilated with India by Agreement and But in Kashmir Pakistan and India taken eatery to captured and hence dispute executed as seas fire done at critical point as it remained two countries border locality one ways remain through Rawalpindi and other remained Jumbo Tawie. Pakistan captured Baluchistan as it not participated to Pakistan and border of Pakistan only and wanted to assimilated Kashmir also. He also involved to captured Tibet to extended Indian landmark but it remained great mistake that it targets to captured by China under Red landmarks. Red Revolution happened to Qian/China as influence by Russian support. Jawaharlal Nehru making Affinity towered USSR as India freedom movement made Pro British mentality to publics but there had required to Indian economic development as well as there have required to helping to crisis of refuses as after India Division Hindu peoples left Pakistan in majority number and entered to Indian / Bharat field. When British Ruled in India that time British Indian Forces, Australia Forces New Zeeland forces used to Qian / China opium war that time only Hong Kong and Taiwan Able to captured only and As per geographical infostructures Tibet are high land where Qian forces can able to entered easily as once up on a time Mongolian ruled executed in Tibet also. Due to Power disbalancing and Geographical off fever infostructure Loos in Tibet invade by Jawaharlal Nehru. Qian transform to China as captured Xingjian, Tibet, Manchu, Inner Mongolia and other ailed landmarks which remain independent nation as form China Federation. Jawaharlal Nehru establish Union of India as federal states assimilation. USSR enforcing to Establish Socialistic system to implement by Jawaharlal Nehru in India as political pact done with USSR to done industrial and defiance sector development. But he remained believer of Democracy and hence made conception of union only and kept mixed economical system establishment to India.

British Ruling and Positive Works for Society:

Hinduism save from darkness of Hindu social system

History of India written to realized ancient India through archeological, geology.

Western Education implementation give ways of social development

Mining and industrial development ways given ways of development

New seen availability given ways to development of agriculture.

Social Economical and business development done.

Tea, Coffee, rubber cultivations give new root of international business.

Hospital system given new root of health administration and health care.

Court system given human right to give priority to humanity to society.

Union of India formation and Power Transfer from British to Indian

The **Indian Independence Act 1947** (1947, Chapter 30, 10 and 11; Geo 6) is an action of the Parliament of the United Kingdom that partitioned British India into the two new independent dominions of India and Pakistan. The Act received Royal Assent on 18 July 1947 and thus modern-day India and Pakistan, comprising west (modern day Pakistan) and east (modern day Bangladesh) regions, came into being on 15 August.

The legislature representatives of the Indian National Congress, the Muslim League,[3] and the Sikh community came to an agreement with Lord Mountbatten on what has come to be known as the *3 June Plan* or *Mountbatten Plan*. This plan was the last plan for independence.

Clement Attlee, the Prime Minister of the United Kingdom, announced on 20 February 1947 that:

The British Government would grant full self-government to British India by 30 June 1948 at the latest,

The future of the Princely States would be decided after the date of final transfer is decided.[5]

3rd June Plan

The 3rd June 1947 Plan was also known as the Mountbatten Plan. The British government proposed a plan, announced on 3 June 1947, that included these principles:

Principle of the partition of British India was accepted by the British Government

Successor governments would be given dominion status

Autonomy and sovereignty to both countries

Can make their own constitution

Princely States were given the right to join either India or Pakistan (Princely states had no option to remain independent), based on two major factors: Geographical contiguity and the people's wishes.

The Act's most important provisions were:

Division of British India into the two new dominions – the Dominion of India and the Dominion of Pakistan – with effect from 15 August 1947;

Partition of the provinces of Bengal and Punjab between the two new countries;

Establishment of the office of Governor-General in each of the two new countries, as representatives of the Crown;

Conferral of complete legislative authority upon the respective Constituent Assemblies of the two new countries;

Termination of British suzerainty over the princely states, with effect from 15 August 1947. These states could decide to join either India or Pakistan;

Abolition of the use of the title "Emperor of India" by the British monarch (this was subsequently executed by King George VI by royal proclamation on 22 June 1948);

The Act also made provision for the division of joint property, etc. between the two new countries, including in particular the division of the armed forces.

Two new dominion states:

Two new dominions were to emerge from the Indian empire: India and Pakistan.

Appointed Date: 15 August 1947 was declared as the appointed date for the partition.

Territories:

Pakistan: East Bengal, West Punjab, Sindh, and Chief Commissioner's Province of Baluchistan.

The fate of the North-West Frontier Province (now Khyber Pakhtunkhwa) was subject to the result of a referendum.

Bengal & Assam:

The province of Bengal as constituted under the Government of India Act 1935 ceased to exist.

In lieu thereof two new provinces were to be constituted, to be known respectively as East Bengal and West Bengal.

The fate of District Sylhet, in the province of Assam, was to be decided in a referendum.

Punjab:

The province as constituted under the Government of India Act 1935 ceased to exist.

Two new provinces were to be constituted, to be known respectively as West Punjab and East Punjab.

The boundaries of the new provinces were to be determined, whether before or after the appointed date, by the award of a boundary commission to be appointed by the Governor-General.

Constitution for the New Dominions: until the time of the making of the new constitution, the new dominions and the provinces thereof were to be governed by the Government of India Act 1935. (Temporary Provisions as to the Government of Each New Dominion).

The Governors-General of the new dominions:

For each of the new dominions a new Governor-General was to be appointed by the Crown, subject to the law of the legislature of either of the new dominions.

Same person as Governor-General of both dominions: if unless and until provision to the contrary was made by a law of the legislature of either of the new dominions, the same person could be the Governor-General of both.

Powers of Governor-General: (Section-9)

The Governor-General was empowered to bring this Act into force.

Division of territories, powers, duties, rights, assets, liabilities, etc., was the responsibility of Governor General.

To adopt, amend, Government of India Act 1935, as the Governor-General may consider it necessary.

power to introduce any change was until 31 March 1948, after that it was open to the constituent assembly to modify or adopt the same Act. (Temporary Provisions as to the Government of Each New Dominion.)

Governor-General had full powers to give assent to any law.

Legislation for the new dominions:

The existing legislative setup was allowed to continue as Constitution making body as well as a legislature. (Temporary Provisions as to the Government of Each New Dominion.)

The legislature of each dominion was given full powers to make laws for that dominion, including laws having extraterritorial operation.

No Act of Parliament of UK passed after the appointed date would be extended to the territories of new dominions.

No law and provision of any law made by the legislature of the new dominions shall be void or inoperative on the ground that it is repugnant to the law of England.

The Governor-General of each dominion had full powers to give assent in His Majesty's name to any law of the legislature. [Configuration of Pakistan's Constitution Assembly (CAP I): 69 members of the central legislature + 10 immigrant members= 79].

Consequences of setting up of the new dominions:

His Majesty's Government lost all the responsibility to the new dominions.

The suzerainty of His Majesty's Government over the Indian States lapsed.

All the treaties or agreements with the Indian States and the tribal areas that were in force at the passing of the act lapsed.

The title of "Emperor of India" was dropped from the titles of British Crown.

The office of Secretary of State for India was abolished and the provisions of GOI Act 1935 relating to the appointments to the civil service or civil posts under the crown by the secretary of the state ceased to operate.

Civil servants: Section 10 provided for the continuance of service of the government servants appointed on or before 15 August 1947 under the Governments of new Dominions with full benefits.

Armed Forces: Sections 11, 12, and 13 dealt with the future of the Indian armed forces. A Partition Committee was formed on 7 June 1947, with two representatives from each side and the viceroy in the chair, to decide about the division thereof. As soon as the process of partition was to start it was to be replaced by a Partition Council with a similar structure.

First and Second Schedules:

First Schedule listed the districts provisionally included in the new province of East Bengal:

Chittagong Division: Districts of Chittagong, Chittagong Hill Tracts, Noakhali and Tipperah.

Dacca Division: Districts of Bakarganj, Dacca, Faridpur, and Mymensingh.

Presidency Division: Districts of Jessore (except Bangaon Tehsil), and Kustia and Meherpur Tehsils (of Nadia district).

Rajshahi Division: Districts of Bogra, Dinajpur (except Raiganj and Balurghat Tehsil), Rajshahi, Rangpur and Nawabganj Tehsil (of Malda district).

Second Schedule listed the districts provisionally included in the new province of West Punjab:

Lahore Division: Districts of Gujranwala, Lahore (except Patti Tehsil), Sheikhupura, Sialkot and Shakargarh Tehsil (of Gurdaspur district).

Rawalpindi Division: Districts of Attock, Jehlum, Rawalpindi and Shahpur.

Multan Division: Districts of Dera Ghazi Khan, Jhang, Lyallpur, Montgomery, Multan and Muzaffargarh.

New Form of Indo-Iranian Racism called Hindiana:

Gujrat words come from Gurjar + Jat and Jat invaded remained Continued in Ancient India who called Ashur community at Puranic Texts. Sanskrit had not any proper script but in 1st AD peoples of Sanskrit speaking adopted Proto Dravidian Script and hence there have some similarity among Afro Asian Script Dravidian and Indo-European Sanskrit. Sanskrit language was remained verbal language only from long time and later adopted Kharosthi as Sinai script originated and hence At Maryjo Emperor and Ashoka ruled inscription remain Kharosthi but Indian peoples called this as Brahmi script as Brahmin used Sanskrit mainly. Tibet language are called Sino Tibetans language and it is sister language of Sanskrit language and hence it was easy to communicated Tibet by Samrat Ashoka as Kharosthi and Tibet script have similarity. Brahminism restarted under fascist and Racist Nazi RSS BJP joint venture ruling under leadership of Narendra Modi. Gujrati who actually remaining agent of British and hence under leadership of M. C. Gandhi and Balava Bhai Patel only done satyagraha that acting to captured power but under British remained reality and hence common peoples making fool by Gujrati leaders and hence in First and second World wars pact done to full support to British when it was right time to done vigorous movement. Several Britisher remained flower of M. C. Gandhi and British News Agency highlight to M. C. Gandhi as they wanted to executed long time British ruled. But after First World war Democracy form in British and hence as Semi-independent ruling system executing as political business form in India as Bureaucratic people's community form where maximum peoples remained as Brahmin but Caste system Diminishing under British ruled as Depress Commission stated works in 1885. In 1902 a notification established 50% of service reservation for economically disadvantaged people's reservation started for depress community where there have two district subdivision as caste and tribal. Reservation instituted in 1908 The Morley Minto Reforms also known as the government of India act of 1909, contained provisions made in 1909. The government of India Act introduced provision for reservation which reintroduced in 1935.

But as conservative Brahmin and Katriya Jat leading political parties Jansangha, Rastriya Sayang Savak Sanga, Hindu Mahasabha, Visha Hindu Parisad target to implement racism and through Religion sentiment of temple priest and Akhara Math that guides Worshiping groups unitedly making fool to common peoples and captured political power as telling lie and eating all to implement divide to ruled. Jansangha name changed to Janata Party and later added Bharati to making fool to common peoples and Lotus flower get symbol as Common peoples of India given most statues to Lotus Flower in worshiping and Lord Ram used as slogan and festoon used as Epic base worshiping started in India as Hindi translated Ramayana from Sanskrit by Tulsi Das become most propuler in North and West Indian part.

Reality of Ajodhya name came from grandfather of Lord Rama who fight against Northern Malacho that monologed community of Nepal as they invaded continuously. Northern side of Kosala remained in Nepal as real Mithila are situated at Nepal and in some ways real Ajodhya situated to Nepal as Ayodyanagar as village in Sagarmatha Zone in Siraha District. Ajodhya in Uttar Pradesh are duplicated as its name given by Vikram Aditya of Ujjain when visit

Bhojpuri language region with helping of a monk and cow on influence of Raghuvanshi novel written by Kalidas. Actual name of Uttar Pradesh Ayodhya was Oudh or Awadh and at ancient India Ajodhya original name was Saketa which means heaven or Vaikuntha where Lord Vishnu ruled executed which changed by Vikram Aditya king and only Siva temple had evidence that there have Hindu temple but might is right flash statement making myth and if brain washing done properly than flower given same speech also it remained lie. Saketa that Vaikuntha ruled under Lord Vishnu who defeated Goyasur and captured Goyadham where died and Vishnu Foot step symbol kept at Goya. Lord Rama declared as eswara or Issara as North Indianization by South Indian and they give name Ramanathan puram where vigorous battle done by Lord Rama and Captured Lanka which is Hill lock and Lord Siva temple remained which worshiped by Ravanna and Lanka transform to name Rameswaram later by North Indian given status to Lord Rama as Lord Vishnu. But for capturing political power used myth and telling lie by BJP RSS and Alliance.

Fascist Racist Nazi Ruled by Narendra Modi to implement Capitalism:

By propaganda and cheating power captured by BJP RSS joint Venture to executing Capitalism by cheating with common peoples.

1. Abolish demolish opposition by planning as black hand through ED
2. National property transfer to name of personal property to closer Gujrati.
3. Gujrati deputed or recommended to higher to highest authority's posts.
4. National funds use directly or indirectly through closer friend on loan section and later relief by black hand for BJP-RSS political funds
5. Hug Money transfer to MP, MLA of opposition for Supporting to BJP-RSS to formed government.

6. Political operation through carders by Froude hooligans, mob lynching activist.
7. Superstition myth and black believing spread up through Spiritual business organizations e.g. Dara Sacha Ramrahim organization, Asharam Bapu Ashram, Bageshwar Dham Sarkar, Nirmal Baba, Patanjali Ramdav Baba, etc.
8. Capitalist Bourgeois peoples hacking and remained top level to enjoying entertainment life as hacking where national monetary fund using and national properties capturing by black hand helping. E.g. Ambani, Adani, etc. Hence quick richest personality form by cheating through black hand helping.
9. Country liquor or win business as composite system, Professional Hooliganism, gambling through on line e.g. IPL making team, all social dark roots implement by BJP-RSS joint venture to destroying young and break down nation back bone by planning to enjoying and entertain life as selfish and self-centered.
10. It is bourgeois system where Capitalist like Ambani Adani remained top most level, Next Political businessman remaining second stage and in third stage Spiritual Businessman remain and all these three groups capturing money and enjoying entertainment their life where as for the groups common general peoples like farmers, serviceman of public and privet organization who heavily tax paying where they unable to leading or survival life to living with food, cloth and shelter which is most essential social need.

Language and Communities group of India:

- Indo-Iranian Groups: Arabian (Nayer, Nather, Jat), Turkey (Marathi, Marwari), Indu (Brahmin, Pandit,) Kshatriya (Mongolian-European/ Turkey-Mongolian) etc.
- Dravidian / Mediterranean
- Mongolite
- Austro-Asiatic:

As per human Population map of India

Gujrati, Jat, Brahmin jointly force executing Indo-Iranian Racism to Australasian, Monologed and Dravidian and economy pull in to their hand.

Most Oldest Language of India:

Santhal: 50000 years old

Tamil: 5000 years old

Sanskrit: 2000 years old

Similarity among BJP- RSS and Taliban-Alkayda and another Conservative Islamic Group:

1. All are conservative group on the base of religious system

2. All are trying to push back society toward back about 3000 years.

3. All are fighting against liberal group of their own religious groups and give statements against other religious believes and cultural system.

4. All obstruct reformation of religious system and hence there have no mention about the religious reformer name and methodology as blind supporter the cultural system and dresses.

5. All try Capture power on the base of religious sentiment creation.

6. All try to convert other to Conservative groups as they all explains and demand all human being was remain same as IS and their allied group are saying all human was Islamic at primitive period and BJP and Allied groups are saying all human was Hindu at primitive period.

7. All restrict to Woman freedom and dresses and opposed to European culture and dress wear.

Difference among BJP and Allied Party with IS and another Conservative Islamic Group:

1. BJP and Allied groups are Hindu Conservative Groups and IS leaders and Allied groups are Islamic Conservative groups.

2. BJP and Allied groups are capture power by voting on the base of Hindu sentiment whereas by military operation and terrorist activity force to capture power.

3. BJP leaders and Allied groups create Hindu sentiment in political field but IS and allied groups create Islamic sentiment.

4. BJP leaders and Allied groups covert Islamic and Christen peoples to Hindu but IS and allied groups killed to other religious peoples.

5. Hindu Jahad declare by BJP leaders and Allied groups create Hindu sentiment but Islamic Jahad declared by IS and allied groups create Islamic sentiment.

* North Indian Culture, Conservative system and Religious system force to implement all over India by BJP and Allied Parties:

1. Strong Hindu believed of North Indian system force to implement all over India.

2. Not take any Action to Santa Rampal as who implement Bali System who required to give death sentence as hang to death but Mr. Noranda Modi lead government have no ordinance applied as well Asharan Baba and his son Narayan Sai who are victim of rape case and Hindu religious faith demoralized they required to give death sentence as hang to death but Mr. Noranda Modi lead government have no ordinance applied to save Hindu society.

3. Lord Ram Mandir Issued make due to North Indian Worship mainly Lord Ram and Hanuman, hence some time they use banner of lord Ram also.

4. Shankaracharya Give statement on Multi marriage to start in Hindu religion system as Kulin system remain at previous period but Mr. Noranda Modi lead government have no ordinance applied to save Hindu society.

5. Hindu Maha Sava Activity increased at MP, Haryana and other BJP leading Governmental state and this organization supported child marriage and restriction system to women announcement done again and again but Mr. Noranda Modi lead government have no Ordinance applied to save Hindu society.

6. BJP and their allied parties should not support to Raja Rammohun Roy, Vidhya Sagar and other Hindu Social reformer which indicate that they are conservative and hence that want to started the system of Sati, Bali, child marriage, and other superstition system which were once up on a time remain in Hindu society in India.

Mr. Noranda Modi and BJP leading Government are careless about Human resources Development and Health Care:

1. Swine flu sped up in North and West Indian states like Madhya Pradesh, Gujrat, Chhattisgarh, Maharashtra, Haryana, UP, and Rajasthan where only UP is ruling state under SP Political party but other are ruling under BJP Government and day by day numbers of death case by Swine Flu increased but State governments as well as central government remain silent and not take any action. BAM's Candle on the entrances Examination of Medical field at MP state is another matter to health careless mater.

2. Madhya Pradesh, Gujrat, Chhattisgarh, Location operational death case increased day by day and ruling under BJP Government but State governments as well as central government remain silent and not take any action.

3. Educational stranded in Madhya Pradesh, Gujrat, Chhattisgarh, Haryana, UP, and Rajasthan where only UP is ruling state under SP Political party but other are ruling under BJP Governments

State governments as well as central government remain silent and not take any action. The Tata Nano company establish at Gujrat but Reman resources problem faces by company as technical persons and offices expert works were not found like as South Indian states and West Bengal here as Mr. Noranda Modi rule Gujrat State about 14 years but he was not care about Education and human resources development.

Mr. Noranda Modi Failure in Field of Gujrat state and National level Social works:

1. Gujrat was main Textile Industrial state and Ahmadabad called as Manchester of India but in his ruling, he unable to save sick textile industries in Gujrat and ultimately closed maximum textile industries which land used as housing complexes only.

2. Image of International politics disappointed as he and his allied peoples increasing national communal tension.

3. Maximum foreign industrialist, trade and Business men unwilling to invest in India as disappointed as he and his allied peoples increasing national communal tension. In the same ways Ex PM Mr. A. B. Bajpai ruled period not only Foreign invested but also NRI were not interested to invest in India as burning of Church of Christen burned as European and American countries as well as Australia and New Zeeland are Christen majority countries as well as Bill Grade, IBM, Coco Cola, Charlocks and other Industrialist all are Christian community peoples.

Activity of Mr. Noranda Modi leading government:

1. Criticizing to old leaders, PM, President and other and irrespective to them. Mr. Modi forget Constitution and infrastructure of democracy and unity in diversity developed under old leaders. Mr. Modi, he has as he become first P.M. in India and he have maximum knowledge than any of other whom remain previously as PM, Presidents.

2. Student union, e.g. Ambedkar Perrier Study Circle (APSC) ban for criticizing Mr. Modi as decision taken forwarded copies under Ms. Smithy Irani. As she compulsorily made audience of Mr. Modi to student primary to higher educational student Modi Government should not ban to RSS, VHP when their leader give religious controversial statement and He should not remove to MP and his ministers when they give controversial statement at parliament. Actually Mr. Modi and his ministries are ruling as dictatorship.

RSS is the base of Foreign flower organization:

1. RSS dresses are Khaki Half pant and White shirt and black shoes are foreign uniform which have not any communication with India. Indian purely dress up by Mr. M. Gandhi and Mr. Ishwar Chandra Vidhya Sagar.

2. RSS practice parade which also Foreign system but have not any Indian system to adopted by them. They insult Mahatma Gandhi and respect to Killer of Mahatma Gandhi. Mahatma Gandhi left every things of Foreign system in his life and wanted to developed by Indian system and agriculture whereas Mahatma Gandhi used to habit dress up Persian at his child hood and European dress up at his young hood but for freedom fighting in nonviolence way he left his all habit to used foreign system and dress up and lead life as pure Indian.

Mr. Noranda Modi Misused the powers:

1. CBI used as remote control body like his Dall.

2. Only give Bharat Ratna to BJP First PM Mr. A. B. Bajpai and VHP founder as supported his group and satisfaction.

3. He interfere on Land adaptation and Labour laws in favor of his Supported industrial groups whom give donation to his political parties.

4. The Padma Bhusan, Padma Sree, Padma Bebhusan awards given to maximum BJP and Allied supporters.

Common Peoples and Students made Great Mistake to elects BJP leading Governments and harm to their own life:

1. Land ordinance become a capturing tool of land in chief rate from farmers and common peoples and favor to land Mafia and builders.

2. Casteism become strong in long time BJP ruling state. e. g. MP, Rajasthan, etc. states.

3. Pension system converted to NPS system by Mr. A.B. Bajpai BJP lead government where PF records are not Available and in the time of Daughters or Son marriage or at emergency of self-problem should not have option to take money and Mr. Noranda Modi make 10 percent interest base PF loan where common peoples of government servant future crash by the system.

4. Mr. A.B. Bajpai BJP lead government stop recruitment two years and Mr. Noranda Modi stop one year's recruitment and even today have not any circular to start to recruitment at Government sectors to crash future of students. 5. Day by Days Petroleum and common commodities rate increasing continuously as ' Maghai Dayan Khay Jaraha Hai'.

6. The dream and promise given by Mr. Modi, Ms. Susma Saraj, Mr. Rajnath Singh, Mr. Amit Saha as become flesh statement to all and depresses common peoples where land rate and other increasing as Thakader market become better.

* Indian Hindu Cultures:

North Indian: Hindi become common language and only 9 states of Hindi peoples have same type of culture and worship to same god. They worship to Lord Ram and lord Hanuman mainly. But lord Ganesh, Sree Krishna, Kalika Mata, Sara Bali Dave (Amma Four Hand) and Vishnu Davi, Laxmi Dave and Sarasvati Dave with four hand also worship as Household festival. Several temples of Lord Siva, Lord Sani and Sara Bali establish where worship done commonly. Goddess Sara Bali Temples Gerba Dances done at Night.

Some north Indian Rivers worship and Arati (Oil or Camphor lamp used to lighten near River banks) done by peoples and Basically Ganga, Shipra, Narmada Rivers worship by Hindu peoples. They also worship to Plants as Pippul, Kalpa Bhekha, Amla trees and Tulsi herb, etc. They worship to cow and they give grass to cow to believe get Punna (Heavenly Proudness)

Basically use to read Gita, Hindi Ramayana, Hanuman Chalisha,etc. It is habituated to Ramlila, Krishaliala as Drama. Kalash Jatra(Water pot Procesion), Jhaki (Prophet probation) and Bhajan (Holi song) etc. done mainly.

Chat Puja (Sun Believe as Goddess) by the Bihar peoples and that spread up continuously.

Rivers Ganga, Narmada and Shipra worship done by them.

Blood relation marriage prohibited and they are more conservative peoples.

South Indian: Davidian Languages, Merogon (lord Kartika), Vinayak (lord Ganesh) worship mainly, Amman Devi, Ada Devi (Sarasvati four hands) and Adha Davi worship done also River Godoberi and Krishna worship by them.

East Indian: Sanskrit Diverted language, lord Vishnu main god worship as Satyanarayana, lord Siva, Goddess Durga (Ten hands), Sarasvati and Laxmi (Two hands) and lord Sree Krishna also worship done by them. Rivers Damodaran worship as God and River Ganga worship as goddess in West Bengal but at North Frontier States Brahmaputra worship by them.

West India: Sanskrit Diverted language, Lord Siva and lord Ganesh mainly worship done. Mumba Devi and A Cock Devi also worship done. called Ramakrishna Mission whom worship to Goddess Kali, and the Guru Ramakrishna whereas Probupat group are call ISCON Whom worship to Sree Krishna, Guranga and the Guru Probhupat.

Primitive Hindu groups as per worship:

1. Vaishnava who worship to Lord Vishnu: This group remained Pour vegetarian and Shila Narayan as symbol of Sun and lord Vishnu and Apathies as Hari, and Satya Narayan, etc. worship

Later this groups started worship to apathies as Narasimha, Baraho, Bahaman, Sree Ram and Sree Krishna as Vishnu. They were Vegetarian.

2. Siava who worship to lord Siva: This group worship to Siva Linga as Sun, Moon and Planets Symbol and hence Siva Linga called as Jatir(Light Resources) Linga, Sayanbhu, Mangal(Mars) Nath, Som(Moon)Nath, etc. Later worship to Lord Siva apathies of Lord Siva as Bhishanath, Bhambal, Tarak Nath, etc. They were vegetarian.

3. Sakta who worship Sun as female and later worship to goddess Kati and other Goddess as Amman, Amma, Adiparasakti, Addasakthi, etc. and Bali (Offer animal to cut it hen and blood flows on the land of hole place) of animal than the meat eats by them. They were non-Vegetarian and ferocious group and at about 2500 years ago their influences become maximum. After all Started reformation of Hindu

Base of Hindu Religious books:

1. Rig Veda the oldest system of religious system mainly Shadhu, Sanasi Rishi all mean Monk are use to habit to worship, Meditation and payers done with Yoga and mantra.

2. Sam Bad which are first reformatted system which system adopted by common peoples in marriage, Death Body destructions etc.

Primitive Hindu Social system:

1. Women's Freedom e.g. Kaikai at Ramayana and Ulupi at Mahabharat war field fought against enemies.

2. Multi marriage system remain: Sree Krishna marriage with Ten king's daughters'that princes. Daughter of Sukrachaya the Ashur Guru marriage with two husbands. Kunti at Mahabharat marriage with five brothers. In Ramayana there also have multi marriage system of women as Vali and Sugriva are step brother as their mother remain single but both had different father as Valli had Indra as Father whereas Sigrid had Sun As father.

3. Widow marriage system remained **Hindu Reformation at British ruled and Hindu reformers**:

1. Sati (Widow murder) system, Balbibhao (Child Marriage), etc. abolish by British Government of India on support Raja Rammohun Roy

2. Widow Marriage start by British Government of India on support Ishwar Chandra Vidyasagar.

3. Ganga Ma Santan Bisharjan (Sacrifice child to river ganga) Abolish by British Government of India.

4. Mr. Bethune a Scottish person started Women's education in India under Ruled.

Human Resources upgraded under Congress ruled:

1. Educated persons make small family programmed as per economical capability as they want established new generation and to led life better than them.

2. Numbers of Engineers, Physicians, Prefacers, etc. increased.

3. Women's entry at Every field and even in police, military, engineering medical, Pilots, etc. women have a special entry and reservation to upgrade women.

The Origin of Hindu:

Maximum peoples said that the word Sindhu reformatted into Hindu but it is flash statement. Hindu word came from Hindas as Baltic sea region peoples migrated and rehabilitees to Hindu Kush region and hence Kalash peoples, Nuri peoples and Kashmiri peoples are white, brown eye and somewhere brown hair. different forms European and central Asian called as Indu which word deformed as Indu, Indo and Hindu. Hindu Kush means Origen of Hindu, hence it indicated that Hindu peoples was rehabilitee from Hindu Kush to Indus valley as in Veda's there have mention about the rivers name as Akru now name Ammudarry, Hariruda, Khushi swell as Kailash which are remain at the border of Afghanistan and Uzbekistan and after all rivers as mentioned are originated from Hindu Kush and that give conformation that Hindu origin are Hindu Kush mountain. On the other hand, Lord Hari, Haro, Raha, Ruddro used to worshiped. Some other lords' worship by Hindu whom remain at Hindu Kush place as competition of river name and place similarity indicated those matters.

Kailash remain famous in Hindu literature which indicated one group migrated from Hindu Kush to Kailash and other group started rehabilitees at Indus and later to Post Deccan Island period at Indian peninsula. The system of Hindu believed flow to Mongolian in East frontier and dowers parts of Himalaya where Chinese migrated from China at Primitive Himalayan age and far later the Java, Sumatra, Bali Islands followed the same system and came under Hindu influence and hence group of Islands the Java, Sumatra, Bali Islands call as Indonesia as Hindu Asia / Indo Asia.

Darbari, the Sanskrit word means Giant deformed as Drivir word later and later the folk group of Non-Aryan of Decan Island peoples at Himalayan age converted to Hindu; hence folk system included to Hindu community. On the other hand, Mongolian group whom migrated from China to India their folk social system submerged to Pali community and North Frontier and Indonesian communities' peoples and hence Hindu community made as mixed community at primitive age of Himalayan

Era of Indian History

Wild Tribal Society of India:

From Pre historic age to Vedic Era is remained Semi civilize society where several groups of rulers remained decentralized kingdom and had some common strips roots as there had not any restriction to cross over landmarks. Aryan ruled remained at Northern India whereas Dravidian Ruled remained but there also Aryan invaded as Ashur ruled executed at South India at the End of Wild life tribal society life. Nag Community ruled remained mainly urban system as "Nagar" word came from Nag kingdom. Whereas Raj word used by Aryan where they ruled. Village society executed mainly. Indus was Urban Civilization and have similarity with Norse- Celtic in Upper landmarks Egyptian - Sinai culture in Lower landmarks. As Indus peoples were trading done with Samaritan society and done urbanization but due to Ashur Jat Eurasian peoples invaded Indus Civilization and killed them to captured landmarks. Village society restarted around India up to Emperor system development at 2500 years ago and started Urbanization again.

Imperialism Society of India:

About 2500 years ago urbanization restarted to India and Imperialism society developed which remained continued up to British period started. Several state system developments happened and trading and business started among European through landmarks. Greek ruled executed to Eurasians parts from Turkish region to Indus region as Invaded and killed large number of Hindu in Hindu Kush Region of Persian Kingdom. But at the time of 500 AD Mono ethnic system nonformal fabula concept of single god by assimilated several gods started to Arabian Peninsula as Salam region called bank of water land system as Islam up rise and captured Ancient Persian region from Greek. Islamic conversion holds on to enter Persian region and Turkish Eurasians region. Later Turkish and Uzbek peoples ruled started in new form as Islamic Ruled. Conflict started Pre-Islamic Eurasians Aryan with Islamic Eurasians Aryan.

Modern Indian Society:

Colonial Ruled started due to political conflict seen in India where North India came under Islamic ruled whereas South India remained under Hindu ruled and Islamic ruler trying to captured South Indian kingdoms continued but west part revolution hold on as Marathi kingdom founded by Sivaji and Northern India Sikh Kingdom founded by Ranjit Singh. European came to establish Business around Indian Ocean and Pacific region called East and Far East respectively whereas Europe called as West. Military kept by European when seen conflict to several parts of Asian region holding that Islamic mythology base society politicization done to captured folk religions kingdoms. Colonial ruled Executed around world. New landmarks discovered as American Super islands and Australian islands and captured to rehabilitation by native European. Maximum parts came under British East India Company where direct and indirect ruled Executed. Administration system made corporate and Judication made autonomous system. India connectivity happened with around World and trading started where economic and transportation development started in new ways. Geological serve, Archeological serve, Botanical Serve done under British ruled and written history composed by evidence of Stone, Mattel and wooden Calligraphy and Literature.

The Capital Come Under Bourgeois and Political Business

System Deformation by Planning

1. Bourgeois community develop in Illegal ways of Income as Smuggling and mafia
2. Spiritual Business and illegal business with political link
3. Power Capturing by cheating to enjoying entertainment life
4. Misuse power through Misinformation and misguide
5. Sentimental Political system development through Divide and Rule
6. Destruction Unity in Diversity
7. Planning to destruction of back bone of Farmer, Tribal and common middle-class peoples:
8. Enemy of nation and society as Anti nationalist, Anti farmer, Anti Tribal, and Anti Labour, Anti Common Peoples.
9. Acting Dress up and make up
10. Hack digital voting
11. Works as agent of Bourgeois community as criminal

BJP Political Management System:

1. Religious Sentiment created by VHP, Hindu Mashaba.
2. Illegal works and Hindi Racism executed by Bajrang Dal, RSS, Durgabahini as women organization.
3. Political post captured as BJP
4. Religion supported by Priest groups of Kathabachak/ Reader of Epic and Hindu texts who establish Spiritual

Business organization or Akhara Traditional that spirituals ritual cum Exercised/ yoga organization in Small units, Purahit / priest of Temple Organization

5. Hooligan Activity done by cadres and sentimental speech given by agent of Anchor and Media as paying money and advertisement done.

6. IT Shell establish by which Video in You Tub, Facebook, what app social media utilized vastly to use money to dive to rule

7. Commission getting from Capitalist and given National money and properties to Capitalist and sharing each other by cheating.

8. Depress common peoples to destruct Ecumenical condition of common peoples to implement taxes to every step of common people's movement and making fool by religious sentiment through IT Shell. Superstition and myth spread up to common peoples to push back to darkness to rule by making fool. BJP RSS leaders explained to their Supporters as Donkey that diversion speech as fool to rule if and only if heavily taxes implement or demolish economic condition to supporter than also support to them.

Blind BJP RSS Supporter as Fool

BJP RSS as Anti Nationalist and doing works against Nation and Society to depressing Common Peoples, Farmers labours but due spiritual sentiment through Spiritual Ritual Business Organization politics leading by execution superstition and darkness crated to society to ruled. On the name of Hindi Gujrati racism done where maximum top level governmental post like Governor of Reserved bank, Different countries Ambassadors and other filed on deputation or recommendation posted Gujrati and Economy draining to Gujrat that making most richest to Ambani Adani by black hand helping where no Enforcement directors taking any action that within minimum period how Ambani Adani become quick richest person. On the other hand, divide and Rule executing as Hindu Muslim, Among Tribal groups in Manipur and other state, Assamese with Bengali in Assam state, Tribal with Hindu higher caste, Hindi language person verses Non- Hindi peoples as well as implement force Hindi Racism to making Conflict to rule only that by planning destroying unity in diversity, demolishing infrastructure of Economy and abolish humanity in society. That If BJP- RSS leaders done than that called Super activity (Chamatker) if and only if that remain illegal and crime. If Other any positive works done opposition that also remain guilty.

Post British India situation and Society

Post Independent India and Development under Nationalist:

After decolonization India turn to Industrialization from Agricultural base India. Different Technical institution like IIT, ITE, Poly Technic, Engineering collage, etc. Establish and different heavy Industrial organization establish by Publics collaboration with Foreign alliance. Integral coach, Diesel Locomotive, Electric locomotive and other manufacturing public organization established by technology transferred. India become developing countries category from Under developed country list. Different planed City like Chandigarh, Bangalore, Bhubaneshwar, Etc. establish, National Highways development done8 and rural backward India turn to Modern India.

Capture power by Bourgeois:

Capitalist hack political leaders and political leaders make alliance with religious organization and spiritual business organization who become agent of Political organization BJP, RSS and alliance. By brain washing and telling lie to making fool too common peoples getting vote to win become basic rule. On the other hand, divide to rule and Economy draining to Gujrat become policy and hence capitalism Gujrati capturing public property and getting lump sum loans which getting relief by black hand helping of capitalist pet leaders.

The Capital Come Under Criminal

By using public fund getting support other party leaders who either remain involve in criminal case or rapist. Enforcement Director officers become pet dog poppy of BJP RSS leadership and targeting to opposition leaders that how opposition leaders participating to BJP-RSS and getting post and money both to support to BJP-RSS. Political crisis formed and democracy killed by planning to making rich to bourgeois peoples only.

Post-Colonial Taxation in India:

Equality and education mission were established by nationalist leaders after post independent stage at primitive stage but bourgies leaders making target to capture money and power by sentimental political policy. And hence all capitalist tax relief given where as each and every stage of living system that education to depositing money taxation implement by Noranda Modi as by planning fuel cooking gas rate increasing about 300 percent and other essential commodity rate making double rate or triple rate by which poor become poorest and Rich become richest. As antinationalist mentality antifarmer, Anti labour, Anti tribal, Anti common peoples laws implement by ordinances implementation as well as Federal government of opposition under ruling threading to abolish or demolish power by implement president rule or abolish statehood also but what ever happened in BJP-RSS ruling state like Manipur where law and order degraded in most lower level but supporting where raping and hooligan activity become most common factor each and every day.

HUMAN HYBRIDIZATION:

Around the world after human evolution from the pre-human ancestor of the human app their generation is remaining and modified structure formed and different groups of humans born in different times. Around world five category of human remains as –

1. Negros/ South African continental
2. Mediterranean/ Afro-Asiatic
3. Germanic/ Euro-Asiatic
4. Mongoloid / East Asian
5. Austronesia / Melanesian

At Nomadic period Different group of human being migrated and assimilated where human Hybridization held on at prehistoric age. African peoples migrated and ruled at European countries as at Godism period of Celtic and Norse communities had black gods and goddess. Mongoloid peoples migrated at North America as Well as Austronesia peoples and Viking peoples also migrated to America from Europe. At Colonial Ruling period peoples migrated from here and there more and more and bounded with marriage relation, hence human hybridization happened more and more.

HUMAN SOCIAL SYSTEM EVOLUTION

1. Like other animals' humans also chordate, mammalian, terrestrial, social, intelligent, omnivorous animals. Due to the most intelligent character, social system, language, and in faces structure evaluated by them.

2. Like some social animals e.g. Wolf, Elephant, Monkey and ape have leadership humans also have leadership characters.

3. Due to the most intelligent mammalian human making slaves to other mammals and even its remaining target by stronger humans try to make other humans as slaves.

4. Humans discovered several crowns, foods and clothes and other resources by which they changed their living standard where one after system evaluated due to finding new matter or new materials.

5. Fire discovers ways to work after evening. Copper discovery and the system of copper extraction gave ways to lead life in new ways. Iron discovered and it using system given new ways and it have historical proved that Assyrian peoples when iron discover and sharp weapon invented than other group of humans were making slave and torturing started at junction point of Afro-Euro-Asia region. Blade invention given ways of saving, Scissors invention given ways of hair style, weaving machining turn to wear cloth and swing invention style increasing as dressing and designing, etc.

6. When humans evaluated that only food, collections were works and humans migrated for food collection mainly in the mountain range as they were able to climb mountains and climb trees. Even today tribal peoples are able to climb trees to collect fruits. Tribal peoples are also even today's maximum rehabilitates to mountain ranges.

7. Before Human evolution Ape, our insisters evaluated monkeys and they migrated around the world for food collection and it was required when a food crisis was happening to a particular place. Due hybridization, a new generation of animals evaluated and when that mutation happened, then generation to generation flowing gen structure. Humans are the next generation of apes, so in some ways for food collection humans migrated and climbed mountain ranges and traveled here and there for collecting food.

8. In the mountain range there is a cave making shelter for the safety of life from climatic conditions. Mountains were primitive rehabilitation parts of human and colonization areas as there are remaining directions, trees availability where fruits are available more and more.

9. Sex are most essential to living organism by which offspring taken born and generation to generation same system of living style executing.

10. At primitive stage minimum sound reaming to use to communication to survival of life but when fire discover life style started to changing and statement life started to build up. Copper age humans started to do works as slaves under stronger human groups where the king remains the main

boss and for him other humans do the work. Any things which were ever found at locality first that had the right to use by only king / queen and their allied personality.

11. After rehabilitation to a particular area, conflict created to gather more and more power hence quarreling and battle system evolution started.

Human Migration History:

Migration of humans started the same as our ancestor ape or monkey. From ape there are five places where human different groups are evaluated. The evaluated human places are as follows as-

1. South African Continent region where Black peoples evaluated.
2. North African Region Where Brown human evaluated.
3. European island groups where White humans were evaluated.
4. Eastern China regions where Yellow humans are evaluated.
5. Pacific oceanic islands region where Light Brown peoples evaluated.

It is seen that there is no evidence that in Deccan Island, North and South American continents had not evaluated any human groups. In Deccan Island Ape evaluated and that group mostly migrated to China region and Pacific region through forest and mountain ranges.

Now we come to human migration as follows as –

1. Through mountain rage and land make migration for Fruit collection:
2. Through mountain rage and landmark migration for hunting animals:
3. Through mountain rage and landmark migration for Cattle fodder:

4. Through navigation migration for fish hunting:
5. Versatile movement of Human for power capturing to Race execution:

World human Evolution spots and migration:

1. South African Continent region Black people's evolution and migration: They migrated to Indian peninsula and pacific different island through navigation, North Africa by through landmarks.
2. North African Region Where Brown Peoples evolution and migration: They migrated to Indian peninsula through navigation and lateral civilization period migrated through landmarks, in Central American parts they migrated through navigation.
3. European islands groups' White people's evolution and migration: They migrated to North Africa through navigation. They migrated to Indian peninsula through land makes in lateral stage via central Asia and Some branches migrated to china through land marks and mixed up
4. Eastern China regions yellow people's evolution and migration: They migrated to the Indian peninsula in the North mountain ranges. They migrated to the North American continent's south Parts, South America continent and pacific zone islands through navigation. They migrated to northern parts of North America continents and north Europe by land marked migration through Siberia.
5. Pacific oceanic islands region Light brown people's evolution and migration: They migrated to Indian Peninsula and South American continents and Central America through navigation. They migrated to some parts of China through Malaysia.

Case Study of particular landmark human migration and Hybridization:

Deccan Island Human Migration:

Deccan island was remaining near to African Continents and submerged far later to Asian supercontinent. Human ancestor migration happens to the pacific zone through Deccan Island but humans are not evaluated to Deccan Island. After humans were evaluated on earth from Ape they started to migrate for food and shelter but when one after another invention happen then human migration range became larger and spread up colonies of human beings. Through landmarks migration ranges were minimum but when boats were invented, their ranges increased far.

Indian Peninsula Migration:

South Easter migration happened first but when it submerged with Euro-Asia Super Island then converted to Indian peninsula and different community migrated continued.

1. Navigation through boating: South African and Polynesian peoples migrating through navigation.

2. Through walking: Europeans and North African migrated to Indian through walking at primitive stage where as later animal riding use to migrate for conflict with another group of European. Chinese migration done through walking only for food.

3. Through riding on animal migration: Assyrian communities migrated to Indian peninsula as well as Sinai deserts Assyrian peoples migrated to Indian peninsula at whom called as Aryan. Vedic peoples were Mediterranean who was North African civilize peoples who ruled at Egypt. But when European Germanic Assyrian groups discovers irons and invented irons to use as weapon material than Mediterranean peoples migrated toward Indian peninsula due to invaded by Assyrian. Assyrian Germanic groups peoples started to ruling at Egypt and one after another place

of Arabian Peninsula captured and later some groups of Assyrian entered to Indian peninsula that called as Aryan who were ruling at Euro-Asian junction locality. Due Assyrian domination, Celtic peoples some groups became slave under Assyrian who use for worrier activity against Egyptian Black ruling civilized peoples. But some slaves had to arrest whom relief and rehabilitation done at permissible place near Caucasus and black sea whom called as Slavic community. Some parts of Slavic community peoples migrated to Hindu Kush who later rehabilitated to Indus Valley called as Indu community later Assyrian called them as Hindu.

Population group migration:

1. Polynesian Migration: Santali, Mundari and their other group migrated to Indian peninsula by navigation of boating. Within these groups some remained as cannibal.
2. South Eastern African Migration: South African continental peoples migrated to Indian peninsula through navigation by boating and spread up to Indian oceanic island and south India and west parts of India.
3. North Eastern African Migration Dravidians, Adi community, Solar dynasty Lunar dynasty of Vedic Godism are Mediterranean
4. European migration: Brahmin/ Priest community was totally Europeans but phenotypic characters are change when they mixed with African and Polynesian. Kashmiri Pandit and Kalash, Nuristan peoples are parts of Slavic groups and Panjabi, Shindhi, Gujrati, Bhils, Some Maharashtrian are Assyrian whom also Germanic group of European peoples but in South Kashmir mixed community formed as Slavic Assyrian.
5. Chinese migration: Ladakhi, Gorkha, Chakma, Tipri, Assamese, and other North Eastern Indian peoples are Chinese originated.

6. Dravidian is Mediterranean North Sub Saharan African people's origin, Vedic community is Dravidian mixed with Germanic community peoples, Indu/ Hindu are Brahmin Community is Germanic Slavic who rehabilitated at Kashmir valley at Himalayan Range, but who living al plain of Indian peninsula parts are Slavic-Egyptian community. North Easter and Northern Himalayan rage peoples are Mongoloid. Easter region and central region people are Polynesian. Indus valley peoples reaming as mixed population of Slavic- Egyptian So Misro, Mishra, Mixed community execute in Brahmin. Brahmin related with Brahma but when they deputed to assistant of Vedic Gods and goddess then at Yajurveda period worshiping started by which a stanza including in Veda as Brahmanas which given summaries by Assistant of Lord Groups. Brahmanas peoples called as Brahmin as Purohit means another helpful person.

7. Indus civilization demolish by Assyrian peoples whom called as Aryan and far later mixed with Indu community as they changed pronunciation as Hindu instead of Indu. But even today's Dravidian called word Indu and Indus valley name given on this community of Indu. Sinauli Peoples migrated from Sinai desert who remaining warrior ferocious and they also know cultivation as Auli mean cultivation.

8. Bhil community called as Bow community by Dravidian as they also remained as Aryan but came at Vedic period where battle of Deva Asur happened, Hence Bed community indicated at Mahabharata and other stories of religious text. Hence it indicated Assyrian peoples came to Indian peninsula in different time period. Aryan / Assyrian/ Sinai peoples invaded done and destruction of Slavic-Egyptian culture of Indus valley township civilization and Dravidian migrated to Indian peninsula from North East Africa through Afghanistan as they invaded at Egypt by Assyrian. Dravidian community called as Vedic community as they have knowledge of written script and other field of

Agriculture. Vedic community is next generation of Ra and Hori gods of Egyptian who remained black community of Egyptian civilization. Vedic / Mediterranean peoples were agricultural base society where as assistant Slavic-Egyptian community remaining as Township society but as defatted by Assyrian both communities come together. Slavic-Egyptian peoples working under Vedic Gods and hence mixed Dravidian with Slavic-Egyptian European language to formed as Sanskrit language as called Iranian branch of Indo-European language. Assyrian language mixed as it become integral parts of north Indian community which defined as Arya-Barta/ Aryan locality whereas South India was called as Anerya-Barta/ Non-Aryan / Non-Assyrian locality. Monk / Moni Agastya is giving priority by Dravidian as Vedic literature developed by him and assimilated of Brahmin community to Dravidian as assist worker under Dravidian/ Vedic gods.

9. Slavic peoples are mixed group of Celtic and Norse community as they were made slave by Germanic Assyrian groups of peoples whom discover Iron and Tin and iron instrument and weapon developed as processing of iron invented. Slave used to capture and working each and every thing. Assyrian was target to capture Egyptian Black community locality ruling spots, so battle up by slave. Slave who came under Egyptian black people then Assyrian relief them as doubt if slave given information. Relief slave of Egypt were rehabilitation at permissible place nearby Caucasus. But Slave always wanted to became free, so slave left that place and migrated toward east and after all rehabilitation to Western Himalayan range and Indus valley. Hence Indus god and goddess have similarity with Celtic and Norse community. Some groups of Slavic migrated to Tibet ranges that formed Bon community mixed with Chinese Mongoloid. Hence Bon and Hindu have some similar system. After decline of Godism of Assyrian that Adam revolution done and abolish Godism, Slavic

migration done all over European countries. Hence, Sanskrit, Lithuanian, Slovenian and Germany language have similarity.

10. Dus surname are polish which is a group of Celtics community, Dus meaning Soul or Dusic Suffocate and Inaas Arabic meaning Mirror and Du are surname of Chinese also. In upper Indus, Chinese Mongoloid peoples migrated, hence in Indus civilization gods have some Chinese dress up also. Hence it mostly, Indus meaning are mirror of soul. But mainly Slavic and Celtic gods and goddess used to habit as ruled and township system executed. Bricks developed at Turkey date back to 7000 BC and it clears that Indus related with ancient Turkey. There have similarities among of Celtic Black gods and Indus gods which indicated that black Celtic community were livings at Indus valley and most possibility that peoples were partial groups of Slavic ester region peoples. Pamir is region where Norse, Celtic, Slavic and Mongoloid. Pamir is junction with upper Indus hill region. Hence as per culture of Indus civilization those were mixed culture. Black Celtic god matches with Indus civilization gods. Celtic and Norse have Black God those indicated African originated peoples ruled at European countries and hence white as well as black god remains to Ancient European community. Therefore Afro-Celtic and Euro-Celtic assimilated in Indus civilization.

11. Monique means Advisor which is Celtic language a group of Germanic language. Indus and Indu community were related with Germanic Celtic and Slavic community so several words matching. Moni were given advice to common peoples mainly in ancient India in Indu community. Hence, they were Advisory peoples in ancient India. In Land Lord system of British India Monim posts remaining under Lord as Advisory post who was remaining assistant of Land Lord. Monim Word are evolutes from Moni.

12. Ri meaning King and Shee meaning brave than Rishee means Brave king as Ri + Shree = Rishee but that short formed as Rishi as pronouncing as A+E and long e". From Rishee word Rishi words generated as simplification. Indu community was caltic-slavic as indo-european group and they ruled whom kings called as Rishi. Eg. As Rishi Vishamitra, Rishi Agaysta, Rishi Kaysape, etc. were ancient North Indian Kings who ruled at different time. In ancient India Indu community ruled in North India and Indus where kings denoted as Rishi which means brave kings.

13. Omnicom, Omni, Omega were related with moon where Omni Moons means all phase of moon which transformed to Om as short formed. Omnicom, Omni are Germanic Celtic group of words and Celtic is related with Indu community. Swastika/ Cross symbol are Slavic symbols and Indu community related with Slavic also. Hence Om and Swastika are Germanic symbols of Celtic- Slavic. Actually, Om symbol are Three Crescent moon with a new moon phase as special as with Star called Chandra Bindu. Chandra means Moon and Bindu means Tara. As Tree moons or Three Crescent moon believes as three goddess and most powerful words in Indo Europeans Germanic community. Hence Indu community given most priority to religion base but that remaining continued as there are various assimilation others groups of peoples and at present scenario transform as Hindu. Gamma have value three and three symbols have similarity in Sanskrit, European and it mostly indicate three goddesses of moon.

14. Adu means Grift of God and Ina/ Inaya means pure, Ina/ Inaya + Adu = meaning pure gift of God. Dyaus pita is Hindu god and believes as Sky god and Zeus Celtic God which believed as sky god. Hence Indu = Ina/ Inaya + Dyaus/ Zeus. Dew/ Deaw/ Dheu are similar word which is round shape like as Sky and have same type of sound and hence peoples also given priority of Dew and snow as is also from of water. Far later is given priority of Snow and Dew

as Moon god. Moon also consider with pearl / Moti, hence call Indu Moti where indu/ Indoo meaning formed as Moon.

15. Ogham word use in Celtic divination system in Celtic religion and repeated. Ogma is god of speech and language hence ogham use for divination in Celtic religion. Basically, Indu communities are Afro-Celtic and Euro-Celtic community and hence use Om as short formed. On the other hand, Om indicated as Omni Moon which means all phase of moon where mainly three cesarean moons with Special moon phase with star. Three moon symbols given most priority in Ethnic group of Celtic and Slavic communities and hence in Indu Om symbol and speech given most priority.

Slavic Groups Evolution: Slavic peoples are a mixed group of Celtic and Norse communities as they were made slaves by Germanic Assyrian groups of peoples who discovered Iron and Tin and iron instruments and weapons developed as processing of iron was invented. Slaves used to capture and work each and every thing. Assyrian was targeted to capture Egyptian Black community locality ruling spots, so they were battled up by slaves. Slaves who came under Egyptian black people then Assyrian relieved them as doubt if slaves were given information. Relief slaves of Egypt were rehabilitated at a permissible place nearby Caucasus. But slaves always wanted to become free, so slaves left that place and migrated toward the east and after all rehabilitation to Western Himalayan range and the Indus valley. Hence Indus god and goddess have similarity with Celtic and Norse community. Some groups of Slavic migrated to Tibet ranges that formed a Bond community mixed with Chinese Mongoloid. Hence Bon and Hindu have some similar system. After the decline of the Godism of Assyrian that the Adam revolution did and abolished Godism, Slavic migration was done all over European countries. Hence, Sanskrit, Lithuanian, Slovenian and Germanic languages have similarity.

Dus surnames are Polish which is a group of Celtics community, Dus meaning Soul or Dusic Suffocate and Inaas Arabic meaning

Mirror and Du are the surname of Chinese also. In upper Indus, Chinese Mongoloid peoples migrated, hence in Indus civilization gods have some Chinese dress up also. Hence mostly, Indus meaning is a mirror of soul. But mainly Slavic and Celtic gods and goddesses used to live as ruled and the township system executed. Bricks developed in Turkey date back to 7000 BC and it clears that Indus is related to ancient Turkey. There were similarities among of Celtic Black gods and Indus gods which indicated that black Celtic communities were living at Indus valley and most likely that peoples were partial groups of Slavic ester region peoples. Pamir is a region containing Norse, Celtic, Slavic and Mongoloid. Pamir is a junction with the upper Indus hill region. Hence as per culture of Indus civilization those were mixed cultures. Black Celtic god matches with Indus civilization gods. Celtic and Norse have Black God; those indicated African originated peoples ruled European countries and hence white as well as black god remains to the Ancient European community. Therefore Afro-Celtic and Euro-Celtic assimilated in Indus civilization.

Monique means Advisor which is Celtic language a group of Germanic language. Indus and Indu community were related with Germanic Celtic and Slavic community so several words matching. Moni were given advice to common peoples mainly in ancient India in Indu community. Hence, they were Advisory peoples in ancient India. In the LandLord system of British India Monim post remained under the Lord as an Advisory post who was the remaining assistant of the Landlord. Monim Word evolved from Moni.

Ri meaning King and Shee meaning brave than Rishee means Brave king as Ri + Shree = Rishee but that short form as Rishi is pronounced as A+E and long e". From Rishee word Rishi words generated as simplification. The Indu community was caltic-slavic as an indo-european group and they ruled whom kings called as Rishi. Eg. Rishi Vishamitra, Rishi Agaysta, Rishi Kaysape, etc. were ancient North Indian Kings who ruled at different times. In ancient India Indu community ruled in North India and Indus where kings were denoted as Rishi which means brave kings.

Omnicom, Omni, Omega were related to the moon where Omni Moons means all phases of the moon which transformed to Om as short formed. Omnicom, Omni are a Germanic Celtic group of words and Celtic is related with Indu community. Swastika/ Cross symbol are Slavic symbols and Indu community related with Slavic also. Hence Om and Swastika are Germanic symbols of Celtic-Slavic. Actually, Om symbol is the Three Crescent moon with a new moon phase as special as with the Star called Chandra Bindu. Chandra means Moon and Bindu means Tara / Star. Three moons or Three Crescent moon believes as three goddesses and are the most powerful words in the Indo Europeans-Germanic community. Hence the Indu community gave most priority to religion but that remaining continued as there are various assimilation of other groups of peoples and at present scenario transform as Hindu. Gamma has value three and three symbols have similarity in Sanskrit, European and it mostly indicate three goddesses of moon.

Adu means Gift of God and Ina/ Inaya means pure, Ina/ Inaya + Adu = meaning pure gift of God. Dyaus pita is Hindu god and believed as Sky god and Zeus Celtic God which believed as sky god. Hence Indu = Ina/ Inaya + Dyaus/ Zeus. Dew/ Draw/ Dheu are similar words which are round shaped like Sky and have the same type of sound and hence people are also given priority of Dew and snow as is also from water. Far later is given priority to Snow and Dew as Moon god. Moon also considered with pearl / Moti, hence called Indu Moti where Indu/ Indoo meaning formed as Moon.

Ogham word use in Celtic divination system in Celtic religion and repeated. Ogham is god of speech and language hence ogham is used for divination in Celtic religion. Basically, Indu communities are Afro-Celtic and Euro-Celtic communities and hence use Om as short form. On the other hand, Om is indicated as Omni Moon which means all phases of the moon where mainly three cesarean moons with Special moon phase with star. Three moon symbols are given most priority in Ethnic group of Celtic and Slavic communities and hence in Indu Om symbol and speech are given most priority. Ogham transforms to Om.

Sanatan was actually an African Egyptian who used to inhabit music whereas Indu was white Celtic-Slavic community who worshipped fire gore in every step of life. In lateral time Agastya and Lupamudra had husband wife philosophers who assimilated both groups and shared a traditional system, hence called Sanatan-Hindu. They have assimilated Polynesian and mongoloid.

Turkey and Arabian Germanic peoples migrated through Iran and mixed with Indo groups as Arabian peoples and Turkey peoples invaded and later ruled in North West India and formed as Indo-European branch group as Indo-Iranian.

Hindu Religious Timing:

Godism:

It called as Shata means Hundreds of Gods believed but that meanings changed by priest groups for their own interest. Sattya was making which means truth.

Lordism:

It divided into two parts as Trata where three influential ruled given status as God. And Drapor where two influential ruled gave status as god. After that none of any rulers consider as God statuses. Guides of worshiping of God and Lord worshiping started in many peoples like as Gerang

Maha Provu: Maha means powerful, Provu means owner of Landmarks

Lord means Land orders executer

God means General order of Director

Prophet:

Prophet means Person of Performance Execute of God or link with god. Brahmin rule become prophet rule who explain then as agent of god or lord and hence temple become most importance to kings or rulers where davdasi that slave of god system implements in ancient rule, Dasiattam now called as Bharat Nityam. At system style implement in medieval India which called as Baiji attam now called Kathan. After Lordism Praphatism executing where Brahmin ruling on the name of God and goddess and money drain on the name of god and goddess and rule to depress common peoples.

Guideism Spread Up and Political Power captured:

In European continent there had Poly ethnic system but Church system made a well administration system and political power captured by Pope. Theological system implements to captured power and rule. But later when one after another nation protested against pop than only Vatican City remain under Pop Only.

Theocracy is a form of government in which one or more deities are recognized as supreme ruling authorities, giving divine guidance to human intermediaries who manage the government's daily affairs.

Politics of Vatican City

Following the Capture of Rome on 20 September 1870, the Papal States including Rome with the Vatican were annexed by the Kingdom of Italy. In 1929, through the Lateran Treaty signed with the Italian Government, the new state of Vatican City was formally created and recognized as an independent state The head of state of the Vatican is the pope, elected by the College of Cardinals, an assembly of high-ranking clergy The pope is elected for life, and either dies or may resign. The cardinals are appointed by the popes, who thereby choose the electors of their successors.

Voting is limited to cardinals under 80 years of age. A Secretary for Relations with States, directly responsible for international relations, is appointed by the pope. The Vatican legal system is rooted in canon law and ultimately is decided by the pope; the Bishop of Rome as the Supreme Pontiff "has the fullness of legislative, executive and judicial powers." Although the laws of Vatican City come from the secular laws of Italy, under article 3 of the Law of the Sources of the Law, provision is made for the supplementary application of the "laws promulgated by the Kingdom of Italy"

Monastic Community of Mount Athos:

Mount Athos is a mountain peninsula in Greece which is an Eastern Orthodox autonomous area consisting of 20 monasteries under the direct jurisdiction of the Primate of Constantinople. There have been almost 1,800 years of a continuous Christian presence on Mount Athos, and it has a long history of monasteries, which dates back to at least 800 AD. The origin of self-rule at Mount Athos can be traced back to a royal edict issued by the Byzantine Emperor John Tzimisces in 972, and reaffirmed by Emperor Alexios I Komnenos in 1095. Greece wrestled control of the area from the Ottoman Empire during the First Balkan War in 1912. However, it was formally recognized as part of Greece only after a diplomatic dispute with the Russian Empire was no longer an obstacle; after the latter's collapse during World War I

Mount Athos is specifically exempt from the free movement of people and goods required by Greece's membership of the European Union, and entrance is allowed only with express permission from the monks. The number of daily visitors to Mount Athos is restricted, with all visitors required to obtain an entrance permit. Only men are permitted to visit, and Eastern Orthodox

Christians take precedence in the issuing of permits. Residents of Mount Athos must be men aged 18 and over who are members of the Eastern Orthodox Church and also either monks or workers.

Athos is governed jointly by a community consisting of members of the 20 monasteries and a Civil Administrator, appointed by the Greek Ministry of Foreign Affairs. The monastic community is led by the Protos.

Islamic theocracies

An Islamic republic is the name given to several states that are officially ruled by Islamic laws, including the Islamic Republics of Iran, Pakistan, and Mauritania. Pakistan first adopted the title under the constitution of 1956. Mauritania adopted it on 28 November 1958. Iran adopted it after the 1979 Iranian Revolution that overthrew the Pahlavi dynasty. Despite having similar names, the countries differ greatly in their governments and laws.

The term "Islamic republic" has come to mean several different things, at times contradictory. To some Muslim religious leaders in the Middle East and Africa who advocate it, an Islamic republic is a state under a particular Islamic form of government. They see it as a compromise between a purely Islamic caliphate and secular nationalism and republicanism. In their conception of the Islamic republic, the penal code of the state is required to be compatible with some or all laws of Sharia, and the state may not be a monarchy, as many Middle Eastern states presently are[1]

Afghanistan

Afghanistan was an Islamic theocracy when the Taliban first ruled Afghanistan from 1996 to 2001 and since their reinstatement of the Islamic Emirate of Afghanistan in 2021, Afghanistan is an Islamic theocracy again.

Spreading from Kandahar, the Taliban eventually captured Kabul in 1996. By the end of 2000, the Taliban controlled 90% of the country, aside from the opposition (Northern Alliance) strongholds which were primarily found in the northeast corner of Badakhshan Province. Areas under the Taliban's direct control were mainly Afghanistan's major cities and highways. Tribal khans and warlords had de facto direct control over various small towns, villages, and rural areas The Taliban sought to establish law and order and to impose a strict interpretation of Islamic Sharia law, along with the religious edicts of Mullah Mohammed Omar, upon the entire country of Afghanistan.

During the five-year history of the Islamic Emirate, the Taliban regime interpreted the Sharia in accordance with the Hanafi school of Islamic jurisprudence and the religious edicts of Mullah Omar. The Taliban forbade pork and alcohol, many types of consumer technology such as music,[16] television and film as well as most forms of art such as paintings or photography male and female participation in sport, including football and chess recreational activities such as kite-flying and keeping pigeons or other pets were also forbidden, and the birds were killed according to the Taliban's ruling Movie theaters were closed and repurposed as mosques Celebration of the Western and Iranian New Year was forbidden Taking photographs and displaying pictures or portraits was forbidden, as it was considered by the Taliban as a form of idolatry Women were banned from working, girls were forbidden to attend schools or universities were requested to observe purdah and to be accompanied outside their households by male relatives; those who violated these restrictions were punished Men were forbidden to shave their beards and required to let them grow and keep them long according to the Taliban's liking, and to wear turbans outside their households Communists were systematically executed. Prayer was made compulsory and those who did not respect the religious obligation after the azaan were arrested Gambling was banned Thieves were punished by amputating their hands or feet In 2000, the Taliban leader Mullah Omar officially banned opium cultivation and drug trafficking in Afghanistan the Taliban succeeded in nearly eradicating opium production (99%) by 2001 Under the Taliban governance of Afghanistan, both drug users and dealers were severely prosecuted

Cabinet ministers and deputies were mullahs with a "madrasah education." Several of them, such as the Minister of Health and Governor of the State bank, were primarily military commanders who were ready to leave their administrative posts to fight when needed. Military reverses that trapped them behind lines or led to their deaths increased the chaos in the national administration At the national level, "all senior Tajik, Uzbek and Hazara bureaucrats" were replaced "with Pashtuns, whether qualified or not." Consequently, the ministries "by and large ceased to function.

Rashid described the Taliban government as "a secret society run by Kandaharis ... mysterious, secretive, and dictatorial. They did not hold elections, as their spokesman explained:

The Sharia does not allow politics or political parties. That is why we give no salaries to officials or soldiers, just food, clothes, shoes, and weapons. We want to live a life like the Prophet lived 1400 years ago, and jihad is our right. We want to recreate the time of the Prophet, and we are only carrying out what the Afghan people have wanted for the past 14 years

They modeled their decision-making process on the Pashtun tribal council (jirga), together with what they believed to be the early Islamic model. Discussion was followed by a building of a consensus by the "believers" Before capturing Kabul, there was talk of stepping aside once a government of "good Muslims" took power, and law and order were restored.

As the Taliban's power grew, decisions were made by Mullah Omar without consulting the *jirga* and without consulting other parts of the country. One such instance is the rejection of Loya Jirga decision about expulsion of Osama bin Laden. Mullah Omar visited the capital, Kabul, only twice while in power. Instead of an election, their leader's legitimacy came from an oath of allegiance ("Bay'ah"), in imitation of the Prophet and the first four Caliphs. On 4 April 1996, Mullah Omar had "the Cloak of Muhammad" taken from its shrine, Kirka Sharif, for the first time in 60 years. Wrapping himself in the relic, he appeared on the roof of a building in the center of Kandahar while hundreds of Pashtun mullahs below shouted "Amir al-Mu'minin!" (Commander of the Faithful), in a pledge of support. Taliban spokesman Mullah Wakil explained:

Decisions are based on the advice of the Amir-ul Momineen. For us, consultation is not necessary. We believe that this is in line with the *Sharia*. We abide by the Amir's view even if he alone takes this view. There will not be a head of state. Instead, there will be an Amir al-Mu'minin. Mullah Omar will be the highest authority, and the government will not be able to implement any decision to which he does not agree. General elections are incompatible with *Sharia* and therefore we reject them.

The Taliban were reluctant to share power, and since their ranks were overwhelmingly Pashtun they ruled as overlords over the 60% of Afghans from other ethnic groups. In local government, such as the Kabul city counci or Herat Taliban loyalists, not locals, dominated, even when the Pashto-speaking Taliban could not communicate with roughly half of the population who spoke Dari or other non-Pashtun tongues. Critics complained that this "lack of local representation in urban administration made the Taliban appear as an occupying force.

Iran

Iran has been described as a "theocratic republic" by the CIA World Factbook and its constitution has been described as a "hybrid" of "theocratic and democratic elements" by Francis Fukuyama. Like other Islamic states, it maintains religious laws and has religious courts to interpret all aspects of law. According to Iran's constitution, "all civil, penal, financial, economic, administrative, cultural, military, political, and other laws and regulations must be based on Islamic criteria.

In addition, Iran has a religious ruler and many religious officials in powerful governmental positions. The head of state, or "Supreme Leader", is a faqih (scholar of Islamic law) and has more power than the president of Iran. Iran's current Supreme Leader is Ali Khamenei, a role he's held since 1989. The Leader appoints the heads of many powerful governmental positions: the commanders of the armed forces, the director of the national radio and television network, the heads of powerful major religious and economic foundations, the chief justice of Iran, the attorney general (indirectly through the chief justice), special tribunals, and members of the supreme national security council who are dealing with defense and foreign affairs. He also co-appoints the 12 jurists of the Guardian Council

The Leader is elected by the Assembly of Experts which is made up of mujtahids,[34] who are Islamic scholars competent in interpreting Sharia.

The Guardian Council, has the power to reject bills passed by the Parliament. It can also approve or reject candidates who want to run for the Presidency, Parliament, and the Assembly of Experts. The council supervises elections, and can allow or ban investigations into elections. Six of the twelve council members are faqih and have the power to approve or reject all bills passed by the Parliament; Whether the faqih believes that the bill is in accordance with Islamic laws and customs (Sharia) or not. The other six members are lawyers appointed by the chief justice, who is a cleric and appointed by the Leader.

Saudi Arabia

In the Basic Law of Saudi Arabia, Saudi Arabia defines itself as a sovereign Arab Islamic state with Islam as its official religion. However, some critiques describe Saudi Arabia as an Islamic theocracy. Religious minorities do not have the right to practice their religion openly. Conversion from Islam to another religion is punishable by death as apostasy. Muhammad Al-Atawneh describes the current Saudi regime as a 'theo-monarchy, that draws power from long-standing religio-cultural norms.'

Jewish theocracies

Israel

Israel describes itself as a Jewish state. Israel recognizes by law the Chief Rabinate of Israel as the supreme rabbinic authority for Judaism in Israel. Gail Page describes Israel as a "theocracy", a "country that has openly declared itself for a particular religious group". On July 2019, the Israeli Knesset voted to pass the nation-state law which declares Israel as the nation-state of the Jewish people; Haidar Eid thus describes Israel as an ethno-religious state.

Central Tibetan Administration

The Central Tibetan Administration, colloquially known as the Tibetan government in exile, is a Tibetan exile organization with a state-like internal structure. According to its charter, the position of head of state of the Central Tibetan Administration belongs ex officio to the Dalai Lama, a religious hierarch. In this respect, it continues the traditions of the former government of Tibet, which was ruled by the Dalai Lamas and their ministers, with a specific role reserved for a class of monk officials.

On 14 March 2011, at the 14th Dalai Lama's suggestion, the parliament of the Central Tibetan Administration began considering a proposal to remove the Dalai Lama's role as head of state in favor of an elected leader.

The first directly elected Kalön Tripa was Samdhong Rinpoche, who was elected on 20 August 2001.

Before 2011, the Kalön Tripa position was subordinate to the 14th Dalai Lamawho presided over the government in exile from its founding. In August of that year, Lobsang Sangay received 55 percent of 49,189 votes, defeating his nearest rival Tethong Tenzin Namgyal by 8,646 votes becoming the second popularly elected Kalon Tripa. The Dalai Lama announced that his political authority would be transferred to Sangay

Non-Formal Spiritual System Development and Political Power Spread up by Islamic theologies:

In Arabian Peninsula there had poly ethnic system and different groups of ethnicities, Non-formal system of mono ethnic implement to Arabian Peninsula to brain washing and to politicization by which Islamic rule spread up around North African and West, Central Asia and later to far east spread up it.

Falk and False Ideological Brain Washing:

Akhanda Bharat and Islamic community capture power in India a flak and false statement spread up through IT cell of BJP-RSS brain washing to Youngs through What App, YouTube, and Facebook, etc. acting and cheating by dress up and make up become fashion of political system where orange colour cloth wearing and telling tie continue by BJP-RSS leaders. Conflict creating by messaging and through agent of Kathabachak companies who executing spiritual business. Present India are assimilated post British ruled India which called Union India or Sanjukta Bharat. Hindi force racism executing by force as to target to abolish diversity in unity and demolish abolish languages, culture, identity of South Indian and North East Indian.

Present Scenario of Indian Politics:

* Insult to Nation, Nationality and National leaders by P.M. Noranda Modi:

1. In a top most responsible post person as national representative as Prime Minister he is always use the name of country as Hindustan as irrespective Nation where as India defined as Bharat /India as secular country in constitution. Hindustan was not accepting by the parliament and constitution as in this nation have Sheikh, Jain, Islamic, Buddhist, Christian, Persian communities also even Hindu remain majority because Kashmir and Telangana are Islamic majority, Nagaland is Christian majority, Punjab is Sheikh majority and U.P. and Karalla are about 40% Islamic

community. As a Prim Minister, name of nation and nationality should use properly as per constitution only but he not only he disobeys the nation but also disobey the constitution.

2. He insult Natajee Subash Chandra Bose as he is not declared as death but wanted to give Bharat Ratna Award as death. If he really interested to respect Mr. Subash Chandra Bose than as Subash Chandra Bose International Award to be stated for political and social worker under Government of India.

3. He insult the retired president Late Dr. Sarvopalli Radha Kishnan as His Birth Day 5th September celebrate as teacher day to encourage education in India but he declared as Guru Dibash and give speech on his life only.

4. He irrespective to assassinate Mr. M. Gandhi who called as father of nation but the his birth day 2nd October is not celebrated as national hole day but clean India day as clean by groom as photographic identity.

Barat Barsha as Geographical area:

If we enter into history than we understand that Barat Barsha was a geographical area in North Indian Part called Kuru state that at modern India Haryana, some parts of basin Jamuna and Ganga plain. Barat Barsha is geographical are of Indian Peninsula only but name of nation or country remained at Ancient time and it mainly call north Indian region where Aryans ruled executed.

Hindu

Its boundary indicated from Hindu Kush mountain to Kashmir range where execute several countries. In ancient time to mogul period there execute several small countries in Barat Barsha. But in Europe the Barat Barsha was indicated as Indus which turn to India by speech slip to European. Hindu means Hind that who hidden and Du means Mountain locality. That Kalash, Aryan valley peoples, Ballti, Kashmiri all are white and maximum have brown eye and brown hair also remained some peoples and as per prehistoric evidences they all are European gen. Actually, in Baltic region at historic period two groups of rulers divided and who defatted either become slave or hidden to another place. Hence Hind meaning in Iris and some other north European language as Slave or servant and those peoples used to hunting Dear and Etan flash of dear and hence in in South European and North African region as well as West Asian parts Hinda means Dear also. As Hindu called them Santana which means Brilliant Skin or body that indicated white peoples who remained Europeans.

Tamil means Brown colour or copper colour or dark coloud. Dravidian means winner of Water that means they migrated through boat. Sindhu means Sinai Black; Elam means Black ruled. Black peoples of India are basically tribal peoples either African Originated or Austroasiatic peoples Santhal peoples are Summon or Surran community where as Dravidian peoples are different folk community who worshiped to Kalika who called Kateri Amman and Tandava and some other gods and goddess which basically called local gods or goddess of Tamil Nadu.

Hindu actually remained at Himalayan ranges and basically Hindu Kush as Kush means grass that Hindu Kush means grass root of Hindu and they basically use Scythe and hence somewhere called Scythian and Scythe even today used in North, West and Central India only.

Sindu or Indu:

Sindu means who break laws and that indicated law breaker migrated and rehabilitated to Indus called Sindu and East bank red sea and Mediterranean Sea junction region called Sinai and Sindi peoples migrated through Russia and West part of China from Baltic region. Hence in Russia there have Sindi surname and one group migrated to south China at Tibet region whom language called Sino Tibetan. and Swasti means single parson and Swastika means old generations. and Swastika/ Cross used to Baltic Region, Slavic Community, Tibetans, Sindi, Hindu also.

Bahaman:

Bahaman are actually genetically European and hence maximum Brahman/ Bahama are white skin but long-time rehabilitation in India they mixed with Black somewhere and due to hybridization minimum Bahaman remain black. All priest Groups are not Bahaman which deformed to Brahmin. Mishra mean mixed community and it is reality Egypt called Mishra that indicated from Egypt Such brahmin migrated whom are Mishra or Misro surname. Mithil are in Scotland region and Gaelic and Schottische that Saxon language branch match with Sanskrit as Lithuanian as well as Syrian languages also matching that indicated at prehistoric age Mithila kingdom fondued by Mithil group of peoples and hence all over India Mithil brahmin founded who indicated them as Mithili.

Kshatriya:

At Ural which is Junction point of Europe and Asia that belt from Eurasians peoples belt as mixed peoples of Mongoloid and Europeans. Khatri means dangerous and ferocious who remained warriors' peoples and hence they ruled in Eurasian belt basically Turkish people's groups region from Siberian region to Turkey. One groups of peoples are Marathi and Marwari.

Jat/ Jut

Jut migrated from Jut land of Baltic region who later become form as Euro Asiatic community as they migrated to Indian peninsula through Caucasus as well as West China. In Jat community, Hathi, Vannar, garud, gardhapa, Varaha, Kakar and Nagvanshi remain. Nagvanshi peoples have surname as Nag and their rulers indicated as Snake whom worshiped by common peoples of India as serpentine.

Bhasha:

Bhasha means Business groups and it seen that Mesopotamian group of peoples had business relation with Indus peoples and done sailing to continued business. It seen that It is tradition to business done by European through sailing. It also tradition to invaded through sailing by European. Basically, Arabic peoples who migrated through Iran called Bhasha.

As a result, Brahmin, Kshatriya, Bhasha and Jat remain in unity and called that Santana as they remained White Skin. Where as Sudra remain basically African originated and Austroasiatic black and brown community and white racism executed in ancient India which called Monubad. Sudra or Sudtra means black and defatted Black peoples became slave of White groups who had not remained human right. Black peoples who migrated to Indian peninsula about 60000 years ago they migrated to eastern and south sine where even todays they are remained majority. Northern, Western, Central parts of India rained white peoples mainly.

Barat Barsha turn to Hindustan:

Islamic rule enters to Parashah and Persian peoples enter to Barat Barsha because the also remain safe as to lead life as they believe Sun god, fire god as previous believer of natural power in Barat Barsha. Islamic peoples indicate the same land mark as Hindustan because the peoples of Hindu Kush mountain were indicated as Hindu and they shift from Hindu Kush to enter Indian peninsula but Bharat Barsha remain as Arajabarta (Land of Aryan) and Anarja Bartha (Land of non- Aryan).

The word remains as Dave as superior people and Davari as inferior peoples and Dave was means god whereas Daveri means Danab(giant) Danab turn to Dabir after long time and indicate the south Indian peoples. After long time the religios fath become submarge and as a whole called as hindu in the whole land mark of Barat Barsha where maximum time ruled by different king of Arjabarta (Land of Aryan) and Anarja Bartha (Land of non- Aryan) separately. Islamic people indicate them as a same religious group as Hindu and the land mark indicate as Hindustan (Land of Hindu). As a heard that the land mark peoples used to habit to use milk to offer to god Siva and the milk river flow from temple of god Siva and temple had lump sum goal and money than gaudiness give to power to Islamic ruler of outer land. The outer ruler attracts to Barat Barsha and give the name as Hindustan (The land of Hindu)

Hindustan turn to India:

weakness come after long time ruled by Islamic ruler in Barat Barsha and European start to come to established commercial establishment in Hindustan and turn as ruler in different part. Pondicherry ruled by France community, Goa-Damon-Due ruled by Portugal's community and Bengal- Bihar-orisha ruled by British community (England-Wales- Scotland the independent three countries peoples). Bengal-Behar-Orissa becomes the first spot of British ruled but after all maximum part of Barat Barsha ruled by British either direct or indirect ruled system. But the European indicate the land mark as India which one called as Hindustan by Islamic ruler. The European ruler indicate the land mark as France India, British India as per capture by the community.

Independent India-Pakistan:

As British India divided into India and Pakistan where about 550 numbers princely states remained but Hindi speaking peoples indicate them as Hindustani where British ruler wanted to kept India as united stage where princely states wanted to assimilated also but Islam league should not agree to remained unitedly. Islamic leaders wanted to ruled whole India as about as Islamic ruled executed in two main period as Afghan/ Pathan sultanate Ruled and Mughal (Uzbeks) Ruled. M. C. Gandhi jointly movement done as Semi Independent ruled executed from 1920 and 1927 commonwealth bile pass to formed commonwealth and 1931 India, Australia, New Zeeland and Canada become members of commonwealth as from 1920 these four nations become Semi-independent and under Governor General where Imperial Legislative council remained as supreme Authority to pass bill as parliamentary system executed. Lower House members remained Indians and Upper House members remained Britishers who elected by voting. Due to decolonization several colonies given independent as to continued trading by British. Due to Business continued proper ways British wanted to form Unions as single country but as Islamic group should not agree reman in Union. As Brahmin Nature that to getting better position to ruling field M. C. Gandhi supporting to Islamic group who wanted to rule Whole India but in provincial and central Elections up to 1946 mainly in Western British India that present Pakistan and Bengal province now Bangladesh and Wes Bengal. Hence ultimately British India Divided as India union and Pakistan whereas British India divided into India and Pakistan where about 550 numbers princely states remained but Hindi speaking peoples indicate them as Hindustani where British ruler wanted to kept India as united stage where princely states wanted to assimilated also but Islam league should not agree to remained unitedly. Islamic leaders wanted to ruled whole India as about as Islamic ruled executed in two main period as Afghan/ Pathan sultanate Ruled and Mughal (Uzbeks) Ruled. M. C. Gandhi jointly movement done as Semi Independent ruled executed from 1920 and 1927 commonwealth bile pass to formed commonwealth and 1931 India, Australia, New Zeeland and Canada become members of commonwealth as from 1920 these four nations become Semi-independent and under Governor General where Imperial Legislative council remained as supreme Authority to pass bill as parliamentary system executed. Lower House members remained Indians and Upper House members remained Britishers who elected by voting. Due to decolonization several colonies given independent as to continued trading by British. Due to Business continued proper ways British wanted to form Unions as single country but as Islamic group should not agree reman in Union. In provincial and central election congress remain maximum provincial majority but Islamic league remain majority in Western British Indian provinces (now called as Pakistan) and Bengal province (now formed as Bangladesh and West Bengal) up to 1946. Federal system (different states form and ruled under state government from Local legislative Assembly) and parliamentary system started. Ultimately as per listed one after other colonies were given independent like India given independent in 1947 and by independent bill pass to London assembly pass that India Divided where remained provision that as British India divided into India and Pakistan where pcnil

Independent Bangladesh:

Hindi Racism: Hindi Hai Hum Hindisha Hamara means we are Hindi peoples and Hindustani is ours. Hindustan means to Hindi peoples are as whole India where as in Non-Hindi peoples indicate Hindustani means only Hindi linguistic peoples

Now a days Hindi peoples indicating that they are superior than non-Hindi peoples where as they are attamed the competition examination in Hindi language which are there mother language and as well as they read write in Hindi.

Problem to Non-Hindi peoples:

India-Barat:

Actual name given after independent that Union India in English and in Indian language Sanjukta Bharat as British India divided into India and Pakistan where about 550 numbers princely states remained but Hindi speaking peoples indicate them as Hindustani where British ruler wanted to kept India as united stage where princely states wanted to assimilated also but Islam league should not agree to remained unitedly. Islamic leaders wanted to ruled whole India as about as Islamic ruled executed in two main period as Afghan/ Pathan sultanate Ruled and Mughal (Uzbeks) Ruled. M. C. Gandhi jointly movement done as Semi Independent ruled executed from 1920 and 1927 commonwealth bile pass to formed commonwealth and 1931 India, Australia, New Zeeland and Canada become members of commonwealth as from 1920 these four nations become Semi-independent and under Governor General where Imperial Legislative council remained as supreme Authority to pass bill as parliamentary system executed. Lower House members remained Indians and Upper House members remained Britishers who elected by voting. Due to decolonization several colonies given independent as to continued trading by British. Due to Business continued proper ways British wanted to form Unions as single country but as Islamic group should not agree reman in Union.

Hindustan Region and Hindi peoples:

Hindustan remained from Kashmir to Madhya Pradesh and from eastern Rajasthan to Bihar region which later spread up to Bengal in east and Hyderabad to south region. Actually, Hindustan region called only kingdom which remained under ruled of Ibrahim Lodhi only which captured by Mughal and enlarged later.

Hindi the language of Hindustan: language of Hindu peoples indicated by Islamic ruler which actually Khariboli that deformative of Kharosthi. Arabian and north Iranian and Turkish language mixed language as in Islamic ruled Persian remained official language in Islamic ruled age which mixed with Pashtu language of Pathan ruled and Uzbek of Mughal ruled. Sanskrit evaluated in Northern Iran from Astana language and spread up through India as Scythian ruled. Due to Pashtu and Uzbek language main flow Urdu evaluated in west ancient India that from Indus to Afghanistan region it remained ruled under Iranian/ Persian

Independent India

Political system of Barat/ India: Union Federal system

Name required of country: United Republic of Bharat

Responsibility of participation of princely states: As per independent bill 1947 maximum princely state participate either in India or in Pakistan. Then Hyderabad submerged by force with India and Baluchistan submerged with Pakistan. Kashmir forcefully try to submerged with both India and Pakistan and hence dispute remained.

States name required to define:

West Bengal as Bangla Pradesh

Panjab as Gurumukhi Pradesh

Andhra Pradesh as Telegu Pradesh

Uttar Pradesh as Brojo Pradesh

Madhya Pradesh as Vrindachal Pradesh

Demand of us required as Non-Hindi:

Birth Right:

1. Mother language as Basic Educational System

2. Equality to every one as per qualification.

3. Right to give speech in mother language or vernacular in parliament But

If vernacular not understand by other member than interpreter to recruited to give translated speech in bi- lingual system.

4.Compititive written and interview Examination should be given by vernacular recognize language in the state compulsorily.

5.Within India all peoples are not Hindi whereas the Hindi leaders defined as -

a. Sara Jahasa Acha Hindustan Hai Hamada (Everywhere are good mater that is our Land of Hindu.

b. Hindi Hai Hum Hindustan Hamada (We are Hindi Peoples and Land of Hindu is Only Our)

c. Buri Najar Na hamsa Dalo Sabsa Aga Hogi Hindustani (Ban view not to see to Hindi Speaking peoples become in top most post)

d Jai Hind (Great Hindu Land) but Hindi peoples have only right to speak in Hindi and use

In the above case it is clear that Hindi leaders are forcefully defined that the land Of Independent India Name as Land of Hindu and only Hindi speaking peoples have right to live in Independent India. Whereas per constitution the Independent India have two Name as 1. India in English, 2. Bharat In Indian Languages.

Within Enter Independent India the Written Competition Examination and Interview get in Either English or in Hindi but so many Peoples are in Non Hindi areas are getting education in there vernacular and mother language which one are State official language and under constitution that are recognized language But if Non Hindi Peoples are become unable to attempt in their own language in their own state than what valuation remain the recognize and state official language .In Hindi State Hindi Officer input Hindi language and grammar question compulsory in competition Examination and get interview in Hindi. But in Non Hindi State there are education system implement in State language and English hence it required that to be given written examination and interview either in English or state language than the actual competition to give the proper result other wish the system favor to Hindi speaking peoples that they get like as mother milk in Mother language . Hence after the Hindi take in Examination field and interview than the Bihari's, UP's And other Hindi peoples come to the higher level in maximum number to ground levels governmental posts. After all Hindi Racism come by the system Hence Every Hindi Speaking Peoples explain that the name of country as Hindustan and they understand that the meaning of Hindustan as Hindi land and everywhere of Independent India required to implement forcefully the Hindi Language or by grayness to give awards in case by Central Government and Akhil Bharati Hindi Parishad.

In my real life When I remain in Ratlam in Madhya Pradesh remain as Apprentice Junior Engineer the Senior Section Engineer Mr. Harish Chanda Panda and others said that Why We live in Hindustan if we are unable to speak in Hindi and when I was in Ujjain in Madhya Pradesh in that time several period said by K. K. Mittal That why I live in Hindustan if I am unable properly speak and write Hindi Language and Said that I require to find out other county. Today such word said one after another and said all state required to implement Hindi language.

The above give alarm that Hindi peoples want to capture whole India as Oppose that to speak in State official language in parliament and in State Assembly Hindi speaking peoples or Muslim are given statement in Hindi and Urdu respectively. Afterall the Hindi speaking peoples support to Urdu speech because both have some things similar.

I Say to Non-Hindi Peoples that even today have time to wake up and alert to save us otherwise we become bake and Hindi peoples said they are superior whereas participate in Hindi by them.

We have required to demand by revolutionary mode as-

1. Give the right to give speech in vernacular state official language with interpreter in parliament.

2. In state Either Cantal or State Governmental or public organization competitive examination and interview should to take in State official language and English.

3. In Local Assembly in State should be use the State official language in speech and written particular.

4. Want Birth right that our Mother language and state official language.

5. Want to demand compulsory State official linguistic question in competition examination at list 10 percent that if a candidate remain to do work, he should able to communicate easily in working field because maximum word use by common worker as vernacular language

6 In departmental examination there to be input State language as compulsory because in Hindi State there are remain compulsory Hindi Language in Departmental examination. Even in some case the question and answer remain and getting in Hindi.

6. Every letter and notice in State should remain in State official Language as Hindi States.

7. Hindi Racism to mention at international level and force to implement the system and required to help UN Department.

8. The Name of the country required to give as the United Bharat Republic because The India was given by European and after all the British ruler give the name British India where as previously Islamic invader called as Hindustan because that they enter land lived the religion of Hindu mainly and after lord Asoka ruled the land mark Buddhism start the flows in the religious under royal society but the Islamic ruler understand the land mark as Hindu land, hence the enter land mark called as Hindustan. But the real name of the land mark was Bharat Barsha and hence required the give name of nation as United Bharat Republic for create better integration of nation.

9. Name of the currency of our nation as Indiana by which reformation of economic system required and known by every citizen as Indiana whereas at present in different state call the currency name as Taka called by Bengali, Tanka called by Oria, Rupkani called by Marathi, Toka called by Assesses and so on. On the Other hand, in Nepal, Indonesia, Pakistan the currency called the same as Rupees and hence identification of nation required a special as for the national integrity.

10 In the verbally Hindi speaking peoples call them as Hindustani but in Non-Hindi State the Hindustani means as Hindi speaking peoples. Hence confusion create as that defining the propels as Hindustani, and the upper-class peoples indicate them as Indian in English but the Non- Hindi peoples indicate them as Bharati and these indicate the dissatisfaction of the peoples. The Islamic state and Islamic community indicate the land mark as Hindustan but they indicate them as Muslim but not things as Hindustani because that Hindu are attaching with the word with Hindustani. After all dissatisfaction create and terrorism increase around that part where the Islamic community remain maximum in number, hence it required to indicate us as Braotian which to be easy to specified us as singe identity and hence the national integrity to be increase.

11. There are required the restrict by law that the name of nation and nationality should be indicate as Hindustan and Hindustani as well as India and Indian in Films and newspaper, magazine, and

journal respectively. The proper name to require as United Bharat Republic and in short to indicate as UBR and nationality should be indicating as Bharotian as single unity.

12. AS per constitution the name of country given as Union India and Sanga Bharat because the British India was ruled either direct ruled or indirect agent ruling and after all the religion remain as Hindu, Muslim, Shaik, Ishai(Christian), Jain, etc. and Hindustan if give the name of country than may arise problem that to feel Hindu Land but time pass out above 64 years but national integrity cannot try to increase by the identity of nation. No Liberty of tower or Liberty of statue are not create by the government and peoples celebrating independent day near India Gate and some where the India Gate make as model by the peoples but the India Gate was made by the British Ruler in Respect of visit India by the king of England Gorge-V and he entered the Indian land through Bombay hence There also made as Gate way of India. But we become Proud that we celebrate Indian Independent day near the India Gate which indicate that we have no feelings of nationality. Hence It is required to make the liberty of tower and liberty of statue in respect of independent nation.

13. The parliament House, Governor General House (President house) in New Delhi and Right Us House Governor House in Calcutta (Kolkata) remain as the Administrations purpose as Central and state of West Bengal but we do nothings after independent as Our own building for local and central administration.

Area of as per language:

1. Hindi language tic States: Hindi use as Official language.

Haryana, Himachal Pradesh, Uttaranchal, Uttar Pradesh, Bihar, Jharkhand, Chhattisgarh, Madhya Pradesh, Rajasthan the list of State and only union territory Delhi includes in the list of Hindi Language part of India.

2. Non- Hindi linguistic States: Indo-English use as official language.

Jammu & Kashmir, Punjab, Gujrat, Maharashtra, Andhra Pradesh, Goa, Karnataka, Tamil Nadu, Kerala, Orissa, West Bengal, Sikkim, Assam, Meghalaya, Tripura, Mizoram, Manipur, Nagaland, Arunachal Pradesh as the state and union territory Daman-Diu, Pondicherry, Lakshadweep, Chandigarh, and Andaman & Nicobar where English use as official language and the peoples of these area participate competition written examination and face interview in English and they have no other option they may participate in recognize language whereas the peoples of these area use the recognize language in study and only one language paper remain English and become weak in English and remain unknown the Hindi language which have option to attempt Competition examination and interview. By the system Hindi speaking peoples give more and more facility and enter to Non-Hindi area where as have same qualification and same marital as the Hindi speaking peoples whereas Hindi speaking peoples also have habit to take education in Hindi and have only one regular or optional English Language paper and they are also maximum weak in English. But in departmental and other competition examination one 10% question get in Hindi and become successes in the competition by the system, hence partiality created by the system and the Non-Hindi peoples become downward in competition by system.

Policy to increasing the number of Hindi States: Divide the Hindi States to increase the number as UP, Bihar, Madhya Pradesh Divide int two parts as new states form as Uttarakhand, Jharkhand, and Chhattisgarh and previously the Hindi state form by division of Panjab State as Haryana and Himachal Pradesh. The resent year when Telangana state demand and central government give willingness to form the Telangana state than the Up Government and other political party as majority of Hindi Peoples want to divide as Up into different parts as Harit Pradesh, Bundel Khand, etc. The policy is to increase as numbers of Hindi States.

Council Corporate Administration

This system is by the peoples and for the peoples but the Democracy is the system which is by the peoples but for the representative of the Parliament and Local Assemble. Revolution is the only path to change of society and political system. In European countries there were revolution and change the political and social system. In Ex Colonial countries basically executing democracy and somewhere military dictatorship executed. But there have not any new system that can change the social and political system.

Time to time different political system developed around world and hence liberalism, democracy, communism, socialistic system, etc. developed around world. After colonial ruling the global political system diverted to new rout and if new corporate system of government adopted then that to be better for the peoples and by the peoples.

New Form of Indo-Iranian Racism called Hindiana:

Language and Communities group of India:

1. Indo-Iranian Groups: Arabian (Nayer, Nather, Jat), Turkey (Marathi, Marwari), Indu(Brahmin, Pandit,) Kshatriya(Mongolian-European/ Turkey-Mongolian) etc.
2. Dravidian / Mediterranean
3. Mongoloed:
4. Austro-Asiatic:

As per human Population map of India

Gujrati, Jat, Brahmin jointly force executing Indo-Iranian Racism to Australasian, Mongoloied and Dravidian and economy pull in to their hand.

Most Oldest Language of India:

Santhal: 50000 years old

Tamil: 5000 years old

Sanskrit: 2000 years old

Essential to Form Liberal Bharat United Federation

It is seen that Hindi racism executing by BJP-RSS political alliance and they making political spiritual hydride business where superstition, darkness of social system rising by which they making system that called "Adhara Kayam Raha/ Black Shadow covered to Society" as they are social and National Enemies who allied with antisocial who done artificial conflict and executing divide to rule and on black hand use national und to their political purpose and enjoying life. Dravidian and Sino-Tibetan North-Eastern language poles Identity, languages, social culture come under dangers. Unity in diversity killed by planning and actually Gujrati economic draining by making fool to Hindi peoples. Hence Consulate Confederation Cooperation Confederation systep0m required to implement and Eastern Indian Alliance North Eastern Region, East- Central Region and South India Region required to form as required to Liberal Bharat United Federation.

Present Scenario of Indian Politics

1. Polymorphic-Chameleonic

The political system become such that Politician become

 1. Falk Nationalist
 2. Cheater
 3. Misguide
 4. Misinformation
 5. Economic Monopoly to Gujarat
 6. National property to self-property conversion
 7. Doug Addiction Encouragement

8. Misuse of power
9. Autocratic Fascist Racist Nazi ruling RSS-BJP Joint Venture Ruling

** Great Drama created:

1. Parliaments called as Mother and head down near the gate of parliament as well as call foreign Delegates.

2. Ganga called as Mother to get favor to Hindu peoples and dirty remain as it is as before.

3. Every time sentimental speech given by nearest personality.

4. Mr. Adita Nath Yogi, Saki Maharaj saying that they are Sanashi /monk but in reality they use wealths in lump sum and only saffron cloths / garua bashra are not the main point to a monk. Sannashi mean Suno ash /zero expectation otherwise they are make drama only.

5. The BJP right hand supporter Ram Deve Baba nothing But Business man who start to business as Yoga schooling and later enter to food industeries and Ayurvad manufacturing companies. If someone become monk than he or she are not required any business.

6. Sentiment politics and business are main motive as Ram mandir issue created as in North and Central Indian people worship to Lord Ram and Lord Hanuman

** Cheat with Common Peoples:

1. Learn some English words which used to attracted to common peoples but opposing English to use at Governmental offices where as his ministry maximum Ministers next generation and BJP Ruling States Ministry next generation like Son and Daughter or Grand Son and Grand Daughter are taking Education in English as it clear to cheating with common peoples to depress and misguide directly.

2. He calling about Smart Cities but executing cities have not any proper drainage system and road ways and there have not any project of pollution control, garbage treatment and west land development but misguide to executed new cities as land capturing policies from Villagers.

3. There have not any control to Housing Board that money wastage in different projects which planning have some things fault, e.g. at Ratlam city nears Shasrie Nagar several Flat House remain vacant under Housing Board but BJP leading under Mr. Sive Raj Shing Chuhan are not treating by Mr. Noranda Modi. Land Mafia and Promoter are born like as husbandry.

** Cause of Win Voting at Lock Shabha:

1. Animation film produces and advertisements

2. Hindu adamants used as Nama- Nama caption, Lard Ram picture add at Stage

3. No commands remain as tea seller when remain C. M. But advertisements had done as Child Tea seller and get sympathies from common peoples.

4. High light Gujrat Progress as Tata company establish Nano Car Company but realty remain different as the textile industries damage by which Gujrat know and Ahammadabad known as Manchester of India.

 **Contribution of Congress leader to ruled nation:

1. Mr. Jawaharlal Nehru:

a. National economic system establishes as new path as mixed economical system even we make public and business relation with USSR (Socialist county). In India Public and private business organization encourage by him.

b. India make secular country as to give right to obey every religious faith Asian this nation has Sheikh, Jain, Islamic, Buddhist, Christian, Persian communities also even Hindu remain majority because Kashmir and Telangana are Islamic majority, Nagaland is Christian majority, Punjab is Shaikh majority and U.P. and Karalla are about 40% Islamic community.

c. In his Prim Ministries he united India as to submerged Kashmir estate with Jumbo, Hyderabad estate with Andhra region and Goa, Daman and due submerged with India as union territory.

d. Educational up gradation started under governmental encourages.

e. NAM organization establish with Indonesia and the Ex Colonial countries to make a Ex colonial countries platform.

f. Pondicherry submerged with India by agreement as international political influence.

g. Educations development done under public institutions.

National Defiance Academy Establish to make stronger the military by training.

h. Mixed economical system development done.

i. National flag, republic system and national Identity done.

2. Ms. Indira Gandhi:

a. She diminished the power of Pakistan as to supported to Shake Muzebar Rahman to create Bengal Dash as new nation at 1971 which was remained as East Pakistan

b. Banking organization reformation done as Estate Indore, Mahishur, Tebankur, Bikaner & Jaipur, Suorashtra, etc. State Banks submerged with Empirical Bank which come to executed as largest bank of India as The State Bank of India Organization. She nationalized the other bank also to give security to common peoples.

c. She established the steel plants at Durgapur, Rawerkally, Bokaro, etc. as public organizations for manufacturing the steel.

d. International political field created as a result SAARC organization formed and SAF gam started at South Asian Region and neighbor nation come to a platform.

e. State Reformatted created as per languages for give right to regional languages and after state reorganization regional languages used in state, e.g. Tamil use Tamil Nadu, Malayalam use in Kerala, etc.

f. War pact with USSR give strength to India by her encouragement, which strengthen Rocket technology, Defiance Operating system, Missile Technology, Space technology started by collaboration with USSR and later by collaboration with Russia and now jointly Indo Russian system rocket system establish in India. By her the India reach to High level international politics and India become stronger as able to test Atom Bomb also. Naval ships, submarine and other weapon come from Russia to India and collaborating military practice done to developed defiance strength.

g. Sikkim submerged with India by Voting

h. Green revolutions crop production became high level, White revolution as milk production became high level, and blue revolution as fish production became high level done by encouraging the farmer to use to highbred seeds which produced by the agricultural, diary and fishery department as different seed get for rice, wheats, fish from Japan and Jerseys, cows and leg horn of hens gets from Australia and started to cultivated, farming and husbandry of cows and paltry farming continuously done to developed farmer economic developments.

i. IMF and World Bank loan got for make India as self-reliance and Economical and technically independent by collaboration steel plants and industries under public organizations establish than steel and other industrial products manufacturing started.

j. Educational and technical educations started in new ways by established Indian Institute of Technology and Central Schools, etc.

k. Mineral and oil field research done under her government and Gujrat, Mumbai and Andhra Pradesh found shore and off shore oil field.

l. Television system started and developed in India as satellite Arya Bhatta Launch by her government and telecommunication system developed.

m. National High ways and roadways system development done which now we get better road ways system.

n. Amor Joyan Joti establish at India Gate to Give respect to Assassination army and deface person for nation.

o. Blue Star operations defatted the Punjab Movement to separation to protected India division

n. Non-Conventional energy used as Solar Energy, Cow's dank (Gobar Gas) Energy, Wind Energy started to use too started under her encouragement and motivation.

3. Rajiv Gandhi:

a. Within small time ruling he give entry the higher technology as Computer and electronics field by which one after another technical field, offices and banking system developed environment and working field.

b. International image created to military help to Sri Lanka as Jaffna region declared independency. Sri Lanka remain single country by his help hand and Indian political image made at international field.

c. Globalization and liberalization started by him give path to enter new technology by which the India reach in modern environments where Mobile phone, Cabal TV and other technology enter to India.

d. Education give power to society to stand selves reliance and Indira Gandhi said reality as "Education is a liberating force, and in our age, it is also a democratizing force, cutting across the barrier of caste and class, smoothing out inequalities imposed by birth and other circumstances. Late Rajiv Gandhi flowed her mother and established Modern schools' system and distance educational system developed as open schooling and open university system developed under distance educational council.

e. Gorkha movement for spiritualization's movement adjustment done by agreement and formed a Gorkha Hill Council.

f. Information revolution and Electronic revolution done by him to started computer and internet works system in India.

g. Woman reservation gave in Panchayat raj (Village Board)

Post Rajiv Gandhi period of Congress ruling period:

Mr. P. V. Narasimha Rao and Mr. Monmohan Sing has prime Minister:

1. Liberalization and globalization continued and make better relation with China as powerful Asian country.

2. Railways extended continuously and truck extended in J & K, Meghalaya, Tripura, etc. and other states.

4. Mobile phone and satellite system upgraded continuously and make better relation with USA in trade and business. Hence 2G and 3G connections and television system developed by which hundreds of TV channel are available today. Now Communication system developed in high level.

5. The protection laws against terrorist; woman empowerment and protection laws developed and passed at parliament.

6. Woman empowerment developed as Police, Military, and other public organization woman quota given to make powerful woman in nation. In Pilot training Rajiv Gandhi Foundation pay stiffen also to developed women empowerment.

* Mr. Atal Bihari Bajpai Lead Government Activity:

1. Kargil Forces down toward lower valley in winter which is the mistake decisions of government and in the meantime Pakistan forces enter and capture Kargil and thereafter war required to done and Extra money expanse by government. It was the indication of Government fault that in winter forces required to left top valley.

2. On the base of Lord Ram Mandir issued the BJP lead Mr. Bajpai Government win in the election than peoples upset when Lord Ram Mandir was not built up.

3. Mr. L.K. Advani visited Pakistan and he expressed that Mr. Jinnah was great leader in freedom fighting stage and appreciated vary much about Mr. Jinnah. Peoples of India upsetting.

4. Two years Central Governmental Recruitment stop where as he promised vacancies to be fill up under his governments and young generation back bone brake down by him.

5. Coffin Candle happened after Kargil war when Gorge Fernanda remain Defiance Minister under his Ministry as low category mater as social angle of view.

Why Ram Mandir and Ram Lala became Political Issued at BJP Political Party?

Answers:

1. Lord Ram and his obedient follower Lord Hanuman worship done by states peoples of Bihar, Uttar Pradesh, Madhya Pradesh, Rajasthan, and other North Indian states and believe as most power full god. Hence Lord Ram issued made by them as political issued. In North India common peoples in the morning wish each other as "Ram- Ram".

2. Due to issue the lord Ram the BJP political party get most respond in North Indian States mainly.

3. North Indian peoples are most conservative Hindu mentality and they get the weak point to establish political platforms by this issued.

P.M. Noranda Modi Represent Him as a Gujrat Representative rather than Indian national Representative:

1. He is the first prime minister who activity shown that his native state is the only place that Gujrat development is the only aim to his motive.

2. He organize the programmed at Foreign countries with Gujarati peoples mainly and Gujrati culture given most priority whereas at USA, Canada, European Countries and other continents and countries have Bengali, Tamil, Keralan, Panjabi Associations but his activity highlight Gujrati only.

3. He get High Speed Train project in Gujrat mainly where as it required to connect the Port cities and Capital city connection to speed up the national connectivity.

4. He arrangement Vibrant Gujrat the global Trade show at Gujrat as he is behaving only Gujrat representative. It is activity as previously any one Prime Minister was not Done such that as they also remain South Indian, Punjabi and other State and any Summit was arranged previously at New Delhi as Indian Capital City.

5. He get projects to build up PMO office at Gandhinagar as activity that previously any Prime minister were not remain in India. He only gives priority to Gujrat and behave like these.

He should not want All Indian Progress that indicated.

6. China President Visit to India done at Gujrat but not at New Delhi that indicated He mostly want Gandhinagar to the Capital City.

* P.M. Noranda Modi make Foolish to Common Peoples of India:

1. He wanted Vote on the base of 370 Act as J & K special states to do Abolish by Him.

2. He promised to common peoples that he should back Black Money from Foreign Countries.

3. International Petroleum price drop 40 to 50 % where as in India only 5 rupees drop in Patrol, Diesel, CNG and Cooking Gas and explain that he reduced price rate of Petroleum products. 4. International price of Gold deaminized and in hence in India Gold price also reduced but he explains that his government reduced the rate of Gold.

5. He explain him as he come from common family but he gives statement to abolish Labour law and start to flexibility of working hours that indicated he only working for rich personality and common peoples are to be as animal character by which common labour should work 24 hours for owner. At is the same system at tea stall child labour kept as servant and not only he does works at stall but also work at owner house as 24 hours servant and get minimum money as salary.

6. Make Common peoples by slogan 'Make in India' and Clean India. He has no programmed to establish Indian organization to production of goods and export Indian goods to foreign countries. He also has no programmed to clean city as to establish Pollution control system, Drainage development system, Destruction of West materials, Recycling of reusable materials, programmed to starting new clean machineries, River pollution control programmed etc. He only uses groom for cleaning as to capture Photographs.

Mr. Noranda Modi required to Rejoin from P. M. Post as He unable to full fill his promised:

1. 370 Act of Special States should not remove by Him.

2. He should not take any action against to Pakistan and China where Pakistan military fired every day and many soldiers killed and china military some time enter to Indian land.

3. Ganga Clean project have no proper guide line.

4. Jamuna pollution controlling not done which water polluted river Ganga also.

5. Infiltration of Bangladeshi are unable to stop by his government which was promised by him. He also not taken any action by diplomatic relation.

6. PMO offices make at Gandhinagar and Varanasi as selfishness works which non of Prim Minister done like such works.

* The condition to Left India by British Rulers:

1. Minimum Broad gauge and maximum Meter gauge railways available and mainly port city.

2. British executed direct ruled and indirect rules under estate of land lords in different parts on India which were off position to executed proper democracy.

3. Minimum land line of telephone system remain around India. Poor Communication system remain around India.

4. Part of India as Kashmir, Hyderabad remain independent Estates and Goa, Damon Due remain under ruled of Portugal and Pondicherry remain under ruled of France.

5. Undeveloped Irrigation and Agriculture system remain around India.

6. Educational Institutions remain minimum in Number. Only Roorkee was remain Engineering college and there had minimum Technical schools also.

7. Minimum Medical college and hospitals remain. Hospital remain under privet organization.

8. Only National Highway Grant Tank Road remain which Connected Calcutta to Peshawar.

9. In several place Railways was not connected properly. e.g. In Malda to Murshidabad was required travel by boat to crossing Ganga River.

*Poor Administrative power lead by Non-Congress Parties Governments:

1. Mr. Morarji Dasia Janata Dal Government:

a. No Economical and financial proper guide and projects remain under him.

b. No industrial and communicational developments projects remain.

c. Mr. Morarji Dasia should not Completed by him and later Mr. Charan Singh became Prime Minister.

2. Mr. V. P. Singh Janata Dal Government:

a. Economical system try to developed socialistic system but fail quickly.

b. Mr. Davilal became Deputy Prime Minister.

c. Unstable government formed due to inter coalitions among Janata Dal members and Government fall down intermediate time and later Mr. Chandrashakher become Prime Minister but Midterm polling happened immediately.

3. Mr. Davagoura Janata Dal Government:

a. Not lasting 5 years and intermediate polling happened.

b. Intermediate Prime Minister Mr. I. K. Gujral Made due to Instability of Government.

c. Janata Dal Broken into Different Political parties as RJD, BJD, JDSP, etc.

4. Mr. Atal Bihari Bajpai lead Bharatia Janata Party:

a. Kargil War happened due to mismanagement of Government as Military left from upper hill at winter season which were not done any time and in the meantime Pakistan Military capture the Kargil Hill area and the country force to involved war due to miss administrative power.

b. IC 814 Air Lines Aeroplan High-jack by terrorist and land at Amritsar but Minister was to take any Action at Amritsar Airport but sand CRP as special team from New Delhi and flight flew away from Amritsar to Lahore and then Abu Dhabi and later to Kabul. Due to miss administrations chances at Amritsar miss and later Masood, the terrorist's leader with his group left by Mr. A. B. Bajpai Government to safe passengers of high-jack Aeroplan.

c. Privatized maximum Public Autonomous organizations and seal government property in chief rate.

d. The recruitment of public organizations stops by two years off favor to new generation and students.

e. New pension system (NPS) system started to Public organizations off favor of common peoples and Pension to MLA and MPs started in favor of political persons.

f. Coffin scandal a lowest level mater happened to assassinated soldier motel mater.

g. Deputy Prime Minister recruited to Mr. L.K. Advani as poor Administrative symbol whereas per parliament system Deputy Prime Minister post have no options.

h. Parliament House Attracted by Terrorist Group which indicated poor security of New Delhi under his ministry.

i. Narmada projects as half cannel and half pipe lines system to water supply from Narmada to Shipra River a Vogues system where money expanses more but only single purposes serving by the projects. It was taken as the Madhya Pradesh ruling under BJP lead Government but there were not another river projects by his Ministry.

5. Mr. Narendra Modi BJP Lead Government:

a. Miss Guide to Common Peoples -

(i) Clean India : Clean by Groom as an acting by BJP leaders and allied personality but have no any guide line and any project to clean city and village by establish proper drainage system development and sweeping by machineries under Municipalities and Village board and have not any team to establish to protects pollutions and crash the waste materials and recycles those.

(ii) Make India: Foreign companies call to investment and only make rubber stamp as make in India but have not any proper innovative and upgrading projects to make self-technological base industries and have no educational development programmed that at Universities level innovations and up gradations to done by which technological and economically county will become self-reliance.

(iii) Adopted Village: It is the policies to restated Land Lord system by His ministry as give power to rich and factory owner and MPs whose next generations should demand that their old generations expenses money for Village establishment and get authority from government and will become land lord as old system started.

(iv) Break the protocol miss guide to common peoples that actually he disobeys the basic rules and regulation of society and administration system and supreme personality as his habit

b. Priority to Give self-importance rather than National interests:

(i) Sub PMO offices established at Gandhi Nagar and Varanasi as He is Gujrati and Gujrat Capital is Gandhi Nagar as well as His Constituency are also Varanasi.

(ii) Make lager Cabinet ministry to satisfy to his allied personality and 66 cabinet ministers recruited.

(iii) Give priority to NRI rather than common peoples who lead life to Indian land.

c. U-Turn Done which Promise to Common peoples to Do:

(i) 370 Act Abolish issues remain silent

(ii) No action taken against Pakistan to violet LOC

(iii) No Black Money Return to India from Foreign Countries.

d. Common people's mentality Diversion done:

(i) Speech giver as Hindu women required to give birth four children by his MP and Allied Political parties members but not take any action.

(ii) Religious Tension created by Ghar Baposhi system started and controversial statement given by RSS, VHP and other parties members.

(ii) High money expenses to invited Diplomates at Shapth Grahan

e. Apply Rules To forget Promised at Voting:

(i) After 3 days a family forget event mater or death case.

(ii) After 3-month common peoples forget a locality events matter and come too busy to their self-works.

f. Miss Management of Administration:

(i) Adhadesh/ ordinance Implement by which break the Democratic system.

(ii) Citizenship Electronic Card system have not any programmed but Aadhar Card implement in every field.

Required Government system:

1. Corporate Government Administrative system and

2. Liberal Social system Development

3. Multi River Project Development

4. Multi Economical Project Development

5. Self-Reliance Industrial Development

Political Parties Leaders Who are memorable:

Swaraj Party, Indian political party established in late 1922–early 1923 by members of the Indian National Congress (Congress Party), notably Motilal Nehru, one of the most prominent lawyers in northern India (and the father of political leader Jawaharlal Nehru), and Chitta Ranjan Das, a nationalist politician from Bengal. The party's name is taken from the term *swaraj*, meaning "self-rule," which was broadly applied to the movement to gain independence from British rule.

The party's primary goal was to contest the elections to the new Central Legislative Assembly in 1923 and, once in office, to disrupt official policy and derail the Raj (British government in India) by anti-government agitation within the council chambers. Though the non-cooperation approach of Mohandas K. Gandhi had remained the primary strategy of the Congress, in reality those Congress leaders who were less-orthodox Hindu or who were more secular-minded in outlook chose the alternative tactic of partially cooperating with political reforms being instituted by the British after World War I. The Swarajists won more than 40 seats in the Central Legislative Assembly in 1923, but their numbers were never quite enough to prevent the British from passing the legislation they desired or believed was needed to maintain internal order in India. By 1927 the party had disbanded.

Chitta Ranjan Das, (born Nov. 5, 1870, Calcutta [now Kolkata], India—died June 16, 1925, Darjeeling [now Darjeeling]), politician and leader of the Swaraj (Independence) Party in Bengal under British rule.

After failing the competitive entrance examination for the British-dominated Indian Civil Service, Das entered the legal profession. He defended many accused of political offenses and took an active part in nationalistic journalism.

Bitterly opposing British rule in India and rejecting all ideas of political or economic development of India along Western lines, he idealized the life of the ancient Indian village and saw a golden age in ancient Indian history. He supported the noncooperation movement launched against British rule by Mahatma Gandhi and in 1921 was imprisoned for six months as a political offender. In 1922 he became president of the Indian National Congress. Under his leadership the Congress abandoned its intentions to boycott colonially sponsored elections for provincial councils. It decided instead to participate in order to seek positions that would permit them to obstruct governmental business from within.

Later, when the Swarajists were returned as the largest party in Bengal, Das declined the post of chief minister, stating that his aim was to wreck the existing government, not to cooperate with it. In 1924 he was elected mayor of Calcutta (now Kolkata) and tried to improve the lot of the city's neglected Indian population. In 1925 there were some signs of a possible compromise between Das and Lord Birkenhead, the secretary of state for India, but Das died before any agreement could be reached.

Motilal Nehru, in full **Pandit Motilal Nehru**, (born May 6, 1861, Delhi, India—died Feb. 6, 1931, Lucknow), a leader of the Indian independence movement, cofounder of the Swaraj ("Self-rule") Party, and the father of India's first prime minister, Jawaharlal Nehru.

Motilal, a member of a prosperous Brahman family of Kashmiri origin, early established a lucrative law practice and was admitted to the Allahabad High Court in 1896. He shunned politics until middle age, when, in 1907, at Allahabad, he presided over a provincial conference of the Indian National Congress (Congress Party), a political organization striving for dominion status for India. He was considered a moderate (one who advocated constitutional reform, in contrast to the extremists, who employed agitational methods) until 1919, when he made his newly radicalized views known by means of a daily newspaper he founded, *The Independent*.

The massacre of hundreds of Indians by the British at Amritsar in 1919 prompted Motilal to join Mahatma Gandhi's non-cooperation movement, giving up his career in law and changing to a simpler, non-Anglicized style of life. In 1921 both he and Jawaharlal were arrested by the British and jailed for six months.

In 1923 Motilal helped found the Swaraj Party (1923–27), the policy of which was to win election to the Central Legislative Assembly and obstruct its proceedings from within. In 1928 he wrote the Congress Party's Nehru Report, a future constitution for independent India based on the granting of dominion status. After the British rejected these proposals, Motilal participated in the civil disobedience movement of 1930 that was related to the Salt March, for which he was imprisoned. He died soon after release.

1. Dream of Pandit Jawaharlal Nehru.:

a. Strong India: Defiance Academy establish to give training army, navy and air forces to make self-independent in Defiance system.

b. United India: Kashmir, Goa-Daman -Due, Hyderabad make the parts of India and by agreement Pondicherry make the parts of India. Secularism system developed as unity in diversity is the nature of Indian system.

c. Educated India: Educational secondary and Higher Educational Institutions established and kept to hand of government to developed human resources.

d. Economic Independent India: Mixed Economical system developed even Business pact deal with USSR a Socialist country.

Non-Aligned Movement

The **Non-Aligned Movement (NAM)** is a forum of 120 countries that are not formally aligned with or against any major power bloc. After the United Nations, it is the largest grouping of states worldwide.

The movement originated in the aftermath of the Korean War, as an effort by some countries to counterbalance the rapid bi-polarization of the world during the Cold War, whereby two major powers formed blocs on a policy to pull the rest of the world into their orbits. One of these was the pro-Soviet socialist bloc whose best known alliance was the Warsaw Pact, and the other the pro-American capitalist group of countries, many of which belonged to NATO. In 1961, drawing on the principles agreed at the Bandung Conference of 1955, the Non-Aligned Movement was formally established in Belgrade, Yugoslavia, through an initiative of Yugoslav President Josip Broz Tito, Indian Prime Minister Jawaharlal Nehru, Egyptian President Gamal Abdel Nasser, Ghanaian President Kwame Nkrumah, and IIndonesian President Sukarno.

This led to the first Conference of Heads of State or Governments of Non-Aligned Countries. The purpose of the organization was summarized by Fidel Castro in Havana Declaration of 1979 as to ensure "the national independence, sovereignty, territorial integrity and security of non-aligned countries" in their "struggle against imperialism, colonialism, neo-colonialism, racism, and all forms of foreign aggression, occupation, domination, interference or hegemony as well as against great power and bloc politics.

The countries of the Non-Aligned Movement represent nearly two-thirds of the United Nations' members and contain 55% of the world population. Membership is particularly concentrated in countries considered to be developing countries, although the Non-Aligned Movement also has a number of developed nations.

The Non-Aligned Movement gained the most traction in the 1950s and early 1960s, when the international policy of non-alignment achieved major successes in decolonization, disarmament, opposition to racism and opposition to apartheid in South Africa, and persisted throughout the entire Cold War, despite several conflicts between members, and despite some members developing closer ties with either the Soviet Union, China, or the United States. In the years since the Cold War's end in 1991, the movement has focused on developing multilateral ties and connections as well as unity among the developing nations of the world, especially those in the Global South.

Origins and the Cold War

The term 'Non-Alignment' was used for the first time in 1950 at the United Nations by India and Yugoslavia, both of which refused to align themselves with any side in the multi-alliances involving Korean War. Drawing on the principles agreed at the Bandung Conference in 1955, the Non-Aligned Movement as an organization was founded on the Brijuni islands in Yugoslavia in 1956 and was formalized by signing the Declaration of Brijuni on 19 July 1956. The Declaration was signed by Yugoslavia's president, Josip Broz Tito, India's prime minister Jawaharlal Nehru and Egypt's president, Gamal Abdel Nasser. One of the quotations within the Declaration is "Peace cannot be achieved with separation, but with the aspiration towards collective security in global terms and expansion of freedom, as well as terminating the domination of one country over another". According to Rejaul Karim Laskar, an ideologue of the Congress party which ruled India for most part of the Cold War years, the Non-Aligned Movement arose from the desire of Jawaharlal Nehru and other leaders of the newly independent countries of the third world to guard their independence and sovereignty "in face of complex international situation demanding allegiance to either two warring superpowers".

The Movement advocates a middle course for states in the developing world between the Western and Eastern Blocs during the Cold War. The phrase itself was first used to represent the doctrine by Indian diplomat V. K. Krishna Menon in 1953, at the United Nations.

But it soon after became the name to refer to the participants of the *Conference of Heads of State or Government of Non-Aligned Countries* first held in 1961. The term "non-alignment" was established in 1953 at the United Nations. Nehru used the phrase in a 1954 speech in Colombo, Sri Lanka. In this speech, Zhou Enlai and Nehru described the Five Principles of Peaceful Coexistence to be used as a guide for Sino-Indian relations called *Panchsheel* (five restraints); these principles would later serve as the basis of the Non-Aligned Movement. The five principles were:

Mutual respect for each other's territorial integrity and sovereignty.

Mutual non-aggression.

Mutual non-interference in domestic affairs.

Equality and mutual benefit.

Peaceful co-existence.

India and the Non-Aligned Movement

For **India**, the concept of non-alignment began as a policy of non-participation in the military affairs of a bipolar world and in the context of colonialism aimed towards optimum involvement through multi-polar participation towards peace and security. It meant a country should be able to preserve a certain amount of freedom of action internationally. There was no set definition of non-alignment, which meant the term was interpreted differently by different politicians and governments, and varied in different contexts. The overall aims and principles found consensus among the movement members. Non-aligned countries, however, rarely attained the freedom of judgement they desired and their actual behavior towards the movement's objectives, such as social justice and human rights, were unfulfilled in many cases. India's actions often resembled those of aligned countries. The response of the non-aligned nations during India's wars in 1962, 1965 and 1971 revealed non-aligned positions on issues such as secession. The non-aligned nations were unable to fulfil the role of peacekeepers during the Indo-China war of 1962 and the Indo-Pakistan war of 1965 despite meaningful attempts. The non-aligned response to the Bangladesh Liberation War and the following 1971 Indo-Pakistan War showed most of the non-aligned nations prioritized territorial integrity above human rights, which could be explained by the recently attained statehood for the non-aligned. During this period, India's non-aligned stance was questioned and criticized. Jawaharlal Nehru had not wanted the formalization of non-alignment and none of the non-aligned nations had commitments to help each other. The international rise of countries such as China also decreased incentives for the non-aligned countries to stand in solidarity with India.

India played an important role in the multilateral movements of colonies and newly independent countries that wanted to participate in the Non-Aligned Movement. The country's place in national diplomacy, its significant size and its economic growth turned India into one of the leaders of the Non-Aligned Movement.

Prior to Independence and India becoming a republic, Jawaharlal Nehru contemplated the path the country would take in world affairs. In 1946, Nehru, as a part of the cabinet of the Interim Government of India, said during a radio broadcast; "we propose, as far as possible, to keep away from the power politics of groups, aligned against one another, which have led in the past to world wars and which may again lead to disasters on an even vaster scale". In 1948, he made a speech to the Constituent Assembly (Legislative) titled "We Lead Ourselves" in which he said the world was going through a phase in which the foreign policies of major powers had "miserably failed". In the speech, he talked about what alignment entailed, saying:

What does join a bloc mean? After all it can only mean one thing: give up your view about a particular question, adopt the other party's view on that question in order to please it […] Our instructions to our delegates have always been first to consider each question in terms of India's interest, secondly, on its merit - I mean to say if it did not affect India, naturally on its merits and not merely to do something or to give a vote just to please this power or that power .

In 1949, he told the Assembly:

We have stated repeatedly that our foreign policy is one of keeping aloof from the big blocs [….] being friendly to all countries... not becoming entangled in any alliances… that may drag us into any possible conflict. That does not, on the other hand, involve any lack of close relationships with other countries.

Some saw confusion in these speeches and the West questioned Nehru's "neutrality"; in the United States in 1949, Nehru said; "we are not blind to reality nor do we acquiesce in any challenge to man's freedom from whatever quarters it may come. Where freedom is menaced or justice threatened or where aggression take place, we cannot and shall not be neutral". The term 'Non-Alignment' was used for the first time in 1950 at the United Nations when both India and Socialist Federal Republic of Yugoslavia rejected alignment with any side in the Korean War. Over the years, Nehru made a number of comments on non-alignment; in 1957 he said, "Non-alignment seems to me as the natural consequence of an independent nation functioning according to its own rights. After all alignment means being regimented to do something you do not like and thereby giving up certain measures of independent judgement and thinking."

Tito, Nasser, and Nehru at the Conference of Non-Aligned Nations held in Belgrade 1961

PM Singh and the MOS for External Affairs at the XIVth NAM's Business Forum in Cuba, 2006.

President Aliyev and Vice President Naidu at the 18th Summit of Non-Aligned Movement in Баку, 2019

Indian non-alignment was a product of the Cold War, a bipolar world and India's colonial experience and the non-violent Indian independence struggle] According to Rejaul Karim Laskar, the Non-Aligned Movement was devised by Nehru and other leaders of newly independent countries of the Third World to "guard" their independence "in face of complex international situation demanding allegiance to either of the two warring superpowers".

The term "non-alignment" was coined by V K Menon in his speech at the United Nations (UN) in 1953, which was later used by Indian Prime Minister Jawahar Lal Nehru during his speech in 1954 in Colombo, Sri Lanka, in which he described the Panchsheel (five restraints) to be used as a guide for Sino-Indian relations, which were first put forth by Chinese Premier Zhou Enlai. These principles would later become the basis of the Non-Aligned Movement. The five principles were: mutual respect for each other's territorial integrity and sovereignty; mutual non-aggression; mutual non-interference in domestic affairs; equality and mutual benefit; and peaceful co-existence. Nehru's concept of non-alignment brought India considerable international prestige among newly independent states that shared its concerns about the military confrontation between the superpowers and the influence of the former colonial powers. By laying the foundation stone of 'Non-Alignment Movement', India was able to establish a significant role for itself as a leader of the newly independent world and in the multilateral organizations like the UN.

According to Jairam Ramesh, neither Menon or Nehru "particularly cared for or were fond of the term 'non alignment' much less of the idea of 'non-aligned movement' or a 'nonaligned grouping'".

Vijaya Lakshmi Pandit (née Sw**arup Nehru**; 18 August 1900 – 1 December 1990) was an Indian freedom fighter, diplomat and politician. She served as the 8th President of the United Nations General Assembly from 1953 to 1954, the first woman appointed to either post. She was also the 6th Governor of Maharashtra from 1962 to 1964. Noted for her participation in the Indian independence movement, she was jailed several times during the movement.

Hailing from the prominent Nehru-Gandhi political family, her brother Jawaharlal Nehru was the first Prime Minister of independent India, her niece Indira Gandhi was the first female Prime Minister of India and her grand-nephew Rajiv Gandhi was the sixth and youngest Prime Minister of India. She was sent to London as India's most important diplomat after serving as India's envoy to the Soviet Union, the United States and the United Nations. Her time in London offers insights into the wider context of changes in India–UK relations

She attended the 1916 Congress session that took place in Lucknow. She was impressed by Sarojini Naidu and Annie Besant.

In 1920, she spent time in Mahatma Gandhi's ashram close to Ahmedabad. She participated in daily chores including dairy work and spinning. She also worked in the office that used to publish Young India.

Pandit was the first Indian woman to hold a cabinet post in pre-independent India. In 1936, she stood in general elections and became member of parliament by 1937 for constituency of Cawnpore Bilhaur. In 1937, she was elected to the provincial legislature of the United Provinces and was designated minister of local self-government and public health. She held the latter post until 1938 and again from 1946 to 1947.

She spent significant time in jail for her participation in the Indian independence movement. She was jailed for 18 months from 1931 - 1933. She was jailed again for 6 months in 1940 before getting jailed in 1942 for 7 months over her participation in the Quit India Movement. After her release, she helped the victims of the Bengal famine of 1943 and served as president of the Save the Children Fund Committee which rescued poor children from the streets.

Following the death of her husband in 1944, she experienced Indian inheritance laws for Hindu widows and campaigned with All India Women's Conference to bring changes to these laws.

In 1946, she was elected to the Constituent Assembly from the United Provinces.

Following India's freedom from British occupation in 1947 she entered the diplomatic service and became India's ambassador to the Soviet Union from 1947 to 1949, the United States and Mexico from 1949 to 1951, Ireland from 1955 to 1961 (during which time she was also the Indian High Commissioner to the United Kingdom), and Spain from 1956 to 1961. Between 1946 and 1968, she headed the Indian delegation to the United Nations. In 1953, she became the first woman President of the United Nations

General Assembly (she was inducted as an honorary member of the Alpha Kappa Alpha sorority in 1978 for this accomplishment).

Hon. Members that Shrimati Vijaya Lakshmi Pandit has resigned her seat in the House with effect from 17 December 1954.

In India, she served as Governor of Maharashtra from 1962 to 1964. She returned as a member of parliament for 1964 to 1968 with her election victory in Phulpur. Pandit was a harsh critic of Indira Gandhi's years as Prime Minister especially after Indira had declared the emergency in 1975.

Pandit retired from active politics after relations between them soured. On retiring, she moved to Dehradun in the Doon Valley in the Himalayan foothills. She came out of retirement in 1977 to campaign against Indira Gandhi and helped the Janata Party win the 1977 election. She was reported to have considered running for the presidency, but Neelam Sanjiva Reddy eventually ran and won the election unopposed.

In 1979, she was appointed the Indian representative to the UN Human Rights Commission, after which she retired from public life. Her writings include *The Evolution of India* (1958) and *The Scope of Happiness: A Personal Memoir* (1979

2. Dream of Ms. Indira Gandhi:

a. Self-Reliance India: Steel Plant Development done and India public sectors started Steel production, Agricultural development done and green revolution, white revolutions and blue revolutions done. Heavy Industrial development done under her administration and nationalized the sick industries to developed those.

b. Clean India: Gave priority to Environmental pollutions. Take step of Ganga Action Plant to save River Ganga. ETP plants developed at different organizations and production units.

c. Establish India: Irrigation system developed under Multi River projects and water supply through canal as well as Hydro Electric production started at different projects. TV and satellite programmed started in new ways and information revolution started.

d. Strong India: defiance pact done with USSR and Space research, Defiance researches done and missile and atom bomb made in India. Estate system and land lord system abolished and state reformation done to make strong India.

e. Make in India: Railway Locomotive Electrical and Diesel Engine manufacturing unit established at Chita Ranjan and Varanasi, Railway Coach factory and Modernization unite establish at Parambu, Kapurthala and Patiala established and make in India system developed by which today we manufacture Railway Engine and coaches for our country and export to other country as Bangladesh, Caney and other countries.

f. Educated India: Established UGC, NCERT, CBSE and other organizations by which standard education system provided to our generations. Central School (Khatria Vidyalaya) established.

3. Dream of Rajiv Gandhi:

a. Advance India: Computer and advance technology gave entry to India and new educational field started in India. Digital India started and information revolution happen in new ways and Net system give the new communication system development.

b. Educated India: Distance educations started and established IGNOU and modern schools (Navodaya Vidyalaya) established and as well as Distance Education council developed.

c. Strong India: defiance research makes continued and Missile technology developed and deface drill to purchase Canon from foreign county.

Special Contribution of Congress Party:

1. Contribution and infrastructure of Democracy development. 2. Mixed Economical System development.

3. Unity in Diversify system development

4. National flag, national Identity and system development.

Anti-National Activities Done by Mr. Noranda Modi:

1. Insult to Father of Nation Mr. Mahatma Gandhi and his ideology as make his birthday as clean India day and NH money should not pay to public organizations worker who works and service done on that day 2nd October.

2. His supported Political group celebrate the Killer of Mr. M. Gandhi Mr. Nathu Ram Goodes birthday but he is not taking any action to that organization.

3. He Insult Dr. Sabapalli Radhakrishnan as Teacher days celebrated on respect of his birth day declared as Guru days and try to miss guide to student the future of India.

4. He Insult Pandit Jawaharlal Nehru and Indira Gandhi as he should not offer flower to their memorial which he done first time in Indian History.

Mr. Noranda Modi and BJP lead Central and State Governments should not take any steps to developed Human resources:

1. Child marriage, child labour are mostly held on the state of northern, Central and Western Indian states, e. g. MP, Rajasthan, Haryana, Chhattisgarh and all are Govern by BJP lead governments but should not take any action to stop Child marriage, child labour and they are not give any caption to developed Human mentality against to protected child future.

2. Maternal blood relation marriage should not abolish by lay and social caption should not don by both central and State government as consider genetical science and social point of view are not good for society as nearest blood relation marriage. In south Indian states and Maharashtra have maternal relation marriage system.

Portugal, Danish, France and British peoples came in India at Mogul Period for Business purposes and later Portugal ruled Goa,

Daman and Duie; France ruled at Pondicherry and Chandan Nagar; and rest of India ruled under British community either directly or by agent ruler whom called Estate/ Riashat and land lord society formed. Now Mr. Modi requested to Different countries like as France, China and other to establish Business and he called make in India as rubber stamp. As per tendency of Mr. Modi that he selling Indian land and peoples to foreign countries and in future any of power full country may rule India where remote controller remain foreign country and TV channel remain Indian Government. As per political laws of agreement one become rider and another become horse. If India will become purely host country than foreign countries will be rider as per political agreement.

2. Already several multi-national companies establish in India and Mr. Modi force fully try to make India as purely Host Country where Economy should drain out from India to foreign country as Foreign company establishing to do production in India for Indian market only where profit to get to self-county only.

3. For a long time China wanted to capture Indian market to selling products and Mr. Modi make it easy where Indian self-industries destructed and he have not any aim to establish to make India as guest country by which Economy should come in country.

4. He make India fully dependent on foreign countries and later power may capture by powerful country and we again will be dependent and ruling by foreign community like as Mr. Babar called to establish Mughal ruled and our culture destructed and back bone broken to rule independently. Mr. Modi are broken bake bone of India that we should not walk independently and make purely host country under China, France and other countries.

5. Mr. Modi shown dream before voting of 2014 to make self-industrial development and Foreign Direct Investment (FDI) opposing but have done such matter and try to make India as purely host country that we should not stand industrial field on our own leg and in future India will rule by foreigner.

6. He is proving that India are unable to stand its own leg and hence he is bagging to foreign countries to make India to purely host country like as bagger and travel to foreign countries door to door.

Clean India of Modi make Sweeping India:

1. Toilet programmed is under WHO and UNDP which highlight by Mr. Modi as Polio, Anganbari and Toilet programmed were the programmed of WHO, UNICEF and UNDP respectively but was not declared as Congress Government Credit but Mr. Modi declared as His Credit as he tells lie.

2. He make Officers and other class peoples as Sweeper by sweeping with groom than there have required to abolish or surrender posts of Cleaner and sweeper in railways, Municipality and Administrative offices as GM, to TCN sweeping at Stations and railways compounds as well as Collector, DM etc. sweeping road side.

3. Mr. Modi have not any projects to developed Drainage system development, Pollution control development, Plastic west controlling system development and wasteland development than there have not any Clean India programmers.

Modi's Savka Shath Savka Vikash Statement mean Modi Ka Shath Ushika Vikash (Progress All Together transform to Modi's partner Progress fast):

1. The Bengali singer attach with Baba Ramdev convinced to Modi make him to Minister of BJP Government who have not any social development or political contribution at West Bengal.

2. Left Siva Sana Party at Conflict participate to BJP by Surash Provu become Railways Cabinet Minister.

3. Ms. Kiron Badi became CM. Candidate of BJP as she left AAB political party and meet with P.M. Modi.

4. Bhumi Adhigrahan as unconditional make favor of builder and thakader by which real rate land mark to seal in very high rate

which become impossible to buy by common peoples and rich become richer and poor become poorer.

5. Tell lie and confuse to common peoples make main policy by Mr. Modi as he said, 'Acha Din Ana Bala Hai' mean better days will come where subject made silent where he wants to told that his better days would come when he was fight election 2014. After win the election 2014 he decleared that Acha Din Aye Gaya mean Better days come where he also silent subject to confuse to common peoples that he wants to said his better day come.

The above indicated that it is reality of Modi's partner progress fast that he has not any aim to progress whole country and common peoples.

Sannash(Monk) means Suno Ash (Zero willingness) But Mr. Modi Allied Monks are only Acting monks whom dressing the monks and luxury life leading peoples:

1. Baba Ram Dave acting monk who have really a great business man and leading business on the name Patanjali. Advertisement done with photography of Baba Ramdev. Not only Million Rupees monitory Agricultural Product business organization supervision done by him but also Yoga organization executed by him and booking done in high rate which advertisement done continuously.

2. Sakhi Maharaj acting as monk but become a M.P. Dress up like as monk but mind remain as common as general purpose., hence command like as childhood.

Clever give more priority than intelligent by Indian mass Media:

1. Noranda Modi Speech quality better, no social works, tell lie at any time, U-turn at any time and acting better dressing better. Give mass Media most priority and shown animation and highlight speech only but analyzing of make India, Clean India procedure should not mechanize details shown.

2. Arobindra Kejriwal Speech better, Acting better. The News agency highlight free water supply but there had not any highlight about West Bangle that at Former CM Late Joti Bose period had free water supply at tree time at Kolkata and other parts of W.B. and even today Ms. Mamata Banerjee Period there have nominal charge as quarterly Rs 150 /- tree time one hour water supply as news agency neither analyze not get proper information about every state of India and there infrastructures.

3. High light Modi laher (Modi's wave) before 2014 elections and caption given continuously as Modi' tea and A child seal tea on station to create sympathies to common peoples mind, animation shown to create Modi's waves as highlight and propaganda done continuously as Gujrat development but analytical programmed on Gujrat development was not shown that in which angle Gujrat development happening under CM Modi as in field of education , industrial and human resources and infrastructures and there had not any comparison with other states of India or province of foreign counties like comparison with Shanghai, Hong Kong, etc. Due to High light Modi become CM to PM as acting mass media as agent of Modi.

The above matter indicated that get money and advertisement system implement by mass media in India.

Basic requirement of establish clean, hygienic, progressive and develop India:

1. Wasteland use and development for housing complexes by municipality or corporation in city area.

2. ETP plants for drainage water treatment to establish that should drainage water not to enter directly to river.

3. Drainage waste, solid waste treatment plant required to include in projects.

4. Maximum cities and town ship have not any proper drainage system hence there require proper drainage system as passage there should be under ground or open drainage system in proper link.

E.g. at Ratlam and Bhopal City have not proper drainage system and remain lot of waste lands.

5. Industrial independency required to establish through innovation and upgrading and encouragement system by bodies of central government by which Economy drain out to stope as FDI, licensing and import of technology system continuously drain our economy and hence break down our infrastructure of country.

6. Centralize village system requires by which electricity, drinking water supply should provide by government. 7. Agriculture, and farming educational institution at ground level at Villages require to establish by government by which pesticide, herbicide using, genetical better plant cultivation system development to be properly use at village by which pesticide and herbicide effect should not create health problem to common peoples. Now a day's European union banned the import Vegetable and fruits from India due high level of pesticides used by farmer basically at Gujrat as Hapush mango cultivated at Gujrat only.

8. Toilets Bathroom programmed in chief rate at village society and encouragement requirement.

9. Vacuum Cleaner cum crasher require to using by Municipality or corporation than waste treatment plant requirement become essential. Static Dust bin and Mobile Dust bin in two categories like Biodegradable and non-biodegradable required to establish.

10. Horticulture education required to urban localities and encouragement. Horticultural Institutions require to establish.

11. Proper Marketing of Vegetable, Garments and food cum general Retailers, Educational institutions and hospital organization system require to establish on the base of populations of locality

Persians Peoples comparison with Jews (Yehudi):

Persian left Paras the present name Iran due to invaded of Islamic rule by Calipha ruled and they entered to India and other countries mainly as the Jews left West Arabian land Jerusalem to Different European Countries but Parisians have not any mentality to create independent Paras Land where as Jews create Israel. In India Irani, Turani, Tata, Bhaba, Shah they are all Persian whom some bodies mixed with Hindu culture but they are more Hindu conservation now a days who have not any knowledge of their own origin. e.g. Smite Irani and Amit Shah are some example whom have not knowledge that why they have such titles. **Indian Culture as Mixed Culture from Ancient Periods:**

1. Mongolian culture enter to India at primitive Himalayan age as Chines origin Hun, Shak community center in Indian field. In Indian History Gautam Buddha and ruler of larger are Samrat Kanishka were Shak community. Mongolian culture enters and Chines dresses and dices enter at ancient period.

2. Aryan Entered from Central Asia from Hindu Kush mainly and system of central Asia enter to India.

3. Greek Entered at Nanda vansha Ruling period as Alexander invaded and Salocus remain Greek ruler in India.

4. Samrat Ashoka was the grand child of Chandra Gupta Marjah who marriage with Salocus's Daughter and enter Greek culture to his family. Hence the works of Samrat Ashoka were seen as Greek sculpture as idol of Gautam Buddha and stupa sculpture.

5. Pathan ruled as Islamic culture enter to India before 1200 years ago and Islamic culture as use rose and Islamic dresses as used Kurta-pajama by meal person and Kurta-sallower used by female culture started.

6. Mogul Ruled started before 650 year ago and Mogul dices and dresses used by us today also.

7. British Culture, languages, dresses and food dice enter at British ruled in India

Independent movement was done against British ruled. Hence European culture and pro-British mentality created by Indian leaders to make favor Indian toward them but today that is useless as different cultures, dresses and food dices enter in Indian field from long ago and make India as Mixed cultures. After Independent Russian, American, Japan, Chines cultures, Dresses and food dice enter as Indian Government make closer to those countries by make bilateral relation developments and mixed cultured made to developed India but now a days some political parties obstructed developed India as to they have interested to capture power by policy and said foreign culture enter to Indian culture but they try to push bake India to Thousands years ago where as they and their family use the system of foreign cultured and getting education either in English medium or at foreign countries and used Allopathy medicine in their daily life but advice to common peoples to used Ayurveda medicine and vernacular language as educational medium as their aim to that their children to be remain as upper level and officers grades and they should remain opportunity to do job at foreign countries also as they used English medium schooling system only. Actually Yoga, Suja Pranam, Namaj Ada Karna and Christen Payer at Church all are Exercise with mental controlling system which were developed by society at different places as social system is manmade. As well as Food habit of human is omnivorous system and as per availability food habit developed. The culture of human has differentiated as per geographical climate mainly and global integrity developed as feel we are all human being and hence make India as an example that where mixed culture remains and unity in diversity formed as humanity give most priority.

Cause of European system Spade up:

Ancient European God, goddess and dresses were having so much similarity with Persian and Indian system as human consider seven days as seven planets defined where Sun and Moon also consider as a Planets but Earth was not considered as planet as it considers as flat. Sun (Ravi), Moon (Soma) remain the same consideration days in Indian and European system. Other days in a week consider in India as Mangal(Mars), Budh (Mercury) Guru / Bahashpati (Jupiter), Sukro (Venus) and Sani (Saturn) the name of planets as ancient system consideration in India as well as at European system Tuesday as consider on Turas god, Wednesday consider on Wedding god(Kam Dave), Thus Day consider on Thunder god (Indra Dave) Fri Day consider on Fire God (Agni Dave) Saturday consider on Saturn God (Sani Dave) . It is clear that God and Goddess was same as in European system and in India but Social system change as per Science and Technology inventions and discover and Industrial developments. If we ancient period consider than seen the same case that dresses of European countries, Arabian countries remain same as when cotton and woolen cloth invented as to covered with binding like same as Indian. But due to cold climatic condition the food and salter were survived difficulty at European countries. Shirts, Pant, Coat, Rain Coat and other development done for easy to lead life and survived life to food and salter as Basic need.

The European system are not only spade up at all Ex colonial Countries as different European countries ruled sometimes but also the China, Korea, Japan and other countries which were not remain under ruled of any European countries those countries also flowed the system and culture and dresses as Industrial development and revolutions done at European countries and basic Science, technological, medicinal, system development and Managerial protocol system given by mainly UK, USA, France, German only which Spade up All over world and hence maximum theories , Normal culture of Industrial parts and body and system name are European languages. After all computer invent to UK and system of Computer developed at USA and Automation and information revolutions spade up in English mainly.

Japan, China, Korea and some other countries adopted English language and European culture to Import Technologies and development done and Export to other countries and use English as International Language for Self-Reliance's and development international trade and business where newly developed Industrial locality. Not only they adopted English languages but also adopted Dresses like Shirt, pants, T-shirts and other adopted to do works and operate vehicles, machineries are remaining easy and comfortable. But Some countries opposed the European culture and languages like Iraq, Syria and Western Asian countries and in Indian conservative Peoples who obstruct to developed their countries and hence their countries are not become self-reliance as they should not developed Educational system to progress to make country as self-reliance.

Indian conservative peoples are mainly BJP, RSS, Bajrang Dal, VHP and their allied groups who are smellier mentality peoples like as Alkayda, ISI, Taliban group as strong Conservative mentality but only have difference that Alkayda, ISI, Taliban group are more violation created.

Similarity among BJP- RSS and Taliban-Alkayda and another Conservative Islamic Group:

1. All are conservative group on the base of religious system

2. All are trying to push back society toward back about 3000 years.

3. All are fighting against liberal group of their own religious groups and give statements against other religious believes and cultural system.

4. All obstruct reformation of religious system and hence there have no mention about the religious reformer name and methodology as blind supporter the cultural system and dresses.

5. All try Capture power on the base of religious sentiment creation.

6. All try to convert other to Conservative groups as they all explains and demand all human being was remain same as IS and their allied group are saying all human was Islamic at primitive period and BJP and Allied groups are saying all human was Hindu at primitive period.

7. All restrict to Woman freedom and dresses and opposed to European culture and dress wear.

Difference among BJP and Allied Party with IS and another Conservative Islamic Group:

1. BJP and Allied groups are Hindu Conservative Groups and IS leaders and Allied groups are Islamic Conservative groups.

2. BJP and Allied groups are capture power by voting on the base of Hindu sentiment whereas by military operation and terrorist activity force to capture power.

3. BJP leaders and Allied groups create Hindu sentiment in political field but IS and allied groups create Islamic sentiment.

4. BJP leaders and Allied groups covert Islamic and Christen peoples to Hindu but IS and allied groups killed to other religious peoples.

5. Hindu Jahad declare by BJP leaders and Allied groups create Hindu sentiment but Islamic Jahad declared by IS and alliance groups create Islamic sentiment.

* North Indian Culture, Conservative system and Religious system force to implement all over India by BJP and Allied Parties:

1. Strong Hindu believed of North Indian system force to implement all over India.

2. Not take any Action to Santa Rampal as who implement Bali System who required to give death sentence as hang to death but Mr. Noranda Modi lead government have no ordinance applied as well Asharan Baba and his son Narayan Sai who are victim of rape case and Hindu religious faith demoralized they required to give death sentence as hang to death but Mr. Noranda Modi lead government have no ordinance applied to save Hindu society.

3. Lord Ram Mandir Issued make due to North Indian Worship mainly Lord Ram and Hanuman, hence some time they use banner of lord Ram also.

4. Shankaracharya Give statement on Multi marriage to start in Hindu religion system as Kulin system remain at previous period but Mr. Noranda Modi lead government have no ordinance applied to save Hindu society.

5. Hindu Maha Sava Activity increased at MP, Haryana and other BJP leading Governmental state and this organization supported child marriage and restriction system to women announcement done again and again but Mr. Noranda Modi lead government have no Ordinance applied to save Hindu society.

6. BJP and their allied parties should not support to Raja Rammohan Roy, Vidhya Sagar and other Hindu Social reformer which indicate that they are conservative and hence that want to started the system of Sati, Bali, child marriage, and other superstition system which were once up on a time remain in Hindu society in India.

Mr. Noranda Modi and BJP leading Government are careless about Human resources Development and Health Care:

1. Swine flu sped up in North and West Indian states like Madhya Pradesh, Gujrat, Chhattisgarh, Maharashtra, Haryana, UP, and Rajasthan where only UP is ruling state under SP Political party but other are ruling under BJP Government and day by day numbers of death case by Swine Flu increased but State governments as well as central government remain silent and not take any action. BAM's Candle on the entrances Examination of Medical field at MP state is another matter to health careless mater.

2. Madhya Pradesh, Gujrat, Chhattisgarh, Location operational death case increased day by day and ruling under BJP Government but State governments as well as central government remain silent and not take any action.

3. Educational stranded in Madhya Pradesh, Gujrat, Chhattisgarh, Haryana, UP, and Rajasthan where only UP is ruling state under SP Political party but other are ruling under BJP Governments

State governments as well as central government remain silent and not take any action. The Tata Nano company establish at Gujrat but Reman resources problem faces by company as technical persons and offices expert works were not found like as South Indian states and West Bengal here as Mr. Noranda Modi rule Gujrat State about 14 years but he was not care about Education and human resources development.

Mr. Noranda Modi Failure in Field of Gujrat state and National level Social works:

1. Gujrat was main Textile Industrial state and Ahmadabad called as Manchester of India but in his ruling, he unable to save sick textile industries in Gujrat and ultimately closed maximum textile industries which land used as housing complexes only.

2. Image of International politics disappointed as he and his allied peoples increasing national communal tension.

3. Maximum foreign industrialist, trade and Business men unwilling to invest in India as disappointed as he and his allied peoples increasing national communal tension. In the same ways Ex PM Mr. A. B. Bajpai ruled period not only Foreign invested but also NRI were not interested to invest in India as burning of Church of Christen burned as European and American countries as well as Australia and New Zeeland are Christen majority countries as well as Bill Grade, IBM, Coco Cola, Charlocks and other Industrialist all are Christian community peoples.

Activity of Mr. Noranda Modi leading government:

1. Criticizing to old leaders, PM, President and other and irrespective to them. Mr. Modi forget Constitution and infrastructure of democracy and unity in diversity developed under old leaders. Mr. Modi, he has as he become first P.M. in India and he have maximum knowledge than any of other whom remain previously as PM, Presidents.

2. Student union, e.g. Ambedkar Periyer Study Circle (APSC) ban for criticizing Mr. Modi as decision taken forwarded copies under Ms. Smithy Irani. As she compulsorily made audience of Mr. Modi to student primary to higher educational student Modi Government should not ban to RSS, VHP when their leader give religious controversial statement and He should not remove to MP and his ministers when they give controversial statement at parliament. Actually Mr. Modi and his ministries are ruling as dictatorship.

RSS is the base of Foreign flower organization:

1. RSS dresses are Khaki Half pant and White shirt and black shoes are foreign uniform which have not any communication with India. Indian purely dress up by Mr. M. Gandhi and Mr. Ishwar Chandra Vidhya Sagar.

2. RSS practice parade which also Foreign system but have not any Indian system to adopted by them. They insult Mahatma Gandhi and respect to Killer of Mahatma Gandhi. Mahatma Gandhi left every things of Foreign system in his life and wanted to developed by Indian system and agriculture whereas Mahatma Gandhi used to habit dress up Persian at his child hood and European dress up at his young hood but for freedom fighting in non-violence way he left his all habit to used foreign system and dress up and lead life as pure Indian.

Mr. Noranda Modi Misused the powers:

1. CBI used as remote control body like his Dall.

2. Only give Bharat Ratna to BJP First PM Mr. A. B. Bajpai and VHP founder as supported his group and satisfaction.

3. He interfere on Land adaptation and Labour laws in favor of his Supported industrial groups whom give donation to his political parties.

4. The Padma Bhusan, Padma Sree, Padma Bebhusan awards given to maximum BJP and Allied supporters.

Common Peoples and Students made Great Mistake to elects BJP leading Governments and harm to their own life:

1. Land ordinance become a capturing tool of land in chief rate from farmers and common peoples and favor to land Mafia and builders.

2. Casteism become strong in long time BJP ruling state. e. g. MP, Rajasthan, etc. states.

3. Pension system converted to NPS system by Mr. A.B. Bajpai BJP lead government where PF records are not Available and in the time of Daughters or Son marriage or at emergency of self-problem should not have option to take money and Mr. Noranda Modi make 10 percent interest base PF loan where common peoples of government servant future crash by the system.

4. Mr. A.B. Bajpai BJP lead government stop recruitment two years and Mr. Narandra Modi stop one year's recruitment and even today have not any circular to start to recruitment at Government sectors to crash future of students. 5. Day by Days Petroleum and common commodities rate increasing continuously as ' Manghai Dayan Khay Jaraha Hai'.

6. The dream and promise given by Mr. Modi, Ms. Sushma Saraj, Mr. Rajnath Singh, Mr. Amit Shah has become flesh statement to all and depresses common peoples where land rate and other increasing as Thakader market become better.

* Indian Hindu Cultures:

<u>North Indian:</u> Hindi become common language and only 9 states of Hindi peoples have same type of culture and worship to same god. They worship to Lord Ram and lord Hanuman mainly. But lord Ganesh, Sree Krishna, Kali Mata, Sara Bali Dave (Amma Mata have Four Hand) and Vishnu Dave, Laxmi Dave and Sarasvati Dave with four hand also worship as Household festival. Several temples of Lord Siva, Lord Sani and Sara Bali establish

where worship done commonly. Goddess Sara Bali Temples Gerba Dances done at Night.

Some north Indian Rivers worship and Arti (Oil or Camphor lamp used to lighten near River banks) done by peoples and Basically Ganga, Shipra, Narmada Rivers worship by Hindu peoples. They also worship to Plants as Pippul, Klapa Bhekha, Amla trees and Tulsi herb, etc. They worship to cow and they give grass to cow to believe get Purnna (Heavenly Proudness)

Basically, use to read Gita, Hindi Ramyan, Hanuman Chalisha, etc. It is habituated to Ramlila, Krishaliala as Drama. Kalash Jatra (Water pot Procession), Jhaki (Prophet procession) and Bhajan (Holi song) etc. done mainly.

Chat Puja (Sun Believe as Goddess) by the Bihar peoples and that spread up continuously.

Rivers Ganga, Narmada and Shipra worship done by them.

Blood relation marriage prohibited and they are more conservative peoples.

South Indian: Davidian Languages, Merogon (lord Kartika), Vinayaka (lord Ganesh) worship mainly, Amman Devi, Ada Devi (Sarasvati four hands) and Aydha Dave worship done also River Godoberi and Krishna worship by them.

East Indian: Sanskrit Diverted language, lord Vishnu main god worship as Satyanarayana, lord Siva, Goddess Durga (Ten hands), Sarasvati and Laxmi (Two Hans) and lord Sree Krishna also worship done by them. Rivers Damodaran worship as God and River Ganga worship as goddess in West Bengal but at North Frontier States Brahmaputra worship by them.

West India: Sanskrit Diverted language, Lord Siva and lord Ganesh mainly worship done. Mumba Devi and A Cock Devi also worship done. called Ramakrishna Mission whom worship to Goddess Kali, and the Guru Ramakrishna where as Probhupat group are call ISCON Whom worship to Sree Krishna, Guranga and the Guru Probhupat.

Primitive Hindu groups as per worship:

1. Vaishnab who worship to Lord Vishnu: This group remained Pour vegetarian and Sila Narayan as symbol of Sun and lord Vishnu and Apathies as Hari, and Satya Narayan, etc. worship

Later this groups started worship to apathies as Narasimha, Varaha, Bhaman, Sree Ram and Sree Krishna as Vishnu. They were Vegetarian.

2. Sivo who worship to lord Siva: This group worship to Siva Linga as Sun, Moon and Planets Symbol and hence Siva Linga called as Jatir(Light Resources) Linga, Sayanbhu, Mangal(Mars) Nath, Som(Moon)Nath, etc. Later worship to Lord Siva apathies of Lord siva as Bhishanath, Bhambal, Tarak Nath, etc. They were vegetarian.

3. Shakta who worship Sun as female and later worship to goddess Kati and other Goddess as Amman, Amma, Adiparasakti, Addasakthi, etc. and Bali (Offer animal to cut it hen and blood flows on the land of hole place) of animal than the meat eats by them. They were non-Vegetarian and ferocious group and at about 2500 years ago their influences become maximum. After all Started reformation of Hindu

Base of Hindu Religious books:

1. Rig Veda the oldest system of religious system mainly Sadhu, Sanyasi Rishi all mean Monk are use to habit to worship, Meditation and payers done with Yoga and mantra.

2. Sam Bad which are first reformatted system which system adopted by common peoples in marriage, Death Body destructions etc.

Primitive Hindu Social system:

1. Women's Freedom e.g. Kaikai at Ramayana and Ulupi at Mahabharat war field fought against enemies.

2. Multi marriage system remain: Sree Krishna marriage with Ten king's daughters. Daughter of Sukracherja the Ashur Guru marriage with two husbands. Kunti at Mahabharat marriage with five brothers.

3. Widow marriage system remained **Hindu Reformation at British ruled and Hindu reformers**:

1. Sati system (murder of widow), Balbibhao (Child marriage), etc. abolish by British Government of India on support Raja Rammohan Roy

2. Widow Marriage start by British Government of India on support Ishwar Chandra Vidyasagar.

3. Ganga Ma Santan Bisharjan (Scarifies child to River Ganga) Abolish by British Government of India.

4. Mr. Bethune a Scottish person started Women's education in India under Ruled.

Human Resources upgraded under Congress ruled:

1. Educated persons make small family programmed as per economical capability as they want established new generation and to led life better than them.

2. Numbers of Engineers, Physicians, Professors, etc. increased.

3. Women's entry at Every field and even in police, military, engineering medical, Pilots, etc. women have a special entry and reservation to upgrade women.

Required Government system:

1. Corporate Government Administrative system and

2. Liberal Social system Development

3. Multi River Project Development

4. Multi Economical Project Development

5. Self-Reliance Industrial Development

Suitability to Elect Member of Parliament for National Development and Progress:

If anybody consider Unity of diversity, democracy stability, secularism, liberalization and progress of India than consider the following matter as-

1. Regional parties are neither become a majority parties as they are decentralizing groups whom only consideration their state matter only. These parties should not able to formed central government and hence these parties support to any larger party and get advantage from larger parties. Now a day's common peoples of India give priority to Regionalism and should not consider nationality, diversity in unity, secularism hence they selected political parties who should not make stability to make central government and therefore about two-decade coalition government formed at central which become poor in strength.

2. Religious conservative parties supporter remain the blind supported and hence religious conservative leaders created sentiment of religious mater as issue of voting and capture power but there create conflict and which turn to riot also or collisions happen between/ among religious groups /community. Therefore, communal harmony disturbing by their activities. Hence national development and progress obstructed by the system. If BJP and Allied group come into power Hindu supersession believer become strong than Sati, Bali and other system also use by somewhere as well as Church burning, Islam-Hindu riots held on somewhere or high conflict social environment established by them where foreign Investment groups also mentally not agree to invest money for business purpose. Islamic conservative group only give priority to them only.

3. Post Janata Dals become as like regional parties as they remain in some state only in north India mainly. These parties are splitting and remain in different states which neither may become majority group as these parties' leaders try to third front but remain

unsuccessful. Now a day's common peoples of India give priority to Regionalism and should not consider nationality, diversity in unity, secularism hence they selected political parties who should not make stability to make central government and therefore about two-decade coalition government formed at central which become poor in strength.

4. Communist parties should not make influence as in India not Industrial Revolutions executed and Not proper class formation happened. As around the world different communist countries as USSR, Yugoslavia, Czechoslovakia, Poland communism defatted by democratic parties and there after USSR split into 16 independent countries and conflict created among each other, Yugoslavia spilled into five independent countries, Czechoslovakia spilled into two independent countries.

5. Cast base political parties remain only in North India as North Indian mainly Hindi speaking peoples are mentally conservative mind. Schedule Cast, Schedule Tribes and Other Backward Class group of peoples support to these political parties and due to north India Hindu peoples are more conservative mentality therefore such type of political parties executed which have not any national interest as a whole.

The Future of Indian Political flows:

If the issue of different political parties remain regional, religious and language peoples as to force to implement Hindi for voting purpose to support of North Indian as 224 Hindi Member of Parliaments numbers, etc. than the future of India will enter to dark and broken the unity in diversity system and then as per language, religions and regions India will divided into parts as like as USSR, Czechoslovakia, Yugoslavia and other countries. There will possibility to divide into 21 parts as per language base or 5 parts as per religious base and other possibility as 4 divisions if non-Hindi states remain united.

The effect of BJP leading and allied parties to pressurized North Indian Hindu culture may divided country as-

1. Punjab may demand separate independent country as a Sheikh majority state.

2. Sikkim may demand separate independent country as a Buddhist majority state and participate in India at 1971 but before remain Independent country under monarchy.

3. South Indian culture are separate than north Indian culture and maximum time period in history remain independent country where Rajendra Chola, Pulakashi-II remain powerful King than they may demand separate independent country as Davidian majority states.

4. East Frontier parts culture are different from North Indian than they may formed as separate country as in history Sasanko, Dharam Pal and Ahom group of rulers remain Stronger ruler in Eastern Frontier region and separator culture of same type formed.

5. Kashmir may demand separate independent country as Islamic majority state.

6. Nagaland may demand separate independent country as a Christen majority state and they also demanding separator country.

If such situation come in near future than Mr. Noranda Modi (Prime Minister) and Mr. Rajnath Singh (Home Minister) remain most responsible person whom should not control Mr. Shakhy Maharaj, Mr. Yogi and other VHP, RSS, leaders' statements.

The effect of BJP leading and allied parties to pressurized to implement Hindi to Non-Hindi state and all office of central government than have possibilities may divided country as-

1. Independent Kashmir as national and official languages will be Urdu.

2. Independent Punjab as National and official languages will be Panjabi.

3. Independent Hindustan as National and official languages will be Hindi

4. Independent Liberal United Republic Bharat with official language English at central state official Department and language to be state recognized languages as per state language. Required to World Human strategies:

1. Unity in Diversity.

2. Liberal mentality.

3. Secular (worldly) feeling.

4. Global Citizen feeling

5. Humanity give maximum priority.

First, we have to consider that we are the member of earth and if world execute than we remain alive. Human divided into groups as per social system, culture, economic status, technological advancement, etc. which is man mad and on the other hand human divided as per height, skin colours (Black, White, Yellow, and brown) which are mutational genetical characteristic of evolution of human being as natural matter. Therefore, the world human community become diversified but some peoples remain conservative as they should not try to understand for their selfishness and world social environment of a country or countries make saluted as social various effect by brain wash by religious, social and cultural sentiment. The various may be triable / violence / general which are push back society around world whom have not any progressive contribution in the field of science and technology. BJP and Allied groups are same type of conservative but they are not triable as like as Is and their leaders. We required to save humanity and world community from such groups and should not support to such group which harm to human around world. Mr. Barak Hasan Obama the USA president is the right person who made formality with Mr. Noranda Modi when Mr. Modi visit USA and when He visit India but should not support to him.

Formulate of India developments in Economical and Industrial field:

1. Material technology upgrading by resource works and department to established.

2. Invention and innovation department for Industrial upgrading should require to establish

3. Computer, Robot, Electronics goods like Laptop, Tablets, Mobil phone manufacturing unit should do under Government organization as when privet organization were not interested to education institution than Late Jahar Lal Nehru kept Education under Government hand and Export to other under develop countries and Export to other under develop countries.

3. Hybrid Technology, Integrated Technology and Flexible technology manufacturing unit should do under Government organization and Export to other under develop countries.

4. Agricultural harvesting technology, Medical technology, Aeronautical technology Environmental controlling technology manufacturing unit should do under Government organization and Export to other under develop countries.

5. Missile, Glider Bomb and weapon manufacturing unit should do under Government organization and Export to other under develop countries.

Encourage Required to start for Human Resource development:

1. Agricultural technology, Medical technology, Medicine Manufacturing Engineering, Computer and electronics good manufacturing Engineering, etc. courses will be required to start.

2. Integrated technology, Hybrid Technology, Flexible technology, Charter Engineering, Megastructure Engineering, Industrial Diagnoses technology etc. courses will be required to start.

3. Public Administration and system development; social and religious system development etc. courses will be required to start.

4. Integrated Medicine, Medical Diagnoses technology, etc. courses will be required to start.

5. Integrated Accountancy, Global Business, etc. courses will be required to start.

6. Environment control technology and Digested control technology etc. courses will be required to start.

7. Civil Roadways transportation technology, Railways transport technology and Civil Aviation Transport technology, etc. courses will be required to start.

8. Integrated farming, Multi Farming research methodology, etc. courses will be required to start.

9. Multi Constructional Technology, High tech Building construction Engineering, etc. courses will be required to start.

Corporate Administration requirement for Development of National Development:

1. The Country required to sub cell at Zone: North, South, East and West as per similarity of language to avoiding partiality with other than Hindi to recruitment at Administrative posts:

North Corporate: Punjab, J & K, Haryana, Himachal Pradesh, UP, Uttaranchal, Bihar, Union Territories New Delhi and Chandigarh.

South Corporate: Tamil Nadu, Andhra Pradesh, Telangana, Karnataka, Kerala, Orissa, Union Territories Pondicherry and Lakshadweep

Eastern Corporate: Assam, Manipur, Tripura, Nagaland, Mizoram, Meghalaya, Sikkim, West Bengal and Union Territories Andaman and Nicobar.

Western Corporate: Goa, Karnataka, Rajasthan, MP, Chhattisgarh, Jharkhand and union territories Damon and due; Dadar and Nagar Habile.

Language option:

Northern Corporate: Hindi, Urdu, Panjabi, Kashmiri, Dhongre.

Southern Corporate: Tamil, Telegu, Malayalam, Kennedi, Oria.

Eastern Corporate: Assamese, Bengali, Nepali, Mizo, Manipuri, Brodro.

Western Corporate: Marathi, Gujrati, Hindi, Konkani, Santhal.

Promotional Departments: Officers should Corporate Promotional system through by Examination and interview. Direct and on promotional officers ranking to submerged

Corporate system Ruled: Governor General who requite Governor and CM of Zone and Joint comity of State to establish where Different state CM meeting Selection to be held on for discussion. Governor General and Central Government Joint Comity to establish which home affair to maintain.

Recruitment to be done as IAS, IFS, IPS, IRS, IMA etc. and Staff Selection under Corporate Public Services Corporation.

Commission Recruitment to Establish by:

1. West Land Utilization Commission

2. Environment Control and Digester Control Commission

3. Educational and Self-Help Commission

4. Industrial Innovation Commission

5. Science Expedition Commission

TV Channel Require to Establish

1. Science and Technology

2. Society and Development

3. Industries and Transportation

4. Biology and Heath Care

Mr. Noranda Modi Characteristic comparison with Tea Stall Owner:

1. Capture Vacant land and first tent establish than started tea stall as the same way Jami Adhigrahan system establish.

2. A tea stall owner kept a servant by whom tea stall works and home works done from morning to night as like as his statement labour laws try to establishing.

3. Somewhere tea stall owner thought servants are slave and physical torture also done and basically use to habit to kept child labour, in the same ways Mr. Modi have no project on child labour.

4. He should hide his personal life and his marriage life that what were profession before he remained as CM of Gujrat. Tea stall owner also suddenly make stall on road side and starting tea stall for common peoples.

5. Confusing and diverted the mind to other path to forget basic need of peoples where consuming goods cost increasing, petroleum rate increasing from Rs. 62 /- to 73/- and land cost have not any MRP which are not available without agents as housing board make an inert body. At tea stall cheating and time pass discussion done at tea stall that tea may seal more and more.

BJP Leading Government always remain anti Common Peoples Policies:

1. A. B. Bajpai Government:

(i) New Pension Scheme (NPS): there have not any option to get money from Provident fund as the NPS pension remain in shear market which total should not show in pay bill that how much money deposited in fund. There have two option as phase- I which have to be every month cutting and another Phase-II which is like as VPF as extra money cutting which have only option to get return.

If any purpose like marriage of daughter of a Railway employee required money but on hand have not such amount of money than high interest loan require to get from any one or get loan from bank that indicate the Mahajan system should start in near future.

There has option as to get double money from fund but only 60 % will get at retirement and 40 % will remain in fund which interest will paid as pension. Then only approximated deposited will be in hand at retirement life. Whereas in old pension scheme there had double money as added gratuity, some percent of pension money to seal and get large amount, whole life family pension.

(ii) Maximum public property shear seal to privet organization as Gazette rank abolish from Bank, LIC, Airport and other.

2. Noranda Modi Government:

(i) 33 years retirement or 60 years which remain first:

(a) So many employees get loan on the base of retirement time than if suddenly retirement happen at 33 years base than he should be helpless as all amount money of PF to be paid for loan and empty hand remain after retirement. The life program to be change and who deposited money as LIS that premium to be pending and disturb the life.

(b) Suddenly large number of employee's retirement make skilled worker shortage and working standard disturb by the system.

As new employment recruitment will not to be done immediately and skill works will not be available in organization.

(ii) Labor laws interfere: it is totally any works programmed where only owner favor by the government.

(iii) Land Bill is anti-farmer program selected by the government.

(iv) Millions of money expense for travel and tour by Mr. Noranda Modi by the name that he wants to FDI by foreign companies to make India whereas infrastructure of India is not wanting to developed by which innovation to upgrading to be done at India and industrial development to be done. FDI were opposed by he and his party members previously where they remain in opposition than how he tries to do this that he always tells lie in every step of his movement. When India government have less money in fund as he was explained than millions of moneys for programmed of foreign traveling done by him which have not any result.

*Poor Administrative power lead by Non-Congress Parties Governments:

1. Mr. Morarji Dasia Janata Dal Government:

a. No Economical and financial proper guide and projects remain under him.

b. No industrial and communicational developments projects remain.

c. Mr. Morarji Dasia should not Completed by him and later Mr. Charan Singh became Prime Minister.

2. Mr. V. P. Singh Janata Dal Government:

a. Economical system try to developed socialistic system but fail quickly.

b. Mr. Davilal became Deputy Prime Minister.

c. Unstable government formed due to inter coalitions among Janata Dal members and Government fall down intermediate time and later Mr. Chandrashakher become Prime Minister but Midterm polling happened immediately.

3. Mr. Davagoura Janata Dal Government:

a. Not lasting 5 years and intermediate polling happened.

b. Intermediate Prime Minister Mr. I. K. Gujral Made due to Instability of Government.

c. Janata Dal Broken into Different Political parties as RJD, BJD, JDSP, etc.

4. Mr. Atal Bihari Bajpai lead Bharatia Janata Party:

a. Kargil War happened due to mismanagement of Government as Military left from upper hill at winter season which were not done any time and in the meantime Pakistan Military capture the Kargil Hill area and the country force to involved war due to miss administrative power.

b. IC 814 Air Lines Aeroplan High-jack by terrorist and land at Amraitswer but Minister was to take any Action at Amritswer Airport but sand CRP as special team from New Delhi and flight flew away from Amrits8w9er to Lahore and then Abu Dhabi and later to Kabul. Due to miss administrations chances at Amritswer miss and later Masood, the terrorist's leader with his group left by Mr. A. B. Bajpai Government to safe passengers of high-jack Aeroplan.

c. Privatized maximum Public Autonomous organizations and seal government property in chief rate.

d. The recruitment of public organizations stops by two years off favor to new generation and students.

e. New pension system (NPS) system started to Public organizations off favor of common peoples and Pension to MLA and MPs started in favor of political persons.

f. Coffin scandal a lowest level mater happened to assassinated soldier motel mater.

g. Deputy Prime Minister recruited to Mr. L.K. Advani as poor Administrative symbol whereas per parliament system Deputy Prime Minister post have no options.

h. Parliament House Attracted by Terrorist Group which indicated poor security of New Delhi under his ministry.

i. Narmada projects as half cannel and half pipe lines system to water supply from Narmada to Shipra River a Vogues system where money expanses more but only single purposes serving by the projects. It was taken as the Madhya Pradesh ruling under BJP lead Government but there were not another river projects by his Ministry.

5. Mr. Narendra Modi BJP Lead Government:

a. Miss Guide to Common Peoples -

(i) Clean India : Clean by Groom as an acting by BJP leaders and allied personality but have no any guide line and any project to clean city and village by establish proper drainage system development and sweeping by machineries under Municipalities and Village board and have not any team to establish to protects pollutions and crash the waste materials and recycles those.

(ii) Make India: Foreign companies call to investment and only make rubber stamp as make in India but have not any proper innovative and upgrading projects to make self-technological base industries and have no educational development programmed that at Universities level innovations and up gradations to done by which technological and economically county will become self-reliance. (iii) Adopted Village: It is the policies to restated Land Lord system by His ministry as give power to rich and factory owner and MPs whose next generations should demand that their old generations expenses money for Village establishment and get authority from government and will become land lord as old system started.

(iv) Break the protocol miss guide to common peoples that actually he disobeys the basic rules and regulation of society and administration system and supreme personality as his habit

b. Priority to Give self-importance rather than National interests:

(i) Sub PMO offices established at Gandhi Nagar and Varanasi as He is Gujrati and Gujrat Capital is Gandhi Nagar as well as His Constituency are also Varanasi.

(ii) Make lager Cabinet ministry to satisfy to his allied personality and 66 cabinet ministers recruited.

(iii) Give priority to NRI rather than common peoples who lead life to Indian land.

c. U-Turn Done which Promise to Common peoples to Do:

(i) 370 Act Abolish issues remain silent

(ii) No action taken against Pakistan to violet LOC

(iii) No Black Money Return to India from Foreign Countries.

d. Common people's mentality Diversion done:

(i) Speech giver as Hindu women required to give birth four children by his MP and Allied Political parties members but not take any action.

(ii) Religious Tension created by Ghar Baposhi system started and controversial statement given by RSS, VHP and other parties members.

(ii) High money expenses to invited Diplomates at Shapth Grahan/ Promising meeting

e. Apply Rules To forget Promised at Voting:

(i) After 3 days a family forget event mater or death case.

(ii) After 3-month common peoples forget a locality events matter and come too busy to their self-works.

f. Miss Management of Administration:

(i) Adhadesh/ ordinance Implement by which break the Democratic system.

(ii) Citizenship Electronic Card system have not any programmed but Aadhar Card implement in every field.

Future of Nation at Influence of BJP and It allied Group leading groups:

1. Communal harmony break and riot may form

2. Superstitions system increased and Sati system, Bali system, Santan Bisherjan, etc. will increased and Hindu society enter to Burk black age. e.g. A Sati case came at Rajasthan at Mr. A. B. Bajpai period, Bali case by Ram Pal at Haryana and Asharan Bapu and his son Narayan Sai rape case come at Mr. Noranda Modi period.

3. Strong Casteism may implement and SC, ST, OBC reservation system to be abolish than even restriction to learn and get education may implement as like Islamic period.

Cheating character of Selfish Self-Centered Noranda Modi Personality:

1. For self-rules remain difference and for other rules executed something restriction implementation
2. Tax for politician and allied business personality Exide by Narendra Modi
3. Age limit consideration to political candidate for other restricted that not to ne above 70 years. But he himself cross 70 years no command.

The Capital Come under Bourgeois Ruling:

1. Duel ruling executing in India First Ruler become Bourgeois peoples as Ambani and Adani become land Lord of India
2. Agent Rulers Modi Shah making common peoples too fool by sentiments speech and hand over national properties to Ambani and Adani as pack to expanses money to voting.
3. RSS, Bajrang Dal, Hindu Mahasava, Vish Hindu partisan Durga Bahini Etc. Form as motivated common peoples by sentiment.
4. Spiritual Business organization and leaders like Asharam Bapu, Ram Rahil who executing fraud organization and making different illegal business behind religious sentiment

to executing programmed that those making alliance to getting help to setting vote.

5. Bourgeois capitalist Ambani Adani using monetary fund to Narendra Modi to taking power in their hand to formed hack government. Now as agent of Ambani Adani Anti- Farmer laws, Anti Labour laws implement by ordinance implementation and Loan section to Ambani Adani to hand over National organization and monetary fund one after another thereafter Tax relief, Loan Relief with interest as Anti-nationalist.

6. Foreign Investment and Making India propaganda spread up to making fool to common peoples by collaboration with Ambani Adani to showing Global Investment Summit as Froud Programmed where picnic arranged to eating foods together with Ambani Adani and BJP RSS leaders.

7. Tax implement to every steps of common peoples and several new system Note Restriction to making black money of Ambani Adani to White conversion and common peoples enforces to troublesome. Some difficult system enforcement to common peoples by which they to be unable to realize the reality to understand what they having to done.

8. It Cell establish to advertisement and propaganda spread up through misguided and misinformation and agent News media and anchors used to by rant to spread up propaganda as common peoples should not understand reality of their policy to depress common peoples and step up his friend Ambani Adani to making richest around world by cheating with nation and society. Hence Ambani Adani come to top list of Richest people has become Ballooner and Agent Anchor become millionerd. Opposition leaders who are competitors participating with Narendra Modi becoming millionerd as commission taken to support Narendra Modi to breaking hart to Voter. Democracy system cum under risk by cheating as Self Center and selfish mentality to adopt policy to destroying nation and society to self-life enjoyment and entertainment like most royal family

members of the world. Billions of nation monetary fund use for self-entertainment and enjoyment to fulfill life willingness.

Monopoly of Political Business

Monopoly of Political business is actually ways to killing democracy by mythical or conservative system to sentiment creation through Spiritual organization and when power come to hand then News agency, defaces force with intelligent groups paralyzing by capturing employee of lower category to given promotion by overtaking senior and given monetary benefited by cheating and opposition lower leaders who remain competitor captured by monetary benefited given. Narendra Modi is such personality who create fare that India becoming Muslim nation under Congress hand and greediness offer to given peoples to tap that in cheap rate given petroleum products and lowering rate of essential commodities to making fool to common peoples. Narendra Modi actually agent of Capitalist group of business holder who wanting capture national property and financial fund by cheating with help of black hand by a leadership and hence helping to Narendra Modi by given commission to added and offer to use personal Aeroplan and helicopter to operating matting and rally. Several dummy Narendra Modi created by makeup and set up to spread up influences. News agent buy and propaganda spread up. Information Act advantage taken and through agent fraud case artificially build up to make propaganda that congress destroying nation and after getting power enforcement Director form by his agent employee to depress opposition and arrested by planning and if taken entry to become his groups and become Member of RSS and BJP then case diluted and given relief. In the same ways his friend who financially help to election that Ambani Adani groups given loan by recommendation and some getting commission to Party fund and some money invest to transfer name of national organization then Loan relief with interest and tax relief done that making cheating with nation and society as active anti- nationalist.

Policy to making Slave by restriction of Freedom and right in Life:

1. As a social enemy BJP and RSS restriction implement to feudal system Each and every field implement taxation in higher rate
2. To capture land and property from common peoples target to implement NRC system as NPS system implement by A. B. Bajpai to make unsecure retied life of common peoples who given service to nation about 30 years but pension system implements to MLA, MP, and politician if and only if attend one day in Local Assembly and parliament.

Required Government system:

1. Social Corporate Government Administrative system and
2. Liberal Social system Development
3. Multi River Project Development
4. Multi Economical Project Development
5. Self-Reliance Industrial Development

Commission Recruitment to Establish by:

1. West Land Utilization Commission
2. Environment Control and Digester Control Commission
3. Educational and Self-Help Commission
4. Industrial Innovation Commission
5. Science Expedition Commission

TV Channel Require to Establish

1. Science and Technology
2. Society and Development
3. Industries and Transportation
4. Biology and Heath Care

Required to World Human strategies:

1. Unity in Diversity.
2. Liberal mentality.
3. Secular (worldly) feeling.
4. Global Citizen feeling
5. Humanity give maximum priority.

Over All Congress Ruling contribution as British left India as minor developed stage:

1. Railways converted meter gauge to brad gauge.
2. defiance system development done.
3. Irrigation system development
4. Information System development
5. Educational system development.
6. Governmental Hospital development
7. Metro Railways development in different cities.
8. 3rd AC pass provided to Group D and C staffs in Railways.

9 Ganga Action plant and ETP plant on Factories started to control pollution and clean India.

10. Land lord and Estate system abolish to give power to common peoples.

11. Rajdhani and Shatabdi Express stated to speed up connection central capital to other state capital and states capital to state capital.

12. IIT and IIM Institutions establish for Engineering and technical man power developments. 13. Postal Department economical condition developed by establishing Banking system as MIS, Requiring system development.

14. National High ways and Four Lens Road system developed and State Capital to Capital communication and transportation system developed.

15. Pension system started by Congress Government and bonus system started in favor of Labours and employees of public sectors.

* The condition to Left India by British Rulers:

1. Minimum Broad gauge and maximum Meter gauge railways available and mainly port city.

2. British executed direct ruled and indirect rules under estate of land lords in different parts on India which were off position to executed proper democracy.

3. Minimum land line of telephone system remain around India. Poor Communication system remain around India.

4. Part of India as Kashmir, Hyderabad remain independent Estates and Goa, Damon Due remain under ruled of Portugal and Pondicherry remain under ruled of France.

5. Undeveloped Irrigation and Agriculture system remain around India.

6. Educational Institutions remain minimum in Number. Only Roorkee was remain Engineering college and there had minimum Technical schools also.

7. Minimum Medical college and hospitals remain. Hospital remain under privet organization.

8. Only National Highway Grant Tank Road remain which Connected Calcutta to Peshawar.

9. In several place Railways was not connected properly. e.g. In Malda to Murshidabad was required travel by boat to crossing Ganga River.

** Insult to Nation, Nationality and National leaders by P.M. Noranda Modi:

1. In a top most responsible post person as national representative as Prime Minister he is always use the name of country as Hindustan as irrespective Nation where as India defined as Bharat /India as secular country in constitution. Hindustan was not accepting by the parliament and constitution as in this nation have

Sheikh, Jain, Islamic, Buddhist, Christian, Persian communities also even Hindu remain majority because Kashmir and Telangana are Islamic majority, Nagaland is Christian majority, Punjab is Sheikh majority and U.P. and Kerala are about 40% Islamic community. As a Prim Minister, name of nation and nationality should use properly as per constitution only but he not only he disobeys the nation but also disobey the constitution.

2. He insult Subash Chandra Bose as he is not declared as death but wanted to give Bharat Ratna Award as death. If he really interested to respect Mr. Subash Chandra Bose than as Subash Chandra Bose International Award to be stated for political and social worker under Government of India.

3. He insult the retired president Late Dr. Sarvopalli Radha Krishnan as His Birth Day 5th September celebrate as teacher day to encourage education in India but he declared as Guru Dibash and give speech on his life only.

4. He irrespective to assassinate Mr. M. Gandhi who called as father of nation but the his birth day 2nd October is not celebrated as national hole day but clean India day as clean by groom as photographic identity.

5. He irrespective to Assassinate Indira Gandhi Death Anniversary as he not offers garland to his memorial which is a duty of a Prim Minister to give respect to another late prime Minister.

6. He irrespective Mr. Jahar Lal Nehru Birth day 14th November as children celebrate Children day but he not encourages to any children to love other.

 ** Great Drama created:

1. Parliaments called as Mother and head down near the gate of parliament as well as call foreign Delegates.

2. Ganga called as Mother to get favor to Hindu peoples and dirty remain as it is as before.

3. Every time sentimental speech given by nearest personality.

4. Mr. Adita Nath Yogi, Saki Maharaj saying that they are Sanashi /monk but in reality, they use wealth's in lump sum and only saffron cloths / garua bashra are not the main point to a monk. Sanashi mean Suno ash /zero expectation otherwise they are making drama only.

5. The BJP right hand supporter Ramdev Baba nothing But Business man who start to business as Yoga schooling and later enter to food industries and Ayurveda manufacturing companies. If someone is become monk than he or she are not required any business.

6. Sentiment politics and business are main motive as Ram mandir issue created as in North and Central In

** Cheat with Common Peoples:

1. Learn some English words which used to attracted to common peoples but opposing English to use at Governmental offices where as his ministry maximum Ministers next generation and BJP Ruling States Ministry next generation like Son and Daughter or Grand Son and Grand Daughter are taking Education in English as it clear to cheating with common peoples to depress and misguide directly.

2. He calling about Smart Cities but executing cities have not any proper drainage system and road ways and there have not any project of pollution control, garbage treatment and west land development but misguide to executed new cities as land capturing policies from Villagers.

3. There have not any control to Housing Board that money wastage in different projects which planning have some things fault, e.g. at Ratlam city nears Shasrie Nagar several Flat House remain vacant under Housing Board but BJP leading under Mr. Siva Raj Sing Chauhan are not treating by Mr. Noranda Modi. Land Mafia and Promoter born like as husbandry.

The effect of BJP leading and allied parties to pressurized to implement Hindi to Non-Hindi state and all office of central government than have possibilities may divided country as-

1. Independent Kashmir as national and official languages will be Urdu.
2. Independent Punjab as National and official languages will be Panjabi.
3. Independent Hindustan as National and official languages will be Hindi
4. Independent Liberal United Republic Bharat with official language English at zonal state official Department and language to be state recognized languages as per state language.

If such situation comes in near future than Mr. Noranda Modi and Mr. Rajnath Singh remain most responsible person whom create and pressurized to implement Hindi to Non-Hindi peoples.

Political Crisis in India and Demolish Infrastructure of Economy

Fascist, Racist and Nazi Rule in India by Narendra Modi is making destruction of Infrastructure of economy of India. Hind racism executed by RSS and BJP and it make issued as Lord Ram Temple as due to Tulsi Das Sanskrit to Hindi translated Ramayana Influence Worshiping of Lord Ram and His family as well as his Devotee Lord Hanuman done in North, Central and West India. Actually, he is cheating with nation and society by given false stamen and Acting. Dress up make up and spiritual business making base to life entertainment only but targeting to common peoples, farmers, tribal, labours that anti labour laws enforcement done by ordinance. As Agent of Business man Ambani, Adani, Dhamani workings and target to labours to implement 12 hours working time to making slaves to common peoples. As self-center and selfish mentality and only life enjoyment by making foolish is main motive of life. Business policy making as to imports finish product to India by licensing to Guajarati peoples only and making richer to Guajarati peoples. Policy make to capture governmental properly and too making Guajarati self-property as enemy of nation and society. Economy drain out theory implement by which nation become poorer to poorest and only Guajarati become richest as they buy product from china and selling in Indian different states.

Indian Trading Business and Commercial Strategy:

History of Indian Trading and Business:
1. Greek trading Spices directly from India
2. Islamic period Spices trading European from turkey which supply by Indian Islamic rulers.
3. British Merchandise system
4. Under Congress Ruling it become Foreign Direct Investment System, Collaboration and Licensing system

Present Scenario of Indian Business

General Business:

Like as before general business executing as essential commodities and farming products trading and business done by common peoples.

Heavy Industries:

As heavy industries establish by Jawaharlal Nehru Mahalanavish economic policy congress ruled established infostructure of heavy industries those remains either privet public collaboration or become under private as selling public organization by loan section and relief to hand over capitalist.

Capitalist Business:
Ambani Adani Dhamani are actually General Business man who become Capitalism by cheating with nation and Society to hacking BJP RSS leaders who executing Divide misguide Superstition and

rule to implement maximum tax to every step to common peoples and on the other hand

Loan section, national property transfer to capitalist and then loan with interest and taxes relives to making rich to richest who buying properties to foreign nation by Indian national fund.

Capitalist Political Hybrid business

BJP- RSS and Alliances actually Executing political business and hence national fund theft b black hand. Loan section to e3fraind group of capitalists and getting share money on name of donation or social works from Ambani, Adani and other and later loan relief given and money use to buying MP, MLA and party works. Political autocratic bourgeois system implements that making fool to common peoples by brain washing through social electronic media on What app, Facebook and other link and party carders controlling society on the name of different organization as Sava samiti, brahmin society, thakur society, and others but alliance make with RSS, Bjorndal, VHP, and others

Spiritual General Hybrid Business

Spiritual business become high level as Kathabachak organization, e.g. Asharam Bapu Ashram, Ramdave Baba Patanjali, Shree Shree Shankaracharya, Ramrahin Ashram Dara Sacha, Nirmal Baba Ashram, etc. and so many such organization establish all over India. They establish spiritual organization to9 selling speech as well as yoga, Ayurveda products and general foods processes product and others organic & inorganic products as well as political alliance done to getting advantage in back door.

Political Spiritual Hybrid Business

Sakhi Maharaj, Sadhi Proga, Yogi Adhtya Nath execute hybrid political business. Make up and dress up done to acting as devotees to showing other and conflict creating in society to established hybrid business. Kathabachak alliance done where side business on the name of yoga or Ayurveda product as well as food processing business done as well as money collection done on the name f spiritual activity and political activity. Afterall

Hake Government and present strategy of Indian Politics

Capitalist hake government and cheating with nation and society. Target to implement pyramid system of society where top level remains capitalist and under then remain Politician then kept position to priest and common peoples- labour- farmers depressing by heavy taxation and hence implement Anti-Farmer, Anti- Labour and Anti Common people's laws by ordinances. Politicians misguide and misinformation is given to nation and society through superstation increasing and blind believes development either religious mythology or religious sentiment. They target to killing Democracy and killing scientific temperament of common peoples and hence myth making base of advertisement only as they are enemies of nation and society.

Corporate Industries:

Tata, Birla, who establish industries to develops nation and corporate sectors establish manufacturing business and made a vital role to Indian economy. Steel and heavy industries make a strengthen economical back bone of nation who also work in field of education and technological and medicate field.

Underworld turning to Capitalist:

Ambani, Adani and some closer group of BJPs RSS who remain poorer and had not money to Cary out education in higher level but when entered to Gujrat ports locality or Mumbai and migrated to Dubai and gulf region by any how then return to India and started to some business who started logistic business of gold and diamond that indicated in black root they earn hugs money and for showing white money established some field of business only.

The Black Shadow of the Under World and Social hidden Story

1. Sextual Business
2. Gangster Hooliganism
3. Gambling
4. Black marketing
5. Smuggling
6. Slavery system

Under world and political linkages

Hack Government

Historical story creating without evidence

Historical Misguide BJP and RSS are antinationalist and cheating with nation and society:

1. Vikram adyta ruled at Ujjain: 5th Century Ad
2. Chandra Gupta ruled as capital Patoliputra at 3rd Century
3. Vikram Samvat means Victory Declaration at 56 BC against Shaka ruled. In Indian History
4. there have 6 numbers of Vikram adyta only in Chaloka Dynasty
5. After Harshvardhan Vikram adyta ruled at Ujjain that time period are indicated that Vikram adyta I that only Chaloka Dynasty ruler as Chaloka ruler Pulakaashi II Captured Nasik to Ujjain parts as Harshvardhan defatted
6. But BJP RSS Leaders assimilate all

Mythological Misguided:

1. Pushpak Viman actually name of chariot which operated by five horses but explaining that flying at space. Viman means Speed of Air.

2. Lanka means Iland and as per Ramayana geographical description match with Ramaisher Island and there also have Siva temple which worshiped by Ravana

Society turn in backward that pushing to ancient:

As selfish self-center mentality misguides to society and misinformation given to society to enjoying and entertainment life to collecting money on the name of religion, spiritual and ritual system and making politics as cheating with nation and society for their self-interest. Leaders children getting study in English version and computer internet system implement to every field but telling to other to take study in Hindi version and done work in Hindi that their generation to remain upgrade condition and other should push back to lower rank that remaining servant of them. They implement system by planning as-

1. Spiritual Business Spread up
2. Rituality system demolishing
3. Traditional Medical System Exploitation and Ayurveda traditional system upgradation
4. Superstition upgradation
5. Darkness of society increasing as Andhara kayam raha

Bourgeois turn to Capitalist:

Ambani, Adani, Dhamani etc. actually bourgeois peoples who allied with illegal field who hack BJP RSS leaders and become capitalist who section loan and name transfer to national property as commission share to political BJP RSS by which MP MLA and leaders buying by millions of monies. Thereafter Loan relief done to Ambani, Adani, Dhamani and cheating with nation and society where as each and every step of life Taxations implement to common peoples to depressing them from poor to poorest.

Schooling system making Privatization as Business:

Coaching business done and dummy schooling system implement where several student suicide days by days but Narendra Modi remain silent and on the other hand misguide to student to given advices that to attamed harder question at examination that target to pushing future of student in dark as enemy of nation and society.

Killing Democracy and breaking Young Generation:

Enforcement Directory form to send opposition leaders to jail and job creation making zero and import making highest and export system making zero and every tender given only Ambani Adani, Son of Shah.

Political Business Establish:

By cheating from back door monitory form high level to BJP RSS party and buying MP MAL and other leaders to support to him as offering millions of monies and implement getting money to support to BJP RSS.

Depressing Farmers, Labour and Government Servants:

OPS system implements to politician whereas Government servant getting NPS pension system Anti farmer laws, Anti Labour laws implement by ordinances.

Gramling and Liquor spread

Gramling and liquor business spread up to destroying Society and breaking back bone of young generation.

Influence of Freedom fighters deleted by policy sentimental politics done and divide to rule as well as misguide by misinformation to young generation.

Economic Drain Out:

Monetary fund of different state spending done and economy drain out to Gujrat by black hand. Ambani Adani importing Chines materials and selling to India. Days aby day dependency of China increasing most high level as implement taxation to common peoples and millions of loans with tax relief to Ambani Adani as they are Gujrati.

Last Hundred Years of India

Semi Independent Rule and introduce Democracy: !920 that after first World War British implement Parliamentary system as in main land of Great Britain Parliamentary system started due to revolution of political movement. Democratic party and Labour parties formed and by election Democratic Party come to power but British Royal family remaining as Monarchy as Supreme Authority only. Different parties form in India to participating in Voting system to becoming Lower house member as Imperial Legislative Assembly form by British at New Delhi which called Parliament house at present time.

Post British Ruled to Upgradation of India: Nationalist leaders basically Feudal Community and Bureaucratic community which form at British ruling time to used landlord system by British to Ruling agent system to India formed Feudal society and officers' appointments to Indian through Civil Service Examination cum to formed as Bureaucratic Society. Bureaucratic society

Bourgeois Rule to capturing National Property: Atal Bihari Bajpai started to introduce Religious mater to political field for capturing power. Lord Ram Temple movement started at Ayadha which given name by King Vikramadita of Ujjaln who had relationship with Bhojpuri region. After Poet Kalidas works Raghuvanshi King Vikramadita tried to find out Ayadha but fail then went to take advice from a monk. Monk advice a cow left to find out Ayadha and after three days try to find out Cow then where cow found that place is Ayadhya. He founds out Cow and given name that place where it found as Ayadhya. There remained Siva Temple but Atal Bihari and their team explained as Birth Plash of Lord Rama. Actually, in Ramayana mansion Ajay the grant father of Lord Rama fight to Northern part of Kushal Kingdome as Malloch Community attracting to Kosalam. In that sense Norther part of Kosala was name as Ayadhya on his name where Lord Rama born that place actually situated in Nepal at Nepal at present time as ValmikiAshram situated at Nepal nearest to Bihar Border and Mithila also situated in Nepal. Iskabhu the old generation of Lord Rama consider as Sun God remain Mundari Community as this name is originated of Munday language and in their families Indo European peoples mixed as queen came from Indo European families.

Required to Implement Social Consulate Confederation Liberal

Three phase three stage system that social consulate confederation Liberal system required to implement in India as here have Four region of linguistic and cultural difference where North central region is Hindi and Hindi racism executed by which three region facing problem to competitive examination in recruitment and proportional departmental examination. Hence there have required to form 1. Eastern Precedency Indo-Australasian Region 2. Western Precedency Indo-Eurasian, 3. Central Presidency Indo-Arabic and 4. Southern Presidency Indo-Afrasian.

Corporate Administration Council required to formed in three stage by which partiality and discrimination required to abolishing and demolishing by system. There remaining as Central Administration Council, Zonal Administration Council and State Administration Council. State required to divide as Magisterial Legislative Council, District Legislative Council, Local Legislative Council (Urban/ Suburban/ Village Council)

Public Recruitment Service Council require to establish where general post and Administrative post to be fill up through competitive examination. System required to corporate system where remain Central body, Zonal Body and State Body.

Election Administration Council required to form as Autonomous body. System required to corporate system where remain Central body, Zonal Body and State Body.

Jurisdiction Administration Council required to form as Autonomous Body. System required to corporate system where remain Central body, Zonal Body and State Body.

Majority base Governmental System:

Which political party remaining majority of member this party should able to form government as it seen that one third majority system to form government misuse civilian caste voting where elected members change their party to getting money to given support and earn money in illegal root. Hence in democratic system turn to political business where civilian voting has not remained value to elected member by caste voting. Due getting profited as become political business establishment there have formation of Shopping of political party where elected member of any level sold on cost.

Asynchronies Electoral Machin required to implement where peoples given right to vote on national or zonal or state development decision as they should have to be personal index number which can be change able by candidate. After 18 years each citizen should provide National Citizenship Electronic Chip Card by which only candidate able to implement caste vote by using self-Personal Index Number applied only.

Social Corporate Confederation Liberal system is the system that government form by the peoples and for the peoples but democracy is system to form by the peoples for the representative only as several number of members decided to pass the national or state bill.

Unit House three Conferential branch system:

Each level of legislative building has to *remain a single* unit but three conferential branches where Top conferential *branches* have to remain Self house members only. Intermediate Conferential Branch have to be members of Administrative members who remain Administrative members of state level and Zonal / Zonal level and Central Level. Lower Conferential Branch where Administrative remain as members of District Level- Magisterial Level – State Level / Magisterial Council level- State level - Zonal Level / State Level- Zonal Level – Central Level by which Co-operation to execute too development of nation.

Taxation Implement to Provide Facility:

Transportation tax to implement path or roadways facility *provided* to a locality, Commodity Supply Tax required to implement too provided water Supply, fuel supply, Power Supply, drainage facility, souse facility, Garbage management facility providing. Licensing Tax Implementation to be *implemented* Trading Tax, Business Establishment tax, Vehicle transport Tax, required to implement.

Prehistoric Society of India:

Afro Asian Ruled

Indo European Ruled

Ashur Eurasian Ruled

Historic Society of India:

Aryan Ruled

Islamic Ruled British [Afghani Ruled, Uzbek Ruled (Mogul)]

European Ruled:

Brahmin and Rajput Spread Up Islamic Influence

Bahmani community actually remained Brahmin

Birbal and *TanSen* remained Brahmin who accept Islamic Religion for taken higher post at Akbar Ministry

Man Sing and Jai Singh always supported to Mughal Rulers

Murshid Khulikha was Brahmin and for post capturing as Nawab converted to Islam.

Why Pithy Raj Chauhan Defied with Mahammad Ghori?

Answer: He gave shelter to brother of Mahammad *Ghori* and himself sleeping at night *whereas* alert *that night* might *attract Mohammad Ghori*.

Why Maharana Pratap Defied with?

Answer: Maan Singh and his Step brother Supported to Akbar

British Ruled and Social Reformation

Western Education Stated and Education field open to all:

English *became the* official language in support of *Raja* Ram Mohan Roy who had knowledge to *read, write* and *speak* continuously in eight *languages*. Superstition and unwanted black dark system *abolished* as Sati System (Murdering of Widow), Education *enlightened* to society and Came one after Scientist and Social Reformer. Isher Chandra Sharma (Vidhya Sagar) who started *a social* movement and British ruler reformed Hindu social system. Widow remarriage started, Child Marriage abolish, Child killing to sacrifices at River like Ganga, Thagi Community who cheating with peoples and property captured by Murder.

RSS and Jan *sangh* /BJP are Anti Nationalist and Antisocial:

1. Supporting to Multi Marriage
2. Superstition spread up
3. Child Marriage increasing
4. Depressing Women started and Rape done by BJP RSS leaders
5. Education *is made* most costly by which Society destroying by policy that Education *makes* Business and *abolish it as it* was social works.

6. Killing common peoples by alliance Bjorndal, Hindu Mahasabha etc. through Hindi Racism and

Gujarati peoples are Anti Nationalist:

Gujarati peoples always remain anti nationalist as *during the British* period they *worked* as *agents of the British* and hence *want a semi* Independent Nation where Imperial House *members* roaming British at Upper House and lower house *members* remaining Indian. At First World War and Second World War Full Supported *to the British* and done agreement by M. C. Gandhi. No one Gujrati had Sacrifices life for Freedom movement.

Now a Days Economy drain out to Gujrat by Narendra Modi by Policy that loan Section to *Gujarati* capitalist Bourgeois peoples Ambani Adani and then National Property hand over to then and thereafter Loan with interest and tax Relief given that totally cheating with nation and society.

History of Religion Formation:

Regionality and group formation is wild character of human being realism that called traditionality of social system. Actually, due to apparat ruling in tribal society different groups form as leadership execution. Ancient ruler who became more powerful those implement taxation system and society wind up in a rule of laws. Whatever *collection is done* from *forest,* some part should give leaders at *wildlife* of society which even *today's* follow up by tribal society where civilization should not rich todays. But mettle discovered turning to settlement life where worker

Indian Peninsula Ancient Communities and religions:

Deva /Hindu/ Sindhu Sinai Black rehabilitated at Lower Indus Dravidian are this type of peoples

Indu Indo-European a Mixed community of Celtic- Slavic- Norse White peoples rehabilitated upper Indus and Kashmir. Kashmiri Hindu are these type of peoples

Ashur / Assyrian ***Arabic, Iranian*** White peoples, Jat/ Jut, Gujar, Marat etc. are those categories of peoples.

Saman / Saren Community: Austrasia peoples Santhal Mundari Brown Skin peoples.

Chinese Burmese ***NorthEastern***, Nepal and Ladakh region of peoples Ahom-Matai community.

White Racism and Slavery system of India (Caste System):

At the prehistoric Nomadic age *Europeans* migrated to Himalayan range of Hindu Kush *and the Indus* region through two ways as Caucasus and Ural ranges as primitive society mountain ranges flowing. After fire discovered African ***rulers*** executed to Enter European ***landmarks*** and hence it has ***mentioned*** black gods and ***goddesses*** in different European mythology. White ***rulers were*** executed at different Kabila and at copper black rulers arrested and made ***to be slaved***. Sutra which ***transforms*** to Sudra means black and white racism ***started and continued***. Later Ashier group and Vanir group divided and Ashier group ruled and Vanir group defeated who either ***became*** slave or hidden to other place through migration. Hindu means Hidden Mountainous peoples who actually pour Europeans and rehabilitated to Hindu Kush and Sindi who remain law ***breakers*** left European range and started to rehabilitation in Indus called Sindu means Sinner mountainous peoples and later migrated to Sinai desert. ***Behind Vanir*** group Ashier groups flowing as ***invaders*** continued to ***capture*** Vanier group to ***make slaves***. *The Ashier* group basically migrated *to the Arabian* Peninsula and *Iran* and they also migrated *to the Indian* peninsula ***which is*** indicated as Ashur. As a Result, Old Slavic ***groups*** remain Black and White as there remain black and White Gods and ***Goddesses*** which have similarity with Afro Asian and Euro Asian gods and ***goddesses***. Dravidian are ***Afro-Asian whereas*** Hindu, Sindi and Ashier ***groups*** remain European who united later. As a result, Sanskrit ***matches*** with Lithuanian and Syrian also ***which were evaluated in Northern*** Iran ***under Sasanian rule***. European ***groups invaded the Indian*** peninsula and

Afro Asian migrated *toward the south* Indian side through Vrindrachal *range* trips. Hence Dravidian branch group language remained different *from* North Indian language. *United* European groups executed white racism and *depress the community* form as they remained slaved. Different groups of *tribes migrated* and made defeated groups as *slaves* and hence Some white *groups were also* made *slaves* by leading *groups* of rulers. Later mixed due to marriage relation and human hybridization hold on and caste system form which is nothing but slavery system of society which supporting by BJP-RSS and alliance as basically they are brahmin Jat/ Jut and Eurasian Kshatriya group even today executing racism and target to Dravidian and Ahom and north Eastern Indian to demolish and abolish their language, Social system, Culture and Identity.

M. C. Gandhi Worked as White Racist:

M. C. Gandhi as Persian Originated Priest always support to White Racism and hence not Supporting to B. R. Ambedkar as B. R. Ambedkar remained depress community and always remained helpful to British as works as slow poison as working as agent of British as calling nonviolence but support to British as wanted Semi-independent ruling system like as Australia, New *Zealand*, Canada ruling system demanded by Native Britisher as well as full supporting to British in First World War and Second World Wars. He *acted* as nationalist *when* Britisher started to *form the commonwealth* and later *made plans* to *decolonize* to safeguard British economic policy. In his childhood used Persian dressing and at young age used Britisher dressing and then started to acting as monk to wear White Cloth when he was kick out from First Class coach of a train in South Africa when he was gone for Barrister law practices.

He made alliance with Islamic Leaders who wanted to rule whole India as previously ruled mainly in Northern India. Indian Islamic community leaders wanted to ruled whole India and kept Calipha certificated rulers in Turkish rulers and Uzbek Mughal ruler. Caliphate Movement only done as Britisher destroyed Ottoman ruled in Turkish Islamic ruled in First World War whom encourage Islamic ruled spread up around world. As selfish mentality to power gain only by any how that he supported to Islamic community on the name of joint venture movement. As acting as nationalist but working in favor of British ruler as white racist fully support to British in First World War and Second World Wars but as actor done Social Disobedient and *Non Cooperation* movement as walking and fasting system adopted called Anasan. In West India fasting means getting dried fruits taken three times also. When fast World War ended than Semi-independent rule started where Imperial Legislative Assembly members remained as British members remained in Upper House as Deputation and Lower House members elected. By Duel ruling system democracy implement as in Great Britain also started Democracy after end of First World War. At the ending period of Second World War acting as nationalist and *Quit* India Movement done *when CommonWealth* formed and India *became* one of members like Australia, New *Zealand* and Canada and started to power transfer in Semi-independent system and decolonization became at primitive stage.

There has no doubt that M. C. Gandhi remained as White Racist that Caste system of India is actually Slavery system where Aryan / Iranian invaded Indian Peninsula and arrested innocent peoples to made slave and human right abolished. Aryan made slave of them to done every works and used to physical harassment done and physically used to women also. Indian peninsula was under rehabilitation of Dravidian that Australasian and Afrasian Mixed community. Dravir means Winer of *Water"* by boating *across oceans* and *seas*. Dravidian are black peoples and Aryan remained White and depressing to black peoples as defeated. Hence M. C. Gandhi always neglect to B. R. Ambedkar and his demand.

Saraj Party Activity: Motilal Nehru and C. R. Das

Jawaharlal Nehru Ideology:

National Government formed:

From 1920 British *implemented a* voting system to India and *governed* through Deuel system ruling *under the Imperial* Legislative Council where Lower House *members* remained Indian and upper house *members* remained British. Every three years *elections are held and the federal* government system *implemented* as Local Assembly formed at Provincial level and Province *transformed* to Statehood status. National Congress Party *remained the majority* to maximum state in1946 and in central there also *remained the majority* political party. But when British India divided *into Independent* India and Pakistan. As the part Islamic league remained *majority, the* parts formed as Pakistan where Bengal and Punjab *provinces were divided* as per Islamic and Hindu majority by Red Clip. In *1*947 National Government formed *by the Multi* Party as it required to *form* National infrastructure and hence with every *leader* of different political *parties* jointly form government to root decided to *make* law and orders, and other *fields* to *make* national progress.

Law and Orders Restructuring under constitutions:

Constitution adopt commission establish

Economical Reformation as Industrialization:

Social Reformation as Worldly:

Secular means Worldly and in India have different languages, cultures and community and hence target to execute unity in diversity.

Dravir/ Dravidian Forget their own Identity Sanatan:

Sana means Brilliant and tan means copper colour (pale tone brown) in this sense Sindhu which means Sinai Black *then* it also *has the* same *meaning as* Sinai black that Mediterranean peoples migrated to lower Indus who called Sindhu or Sanatan. Hindu remained Hindu raj mountain range of Hindu *Kush remained*. Kalash, Nuri, Kashmiri peoples remained oldest Hindu who actually white Skin and they have some peoples brown eye, brown hair also that indicated Hindu was actually European peoples as Brown Eye, White Skin and Brown hair are European originated as well as Sanskrit words match with Celtic and Norse family language as well as Some word match with Arabic and Turkish Eurasian. But *later* Hindu migrated to *Ganga* and Decan land but Arabian and Turkish already *formed* as Eurasian community as Mongolian migrated toward West whereas European migrated toward East. Indian peninsula when Eurasian migrated than where Afrasian mixed with Eurasian and European nomadic peoples.

Political Advice given by Sree Krishna in Mahabharata as Bhagabat Gita:

Colonial Ruling Effect in Society in Different countries:

Prehistoric Aryan History: Ruled at Jannat

Slavery system *implemented in the Arabian* Peninsula by Jannat rulers.

Godism at Mount Olympus:

Historical Aryan Strategy

Present Scenario of Aryan Strategy

Aryans Conservation System reorganizes:

Non-Aryans Liberal System Organization:

Barat Barsha as Geographical area:

If we enter into history *then* we understand that Barat Barsha was a geographical area and *its boundary* indicated from Hindukush mountain to *I*raboti *were several* countries. In ancient *times,* there *were* several small countries in Barat Barsha. But in Europe the Barat Barsha was indicated as Indus which *turned* to India by space slip to *Europe*.

Barat Barsha *turns* to Hindustan: Islamic rule *enters Parasha* and Persian peoples *enter Barat* Barsha because *they* also remain safe as to lead life as they believe Sun god, fire god as previous believer of natural power in Barat Barsha. Islamic peoples indicate the same land mark as Hindustan because the peoples of Hindukush mountain was indicated as Hindu and they shift from Hiducos to Indonesia but Bharat Barsha remain as Arjabarta (Land of Aryan)and Anarja Bartha(Land of non- Aryan).

The word *remains* as Dave as superior people and Davari as inferior peoples and *Dave means* god *whereas* Daveri means Danab(*giant*) Danab *turns* to Dabir *after a long* time and *indicates* the south Indian peoples. *After a long* time the religious faith *became submerged* and as a whole called as Hindu in the whole *landmark* of Barat Barsha where maximum *time was ruled* by different *kings* of *Aryavarta* (Land of Aryan) and Anarja Bartha (Land of non- Aryan) separately. Islamic peoples indicate them as a same religious group as Hindu and the *landmark as* Hindustan (Land of Hindu). *I* heard that the *landmark* peoples *used to* use milk to offer to god *shiva* and the milk river flow from temple of god Siva and temple *had a lump* sum goal and *money rather than* greediness *to give* power to Islamic ruler of outer land. The outer ruler attracts to Barat Barsha and give the name as Hindustan (The land of Hindu)

Hindustan turn to India: weakness *comes after a long* time ruled by Islamic ruler in Barat Barsha and *Europeans* start to come *to the sated* commercial establishment in Hindustan and turn as ruler in different *parts*. Pondicherry ruled by *the French* community, Goa-Damon-Due ruled by Portugal's community and Bengal-*Bihar-orissa* ruled *by the British* community (England-Wales-Scotland the independent three countries peoples). *Bengal-Bihar-Orissa became* the first spot of British rule but after *all, the maximum* part of Barat Barsha ruled *by the British* either direct or indirect ruled system. But the *Europeans* indicated the land mark as India which one *called Hindustan* by Islamic *rulers*. The European ruler indicated the land mark as France India, British India as per capture by the community.

Independent India-Pakistan:

Independent *Bangladesh*:

Hindi Racism: Hindi Hai Hum Hindisha Hamara means we are Hindi peoples and Hindustani is ours. Hindustan means to Hindi peoples are as whole India *whereas* in Non-Hindi peoples indicated Hindustani means only Hindi linguistic peoples

Nowadays Hindi peoples *indicate* that they are superior *to* non-Hindi peoples where as they are *at* the competition examination in

Hindi language which *is their* mother language and as well as they *read and write* in Hindi.

Problem to Non-Hindi peoples:

India-Barat:

Hindustan to Hindi peoples:

Hindi the language of Hindustan: language of Hindu peoples indicated by Islamic ruler

Political system of Barat:

Name required of country: United Republic of Bharat

as a single name

States name required to defined: West Bengal as Banga Pradesh

Panjab as Gurumukhi Pradesh

Andhra Pradesh as Telegu Pradesh

Uttar Pradesh as Brojo Pradesh

Madhya Pradesh as Brindachal Pradesh

Demand of us required as Non-Hindi:

Birth Right:

1. Mother language as Basic Educational System

2. Equality to every one as per qualification.

3. Right to give speech in mother language or vernacular in parliament But

If vernacular not understand by other member than interpreter to recruited to give translated speech in bi- lingual system.

4. Compititive written and interview Examination should be given by vernacular recognize language in the state compulsorily.

5. Within India all peoples are not Hindi whereas the Hindi leaders defined as -

a. Sara Jahasa Acha Hindustan Hai Hamara (Everywhere are good mater that is our Land of Hindu)

b. Hindi Hai Hum Hidusthan Hamara (We are Hindi Peoples and Land of Hindu is Only Our)

c. Buri Najar Na hamsa Dalo Sabsa Aga Hogi Hindusthani (Ban view not to see to us Hindi Speaking peoples become in top most post)

d Jai Hind (Greeting Hindi Land)

In the above case it is clear that Hindi leaders are forcefully defined that the land Of Independent India Name as Land of Hindu and only Hindi speaking peoples have right to live in Independent India. Whereas as per constitution the Independent India have two Name as 1. India in English and, 2. Bharat In Indian Languages.

Within Enter Independent India the Written Competition Examination

In tension and Interview get in Either English or in Hindi but so many peoples are in Non-Hindi areas are getting education in there vernacular and mother language which one are State official language and under continuation that are recognized language But if Non Hindi Peoples are become unable to attempt in their own language in their own state than what valuation remain the recognize and state official language .In Hindi State Hindi Officer input Hindi language and grammar question compulsory in competition Examination and get interview in Hindi. But in Non Hindi State there are education system implement in State language and English hence it required that to be given written examination and interview either in English or state language than the actual competition to give the proper result other wish the system favor to Hindi speaking peoples that they get like as mother milk in Mother language . Hence after the Hindi take in Examination field and interview than the Bihari, UP's And other Hindi peoples come to the higher level in maximum number to ground leveling governmental posts. After all Hindi Racism come by the system Hence Every Hindi Speaking Peoples explain that the name of country as Hindustan and they understand that the meaning of Hindustan as Hindi land and everywhere of Independent India required to implement forceful the Hindi Language or by greediness to give awards in case by Central Government and Akhil Bharatio Hindi Parishad.

In my real life When I remain in Ratlam in Madhya Pradesh remain as Apprentices as Junior Engineer the Senior Section Engineer Mr. Harish Chanda Panda and others said that Why We live in Hindustan if we are unable to speak in Hindi and when I was in Ujjain in Madhya Pradesh that time several period said by K. K. Mittal That why I live in Hindustan if I am unable properly speak and write Hindi Language and Said that I require to find out other county. Today such word said one after another and said all state required to implement Hindi language.

The above give alarm that Hindi peoples want to capture whole India as Oppose that to speak in State official language in parliament and in State Assembly Hindi speaking peoples or Muslim are given statement in Hindi and Urdu respectively. Afterall the Hindi speaking peoples support to Urdu speech because both have some things similar.

I Say to Non-Hindi Peoples that even today have time to wake up and alert to save us otherwise we become bake and Hindi peoples said they are superior where as perticipat in hindi by them.

We have required to demand by revolutionary mode as-

1. Give the right to give speach in vernaculer state official language with interpeter in parliament.

2. In aState Either Cental or State Governmental or public organization compititive examination and interview shoud to takk in State official language and english.

3. In Lokal Assembly in State should be use the State official language in spech and written particuler.

4. Want Birth right that our Mother language and state official language.

5. Want to demant compalcery State official languagtic question in compitetion examination at list 10 percent that if a candidet remain to do work he should able to comunicat easily in working field because maximum word use by comon worker as vernaculer language

6 In depertmental examination ther to be input State langusge as compelcery because in Hindi State there are remain compalcery Hindi Language in Depertmental examination. Even in some case the question and answer remain and gettin in Hindi.

6. Every letter and notice in State should remain in State official Language as hindi States.

7. Hindi Racism to mention at international level and force to implenet the system and required to help UN Department.

8 . The Name of the country required to give as the United Bharat Republic because The India was given by European and after all the British ruler give the name British India where as previously Islamic invader called as Hindustan because that the enter land lived the religion of Hindu mainly and after lord Asoka ruled the land mark Buddhism start the flows in the riligious under royal society but the Islamic ruller understand the land mark as Hindu land, hence the enter land mark called as Hindusthan. But the real name of the land mark was Bharat Barsha and hence required the give name of nation asUnited Bharat Republic for creat better intregation of nation.

9. Name of the curency of our nation as Indiana by which reformation of economical system required and known by the every cetigen as Indiana where as at present in diferent state call the curency name as Taka called by Bengali, Tanka called by Oiria , Rupkani called by Marathi, Toka called by Assamis and so on. On the Other hand in Napal, Indonasia , Pakistan the curency called the same as Rupes and hence identification of nation requird a spacial as for the national intregrity.

10 In the verbally Hindi speaking peoples call them as Hindusthani but in Nonhindi State the Hindusthani means as Hindi speaking

peoples. Hence confusion create as that diffining the proples as Hidusthani , and the upper class peoples indicat them as Indian in English but the Non- Hindi peoples indicat them as Bharotio and these indicat the dissatishfaction of the peoples. The Islamic state and islamic comunity in dicat the land mark as Hindusthan but they indicat them as muslim but not things as hindiusthani becacuse that Hindu are attach with the word with Hindusthani. After all dissatisfaction creat and tarorisom increas around that part where the islamic comunity remain maximu in number, hence it required to indicat us as Braotian which to be easy to spacified us as singe identity and hence the national intregity to be increase.

11. There are required the restric by law that the name of nation and nationality should bebe indicat as Hindusthan and Hindusthani as well as India and Indian in Flims and newspaper, magazin , and jarnal respactively. The proper name to required as United Bhatar Republic and in short to indicat as UBR And nationality should be indicat as Bharotian as single unity.

12. AS per constituation the name of country given asUnion India and Sanga Bharat because the British India was rulled either direct rulled or indirect agent rulling and after all the religion remain as Hindu, Muslim, Shaik, Ishai(Chrastrian), Jain, etc. and Hindustan if give the name of country than may aris problem that to feel Hindu Land but time pass out above 64 years but national integrity can not try to increas by the identity of nation. No Liberty of tower or Liberty of statue are not create by the government and peoples celebrating independent day near India Gate and some where the India Gate make as model by the peoples but the India Gate was made by the British Ruler in Respect of visit India by the king of England Gorge-V and he entered the Indian land through Bombay hence There also made as Gate way of India. But we become Proud that we celebrate Indian Independent day near the India Gate which indicate that we have no feelings of nationality. Hence It is required to make the liberty of tower and liberty of statue in respect of independent nation.

13. The parliament House, Governor General House (President house) in New Delhi and Right Us House Governor House in Calcutta (Kolkata) remain as the Administrations purpose as Central and state of West Bengal but we do *nothing* after *independence* as Our own building for local and central administration.

Area of as per language:

1. Hindi language tic States: Hindi use as Official language.

Haiyana, Himachal *Pradesh*, *Uttaranchal*, *Uttar* Pradesh, Biher, Jharkhand, Chatrisgar, Madhya *Pradesh*, *Rajasthan As* the list of State and only union *territory* Delhi *included* in the list of Hindi *Language* part of India.

2. Non-Hindi *language* States: Indo-English use as official language.

Jammu & Kashmir, Punjab, Gujrat, *Maharashtra*, Andhra *Pradesh*, Goa, Karnataka, Tamil Nadu, Kerala, Orissa, West Bengal, Sikkim, Assam, Maghalaya, Tripura, Mizoram, Manipur, Nagaland, Arunachal *Pradesh* as the state and union *territory* Daman-Diu, Pondicherry, Lakshadweep, *Chandigarh*, and Andaman & Nicobar where English use as official language and the peoples of *their* area *participate competition* written examination and face interview in english and they have no other *often* they may *participate* in recognise language *whereas* the peoples of these area use the recognise language in study and only one *language* paper remain English and become weak in English and remain unknown the Hindi language which have option to *attempt Competitive* examination and interview. By the system Hindi speaking peoples give more and more facility and enter to Non-Hindi area where as have same qualification and samemarrite as the Hindi speaking peoples *whereas* Hindi speaking peoples also have habit to take education in Hindi and have only one *regular* or optional English Language paper and they are also maximum weak in English. But in *departmental* and other *competitive examinations* one 10% question *gets* in Hindi and *becomes successful* in the *competition* by the system, hence partiality created by the system and the Non-Hindi peoples become downward in competition *by the system.*

Policy to increasing the number of Hindi States: *Divide* the Hindi States to increase the number as UP, Bihar, Madhya *Pradesh Divided into* two parts as as new states form as Uttarakhand, Jharkhand ,and Chatrigar and previously the Hindi state form by division of *Punjab* State as Haryana and Himachal *Pradesh*. The *recent* year when Tanagana state demand and central government *give more willingness* to form the Tanagana state than the Up Government and other political *parties* as majority of Hindi Peoples want to divide as Up into different parts as Harit Pradesh, Bundle Khand, etc. The policy is to increase *the number* of Hindi States.

Indian Social Strategy:

1. Bourgeois Groups: Bourgeois Capitalist, Higher Richest landlord personality, Religious Alliance Political Business Leaders, Spiritual Business Leaders.

2. Bureaucratic Groups: Government Public administration Officers, Public Sector Authoritative personality, Public *Private* Organization Executer.

3. General Peoples Groups: General Farmer, General Retail Businessman, General Service Holder in Public sectors, General Staffs of Public Administration,

4. Laboure Decentralized Groups: Lower Income Groups peoples, peoples done Laborious works under Agency Business Holder and constructional Contractors.

Political Business Alliance with Spiritual Businessman

BJP: Political cum intermediator of Capitalist and Spiritual business leaders

RSS: Intermediator of Spiritual Business Leaders and Political Alliances

Bajrang Dal, Hindu Mahasabha: Intermediator of Spiritual Business leaders and Hooligans Groups

Spiritual Cum Political Alliances: Akhara, Ashram, Temple Committee as organizations, Spiritual Business Organization, For *example*, Asharam Bapu organization, Rampal Organization, Sath Guru organization, Ramrahim organization, Radha maa organization, etc.

Doctrine (from Latin: *doctrina*, meaning "teaching, instruction") is a codification of beliefs or a body of teachings or instructions, taught principles or positions, as the essence of teachings in a given branch of knowledge or in a belief system. The etymological Greek analogue is "catechism".

Often the word *doctrine* specifically suggests a body of religious principles as promulgated by a church. *Doctrine* may also refer to a principle of law, in the common-law traditions, established through a history of past decisions.

Christian theology:

Doctrines such as the Trinity, the virgin birth and atonement

The Salvation Army *Handbook of Doctrine*

Transubstantiation and Marian teachings in Roman Catholic theology. The department of the Roman Curia which deals with questions of doctrine is called the Congregation for the Doctrine of the Faith.[3][4]

The distinctive Calvinist doctrine of "double" predestination

The Methodist Church of Great Britain refers to the "doctrines to which the preachers of the Methodist Church are pledged" as *doctrinal standards.*

Other Christian Doctrine

Yuga in Hinduism

Postulation or *Syādvāda* in Jainism

The Four Noble Truths in Buddhism

Roman Catholic and Orthodox doctrine generally comes from the writings of the Church Fathers, which has been clarified in various Ecumenical councils. Short versions can be found in brief statements of Christian doctrine, in prayer books. Longer versions take the form of catechisms. Protestants generally reject Christian tradition and instead derive their doctrine solely from the Bible

Philosophical usage

Epicurus' 40 Principal Doctrines, the first four of which make up the ***Tetrapharmakos***

Measure of religiosity

According to sociologist Mervin Verbit, doctrine may be understood as one of the key components of religiosity. He divides doctrine into four categories: content, frequency (degree to which it may occupy the person's mind), intensity and centrality. Each of these may vary from one religion to the next, within that religious tradition.

In this sense, doctrine is similar to Charles Glock's "belief" dimension of religiosity.

Military usage

The term also applies to the concept of an established procedure to execute an operation in warfare. The typical example is tactical doctrine in which a standard set of maneuvers, kinds of troops and weapons are employed as a default approach to a kind of attack.

Examples of military doctrines include:

Guerre de course

Hit-and-run tactics

Mahanian of late 19th up to mid-20th century

Manhunting doctrine, or assured individual destruction

Shock and awe

Soviet deep battle of World War II

Trench warfare of World War I

Cold War doctrines[edit]

The Cold War saw the enunciation of several strategic doctrines designed *to contain* Soviet expansion.

Carter Doctrine was announced in 1980 by American President Jimmy Carter after the Soviet invasion and occupation of Afghanistan. It declared that any Soviet aggression towards the Persian Gulf would be considered a danger to the essential interests of the United States. This led to the creation of significant American military installations in the area and the formation of the Rapid Deployment Force. The proclamation reinforced the previous Truman Doctrine and Eisenhower Doctrine and to some extent it rejected the Nixon Doctrine. See also Reagan Doctrine.

Peacekeeping doctrines

In modern peacekeeping operations, which involve both civilian and military operations, more comprehensive (not just military) doctrines are now emerging such as the 2008 United Nations peacekeeping operations' "Capstone Doctrine"[14] which speaks to integrated civilian and military operations.

Political usage

By definition, political doctrine is "policy, position or principle advocated, taught or put into effect concerning the acquisition and exercise of the power to govern or administrate in society." The term political doctrine is sometimes wrongly identified with political ideology. However, doctrine lacks *the actional aspect* of ideology. It is mainly a theoretical discourse, which "refers to a coherent sum of assertions regarding what a particular topic should be" (Bernard Crick). Political doctrine is based on a rationally elaborated set of values, which may precede the formation of a political identity *per se*. It is concerned with philosophical orientations on a *meta-theoretical* level.

Legal usage

A legal doctrine is a body of interrelated rules (usually of common law and built over a long period of time) associated with a legal concept or principle. For example, the doctrine of frustration of purpose now has many tests and rules applicable with regards to each other and can be contained within a "bubble" of *frustration*. In a court session a defendant may refer to the doctrine of justification.

It can be seen that a branch of law contains various doctrines, which in turn contain various *rules* or *tests*. The test of *non-occurrence of crucial events* is part of the doctrine of *frustration* which is part of contract law. Doctrines can grow into a branch of law; restitution is now considered a branch of law separate to contract and tort

Hack Government

As a form of government surveillance, hacking presents unique and grave threats to our privacy and security. It has the potential to be far more intrusive than any other surveillance technique, permitting the government to remotely and surreptitiously access our personal devices and all the intimate information they store. It also permits the government to conduct novel forms of real-time surveillance, by covertly turning on a device's microphone, camera, or GPS-based locator technology, or by capturing continuous screenshots or seeing anything input into and output from the device. Hacking allows governments to manipulate data on our devices, by deleting, corrupting or planting data; recovering data that has been deleted; or adding or editing code to alter or add capabilities, all while erasing any trace of the intrusion.

Government hacking targets are not confined to devices, but can extend also to communications networks and their underlying infrastructure.

At the same time, government hacking has the potential to undermine the security of targeted devices, networks or infrastructure, and potentially even the internet as a whole. Computer systems are complex and, almost with certainty, contain vulnerabilities that third parties can exploit to compromise their security. Government hacking often depends on exploiting vulnerabilities in systems to facilitate a surveillance objective. Government hacking may also involve manipulating people to interfere with their own systems. These techniques prey on user trust, the loss of which can undermine the security of systems and the internet.

A growing number of governments around the world are embracing hacking to facilitate their surveillance activities. But many deploy this capability in secret and without a clear basis in law. In the instances where governments seek to place such powers on statutory footing, they are doing so without the safeguards and oversight necessary to *minimize* the privacy and security implications of hacking.

Governmental responsibility to development of Economic Infrastructure:

Import Export balancing (Economical Balance establishment)

Shelf Help Economic field development (Innovation and Self-reliance)

Self-Reliance Mind for Worn Business Encouragement

Entrepreneurship to Business and Trading Encouragement

Present Scenario of World Politics

United State of America U-turn from Iraq and Afghanistan:

Reformation toward Natural reality and Liberal Confederation

New Kind of Survival Root that Neutral Analytical Natural Uniformities to Reformation Overall Youngs (NKSRNANTUROY)

It is the *activity to realize that the social* system is manmade and hence it is clear that *humans are* mortal also. Myth created by imagination as when languages *change or the same* words have *retained* different *meanings*. Peoples when enter to religious myths than forget that gods and goddess also remained human mainly and it is ways of social system formation by leaderships who called as creators but actually gods and goddess remained rulers who guided to ways of life survivals as gardening, farming and controlling common peoples and it is so cruel story that weaker peoples made slaves to do works where they also had no right to eating or drinking if ruler not given permission to them. Later it is seen royalism started where one after another emperor established and one after another society turning to racism where depressing to defeated personality. But common *people* should not analyze the system of society and *believe* that *our ancestors,* called gods or *goddesses,* are *operators* of our life and *creators of the world* and universe. But it *is a reality* that social system and rule regulation *implemented* to society by ruler groups and its realization started which turn to democratic *systems* to choose *rulers* by voting in democracy or social consulate confederation liberalism. We have required *a* naturalistic and neutrally analytical mentality required to create that by which we can *realize* the social event that any text required to read by self-study and analyzed by self and should *stop* to *hear* speech of spiritual business holders.

NKSRNANTUROYism:

Believes in reality and *chose a ruler by a new* form of voting system to establish roots by which national development *remains the* main issues where myths should be defatted *by the young* generation by creating scientific temperament. *The Younger generation study* sciences and technology but when *entering into* spiritual business *holders then* wash out the scientific thinking and become believers of myths without argument. In several religious *systems it is seen* that there have not done any reformation and remained blind supporters who strongly *believe in* myths and magical talking *given the identity* of spiritual sciences but there *are* not any real *systems* of sprites or souls. Spiritual system development done by society rulers mainly and our feeling that our ancestors *are remembered* by us *as a sprite* or soul of *theirs* remaining with us and hence we *offer* foods and *ancestors' idols* kept to our house as guardians. *As for living,* we kept them food, dress and bathing by us and other *activities* that *in the morning* get up idols and at night thought sleep and kept them *in bed* also. Each and every religion creates supernatural power conception and as believed of their ancestors *have a life* story where someone killed someone or himself sacrificed life. Some selfish peoples made it political themes and *brainwashing* to common peoples where spiritual business personality create a vital rule where flowers caste voting to them as their spiritual leaders guided and somewhere spiritual leaders remained himself political leaders who use sentiment and used myth to brain washing or used new formed of religious conceptions as in Arabian peninsula nonformal system implement by brain washing and deleting history of ancient Arabian life. Islamic Ruling system *implemented* on base of myth and *non formal* system where called mono ethnic system but 99 gods *accepting* by name *whose* stories remained different that indicates they remained different personality and peoples of ancient Arabian remained at list 99 groups also. In *India the same* types of ruling system *are implemented* by BJP RSS joint venture ruling where scientific temperament *is abolished* by planning and through mythical story *brainwashing* by spiritual business holders. Spiritual business *holders sometimes implement alliances* with political leaders who misusing power as well as misguided and misinformation given to society as selfishness to *make fools* and earn money *to enjoy life and* entertainment. GET up *young and* understand the reality of society and reformed society by revolutions and rebellions. We have to target to *form a new* administration system which *will be* by the *people* and for the *people*. Democracy is by the *people* but it is for the representation where only some representative decided *the nation* system to *change* and there also remained lower level *candidates* also who misguide and misinformation spread up to society. Hence *they* have required to *implement a system* as technical *advancement is done* presently and hence electronic system of voting through personal index numbers to national level decisions. Social globalization and *liberalism have given* ways to *lead* life in reformation towards upgradation of our *life, society* and economical status of our life also.

Mythical brainwashing political *system has always* made blind society to *a bold* and stagnant society where progress *is obstructed* by planning with team works of *priests* and political alliances groups and somewhere capitalist hack both of them and *lead* on the head of society. Generally, *such a type* of ruling system *is developed by the bourgeois* community who suddenly become richest by gambling, drudges smuggling, *and illegal* ways of earning money. Hence it seen that who had no money to going to school to taken education they become richest and hack political personality and political personality made alliances with spiritual businessman who wash out brain to common peoples and Afterall cheating too eating system developed by compact groups called as bourgeois ruled.

Ideology of NKSRNANTUROYism:

Truth given First Priority

Principle of NKSRNANTUROYism:

Consulate Co-operation Co-ordination Confederation (CCCC)

By the Peoples for the Peoples system development done. *Democracy* is by the peoples for the representative only and hence it turn in hybrid system somewhere like in India at present scenario

Hybrid system *developed* by Narender Modi and Amit Shah with Capitalist Ambani Adani and Spiritual Businessman.

Social Democratic Consulate Confederation Liberalism:

A **consulate** is the office of a consul. A type of diplomatic mission, it is usually subordinate to the state's main representation in the capital of that foreign country (host state), usually an embassy (or, only between two Commonwealth countries, a high commission). The term "consulate" may refer not only to the office of a consul, but also to the building occupied by the consul and the consul's staff. The consulate may share premises with the embassy itself.

Consuls of various ranks may have specific legal authority for certain activities, such as notarizing documents. As such, diplomatic personnel with other responsibilities may receive consular letters patent (commissions). Aside from those outlined in the Vienna Convention on Diplomatic Relations, there are few formal requirements outlining what a consular official must do. For example, for some countries, consular officials may be responsible for the issue of visas; other countries may limit "consular services" to providing assistance to compatriots, legalization of documents, etc. Nonetheless, consulates proper will be headed by consuls of various ranks, even if such officials have little or no connection with the more limited sense of consular service.

Activities of a consulate include protecting the interests of their citizens temporarily or permanently resident in the host country, issuing passports; issuing visas to foreigners and public diplomacy. However, the principal role of a consulate lies traditionally in promoting trade—assisting companies to invest and to import and export goods and services both inwardly to their home country and outward to their host country. Although it is not admitted publicly, consulates, like embassies, may also gather intelligence information from the assigned country.

Social Consulate Liberalization

The Social consulate Liberalization system is *such a system* where *expert* decisions and consultation taken and public opinion taken *by an online* voting system of digital citizen system World migration of human beings are making globalization. Mixed community formed to every nation. So, it required Social consulate Liberalization.

Foundation Base of Social Consulate Liberalism:

1. Social Liberalism:
2. Three Phase and three Stage system:
3. Equality to judicial:
4. Unity in diversity:

Three house system *development is a basic* system to active nations for development. Zonal *government is required as a basic* system of nations remaining groups of language, groups of culture differentiations among regions and *zones*.

Social system is man-made Realization:

1. Whom we *worship,* they were *born, brought* up, *guided* or ruled as social or political or both.

2. God actually *guides* and orders *demonstrators*. Lord was Law and *Order's* ruling demonstrator. In primitive society god/lord *remained* as owner of all property and common peoples, so common peoples *were considered slaves*. Servant system *came* far later in society *whereas* there was *a* human right given something that due to *work gets* money/rent. Service systems come as various *works are done* and get payment. E.g. *in the United* nation their hade system *was given* later *to the queen* as they convince as *a servant* up *to the later* 20th century but recently using yours obediently.

3. Folk *communities* born as Godism and Lordism execute and *are continued* to *word* shipping. That story *of a lord* reputed and system to offering continues *as they believe* their lord *remains* alive.

4. Comparison with previous ruler and saying new personality rebirth as older one.

5. Numbers of hundreds or thousands or millions counting as same and identical *whereas* thousand years of gaping *remain* among them.

6. The human identity of ruler comes first in society and later landmarks, universe bodies' identity given on the name of ruler in every society. Rivers and *mountains are given names* of rules and those *change from time* to time and even *today the system remains* as *a continuous* process *of the human* social system.

7. *Fire is the first* step *to the formation of human* society and copper *discovers a given* shuttle system of society where slavery become strongest system and caste system developed by rules.

8. Village society revolute to township. Township form as to owner Ship.

Democracy and it disadvantage: Democracy is by the peoples but for representative.

Social Consulate Liberalism: BY the peoples and for the peoples where national laws only to be implement or changes as per voting base of common peoples.

Root of National Development:

1. Citizenship required *to be given* by birth and by court order if *applied with the witness of a permanent* citizen as wife or husband or reputed company authority.

2. Unauthorized development of common *peoples' houses* for shelter in vacant or unusual land *requires* authority but that to be *a taxing* system and colonial development *to be done* with tax implementation.

3. Always there are required to balancing import and exports by which economical development to be at list balancing by system.

Foundation Base of Social Consulate Liberalism:

1. Social Liberalism:
2. Three Phase and three Stage system:
3. Equality to judicial:
4. Unity in diversity:

Three house system *development is a basic* system to active nations for development. Zonal *government is required as a basic* system of nations remaining groups of language, groups of culture differentiations among regions and *zones*.

Social system is man-made Realization:

1. Whom we *worship,* they were *born, brought* up, *guided* or ruled as social or political or both.

2. God actually *guides* and orders *demonstrators*. Lord was Law and *Order's* ruling demonstrator. In primitive society god/lord *remained* as owner of all property and common peoples, so common peoples *were considered slaves*. Servant system *came* far later in society *whereas* there was *a* human right given something that due to *work gets* money/ rent. Service systems come as various *works are done* and get payment. E.g. *in the United* nation their hade system *was given* later *to the queen* as a *convenience as a* servant up to later 20th century but recently using yours obediently.

3. Folk *communities* born as Godism and Lordism execute and *are continued* to *word* shipping. That story *of a lord* reputed and system to offering continues *as they believe* their lord *remains* alive.

4. Comparison with previous ruler and saying new personality rebirth as older one.

5. Numbers of hundreds or thousands or millions counting as same and identical *whereas* thousand years of gaping *remain* among them.

6. The human identity of ruler comes first in society and later landmarks, universe bodies' identity given on the name of ruler in every society. *Rivers and mountains are given names* of rules and those *change from time* to time and even *today the system remains* as *a continuous* process of human social system.

7. *Fire is the first* step *to the formation of human* society and copper *discovers a given* shuttle system of society where slavery *becomes the* strongest system and caste system developed by rules.

8. Village society revolute to township. Township form as to *ownerShip*.

Democracy and *its disadvantage*: Democracy is by the *people* but for *representatives*.

Social Consulate Liberalism: BY the peoples and for the peoples where national laws only to be *implemented* or *changed* as *per the voting* base of common peoples.

Root of National Development:

1. Citizenship required *to be given* by birth and by court order if *applied with a witness* of permanent citizen as wife or husband or reputed company authority.

2. Unauthorized development of common *peoples' houses* for shelter in vacant or unusual land *requires* authority but that to be *a taxing* system and colonial development *to be done* with tax implementation.

3. Always there are required to balancing import and exports by which economical development to be at list balancing by system.

Enlighten of Society

The Enlightenment's emphasis on reason shaped philosophical, political and scientific discourse from the late 17th to the early 19th century. Matthew White traces the Enlightenment back to its roots in the aftermath of the Civil War, and forward to its effects on the present day.

The Enlightenment – the great 'Age of Reason' – is defined as the period of rigorous scientific, political and philosophical discourse that *characterized* European society during the 'long' 18th century: from the late 17th century to the ending of the Napoleonic Wars in 1815. This was a period of huge change in thought and reason, which (in the words of historian Roy Porter) was 'decisive in the making of modernity'. Centuries of custom and tradition were brushed aside in *favor* of exploration, individualism, tolerance and scientific *endeavor*, which, in tandem with developments in industry and politics, witnessed the emergence of the 'modern world'.

The ancient civilisations of Greece and Rome were revered by enlightened thinkers, who viewed these communities as potential models for how modern society could be *organized*. Many commentators of the late 17th century were eager to achieve a clean break from what they saw as centuries of political tyranny, in *favor* of personal freedoms and happiness *centered* on the individual. Chief among these thinkers was philosopher and physician John Locke, whose *Two Treatises of Government* (published in 1689) advocated a separation of church and state, religious toleration, the right to property ownership and a contractual obligation on governments to recognise the innate 'rights' of the people.

Locke believed that reason and human consciousness were the gateways to contentment and liberty, and he demolished the notion that human knowledge was somehow pre-programmed and mystical. Locke's ideas reflected the earlier but equally influential works of Thomas Hobbes, which similarly advocated new social contracts between the state and civil society as the key to unlocking personal happiness for all.

Scientific revolution

These new enlightened views of the world were also encapsulated in the explosion of scientific *endeavor* that occurred during the 18th century. With the rapid expansion of print culture from around 1700, and increasing levels of literacy, details of experimentation and discovery were eagerly consumed by the reading public.

Margaret Cavendish's *Blazing World*

View images from this item (9)

Cavendish's ground-breaking proto-novel wove original scientific theories into a fictional narrative.

This growth of 'natural philosophy' (the term 'science' was only coined later in the 18th century) was underpinned by the application of rational thought and reason to scientific enquiry; first espoused by Francis Bacon in the early 1600s, this approach built on the earlier work of Copernicus and Galileo dating from the medieval period. Scientific experimentation (with instrumentation) was used to shed new light on nature and to challenge superstitious interpretations of the living world, much of which had been deduced from uncritical readings of historical texts.

Copernicus' celestial spheres

View images from this item (2)

First edition of *On the Revolutions of the Heavenly Spheres* (1543), in which Copernicus argued that the positions of the stars and planetary orbits could be better explained by the sun being at the ***center*** of the universe with the planets rotating around it in a circular motion, as shown in this iconic diagram.

Galileo's sunspot letters

View images from this item (2)

These letters record astronomical observations made by the Italian physicist and astronomer Galileo Galilei in 1612.

At the forefront of the scientific revolution stood Sir Isaac Newton, whose achievements in mathematics and physics ***revolutionized*** the contemporary view of the natural world. Born in 1643, Newton demonstrated a talent for mathematical theory at Trinity College, Cambridge, where his astonishingly precocious abilities led to his appointment as professor of mathematics at the age of just 26. Among Newton's weighty ***catalog*** of investigations were his treatises on optics, gravitational forces and mechanics (most famously encapsulated in his *Mathematical Principles of Natural Philosophy*, first published in 1687), all grounded in empirical experimentation as a way to demystify the physical world.

Newton's Principia Mathematica

Title page of the first edition of Newton's *Mathematical Principles of Natural Philosophy* (in Latin).

The discoveries of Sir Isaac Newton were complemented by those of a host of equally dazzling mathematicians, astronomers, chemists and physicists (Robert Hooke and Robert Boyle, for example), many of whom were members of the Royal Society (founded in 1660, and active today). Yet it was Newton's empirical approach to science that remained particularly influential. By embarking on purely rational and mathematical investigations, Newton was able to show that the natural world was 'amenable to observations and experiment', engendering a feeling among the scientific community that 'Nature had finally been fathomed'.

Micrographia by Robert Hooke, 1665

View images from this item (23)

Hooke's *Micrographia* was the first important work on microscopy, the study of minute objects through a microscope.

The pursuit of rational scientific knowledge was never the preserve of an educated elite. As well as fertilising a huge trade in published books and pamphlets, scientific investigation created a buoyant industry in scientific instruments, many of which were relatively inexpensive to buy and therefore available to the general public. Manufacturers of telescopes, microscopes, barometers, air pumps and thermometers prospered during the 18th century, particularly after 1750 when the names of famous scientific experimenters became household names: Benjamin Franklin, Joseph Priestley, William Herschel and Sir Joseph Banks, for example.

Ephraim Chambers's *Cyclopaedia*, 1741

View images from this item (13)

Encyclopedias, grammars and dictionaries became something of a craze in this period, helping to demystify the world in empirical terms. This huge fold-out page contains carefully ***labeled*** illustrations of anatomised human bodies.

Usage terms Public Domain

Secularisation and the impact on religion

Religion and personal faith were also subject to the tides of reason evident during the 18th century. Personal judgements on matters of belief were actively debated during the period, leading to scepticim, if not bold atheism, among an enlightened elite.

An enquiry into the nature of the human soul

View images from this item (4)

The author, Andrew Baxter argues that all matter is inherently inactive, and that the soul and an omnipotent divine spirit are the animating principles of all life. In making this argument, Baxter is rejecting the beliefs of more atheistic and materialist thinkers such as Thomas Hobbes and Baruch Spinoza.

These new views on religion led to increasing fears among the clergy that the Enlightenment was ungodly and thus harmful to the moral well-being of an increasingly secular society. With church attendance in steady decline throughout the 1700s, evidence of increasing agnosticism (the belief that true knowledge of God could never be fully gained) and a rejection of some scriptural teachings was close at hand. Distinct anti-clericalism (the criticism of church ministers and rejection of religious authority) also emerged in some circles, whipped up by the musings of 'deist' writers such as Voltaire, who argued that God's influence on the world was minimal and revealed only by one's own personal experience of nature.

Though certainly a challenge to accepted religious beliefs, the impulse of reason was considered by other contemporary observers to be a complement rather than a threat to spiritual orthodoxy: a means by which (in the words of John Locke) the true meaning of Scripture could be unlocked and 'understood in the plain, direct meaning of the words and phrases'.[4] Though difficult to measure or quantify, Locke believed that 'rational religion' based on personal experience and reflection could nevertheless still operate as a useful moral compass in the modern age.

New personal freedoms within the orbit of faith were extended to the relationship between the Church and state. In England, the recognition of dissenting religions was *formalized* by legislation, such as the 1689 Act of Toleration which permitted freedom of worship to Nonconformists (albeit qualified by allegiances to the Crown). Later, political emancipation for Roman Catholics – who were allowed new property rights – also reflected an enlightened impulse among the political elite: such measures sometimes created violent responses from working people. In 1780, for example, London was convulsed by a week of rioting in response to further freedoms granted to Catholics: a sign, perhaps, of how the enlightened thinking of politicians could diverge sharply from the sentiments of the humble poor.

View images from this item (1)

The Gordon Riots of June 1780 were in response to legislation passed permitting Catholics greater freedom in society (such as being allowed to join the Army). The riots were so bad that 15,000 troops were deployed to quell the disturbances and nearly 300 rioters were shot dead by soldiers.

From his shop in Westminster, Ignatius Sancho witnessed 'the burnings and devastations' of the Gordon Riots. He described the 'ridiculous confusion' in a series of letters, dated 6–9 June 1780.

Usage terms Public Domain

Political freedoms, contracts and rights

Public debates about what qualified as the best forms of government were heavily influenced by enlightened ideals, most notably Rousseau's and Diderot's notions of egalitarian freedom and the 'social contract'. By the end of the 18th century most European nations **harbored** movements calling for political reform, inspired by radical enlightened ideals which advocated clean breaks from tyranny, monarchy and absolutism.

Late 18th-century radicals were especially inspired by the writings of Thomas Paine, whose influence on revolutionary politics was felt in both America and France. Born into humble beginnings in England in 1737, by the 1770s Paine had arrived in America where he began agitating for revolution. Paine's most radical works, *The Rights of Man* and later *The Age of Reason* (both successful bestsellers in Europe), drew extensively on Rousseau's notions of the social contract. Paine reserved particular criticism for the hereditary privileges of ruling elites, whose power over the people, he believed, was only ever supported through simple historical tradition and the passive acceptance of the social order among the common people.

History of education in England

This article is about primary and secondary education. For the history of higher education in England, see Universities in the United Kingdom.

The history of education in England is documented from Saxon settlement of England, and the setting up of the first cathedral schools in 597 and 604.

Education in England remained closely linked to religious institutions until the nineteenth century, although charity schools and "free grammar schools", which were open to children of any religious beliefs, became more common in the early modern period. Nineteenth century reforms expanded education provision and introduced widespread state-funded schools. By the 1880s education was compulsory for children aged 5 to 10, with the school leaving age progressively raised since then, most recently to 18 in 2015.

The education system was expanded and reorganized multiple times throughout the 20th century, with a Tripartite System introduced in the 1940s, splitting secondary education into grammar schools, secondary technical schools and secondary modern schools. In the 1960s this began to be phased out in *favor* of comprehensive schools. Further reforms in the 1980s introduced the National Curriculum and allowed parents to choose which school their children went to. Academies were introduced in the 2000s and became the main type of secondary school in the 2010s.

Scotland has a separate system; see History of education in Scotland, much of the information listed below is relevant to Wales but specific information on the development of Education in Wales can be found here.

Medieval period

Prior to the arrival of Augustine of Canterbury in England in 597 education was an oral affair, or followed the Roman model in diaspora and integrated families.

The earliest known organized schools in England were connected to the church. Augustine established a church in Canterbury (which later became St Augustine's Abbey) in 598, which included a school for the study of religious texts, and in 604 this was joined by another school at what is now Rochester Cathedral. Further schools were established throughout the British Isles in the seventh and eighth centuries, generally following one of two forms: grammar schools to teach Latin, and song schools to train singers for cathedral choirs.

During the Middle Ages, schools were established to teach Latin grammar to the sons of the aristocracy destined for priesthood or monastic work with the ministry of government or the law. Two universities were established in affiliation with the church: the University of Oxford, followed by the University of Cambridge, to assist in the further training of the Catholic Christian clergy. A reformed system of "free grammar schools" was established in the reign of Edward VI; these too provided routes towards priesthood. Apprenticeship was the main way for youths to enter practical occupations.

Early modern period

Endowed schools have a long history. The oldest, having been founded in 597 as a cathedral school) is King's School, Canterbury. Over time a group of the endowed schools became known as "public schools" to differentiate from private teaching by tutors and to indicate that they were open to the public regardless of religious beliefs, locality and social status. Charity school emerged in the 16th century with the purpose of educating poor children. Christ's Hospital is the most famous of these schools.

In Tudor England, Edward VI reorganized grammar schools and instituted new ones so that there was a national system of "free grammar schools." In theory these were open to all, offering free tuition to those who could not afford to pay fees. The vast majority of poor children did not attend these schools since their labour was economically critical to their families.

The Protestant Reformation had a major influence on education and literacy in England, as it encouraged the reading of the Bible in English ("the vernacular").

In 1562 the Statute of Artificers and Apprentices was passed to regulate and protect the apprenticeship system, forbidding anyone from *practicing* a trade or craft without first serving a 7-year period as an apprentice to a master. Guilds controlled many trades and used apprenticeships to control entry. (In practice sons of Freemen, members of the guilds, could negotiate shorter terms of training).

Following the Act of Uniformity in 1662, religious dissenters set up academies to educate students of dissenting families, who did not wish to subscribe to the articles of the established Church of England. Some of these 'dissenting academies' still survive, the oldest being Bristol Baptist College. Several Oxford colleges (Harris Manchester, Mansfield, and Regent's Park) are also descendants of this movement.

From 1692, 'parish' apprenticeships under the Elizabethan Poor Law came to be used as a way of providing for poor, illegitimate and orphaned children of both sexes alongside the regular system of skilled apprenticeships, which tended to provide for boys from slightly more affluent backgrounds. These parish apprenticeships, which could be created with the assent of two Justices of the Peace, supplied apprentices for occupations of lower status such as farm labouring, brickmaking and menial household service.

Until as late as the nineteenth century, all university fellows and many schoolmasters were expected or required to be in holy orders.

Schoolmistresses typically taught the three Rs (reading, writing and 'rithmetic) in dame schools, charity schools, or informal village schools.

Historian David Mitch argues that private philanthropy was a major source of funding by the 1640s, and in that regard England was distinctive among modern nations. The endowments were permanent, and were still active in the 19th century. In addition to the landed elites in gentry, merchants and clergy were generous in supporting educational philanthropy. The national system that was developed in the last two thirds of the 19th century incorporated the earlier endowments.

Eighteenth century

In the early years of the Industrial Revolution entrepreneurs began to resist the restrictions of the apprenticeship system, and a legal ruling established that the Statute of Apprentices did not apply to trades that were not in existence when it was passed in 1563, thus excluding many new 18th century industries.

In the 18th and 19th centuries, the Society for Promoting Christian Knowledge founded many charity schools for poor students in the 7 to 11 age group. These schools were the basis for the development of modern concepts of primary and secondary education. The Society also was an early provider of teacher education.

Sunday School Movement

Main article: Sunday school

Robert Raikes initiated the Sunday School Movement, having inherited a publishing business from his father and become proprietor of the Gloucester Journal in 1757. The movement started with a school for boys in the slums. Raikes had been involved with those incarcerated at the county Poor Law (part of the jail at that time); he believed that "vice" would be better prevented than cured, with schooling as the best intervention. The best available time was Sunday, as the boys were often working in the factories the other six days. The best available teachers were lay people. The textbook was the Bible. The original curriculum started with teaching children to read and then having them learn the catechism, reasoning that reading comprehension acquired through Bible study could be transferred to secular studies.

Raikes used his newspaper to publicize the schools and bore most of the cost in the early years. The movement began in July 1780 in the home *of Mrs.* Meredith. Only boys attended, and she heard the lessons of the older boys who coached the younger. Later, girls also attended. Within two years, several schools opened in and around Gloucester. Raikes published an account on 3 November 1783 of Sunday School in his paper, and later word of the work spread through the Gentleman's Magazine, and in 1784, a letter to the Arminian Magazine.

The original schedule for the schools, as written by Raikes was "The children were to come after ten in the morning, and stay till twelve; they were then to go home and return at one; and after reading a lesson, they were to be conducted to Church. After Church, they were to be employed in repeating the catechism till after five, and then dismissed, with an injunction to go home without making a noise."

Nineteenth century

In the 19th century the Church of England sponsored most formal education until the government established free, compulsory education towards the end of that century. University College London was established as the first secular college in England, open to students of all religions (or none), followed by King's College London; the two institutions formed the University of London. Durham University was also established in the early nineteenth century. Towards the end of the century, the "*red brick*" universities, new public universities, were founded.

Since the establishment of Lady Margaret Hall (Oxford) Bedford College (London), Girton College (Cambridge) and Somerville College (Oxford) in the 19th century, women also can obtain a university degree.

National schools and British Schools

Prior to the nineteenth century, most schools were run by church authorities and stressed religious education. The Church of England resisted early attempts for the state to provide secular education. In 1811, the Anglican National Society for Promoting the Education of the Poor in the Principles of the Established Church in England and Wales was established. The schools founded by the National Society were called National Schools. Most of the surviving schools were eventually absorbed into the state system under the Butler Act (1944), and to this day many state schools, most of them primary schools, maintain a link to the Church of England, reflecting their historic origins. The Protestant non-conformist, non-denominational, or "British schools" were founded *by the Society* for Promoting the Lancasterian System for the Education of the Poor, an organization formed in 1808 by Joseph Fox, William Allen and Samuel Whitbread and supported by several evangelical and non-conformist Christians.

In 1814, compulsory apprenticeship by indenture was abolished. By 1831, Sunday School in Great Britain was ministering weekly to 1,250,000 children, approximately 25% of the population. As these schools preceded the first state funding of schools for the common public, they are sometimes seen as a forerunner to the current English school system.

Ragged schools

Main article: Ragged school

In 1818, John Pounds, known as the crippled cobbler, set up a school and began teaching poor children reading, writing, and arithmetic without charging fees.

In 1820, Samuel Wilderspin opened the first infant school in Spitalfields.

After John Pounds' death in 1839 Thomas Guthrie wrote Plea for Ragged Schools and started a ragged school in Edinburgh, another one was started in Aberdeen. In 1844 Anthony Ashley-Cooper, 7th Earl of Shaftesbury formed the 'Ragged School Union' dedicated to the free education of destitute children and over the next eight years over 200 free schools for poor children were established in Britain. with some 300,000 children passing through the London Ragged Schools alone between 1844 and 1881.

Government involvements

In August 1833, Parliament voted sums of money each year for the construction of schools for poor children, the first time the state had become involved with education in England and Wales (whereas a *program* for universal education in Scotland had been initiated in the seventeenth century). A meeting in Manchester in 1837, chaired by Mark Philips, led to the creation of the Lancashire Public Schools' Association. The association proposed that non-denominational schools should be funded from local taxes. Also 1837, the Whig former Lord Chancellor Henry Brougham presented a bill for public education.

In 1839 government grants for the construction and maintenance of schools were switched to voluntary bodies, and became conditional on a satisfactory inspection.

In 1840 the *Grammar Schools Act* expanded the Grammar School curriculum from classical studies to include science and literature. In 1861 the Royal Commission on the state of popular education in England, chaired by the Duke of Newcastle, reported "The number of children whose names ought [in summer 1858 in England and Wales] to have been on the school books, in order that all might receive some education, was 2,655,767. The number we found to be actually on the books was 2,535,462, thus leaving 120,305 children without any school instruction *whatsoever*."

In fee-charging public schools, which served the upper-class, important reforms were initiated by Thomas Arnold in Rugby. They redefined standards of masculinity, putting a heavy emphasis on sports and teamwork.

Robert Lowe (1811-1892), a powerful Liberal politician who worked closely with Prime Minister Gladstone, was a key reformer. He agreed with the consensus against too much centralization in English education, but wanted to improve educational standards, and prevent the waste of public money on inefficient teaching, especially in church schools. He introduced a revised code in 1861; future grants would be allocated not by the subjective judgment of inspectors but rather on the basis of the number of students passing an examination in reading, writing, and arithmetic. It was known as 'payment by results. The code ended the favoritism often shown by inspectors; it came under attack by ***school teachers***, inspectors, and Anglican and dissenting opponents of state activity.

The Elementary Education Act of 1870

Out of 4.3 million children of primary school age in England & Wales, 1 million were in purely voluntary schools and 1.3 million were in state aided school, but 2 million had no access to schools whatsoever.[25]

William Forster's Elementary Education Act 1870[26] required partially state-funded board schools to be set up to provide elementary (primary, in modern parlance) education in areas where existing provision was inadequate. Board schools were managed by elected school boards. The schools remained fee-charging, but poor parents could be exempted. The previous government grant scheme established in 1833 ended on 31 December 1870.

Section 74 of the Act empowered school boards to, if they wished, make local byelaws making attendance compulsory between the ages of 5 and 13 but exempting any child aged over 10 who had reached the expected standard (which varied by board). Other exceptions included illness, if children worked, or lived too far from a school.

Two measures in the Act became, for religious reasons, matters of controversy within the governing Liberal Party. Firstly, nonconformists objected to their children being taught Anglican doctrine. As a compromise, William Cowper-Temple (pronounced "Cooper-Temple"), a Liberal MP, proposed that religious teaching in the new state schools be non-denominational, in practice restricted to learning the Bible and a few hymns: this became the famous Cowper-Temple clause (Section 14 of the Act). Section 7 also gave parents the right to withdraw their children from any religious instruction provided in board schools, and to withdraw their children to attend any other religious instruction of their choice.

Secondly, Section 25 gave school boards the power to, if they chose, pay the fees of poor children attending voluntary (i.e. church) schools. Although few school boards actually did so, the provision caused great anger among nonconformists, who saw this as local ratepayers' money being spent on Church of England schools. A large conference was held at Manchester in 1872 to lead resistance to the section, and one of the campaigners was the Birmingham politician Joseph Chamberlain, who emerged as a national figure for the first time. The resulting splits (some education campaigners, including Chamberlain, stood for Parliament as independent candidates) helped to cost the Liberals the 1874 election.

Compulsory and free primary education: 1880s and 1890s

The "Sandon Act" (Act of 1876) imposed a legal duty on parents to ensure that their children were educated. The Elementary Education Act 1880 (the "Mundella Act") required school boards to enforce compulsory attendance from 5 to 10 years, and permitted them to set a standard which children were required to reach before they could be employed. Poorer families were often tempted to send their children to work if the opportunity to earn an extra income was available. Attendance officers often visited the homes of children who failed to attend school, which often proved to be ineffective. Children who were employed were required to have a certificate to show they had reached the *educational standard*. Employers of these children who were unable to show this were penalised.

The Elementary Education Act 1891 provided for the state payment of school fees up to ten shillings per head, making primary education effectively free.

The Voluntary Schools Act 1897 provided grants to public elementary schools not funded by school boards (typically Church schools).

Another act in 1899 raised the school leaving age to 12.

In the late Victorian period grammar schools were *reorganized* and their curriculum was *modernized*. Latin was still taught.

Funding of technical colleges

The Technical Instruction Act 1889 was passed. According to D. Evans, "It gave powers to the County Councils and the Urban Sanitary Authorities to levy a penny tax to support technical and manual instruction. The curricula in technical institutions also had to be approved by the Science and Art Department. In the following year the Local Taxation Act introduced the 'whiskey tax', which made extra money available for technical instruction."

From April 1900 higher elementary schools were recognized, providing education from the age of 10 to 15.

Balfour and Local Education Authorities

Balfour Act of 1902

Main article: Education Act 1902

The controversial Conservative Education Act 1902 (or 'Balfour Act') made radical changes to the entire educational system of England and Wales. It weakened the divide between schools run by the 2,9 able to set local tax rates, and the school boards were disbanded. Funds were provided for denominational religious instruction in voluntary elementary schools, owned primarily by the Church of England and Roman Catholics. The law was extended in 1903 to cover London.

G. R. Searle, like nearly all historians, argues the Act was a short-term political disaster for the Conservative Party because it outraged Methodists, Baptists and other nonconformists. It *subsidized* the religions they rejected. However Searle argues it was a long-term success. The Church schools now had some financing from local ratepayers and had to meet uniform standards. It led to a rapid growth of secondary schools, with over 1000 opening by 1914, including 349 for girls. Eventually (in 1944), the

Anglican schools were effectively *nationalized*. Grammar schools also became funded by the LEA. The act was of particular significance as it allowed for all schools, including denominational schools, to be funded through rates (local taxation), and ended the role of locally elected school boards that often attracted women, non-conformists and labour union men. The Liberals came to power in 1906, but their attempt to repeal the act was blocked by the House of Lords, setting up a major constitutional confrontation.

In the long run the Nonconformist schools practically vanished. In 1902 the Methodists operated 738 schools, but these rapidly declined throughout the 20th century. Only 28 remained in 1996.

The Fisher Act of 1918

The Fisher Education Act 1918 made secondary education compulsory up to age 14 and gave responsibility for secondary schools to the state. Under the Act, many higher elementary schools and endowed grammar schools sought to become state funded central schools or secondary schools. However, most children attended elementary (primary, in modern parlance) school until age 14, rather than going to a separate school for secondary education.

The act was also known as the "Fisher Act" as it was devised by H. A. L. Fisher. The act enforced compulsory education from 5–14 years, but also included provision for compulsory part-time education for all 14- to 18-year-olds. There were also plans for expansion in tertiary education, by raising the participation age to 18. This was dropped because of the cuts in public spending after World War I. This is the first act which started planning provisions for young people to remain in education until the age of 18. The 1918 act was not immediately implemented, instead waiting until an act in 1921 before coming into effect.

After the passing of the Local Government Act 1929, Poor Law schools became state funded elementary schools. The concept of junior technical schools was introduced in the 1930s to provide vocational education at secondary level, but few were ever opened.

Spens and Norwood reports

In 1937 historian G.A.N. Lowndes identified a "Silent Social Revolution" in England and Wales since 1895 that could be credited to the expansion of public education:

The contribution which a sound and universal system of public education can make to the sobriety, orderliness and stability of a population is perhaps the most patent of its benefits. What other gains can be placed to its credit?...Can it be claimed that the widening of educational opportunity in the long run repays that cost to the community by a commensurate increase in the national wealth and prosperity? Or can it be claimed that it is making the population happier, better able to *utilize* its leisure, more adaptable? Anyone who knows how the schools have come to life in the past decade, anyone who is in a position to take a wide view of the social condition of the people and compare conditions today with those forty years ago, will have no hesitation in answering these questions in the affirmative.

A report of 1938 of a committee chaired by Will Spens, a former Vice-Chancellor of the University of Cambridge, recommended that entry to schools would be based on intelligence testing. This was followed by the Norwood Report of 1943 which advocated the "Tripartite System" of secondary education which was introduced in the late 1940s.

1944: Butler

See also: Education Act 1944 and Tripartite System

The Education Act 1944 was an answer to surging social and educational demands created by the war and the widespread demands for social reform. The Education Act 1944, relating to England and Wales, was authored by Conservative Rab Butler and known as "the Butler Act", defined the modern split between primary education and secondary education at age 11.

The Butler Act was also an historic compromise between church and state. Three new categories of schools were created. The first were Voluntary Controlled schools whose costs were met by the State, and would be controlled by the local education authority. The school kept the title deeds to the land, but taught an agreed religious education syllabus. These schools were favoured by the Anglicans: over half their schools chose this status, and were soon effectively absorbed into the state system. The second were Voluntary Aided schools, which retained greater influence over school admission policies, staffing and curriculum, and which were preferred by the Roman Catholics and by some Anglican schools. They would have all of their running costs met by the State, but their capital costs would only be 50% state funded (later increased to 75% by the Education Act 1959, and now 90%).The third were Direct Grant Schools: former independent schools, often town grammar schools and predominantly in the north of England, who accepted a state grant in return for providing free education to many students but still charging for others. The state had little control on syllabus or admissions policy. The schools kept their title deeds.

The elite system of public schools was practically unchanged; Butler assembled a committee which produced the Fleming Report of July 1944, recommending that places at public schools be made available to state-funded scholarships, but its recommendations were not implemented.

The school leaving age was raised to 15 under the Butler Act, with an aspiration to raise it in time to 16, although this did not take place until the early 1970s (see below). The Act also recommended compulsory part-time education for all young people until the age of 18, but this provision was dropped so as not to overburden the post-war spending budget (as had happened similarly with the Act of 1918).

Changes in government approaches towards education meant that it was no longer regarded adequate for a child to leave education aged 14, as that is the age when they were seen to really understand and appreciate the value of education, as well as being the period when adolescence was at its height. It was beginning to be seen as the worst age for a sudden switch from education to employment, with the additional year in schooling to only provide benefits for the children when they leave. Although there were concerns about the effects of having less labour from these children, it was hoped that the outcome of a larger quantity of more qualified, skilled workers would eliminate the deficit problem from the loss of unskilled labour.

The 1944 Act took effect in 1947 when the Labour Party was in power and it adopted the Tripartite System, consisting of grammar schools, secondary modern schools and secondary technical schools. It rejected the comprehensive school proposals *favored* by a few in the Labour Party as more *equalitarian. Under* the tripartite model, students who passed an exam were able to attend a prestigious grammar school. Those who did not pass the selection test attended secondary modern schools or technical schools.

The new law was widely praised by Conservatives because it honoured religion and social hierarchy, by Labour because it opened new opportunities for the working class, and by the general public because it ended the fees they had to pay. The act became a permanent part of the Post-war consensus supported by the three major parties.

However, selection of *academically* gifted children to attend grammar school became increasingly controversial in the 1960s. Critics on the left attacked grammar schools as elitist because a student had to pass a test at age 11 to get in. Defenders argued that grammar schools allow pupils to obtain a good education through merit rather than through family income. No changes were made. In some areas, notably that of the London County Council, comprehensive schools had been introduced. They had no entrance test and were open to all children living in the school catchment area. However, despite tentative support for 'multilateralism' in secondaries, and a desire to raise the standard of secondary moderns to that of private institutions, from Minister for Education Ellen Wilkinson, the majority of Labour MPs were more concerned with implementing the 1944 Act; her successor George Tomlinson saw this through, although the secondary technicals remained underdeveloped.

Circular 10/65 and comprehensive education

Main article: Comprehensive school (England and Wales)

In 1965 the Labour government required all local education authorities to formulate proposals to move away from selection at eleven, replacing the tripartite system with comprehensive schools. This was done by the minister Tony Crosland by means of Circular 10/65 and withholding funding from any school that sought to retain selection. This circular was vehemently opposed by the grammar school lobby. Some counties procrastinated and retained the Tripartite System in all but a few experimental areas. Those authorities have locally administered selection tests.

The Circular also requested consultation between LEAs and the partially state-funded direct grant grammar schools on their participation in a comprehensive system, but little movement occurred. The 1970 report of the Public Schools Commission chaired by David Donnison recommended that the schools choose between becoming voluntary aided comprehensives and full independence. This was finally put into effect by the Direct Grant Grammar Schools (Cessation of Grant) Regulations 1975. Some schools (almost all Catholic) became fully state-funded, while the majority became independent fee-paying schools.

In 1973 the introduction of the Education (Work Experience) Act allowed LEAs to organize work experience for the additional final year school students.

In some counties around the country, these changes also led to the introduction of Middle schools in 1968, where students were kept at primary or junior school for an additional year, meaning that the number of students in secondary schools within these areas remained virtually constant through the change. As of 2007, there are now fewer than 400 middle schools across England, situated in just 22 Local Education Authorities.

Raising of school leaving age (ROSLA)

Main article: Raising of school leaving age in England and Wales

In 1964, preparations had begun to raise the school leaving age to 16 to be enforced from 1 September 1973 onwards. This increased the legal leaving age from 15 to 16 and for one year, 1973, there were no 15-year-old school leavers as the students, by law, had to complete an additional year of education.

Many secondary schools were unable to accommodate the new 5th year students. The solution to the problem was to construct new buildings (often referred to as *"ROSLA Buildings"* or *"ROSLA Blocks"*) for the schools that needed to extend their capacity.[53] This provided the space to cope with the new cohort of *ROSLA students*. The ROSLA Buildings were delivered to schools in self assembly packs and were not intended to stand long-term, though some have proven to have stood much longer than was initially planned and were still in use in the 2010s.

Primary schools

The 1967 Plowden Report advocated a more child-*centered* approach to primary education, and also supported the introduction of middle schools. While many of the report's recommendations were never implemented, primary schools began to move away from rote learning in the late 1960s and 1970s.

Apprenticeships

High technology industry (Aerospace, Nuclear, Oil & Gas, Automotive, Power Generation and Distribution etc.) trained its professional engineers via the advanced apprenticeship system of learning – usually a 5-year process. The higher Apprenticeship framework in the 1950s, 60s and 70s was designed to allow young people (16 years) an alternative path to A Levels to achieve an academic qualification at level 4 or 5 NVQ (National Vocational Qualification). The Higher Apprenticeship Framework was open to young people who had a minimum of 4 GCE "O" Levels to enroll in an Ordinary National Certificate or Diploma or a City & Guilds technician course. For advanced engineering apprenticeships "O" Levels had to include Mathematics, Physics, and English language. The advanced apprenticeship framework's purpose was to provide a supply of young people seeking to enter work-based learning via apprenticeships by offering structured high value learning and transferable skills and knowledge. These apprenticeships were enabled by linking industry with local technical colleges and professional Engineering Institutions.

The Advanced Apprenticeship Framework offered clear pathways and outcomes that addressed the issues facing the industry. This system was in place since the 1950s. The system provided young people with an alternative to staying in full-time education beyond 16/18 to gain pure academic qualifications without work-based learning. The Advanced Apprenticeships of the 1950s, 60s and 70s provided the necessary preparation towards Engineering Technician, Technician Engineer or Chartered Engineer registration. Apprentices undertook a variety of job roles in numerous technical functions to assist the work of engineers, in the design, development, manufacture and maintenance of production system.

Industry Training Boards (ITBs) were introduced by the Industrial Training Act (1964 and amended 1982), requiring employers in a number of sectors to pay a training levy to their industry training board or apply a similar sum to the provision of training to their employees. Later phased out, the Construction Industry Training Board survives (as of 2018).

In modern times, apprenticeship became less important, especially as employment in heavy industry and artisan trades has declined since the 1980s. Traditional apprenticeships reached their lowest point in the 1980s: by that time, training programmes were rare and people who were apprentices learned mainly by example.

Conservative governments, from 1979 to 1997

Following the 1979 General Election, the Conservative Party regained power under Margaret Thatcher. In the early period it made two main changes:

New Vocationalism was expanded (Labour had made some small efforts beforehand, but the Conservatives expanded it considerably). This was seen as an effort to reduce the high youth unemployment, which was regarded as one of the causes of the sporadic rioting at the end of the seventies. The Youth Opportunities Programme was the main scheme, offered to 16- to 18-year-olds. It had been introduced in 1978 under the Labour government of James Callaghan, was expanded in 1980 under the Conservative government of Margaret Thatcher, and ran until 1983 when it was replaced by the Youth Training Scheme.

The Assisted Places Scheme was introduced in 1980, whereby gifted children who could not afford to go to fee-paying schools would be given free places in those schools if they could pass the school's entrance exam.

In 1986, National Vocational Qualifications (NVQs) were introduced, in an attempt to revitalize vocational training. Still, by 1990, apprenticeship took up only two-thirds of one percent of total employment.

The Education Reform Act of 1988

The 1988 Education Reform Act made considerable changes to the education system. These changes were aimed at creating a 'market' in education with schools competing with each other for 'customers' (pupils). The theory was that "bad" schools would lose pupils to the "good" schools and either have to improve, reduce in capacity or close.

The reforms included the following:

The National Curriculum was introduced, which made it compulsory for schools to teach certain subjects and syllabuses. Previously the choice of subjects had been up to the school.

National curriculum assessments were introduced at the Key Stages 1 to 4 (ages 7, 11, 14 and 16 respectively) through what were formerly called Standard Assessment Tests (SATS). At Key Stage 4 (age 16), the assessments were made from the GCSE exam.

Formula funding was introduced, which meant that the more children a school could attract to it, the more money the school would receive.

Open enrolment and choice for parents was brought back, so that parents could choose or influence which school their children went to.

Schools could, if enough of their pupils' parents agreed, opt out of local government control, becoming grant maintained schools and receiving funding directly from the central government. The government offered more money than the school would get usually from the local authority as an enticement. This was seen as a politically motivated move since the Conservative central government was taking control from local authorities which were often run by other parties.

Religious education was reformed; Chapter 1 of the law required that the majority of collective worship be "wholly or mainly of a broadly Christian character".

Apprenticeship reform

In 1994, the government introduced Modern Apprenticeships (since renamed 'Apprenticeships'), based on frameworks devised by Sector Skills Councils. These frameworks contain a number of separately certified elements:

a knowledge-based element, typically certified through a qualification known as a 'Technical Certificate';

a competence-based element, typically certified through an NVQ; and

Key Skills (literacy and numeracy).

Education Act 1996

Between 1976 and 1997, the minimum school leaving arrangements were:

A child whose sixteenth birthday falls in the period 1 September to 31 January inclusive, may leave compulsory schooling at the end of the Spring term (the following Easter).

A child whose sixteenth birthday falls in the period 1 February to 31 August, may leave on the Friday before the last Monday in May.

Under section 8(4) of the Education Act 1996, a new single school leaving date was set for 1998 and all subsequent years thereafter. This was set as the last Friday in June in the school year which the child reaches the age of 16.

Under section 7 of the Act, it was made an obligation for parents to ensure a full-time education for their children either at school or "otherwise" which formalized the status of home education.

Labour, from 1997 to 2010

New Labour adopted an "Education, Education, Education" slogan in the mid-1990s, but maintained many of the Conservative changes after returning to power after the 1997 general election. The following changes did take place, however:

The previous Labour focus on the comprehensive system was shifted to a focus on tailoring education to each child's ability. Critics see this as reminiscent of the original intentions of the Tripartite system.

Grant-maintained status was abolished, with GM schools being given the choice of rejoining the local authority as a maintained community school, or becoming a foundation school.

Although the Government-run eleven-plus exam selection exam for all children had now been abolished, voluntary selection tests continue in certain areas, where some of the original grammar schools have been retained. These areas include: Northern Ireland and some English counties and districts including Devon, Dorset, Kent, Buckinghamshire, Essex, Birmingham, Trafford, Wiltshire,

North Yorkshire, Calderdale, Kirklees, Wirral, Warwickshire, Gloucestershire, Lincolnshire and some London boroughs such as Bexley, Kingston-upon-Thames and Redbridge. There have been various (so far unsuccessful) attempts by campaigners to abolish all remaining grammar schools. The remaining grammar schools are now thus still selective, typically taking the top 10-25% of those from the local catchment area. Some of the still-existing grammar schools in the United Kingdom can trace their history back to earlier than the sixteenth century.

Labour expanded a policy started by the Conservatives of creating specialist schools via the specialist schools programme. This new type of secondary school teaches the National Curriculum subjects plus a few specialist branches of knowledge (e.g. business studies) not found in most other schools. These schools are allowed to select 10% of their pupils.

Numbers: In 1997 there were 196 of these schools. In August 2002 there were 1000. By 2006 the plan was to have 2000, and the goal was to make all secondary schools specialist eventually.

The Beacon Schools programme was established in England in 1998. Its aim was to identify high performing schools, in order to help them form partnerships with each other and to provide examples of effective practice for other schools. The programme was replaced in August 2005 with more broadly based programmes; the Leading Edge Partnership programme (for secondary schools) and Primary Strategy Learning Networks (PSLNs) (at the primary level).

A new grade of Advanced Skills Teacher was created, with the intention that highly skilled teachers would be paid more if they accepted new posts with outreach duties beyond their own schools.

City Academies were introduced. These are new schools, built on the site of, or taking over from existing failing schools. A city academy is an independent school within the state system. It is outside the control of the local education authority and set up with substantial funding from interested third parties, which might be businesses, charities or private individuals.

Education Action Zones were introduced, which are deprived areas run by an action forum of people within that area with the intention of making that area's schools better.

Vocational qualifications were renamed/restructured as follows:

GNVQs became Vocational GCSEs and AVCEs.

NVQs scope expanded so that a degree-equivalent NVQ was possible.

The New Deal was introduced, which made advisors available to long-term unemployed (in the UK this is defined as being unemployed for more than 6 months) to give help and money to those who want to go back into Education.

Introduced Literacy and Numeracy Hours into schools, and set targets for literacy and numeracy.

Set Truancy targets.

Set a maximum class size of 30 for 5-7 year old.

Introduced the EMA, (Education Maintenance Allowance), which is paid to those between 16 and 18 as an enticement to remain in full-time education and get A-Levels/AVCEs.

A Performance Threshold was introduced in 2000 to allow experienced teachers access to higher rates of pay on meeting a set of performance standards, including a standard of pupil attainment. The performance-related pay changes have been bitterly opposed by teaching unions, most notably the National Union of Teachers which challenged the Threshold scheme by legal action.

Introduced Curriculum 2000, which reformed the Further Education system into the current structure of AS levels, A2 levels and Key Skills.

Abolished the Assisted Places Scheme.

A report was commissioned, led by the former chief-inspector of schools, Mike Tomlinson, into reform of the curriculum and qualifications structure for 14- to 19-year-olds. The report was published on 18 October 2004 and recommended the introduction of a diploma that would bring together both vocational and academic qualifications and ensure that all pupils had a basic set of core skills. It is proposed that the current qualifications would evolve into this diploma over the next decade, whether the government will follow the recommendations is yet to be seen — the Conservative Party have already introduced alternative proposals to return to norm-referencing in A-levels rather than the current system of criterion-referencing.

In 2003 a green paper entitled Every Child Matters was published. It built on existing plans to strengthen children's services and focused on four key areas:

Increasing the focus on supporting families and carvers as the most critical influence on children's lives

Ensuring necessary intervention takes place before children reach crisis point and protecting children from falling through the net

Addressing the underlying problems identified in the report into the death of Victoria Climbié – weak accountability and poor integration

Ensuring that the people working with children are valued, rewarded and trained

The green paper prompted a debate about services for children, young people and families resulting in a consultation with those working in children's services, and with parents, children and young people. The Government published *Every Child Matters: the Next Steps* in November 2004, and passed the Children Act 2004, providing the legislative spine for developing more effective and accessible services focused around the needs of children, young people and families.

In January 2007 Education Secretary Alan Johnson announced plans to extend the school leaving age in England to eighteen by 2013. This would raise the leaving age for the first time since 1972, when compulsory education was extended to sixteen. The changes included apprenticeships and work based training in addition to continued academic learning. This became law through the Education and Skills Act 2008, with the school leaving age raised to 17 in 2013 and 18 in 2015.

History of education in England

This article is about primary and secondary education. For the history of higher education in England, see Universities in the United Kingdom.

The history of education in England is documented from Saxon settlement of England, and the setting up of the first cathedral schools in 597 and 604.

Education in England remained closely linked to religious institutions until the nineteenth century, although charity schools and "free grammar schools", which were open to children of any religious beliefs, became more common in the early modern period. Nineteenth century reforms expanded education provision and introduced widespread state-funded schools. By the 1880s education was compulsory for children aged 5 to 10, with the school leaving age progressively raised since then, most recently to 18 in 2015.

The education system was expanded and reorganized multiple times throughout the 20th century, with a Tripartite System introduced in the 1940s, splitting secondary education into grammar schools, secondary technical schools and secondary modern schools. In the 1960s this began to be phased out in favors of comprehensive schools. Further reforms in the 1980s introduced the National Curriculum and allowed parents to choose which school their children went to. Academies were introduced in the 2000s and became the main type of secondary school in the 2010s.

Scotland has a separate system; see History of education in Scotland, much of the information listed below is relevant to Wales but specific information on the development of Education in Wales can be found here.

Medieval period

Prior to the arrival of Augustine of Canterbury in England in 597 education was an oral affair, or followed the Roman model in diaspora and integrated families.

The earliest known organized schools in England were connected to the church. Augustine established a church in Canterbury (which later became St Augustine's Abbey) in 598, which included a school for the study of religious texts, and in 604 this was joined by another school at what is now Rochester Cathedral. Further schools were established throughout the British Isles in the seventh and eighth centuries, generally following one of two forms: grammar schools to teach Latin, and song schools to train singers for cathedral choirs.

During the Middle Ages, schools were established to teach Latin grammar to the sons of the aristocracy destined for priesthood or monastic work with the ministry of government or the law. Two universities were established in affiliation with the church: the University of Oxford, followed by the University of Cambridge, to assist in the further training of the Catholic Christian clergy. A reformed system of "free grammar schools" was established in the reign of Edward VI; these too provided routes towards priesthood. Apprenticeship was the main way for youths to enter practical occupations.

Early modern period

Endowed schools have a long history. The oldest, having been founded in 597 as a cathedral school) is King's School, Canterbury. Over time a group of the endowed schools became known as "public schools" to differentiate from private teaching by tutors and to indicate that they were open to the public regardless of religious beliefs, locality and social status. Charity school emerged in the 16th century with the purpose of educating poor children. Christ's Hospital is the most famous of these schools.

In Tudor England, Edward VI reorganized grammar schools and instituted new ones so that there was a national system of "free grammar schools." In theory these were open to all, offering free tuition to those who could not afford to pay fees. The vast majority of poor children did not attend these schools since their labour was economically critical to their families.

The Protestant Reformation had a major influence on education and literacy in England, as it encouraged the reading of the Bible in English ("the vernacular").

In 1562 the Statute of Artificers and Apprentices was passed to regulate and protect the apprenticeship system, forbidding anyone from practice in a trade or craft without first serving a 7-year period as an apprentice to a master. Guilds controlled many trades and used apprenticeships to control entry. (In practice sons of Freemen, members of the guilds, could negotiate shorter terms of training).

Following the Act of Uniformity in 1662, religious dissenters set up academies to educate students of dissenting families, who did not wish to subscribe to the articles of the established Church of England. Some of these 'dissenting academies' still survive, the oldest being Bristol Baptist College. Savereal Oxford colleges (Harris Manchester, Mansfield, and Regent's Park) are also descendants of this movement.

From 1692, 'parish' apprenticeships under the Elizabethan Poor Law came to be used as a way of providing for poor, illegitimate and orphaned children of both sexes alongside the regular system of skilled apprenticeships, which tended to provide for boys from slightly more affluent backgrounds. These parish apprenticeships, which could be created with the assent of two Justices of the Peace, supplied apprentices for occupations of lower status such as farm labouring, brickmaking and menial household service.

Until as late as the nineteenth century, all university fellows and many schoolmasters were expected or required to be in holy orders.

Schoolmistresses typically taught the three Rs (reading, writing and 'arithmetic) in dame schools, charity schools, or informal village schools.

Historian David Mitch argues that private philanthropy was a major source of funding by the 1640s, and in that regard, England was distinctive among modern nations. The endowments were permanent, and were still active in the 19th century. In addition to the landed elites in gentry, merchants and clergy were generous in supporting educational philanthropy. The national system that was developed in the last two thirds of the 19th century incorporated the earlier endowments.

Eighteenth century

In the early years of the Industrial Revolution entrepreneurs began to resist the restrictions of the apprenticeship system, and a legal ruling established that the Statute of Apprentices did not apply to trades that were not in existence when it was passed in 1563, thus excluding many new 18th century industries.

In the 18th and 19th centuries, the Society for Promoting Christian Knowledge founded many charity schools for poor students in the 7 to 11 age group. These schools were the basis for the development of modern concepts of primary and secondary education. The Society also was an early provider of teacher education.

Sunday School Movement

*Main articl*e: Sunday school

Robert Raikes initiated the Sunday School Movement, having inherited a publishing business from his father and **became** proprietor of the Gloucester Journal in 1757. The movement started with a school for boys in the slums. Raikes had been involved with those incarcerated at the county Poor Law (part of the jail at that time); he believed that "vice" would be better prevented than cured, with schooling as the best intervention. The best available time was Sunday, as the boys were often working in the factories the other six days. The best available teachers were lay people. The textbook was the Bible. The original curriculum started with teaching children to read and then having them learn the catechism, reasoning that reading comprehension acquired through Bible study could be transferred to secular studies.

Raikes used his newspaper to publicize the schools and bore most of the cost in the early years. The movement began in July 1780 in the home of a Mrs. Meredith. Only boys attended, and she heard the lessons of the older boys who coached the younger. Later, girls also attended. Within two years, several schools opened in and around Gloucester. Raikes published an account on 3 November 1783 of Sunday School in his paper, and later word of the work spread through the Gentleman's Magazine, and in 1784, a letter to the Arminian Magazine.

The original schedule for the schools, as written by Raikes was "The children were to come after ten in the morning, and stay till twelve; they were then to go home and return at one; and after reading a lesson, they were to be conducted to Church. After Church, they were to be employed in repeating the catechism till after five, and then dismissed, with an injunction to go home without making a noise."

Nineteenth century

Somerville College, part of the University of Oxford, one of the first women's colleges in England (1879)

In the 19th century the Church of England sponsored most formal education until the government established free, compulsory education towards the end of that century. University College London was established as the first secular college in England, open to students of all religions (or none), followed by King's College London; the two institutions formed the University of London. Durham University was also established in the early nineteenth century. Towards the end of the century, the "redbrick" universities, new public universities, were founded.

Since the establishment of Lady Margaret Hall (Oxford) Bedford College (London), Girton College (Cambridge) and Somerville College (Oxford) in the 19th century, women also can obtain a university degree.

National schools and British Schools

Prior to the nineteenth century, most schools were run by church authorities and stressed religious education. The Church of England resisted early attempts for the state to provide secular education. In 1811, the Anglican National Society for Promoting the Education of the Poor in the Principles of the Established Church in England and Wales was established. The schools founded by the National Society were called National Schools. Most of the surviving schools were eventually absorbed into the state system under the Butler Act (1944), and to this day many state schools, most of them primary schools, maintain a link to the Church of England, reflecting their historic origins. The Protestant non-conformist, non-denominational, or "British schools" were founded by Society for Promoting the Lancastrian System for the Education of the Poor, an organization formed in 1808 by Joseph Fox, William Allen and Samuel Whitbread and supported by several evangelical and non-conformist Christians.

In 1814, compulsory apprenticeship by indenture was abolished. By 1831, Sunday School in Great Britain was ministering weekly to 1,250,000 children, approximately 25% of the population. As these schools preceded the first state funding of schools for the common public, they are sometimes seen as a forerunner to the current English school system.

Ragged schools

Main article: Ragged school

In 1818, John Pounds, known as the *crippled cobbler*, set up a school and began teaching poor children reading, writing, and arithmetic without charging fees.

In 1820, Samuel Wilder spin opened the first infant school in Spitalfields.

After John Pounds' death in 1839 Thomas Guthrie wrote Plea for Ragged Schools and started a ragged school in Edinburgh, another one was started in Aberdeen. In 1844 Anthony Ashley-Cooper, 7th Earl of Shaftesbury formed the 'Ragged School Union' dedicated to the free education of destitute children and over the next eight years over 200 free schools for poor children were established in Britain. with some 300,000 children passing through the London Ragged Schools alone between 1844 and 1881.

Government involvements

In August 1833, Parliament voted sums of money each year for the construction of schools for poor children, the first time the state had become involved with education in England and Wales (whereas a programs for universal education in Scotland had been initiated in the seventeenth century). A meeting in Manchester in 1837, chaired by Mark Philips, led to the creation of the Lancashire Public Schools' Association. The association proposed that non-denominational schools should be funded from local taxes. Also 1837, the Whig former Lord Chancellor Henry Brougham presented a bill for public education.

In 1839 government grants for the construction and maintenance of schools were switched to voluntary bodies, and became conditional on a satisfactory inspection.

In 1840 the Grammar Schools Act expanded the Grammar School curriculum from classical studies to include science and literature. In 1861 the Royal Commission on the state of popular education in England, chaired by the Duke of Newcastle, reported "The number of children whose names ought [in summer 1858 in England and Wales] to have been on the school books, in order that all might receive some education, was 2,655,767. The number we found to be actually on the books was 2,535,462, thus leaving 120,305 children without any school instruction *whatsoever*."

In fee-charging public schools, which served the upper-class, important reforms were initiated by Thomas Arnold in Rugby. They redefined standards of masculinity, putting a heavy emphasis on sports and teamwork.

Robert Lowe (1811-1892), a powerful Liberal politician who worked closely with Prime Minister Gladstone, was a key reformer. He agreed with the consensus against too much centralization in English education, but wanted to improve educational standards, and prevent the waste of public money on inefficient teaching, especially in church schools. He introduced a revised code in 1861; future grants would be allocated not by the subjective judgment of inspectors but rather on the basis of the number of students passing an examination in reading, writing, and arithmetic. It was known as 'payment by results. The code ended the favoritism often shown by inspectors; it came under attack by schoolteachers, inspectors, and Anglican and dissenting opponents of state activity.

William Forster drafted the first Education Act in 1870

Out of 4.3 million children of primary school age in England & Wales, 1 million were in purely voluntary schools and 1.3 million were in state aided schools, but 2 million had no access to schools whatsoever.

William Forster's Elementary Education Act *1870 required* partially state-funded board schools to be set up to provide elementary (primary, in modern parlance) education in areas where existing provision was inadequate. Board schools were managed by elected school boards. The schools remained fee-charging, but poor parents could be exempted. The previous government grant scheme established in 1833 ended on 31 December 1870.

Section 74 of the Act empowered school boards to, if they wished, make local byelaws making attendance compulsory between the ages of 5 and 13 but exempting any child aged over 10 who had reached the expected standard (which varied by board). Other exceptions included illness, if children worked, or lived too far from a school.

Two measures in the Act became, for religious reasons, matters of controversy within the governing Liberal Party. Firstly, nonconformists objected to their children being taught Anglican doctrine. As a compromise, William Cowper-Temple (pronounced "Cooper-Temple"), a Liberal MP, proposed that religious teaching in the new state schools be non-denominational, in practice restricted to learning the Bible and a few hymns: this became the famous Cowper-Temple clause (Section 14 of the Act). Section 7 also gave parents the right to withdraw their children from any religious instruction provided in board schools, and to withdraw their children to attend any other religious instruction of their choice.

Secondly, Section 25 gave school boards the power to, if they chose, pay the fees of poor children attending voluntary (i.e. church) schools. Although few school boards actually did so, the provision caused great anger among nonconformists, who saw this as local ratepayers' money being spent on Church of England schools. A large conference was held at Manchester in 1872 to lead resistance to the section, and one of the campaigners was the Birmingham politician Joseph Chamberlain, who emerged as a national figure for the first time. The resulting splits (some education campaigners, including Chamberlain, stood for Parliament as independent candidates) helped to cost the Liberals the 1874 election.

Compulsory and free primary education: 1880s and 1890s

The "Sandon Act" (Act of 1876) imposed a legal duty on parents to ensure that their children were educated. The Elementary Education Act 1880 required school boards to enforce compulsory attendance from 5 to 10 years, and permitted them to set a standard which children were required to reach before they could be employed. Poorer families were often tempted to send their children to work if the opportunity to earn an extra income was available. Attendance officers often visited the homes of children who failed to attend school, which often proved to be ineffective. Children who were employed were required to have a certificate to show they had reached the *educational standard*. Employers of these children who were unable to show this were penalized.

The Elementary Education Act 1891 provided for the state payment of school fees up to ten shillings per head, making primary education effectively free.

The Elementary Education (School Attendance) Act 1893 raised the school leaving age to 11. The Elementary Education (Blind and Deaf Children) Act of the same year extended compulsory education to blind and deaf children, and made provision for the creation of special schools.

The Voluntary Schools Act 1897 provided grants to public elementary schools not funded by school boards (typically Church schools).

Another act in 1899 raised the school leaving age to 12

In the late Victorian period grammar schools were reorganized and their curriculum was modernized. Latin was still taught.

Funding of technical colleges

The Technical Instruction Act 1889 was passed. According to D. Evans, "It gave powers to the County Councils and the Urban Sanitary Authorities to levy a penny tax to support technical and manual instruction. The curricula in technical institutions also had to be approved by the Science and Art Department. In the following year the Local Taxation Act introduced the 'whiskey tax', which made extra money available for technical instruction."

Balfour and Local Education Authorities

The controversial Conservative Education Act 1902 (or 'Balfour Act') made radical changes to the entire educational system of England and Wales. It weakened the divide between schools run by the 2,568 school boards and the 14,000 church schools, administered primarily by the Church of England, which educated about a third of children. Local Education Authorities were established, which were able to set local tax rates, and the school boards were disbanded. Funds were provided for denominational religious instruction in voluntary elementary schools, owned primarily by the Church of England and Roman Catholics. The law was extended in 1903 to cover London.

G. R. Searle, like nearly all historians, argues the Act was a short-term political disaster for the Conservative Party because its outraged Methodists, Baptists and other nonconformists. It subsidized the religions they rejected. However, Searle argues it was a long-term success. The Church schools now had some financing from local ratepayers and had to meet uniform standards. It led to a rapid growth of secondary schools, with over 1000 opening by 1914, including 349 for girls. Eventually (in 1944), the Anglican schools were effectively nationalized. Grammar schools also became funded by the LEA. The act was of particular significance as it allowed for all schools, including denominational schools, to be funded through rates (local taxation), and ended the role of locally elected school boards that often-attracted women, non-conformists and labour union men. The Liberals came to power in 1906, but their attempt to repeal the act was blocked by the House of Lords, setting up a major constitutional confrontation.

In the long run the Nonconformist schools practically vanished. In 1902 the Methodists operated 738 schools, but these rapidly declined throughout the 20th century. Only 28 remained in 1996.

The Fisher Education Act 1918 made secondary education compulsory up to age 14 and gave responsibility for secondary schools to the state. Under the Act, many higher elementary schools and endowed grammar schools sought to become state funded central schools or secondary schools. However, most children attended elementary (primary, in modern parlance) school until age 14, rather than going to a separate school for secondary education.

The act was also known as the "Fisher Act" as it was devised by H. A. L. Fisher. The act enforced compulsory education from 5–14 years, but also included provision for compulsory part-time education for all 14- to 18-year-olds. There were also plans for expansion in tertiary education, by raising the participation age to 18. This was dropped because of the cuts in public spending after World War I. This is the first act which started planning provisions for young people to remain in education until the age of 18. The 1918 act was not immediately implemented, instead waiting until an act in 1921 before coming into effect.

After the passing of the Local Government Act 1929, Poor Law schools became state funded elementary schools. The concept of junior technical schools was introduced in the 1930s to provide vocational education at secondary level, but few were ever opened.

In 1937 historian G.A.N. Lowndes identified a "Silent Social Revolution" in England and Wales since 1895 that could be credited to the expansion of public education:

The contribution which a sound and universal system of public education can make to the sobriety, orderliness and stability of a population is perhaps the most patent of its benefits. What other gains can be placed to its credit? Can it be claimed that the widening of educational opportunity in the long run repays that cost to the community by a commensurate increase in the national wealth and prosperity? Or can it be claimed that it is making the population happier, better able to utilize its leisure, more adaptable? Anyone who knows how the schools have come to life in the past decade, anyone who is in a position to take a wide view of the social condition of the people and compare conditions to-day with those forty years ago, will have no hesitation in answering these questions in the affirmative.

A report of 1938 of a committee chaired by Will Spend, a former Vice-Chancellor of the University of Cambridge, recommended that entry to schools would be based on intelligence testing. This was followed by the Norwood Report of 1943 which advocated the "Tripartite System" of secondary education which was introduced in the late 1940s.

1944: Butler

The Education Act 1944 was an answer to surging social and educational demands created by the war and the widespread demands for social reform. The Education Act 1944, relating to England and Wales, was authored by Conservative Rab Butler and known as "the Butler Act", defined the modern split between primary education and secondary education at age 11.

The Butler Act was also an historic compromise between church and state. Three new categories of schools were created. The first were Voluntary Controlled schools whose costs were met by the State, and would be controlled by the local education authority. The school kept the title deeds to the land, but taught an agreed religious education syllabus. These schools were favored by the Anglicans: over half their schools chose this status, and were soon effectively absorbed into the state system. The second were Voluntary Aided schools, which retained greater influence over school admission policies, staffing and curriculum, and which were preferred by the Roman Catholics and by some Anglican schools. They would have all of their running costs met by the State, but their capital costs would only be 50% state funded (later increased to 75% by the Education Act 1959, and now 90%). The third were Direct Grant Schools: former independent schools, often town grammar schools and predominantly in the north of England, who accepted a state grant in return for providing free education to many students but still charging for others. The state had little control on syllabus or admissions policy. The schools kept their title deeds.

The elite system of public schools was practically unchanged; Butler assembled a committee which produced the Fleming Report of July 1944, recommending that places at public schools be made available to state-funded scholarships, but its recommendations were not implemented.

The school leaving age was raised to 15 under the Butler Act, with an aspiration to raise it in time to 16, although this did not take place until the early 1970s (see below). The Act also recommended compulsory part-time education for all young people until the age of 18, but this provision was dropped so as not to overburden the post-war spending budget (as had happened similarly with the Act of 1918).

Changes in government approaches towards education meant that it was no longer regarded adequate for a child to leave education aged 14, as that is the age when they were seen to really understand and appreciate the value of education, as well as being the period when adolescence was at its height. It was beginning to be seen as the worst age for a sudden switch from education to employment, with the additional year in schooling to only provide benefits for the children when they leave. Although there were concerns about the effects of having less labour from these children, it was hoped that the outcome of a larger quantity of more qualified, skilled workers would eliminate the deficit problem from the loss of unskilled labour.

The 1944 Act took effect in 1947 when the Labour Party was in power and it adopted the Tripartite System, consisting of grammar schools, secondary modern schools and secondary technical schools. It rejected the comprehensive school proposals favored by a few in the Labour Party as more equalitarian. Under the tripartite model, students who passed an exam were able to attend a prestigious grammar school. Those who did not pass the selection test attended secondary modern schools or technical schools.

The new law was widely praised by Conservatives because it honored religion and social hierarchy, by Labour because it opened new opportunities for the working class, and by the general public because it ended the fees they had to pay. The act became a permanent part of the supported by the three major parties.

However, selection of academical gifted children to attend grammar school became increasingly controversial in the 1960s. Critics on the left attacked grammar schools as elitist because a student had to pass a test at age 11 to get in. Defenders argued that grammar schools allow pupils to obtain a good education through merit rather than through family income. No changes were made. In some areas, notably that of the London County Council, comprehensive schools had been introduced. They had no entrance test and were open to all children living in the school catchment area. However, despite tentative support for 'multilateralism' in secondaries, and a desire to raise the standard of secondary moderns to that of private institutions, from Minister for Education Ellen Wilkinson, the majority of Labour MPs were more concerned with implementing the 1944 Act; her successor George Tomlinson saw this through, although the secondary technical remained underdeveloped.

Circular 10/65 and comprehensive education

In 1965 the Labour government required all local education authorities to formulate proposals to move away from selection at eleven, replacing the tripartite system with comprehensive schools. This was done by the minister Tony Crosland by means of Circular 10/65 and withholding funding from any school that sought to retain selection. This circular was vehemently opposed by the grammar school lobby. Some counties procrastinated and retained the Tripartite System in all but a few experimental areas. Those authorities have locally administered selection tests.

The Circular also requested consultation between LEAs and the partially state-funded direct grant grammar schools on their participation in a comprehensive system, but little movement occurred. The 1970 report of the Public Schools Commission chaired by David Dennison recommended that the schools choose between becoming voluntary aided comprehensives and full independence. This was finally put into effect by the Direct Grant Grammar Schools (Cessation of Grant) Regulations 1975. Some schools (almost all Catholic) became fully state-funded, while the majority became independent fee-paying schools.

In 1973 the introduction of the Education (Work Experience) Act allowed LEAs to organize work experience for the additional final year school students.

In some counties around the country, these changes also led to the introduction of Middle schools in 1968, where students were kept at primary or junior school for an additional year, meaning that the number of students in secondary schools within these areas remained virtually constant through the change. As of 2007, there are now fewer than 400 middle schools across England, situated in just 22 Local Education Authorities.

In 1964, preparations had begun to raise the school leaving age to 16 to be enforced from 1 September 1973 onwards. This increased the legal leaving age from 15 to 16 and for one year, 1973, there were no 15-year-old school leavers as the students, by law, had to complete an additional year of education.

Many secondary schools were unable to accommodate the new 5th year students. The solution to the problem was to construct new buildings (often referred to as *"ROSLA Buildings"* or *"ROSLA Blocks"*) for the schools that needed to extend their capacity. This provided the space to cope with the new cohort of *ROSLA students*. The ROSLA Buildings were delivered to schools in self-assembly packs and were not intended to stand long-term, though some have proven to have stood much longer than was initially planned and were still in use in the 2010s.

Primary schools

The 1967 Plowden Report advocated a more child-centered approach to primary education, and also supported the introduction of middle schools. While many of the report's recommendations were never implemented, primary schools began to move away from rote learning in thee late 1960s and 1970s.

Apprenticeships

High technology industry (Aerospace, Nuclear, Oil & Gas, Automotive, Power Generation and Distribution etc.) trained its professional engineers via the advanced apprenticeship system of learning – usually a 5-year process. The higher Apprenticeship framework in the 1950s, 60s and 70s was designed to allow young people (16 years) an alternative path to A Levels to achieve an academic qualification at level 4 or 5 NVQ (National Vocational Qualification). The Higher Apprenticeship Framework was open to young people who had a minimum of 4 GCE "O" Levels to enroll in an Ordinary National Certificate or Diploma or a City & Guilds technician course. For advanced engineering apprenticeships "O" Levels had to include Mathematics, Physics, and English language. The advanced apprenticeship framework's purpose was to provide a supply of young people seeking to enter work-based learning via apprenticeships by offering structured high value learning and transferable skills and knowledge. These apprenticeships were enabled by linking industry with local technical colleges and professional Engineering Institutions.

The Advanced Apprenticeship Framework offered clear pathways and outcomes that addressed the issues facing the industry. This system was in place since the 1950s. The system provided young people with an alternative to staying in full-time education beyond 16/18 to gain pure academic qualifications without work-based learning. The Advanced Apprenticeships of the 1950s, 60s and 70s provided the necessary preparation towards Engineering Technician, Technician Engineer or Chartered Engineer registration. Apprentices undertook a variety of job roles in numerous technical functions to assist the work of engineers, in the design, development, manufacture and maintenance of production system

Industry Training Boards (ITBs) were introduced by the Industrial Training Act (1964 and amended 1982), requiring employers in a number of sectors to pay a training levy to their industry training board or apply a similar sum to the provision of training to their employees. Later phased out, the Construction Industry Training Board survives (as of 2018).

In modern times, apprenticeship became less important, especially as employment in heavy industry and artisan trades has declined since the 1980s. Traditional apprenticeships reached their lowest point in the 1980s: by that time, training programmes were rare and people who were apprentices learned mainly by example.

Conservative governments, from 1979 to 1997

Following the 1979 General Election, the Conservative Party regained power under Margaret Thatcher. In the early period it made two main changes:

New Vocationalism was expanded (Labour had made some small efforts beforehand, but the Conservatives expanded it considerably). This was seen as an effort to reduce the high youth unemployment, which was regarded as one of the causes of the sporadic rioting at the end of the seventies. The Youth Opportunities Programme was the main scheme, offered to 16- to 18-year-olds. It had been introduced in 1978 under the Labour government of James Callaghan, was expanded in 1980 under the Conservative government of Margaret Thatcher, and ran until 1983 when it was replaced by the Youth Training Scheme.

The Assisted Places Scheme was introduced in 1980, whereby gifted children who could not afford to go to fee-paying schools would be given free places in those schools if they could pass the school's entrance exam.

In 1986, National Vocational Qualifications (NVQs) were introduced, in an attempt to revitalise vocational training. Still, by 1990, apprenticeship took up only two-thirds of one percent of total employment.

National curriculum assessments were introduced at the Key Stages 1 to 4 (ages 7, 11, 14 and 16 respectively) through what were formerly called Standard Assessment Tests (SATS). At Key Stage 4 (age 16), the assessments were made from the GCSE exam.

Formula funding was introduced, which meant that the more children a school could attract to it, the more money the school would receive.

Open enrolment and choice for parents was brought back, so that parents could choose or influence which school their children went to.

Schools could, if enough of their pupils' parents agreed, opt out of local government control, becoming grant maintained schools and receiving funding direct from central government. The government offered more money than the school would get usually from the local authority as an enticement. This was seen as a politically motivated move since the Conservative central government was taking control from local authorities which were often run by other parties.

Religious education was reformed; Chapter 1 of the law required that the majority of collective worship be "wholly or mainly of a broadly Christian character".

Apprenticeship reform

In 1994, the government introduced Modern Apprenticeships (since renamed 'Apprenticeships'), based on frameworks devised by Sector Skills Councils. These frameworks contain a number of separately certified elements:

a knowledge-based element, typically certified through a qualification known as a 'Technical Certificate';

a competence-based element, typically certified through an NVQ; and

Key Skills (literacy and numeracy).96

Education Act 1996

Between 1976 and 1997, the minimum school leaving arrangements were:

A child whose sixteenth birthday falls in the period 1 September to 31 January inclusive, may leave compulsory schooling at the end of the Spring term (the following Easter).

A child whose sixteenth birthday falls in the period 1 February to 31 August, may leave on the Friday before the last Monday in May.

Under section 8(4) of the Education Act 1996, a new single school leaving date was set for 1998 and all subsequent years thereafter. This was set as the last Friday in June in the school year which the child reaches the age of 16.

Under section 7 of the Act, it was made an obligation for parents to ensure a full-time education for their children either at school or "otherwise" which formalized the status of home education.

Labour, from 1997 to 2010

The previous Labour focus on the comprehensive system was shifted to a focus on tailoring education to each child's ability. Critics see this as reminiscent of the original intentions of the Tripartite system.

Grant-maintained status was abolished, with GM schools being given the choice of rejoining the local authority as a maintained community school, or becoming a foundation school.

Although the Government-run eleven-plus exam selection exam for all children had now[been abolished, voluntary selection tests continue in certain areas, where some of the original grammar schools have been retained. These areas include: Northern Ireland and some English counties and districts including Devon, Dorset, Kent, Buckinghamshire, Essex, Birmingham, Trafford, Wiltshire, North Yorkshire, Calderdale, Kirklees, Wirral, Warwickshire, Gloucestershire, Lincolnshire and some London boroughs such as Bexley, Kingston-upon-Thames and Redbridge. There have been various (so far unsuccessful) attempts by campaigners to abolish all remaining grammar schools. The remaining grammar schools are now thus still selective, typically taking the top 10-25% of those from the local catchment area. Some of the still-existing grammar schools in the United Kingdom can trace their history back to earlier than the sixteenth century.

Labour expanded a policy started by the Conservatives of creating specialist schools via the specialist schools programme. This new type of secondary school teaches the National Curriculum subjects plus a few specialist branches of knowledge (e.g. business studies) not found in most other schools. These schools are allowed to select 10% of their pupils.

Numbers: In 1997 there were 196 of these schools. In August 2002 there were 1000. By 2006 the plan was to have 2000, and the goal was to make all secondary schools specialist eventually.

The Beacon Schools programme was established in England in 1998. Its aim was to identify high performing schools, in order to help them form partnerships with each other and to provide examples of effective practice for other schools. The programme was replaced in August 2005 with more broadly based programmes; the Leading Edge Partnership programme (for secondary schools) and Primary Strategy Learning Networks (PSLNs) (at the primary level).

A new grade of Advanced Skills Teacher was created, with the intention that highly skilled teachers would be paid more if they accepted new posts with outreach duties beyond their own schools.

City Academies were introduced. These are new schools, built on the site of, or taking over from existing failing schools. A city academy is an independent school within the state system. It is outside the control of the local education authority and set up with substantial funding from interested third parties, which might be businesses, charities or private individuals.

Education Action Zones were introduced, which are deprived areas run by an action forum of people within that area with the intention of making that area's schools better.

Vocational qualifications were renamed/restructured as follows:

GNVQs became Vocational GCSEs and AVCEs.

NVQs scope expanded so that a degree-equivalent NVQ was possible.

The New Deal was introduced, which made advisors available to long-term unemployed (in the UK this is defined as being unemployed for more than 6 months) to give help and money to those who want to go back into Education.

Introduced Literacy and Numeracy Hours into schools, and set targets for literacy and numeracy.

Set Truancy targets.

Set a maximum class size of 30 for 5-7-year-old.

Introduced the EMA, (Education Maintenance Allowance), which is paid to those between 16 and 18 as an enticement to remain in full-time education and get A-Levels/AVCEs.

A Performance Threshold was introduced in 2000 to allow experienced teachers access to higher rates of pay on meeting a set of performance standards, including a standard of pupil attainment. The performance-related pay changes have been bitterly opposed by teaching unions, most notably the National Union of Teachers which challenged the Threshold scheme by legal action.

Introduced Curriculum 2000, which reformed the Further Education system into the current structure of AS levels, A2 levels and Key Skills.

Abolished the Assisted Places Scheme.

A report was commissioned, led by the former chief-inspector of schools, Mike Tomlinson, into reform of the curriculum and qualifications structure for 14- to 19-year-olds. The report was published on 18 October 2004 and recommended the introduction of a diploma that would bring together both vocational and academic qualifications and ensure that all pupils had a basic set of core skills. It is proposed that the current qualifications would evolve into this diploma over the next decade, whether the government will follow the recommendations is yet to be seen —

the Conservative Party have already introduced alternative proposals to return to norm-referencing in A-levels rather than the current system of criterion-referencing.

In 2003 a green paper entitled Every Child Matters was published. It built on existing plans to strengthen children's services and focused on four key areas:

Increasing the focus on supporting families and careers as the most critical influence on children's lives

Ensuring necessary intervention takes place before children reach crisis point and protecting children from falling through the net

Addressing the underlying problems identified in the report into the death of Victoria Climbié – weak accountability and poor integration

Ensuring that the people working with children are valued, rewarded and trained

The green paper prompted a debate about services for children, young people and families resulting in a consultation with those working in children's services, and with parents, children and young people. The Government published *Every Child Matters: the Next Steps* in November 2004, and passed the Children Act 2004, providing the legislative spine for developing more effective and accessible services focused around the needs of children, young people and families.

In January 2007 Education Secretary Alan Johnson announced plans to extend the school leaving age in England to eighteen by 2013. This would raise the leaving age for the first time since 1972, when compulsory education was extended to sixteen. The changes included apprenticeships and work based training in addition to continued academic learning. This became law through the Education and Skills Act 2008, with the school leaving age raised to 17 in 2013 and 18 in 2015.

Three agents of modern education in India

The British Government (East India Company)

Christian missionaries

Indian intellectuals and reformers

Development of Modern Education

The company wanted some educated Indians who could assist them in the administration of the land.

Also, they wanted to understand the local customs and laws well.

For this purpose, Warren Hastings established the Calcutta Madrassa in 1781 for the teaching of Muslim law.

In 1791, a Sanskrit College was started in Varanasi by Jonathan Duncan for the study of Hindu philosophy and laws.

The missionaries supported the spread of Western education in India primarily for their proselytizing activities. They established many schools with education only being a means to an end which was Christianizing and 'civilizing' the natives.

The Baptist missionary William Carey had come to India in 1793 and by 1800 there was a Baptist Mission in Seram pore, Bengal, and also a number of primary schools there and in nearby areas.

The Indian reformers believed that to keep up with times, a modern educational system was needed to spread rational thinking and scientific principles.

The Charter Act of 1813 was the first step towards education being made an objective of the government.

The act sanctioned a sum of Rs.1 lakh towards the education of Indians in British ruled India. This act also gave an impetus to the missionaries who were given official permission to come to India.

But there was a split in the government over what kind of education was to be offered to the Indians.

The orientalists preferred Indians to be given traditional Indian education. Some others, however, wanted Indians to be educated in the western style of education and be taught western subjects.

There was also another difficulty regarding the language of instruction. Some wanted the use of Indian languages (called vernaculars) while others preferred English.

Due to these issues, the sum of money allotted was not given until 1823 when the General Committee of Public Instruction decided to impart oriental education.

In 1835, it was decided that western sciences and literature would be imparted to Indians through the medium of English by Lord William Bentinck's government.

Bentinck had appointed Thomas Babington Macaulay as the Chairman of the General Committee of Public Instruction.

Macaulay was an ardent Anglicism who had absolute contempt for Indian learning of any kind. He was supported by Reverend Alexander Duff, JR Colvin, etc.

On the side of the orientalists were James Prinsep, Henry Thomas Colebrooke, etc.

Macaulay minutes refer to his proposal of education for the Indians.

According to him:

English education should be imparted in place of traditional Indian learning because the oriental culture was 'defective' and 'unholy'.

He believed in education a few upper and middle-class students.

In the course of time, education would trickle down to the masses. This was called the infiltration theory.

He wished to create a class of Indians who were Indian in colour and appearance but English in taste and affiliation.

In 1835, the Elphinstone College (Bombay) and the Calcutta Medical College were established.

Sir Charles Wood was the President of the Board of Control of the company in 1854 when he sent a despatch to the then Governor-General of India, Lord Dalhousie.

This is called the 'Magna Carta of English education in India.'

Recommendations of the Wood's Despatch:

Regularise education system from the primary to the university levels.

Indians were to be educated in English and their native language.

The education system was to be set up in every province.

Every district should have at least one government school.

Affiliated private schools could be granted aids.

Education of women should be emphasised.

Universities of Madras, Calcutta and Bombay were set up by 1857.

University of Punjab – 1882; University of Allahabad – 1887

This despatch asked the government to take up the responsibility of education of the people.

Although there were a few Englishmen who wanted to spread education for its own sake, the government was chiefly concerned only with its own concerns.

There was a huge demand for clerks and other administrative roles in the company's functioning.

It was cheaper to get Indians rather than Englishmen from England for these jobs. This was the prime motive.

No doubt it spread western education among Indians, but the rate of literacy was abysmally low during British rule.

The state of women education was pathetic. This was because the government did not want to displease the orthodox nature of

Indians and also because women could not generally be employed as clerks.

In 1911, the illiteracy rate in British India was 94%. In 1921, it was 92%.

Scientific and technical education was ignored by the British government.

Scientific revolution

These new enlightened views of the world were also encapsulated in the explosion of scientific endeavor that occurred during the 18th century. With the rapid expansion of print culture from around 1700, and increasing levels of literacy, details of experimentation and discovery were eagerly consumed by the reading public.

Margaret Cavendish's Blazing World

This growth of 'natural philosophy' (the term 'science' was only coined later in the 18th century) was underpinned by the application of rational thought and reason to scientific enquiry; first espoused by Francis Blacon in the early 1600s, this approach built on the earlier work of Copernicus and Galileo dating from the Medieval period. Scientific experimentation (with instrumentation) was used to shed new light on nature and to challenge superstitious interpretations of the living world, much of which had been deduced from uncritical readings of historical texts.

Copernicus' *celestial spheres*

First edition of *On the Revolutions of the Heavenly Spheres* (1543), in which Copernicus argued that the positions of the stars and planetary orbits could be better explained by the sun being at the center of the universe with the planets rotating around it in a circular motion, as shown in this iconic diagram.

Galileo's sunspot letters

At the forefront of the scientific revolution stood Sir Isaac Newton, whose achievements in mathematics and physics revolutionized the contemporary view of the natural world. Born in 1643, Newton demonstrated a talent for mathematical theory at Trinity College, Cambridge, where his astonishingly precocious abilities led to his appointment as professor of mathematics at the age of just 26. Among Newton's weighty catalogue of investigations were his treatises on optics, gravitational forces and mechanics (most famously encapsulated in his Mathematical Principles of Natural Philosophy, first published in 1687), all grounded in empirical experimentation as a way to demystify the physical world.

Newton's *Principia Mathematica*

The discoveries of Sir Isaac Newton were complemented by those of a host of equally dazzling mathematicians, astronomers, chemists and physicists (Robert Hooke and Robert Boyle, for example), many of whom were members of the Royal Society (founded in 1660, and active today). Yet it was Newton's empirical approach to science that remained particularly influential. By embarking on purely rational and mathematical investigations, Newton was able to show that the natural world was 'amenable to observations and experiment', engendering a feeling among the scientific community that 'Nature had finally been fathomed'.

Hooke's *Micrographic* was the first important work on microscopy, the study of minute objects through a microscope.

The pursuit of rational scientific knowledge was never the preserve of an educated elite. As well as fertilizing a huge trade in published books and pamphlets, scientific investigation created a buoyant industry in scientific instruments, many of which were relatively inexpensive to buy and therefore available to the general public. Manufacturers of telescopes, microscopes, barometers, air pumps and thermometers prospered during the 18th century, particularly after 1750 when the names of famous scientific experimenters became household names: Benjamin Franklin, Joseph Priestley, William Herschel and Sir Joseph Bank, for example.

Encyclopedias, grammars and dictionaries became something of a craze in this period, helping to demystify the world in empirical terms. This huge fold-out page contains carefully *labeled* illustrations of anatomized human bodies.

Secularization and the impact on religion

Religion and personal faith were also subject to the tides of reason evident during the 18th century. Personal judgements on matters of belief were actively debated during the period, leading to skepticism, if not bold atheism, among an enlightened elite.

An enquiry into the nature of the human soul

View images from this item (4)

The author, Andrew Baxter argues that all matter is inherently inactive, and that the soul and an omnipotent divine spirit are the animating principles of all life. In making this argument, Baxter is rejecting the beliefs of more atheistic and materialist thinkers such as Thomas Hobbes and Baruch Spinoza.

These new views on religion led to increasing fears among the clergy that the Enlightenment was ungodly and thus harmful to the moral well-being of an increasingly secular society. With church attendance in steady decline throughout the 1700s, evidence of increasing agnosticism (the belief that true knowledge of God could never be fully gained) and a rejection of some scriptural teachings was close at hand. Distinct anti-clericalism (the criticism of church ministers and rejection of religious authority) also emerged in some circles, whipped up by the musings of 'deist' writers such as Voltaire, who argued that God's influence on the world was minimal and revealed only by one's own personal experience of nature.

Though certainly a challenge to accepted religious beliefs, the impulse of reason was considered by other contemporary observers to be a complement rather than a threat to spiritual orthodoxy: a means by which (in the words of John Locke) the true meaning of Scripture could be unlocked and 'understood in the plain, direct meaning of the words and phrases'.[4] Though difficult to measure or quantify, Locke believed that 'rational religion' based on personal experience and reflection could nevertheless still operate as a useful moral compass in the modern age.

New personal freedoms within the orbit of faith were extended to the relationship between the Church and state. In England, the recognition of dissenting religions was formalized by legislation, such as the 1689 Act of Toleration which permitted freedom of worship to Nonconformists (albeit qualified by allegiances to the Crown). Later, political emancipation for Roman Catholics – who were allowed new property rights – also reflected an enlightened impulse among the political elite: such measures sometimes created violent responses from working people. In 1780, for example, London was convulsed by a week of rioting in response to further freedoms granted to Catholics: a sign, perhaps, of how the enlightened thinking of politicians could diverge sharply from the sentiments of the humble poor.

Newspaper report of the Gordon riots, 1780

View images from this item (1)

The Gordon Riots of June 1780 were in response to legislation passed permitting Catholics greater freedom in society (such as being allowed to join the Army). The riots were so bad that 15,000 troops were deployed to quell the disturbances and nearly 300 rioters were shot dead by soldiers.

First edition of the *Letters of the late Ignatius Sancho, an African*, 1782

View images from this item (25)

From his shop in Westminster, Ignatius Sancho witnessed 'the burnings and devastations' of the Gordon Riots. He described the 'ridiculous confusion' in a series of letters, dated 6–9 June 1780.

Usage terms Public Domain

Political freedoms, contracts and rights

Public debates about what qualified as the best forms of government were heavily influenced by enlightened ideals, most notably Rousseau's and Diderot's notions of egalitarian freedom and the 'social contract'. By the end of the 18th century most European nations harbored movements calling for political reform, inspired by radical enlightened ideals which advocated clean breaks from tyranny, monarchy and absolutism.

Late 18th-century radicals were especially inspired by the writings of Thomas Paine, whose influence on revolutionary politics was felt in both America and France. Born into humble beginnings in England in 1737, by the 1770s Paine had arrived in America where he began agitating for revolution. Paine's most radical works, *The Rights of Man* and later *The Age of Reason* (both successful best-sellers in Europe), drew extensively on Rousseau's notions of the social contract. Paine reserved particular criticism for the hereditary privileges of ruling elites, whose power over the people, he believed, was only ever supported through simple historical tradition and the passive acceptance of the social order among the common people.

The **Industrial Revolution** dates back to the 18th century. It was a period characterized by significant reforms in the agricultural and industrial sectors and massive development in the rural areas. Most of these rural areas in the world were purely agrarian. Before the Industrial Revolution in America began, the country was dominated by a **cottage industry**, where people mainly worked in their homes using their own hands or using simple tools; this made the production of goods like clothes very slow. The spinning wheel and weaving looms were the most common machines used at this time. The advent of the Industrial Revolution transformed these communities from rural to urban and industrialized societies.

An Industrial Revolution is the process whereby a society changes from an agrarian economy and adopts a modern economy dominated by industries, machines, and technology. During the Industrial Revolution of the 18th century, there was a cultural and economic shift from the old traditional types of agriculture and human labour to manufactured goods produced in factories by complex machines using new sources of energy and technology. The advancement of technologies improved goods production, transportation, and the emergence of new towns and cities.

The Industrial Revolution began in Great Britain and later spread to the United States and other parts of the world. In the 18th century, Europe experienced significant economic advancement in the agricultural process. Major agricultural and technological development occurred during this period. New farming techniques, new animal species, and new factories were introduced, leading to a significant increase in food production. The increase in food production allowed people to leave their rural homes and migrate to the cities to seek job opportunities in the new factories. Food was also available to support people working in rural areas far away from their farms.

The textile industry triggered the Industrial Revolution in Britain. As the European population increased, the demand for clothes increased. This led to a need for new machines that would produce textile materials in large quantities and at a lower cost. Machines were invented, like the spinning jenny, which made assorted spindles of threads at a single time, and the power loom, which operated through steam power to weave faster and more efficiently. These machines were used in factories. This created more job opportunities, which drove people to leave rural areas and move to the cities. The rural-urban migration contributed significantly to the expansion and growth of cities and towns.

The availability of coal also contributed significantly to the success of the Industrial Revolution in Britain. The demand for coal increased during this time period, as well. This was because coal was plentiful, easily accessible, and very efficient. For this reason, it quickly replaced wood which was the primary source of energy. The new head of power and the textile industry contributed significantly to Britain's massive production of clothes. The extra clothes and materials were exported to other countries like the United States and China.

The demand and growth of the textile industry forced inventors like Samuel Slater to leave Europe and relocate to the United States. Samuel Slater established his textile firm in 1789, which initiated the Industrial Revolution in the United States. His contributions and technology revolutionized the American textile sector, earning him the title of "the Father of American Industries." Industrialization spread quickly once it reached the United States. Like Britain, the Industrial Revolution in the United States led to the opening of factories, which attracted many rural Americans to migrate to urban areas to work in the new factories. The rural-urban migration witnessed the transformation of many large cities like New York City and Boston. The Industrial Revolution also played a significant role in provoking the rise of unskilled labor. It also led to the availability of cheap and affordable commodities for the Americans, which improved their living standards.

Impact of the Industrial Revolution

The Industrial Revolution had several impacts. One of the major impacts of the Industrial Revolution was the development of industries that produced higher-quality goods in large quantities. Many new inventions improved the quality of life since large quantities of goods were produced easily and quickly. This improved the living standards of people and generally improved the economy.

There were also negative impacts as a result of the Industrial Revolution. One negative impact was the pollution of the environment, as factories produced dangerous gasses and waste was poorly disposed of. The poor disposal of wastes exposed people to dangerous diseases. Another negative impact of the Industrial Revolution was child labor and low wages. Children were often employed, as they were easier to exploit, but adults were also poorly paid.

Industrial Revolution

The **Industrial Revolution** was the transition to new manufacturing processes in Great Britain, continental Europe, and the United States, that occurred during the period from around 1760 to about 1820–1840. This transition included going from hand production method to machines; new chemical manufacturing and Iron production processes; the increasing use of water power and steam power; the development of machine tools; and the rise of the mechanized factory system. Output greatly increased, and a result was an unprecedented rise in population and in the rate of population growth. The textile industry was the first to use modern production methods, and textiles became the dominant industry in terms of employment, value of output, and capital invested.

On a structural level the industrial revolution asked society the so-called social question demanding new ideas of managing large groups of individuals. Growing poverty on one and growing population and materialistic wealth on the other hand caused tensions between very rich and poorest people inside society. These tensions where sometimes violently released and led to philosophic ideas like socialism, communism, anarchism.

The Industrial Revolution began in Great Britain, and many of the technological and architectural innovation were of British origin. By the mid-18th century, Britain was the world's leading commercial nation, controlling a global trading empire with colonies in North America and the Caribbean. Britain had major military and political hegemony on the Indian Subcontinent; particularly with the proto-industrialized Mughal Bengal, through the activities of the East India Company. The development of trade and the rise of business were among the major causes of the Industrial Revolution.

The Industrial Revolution marked a major turning point in history. Comparable only to humanity's adaptation of agriculture with respect to material advancement, the Industrial Revolution influenced in some way almost every aspect of daily life. In particular, average income and population began to exhibit unprecedented sustained growth. Some economists have said the most important effect of the Industrial Revolution was that the slandered of living for the general population in the Western World began to increase consistently for the first time in history, although others have said that it did not begin to meaningfully improve until the late 19th and 20th centuries. GDP per capita was broadly stable before the Industrial Revolution and the emergence of the modern capitalist economy, while the Industrial Revolution began an era of per-capita economic growth in capitalist economies. Economic historians are in agreement that the onset of the Industrial Revolution is the most important event in human history since the domestication of animals and plants.

The precise start and end of the Industrial Revolution is still debated among historians, as is the pace of economic and social changes. Eric Hobsbawm held that the Industrial Revolution began in Britain in the 1780s and was not fully felt until the 1830s or 1840s, while T.S. Ashton held that it occurred roughly between 1760 and 1830. Rapid *industrialization first* began *in Britain*, starting with mechanized textiles spinning in the 1780s, with high rates of growth in steam power and iron production occurring after 1800. Mechanized textile production spread from Great Britain to continental Europe and the United States in the early 19th century, with important centers of textiles, iron and coal emerging in Belgium and the United States and later textiles in France.

An economic recession occurred from the late 1830s to the early 1840s when the adoption of the Industrial Revolution's early innovations, such as mechanized spinning and weaving, slowed and their markets matured. Innovations developed late in the period, such as the increasing adoption of locomotives, steamboats and steamships, and hot blast iron smelting. New technologies such as the electrical telegraph, widely introduced in the 1840s and 1850s, were not powerful enough to drive high rates of growth. Rapid economic growth began to occur after 1870, springing from a new group of innovations in what has been called the Second Industrial Revolution. These innovations included new steel making processes, mass production, assembly line, electrical grid systems, the large-scale manufacture of machine tools, and the use of increasingly advanced machinery in steam-powered factories.

Etymology

The earliest recorded use of the term "Industrial Revolution" was in July 1799 by French envoy Louis-Gullaume Otto, announcing that France had entered the race to industrialize. "The idea of a new social order based on major industrial change was clear in Southey and Owen Owen between 1811 and 1818, and was implicit as early as Blake in the early 1790s and Wordsworth at the turn of the [19th] century." The term *Industrial Revolution* applied to technological change was becoming more common by the late 1830s, as in Jerome Adolphe Blanqui's description in 1837 of *la revolution industrially*.

Economic historians and authors such as Mendel's, Pomeranz, and Kridte argue that proto-industrialization in parts of Europe, the Muslim world, Mughal India, and China created the social and economic conditions that led to the Industrial Revolution, this is still a subject of debate among some historians.

Requirements

Six factors facilitated industrialization: high levels of agricultural productivity to provide excess manpower and food; a pool of managerial and entrepreneurial skills; available ports, rivers, canals, and roads to cheaply move raw materials and outputs; natural resources such as coal, iron, and waterfalls; political stability and a legal system that supported business; and financial capital available to invest. Once industrialization began in Great Britain, new factors can be added: the eagerness of British entrepreneurs to export industrial expertise and the willingness to import the process. Britain met the criteria and industrialized starting in the 18th century, and then it exported the process to western Europe (especially Belgium, France, and the German states) in the early 19th century. The United States copied the

British model in the early 19th century, and Japan copied the Western European models in the late 19th century.

Montessori method of education

The **Montessori method of education** involves children's natural interests and activities rather than formal teaching methods. A Montessori classroom places an emphasis on hands-on learning and developing real-world skills. It emphasizes independence and it views children as naturally eager for knowledge and capable of initiating learning in a sufficiently supportive and well-prepared learning environment. It discourages some conventional measures of achievement, such as grades and tests.

The method was started in the early 20th century by Italian physician Maria Montessori, who developed her theories through scientific experimentation with her students; the method has since been used in many parts of the world, in Public and private alike.

Montessori education is based on a model of human development. This educational style operates abiding by two beliefs: that psychological self-construction in children and developing adults occurs through environmental interactions and that children (especially under the age of six) have an innate path of psychological development. Based on her observations, Montessori believed that children who are at liberty to choose and act freely within an environment prepared according to her model would act spontaneously for optimal development.

Although a range of practices exists under the "Montessori" name, the Association Montessori International (AMI) and the American Montessori Society (AMS) cite these elements as essential Mixed-age classrooms: classrooms for children ages $2+\frac{1}{2}$ or 3 to 6 years old are by far the most common, but 0–3, 6–9, 9–12, 12–15, and 15–18-year-old classrooms exist as well

- Student choice of activity from within a prescribed range of options
- Uninterrupted blocks of work time, ideally three hours long

- A constructivist or "discovery" model, in which students learn concepts from working with materials rather than by direct instruction
- Specialized educational materials are often made out of natural, aesthetic materials such as wood, rather than plastic
- A thoughtfully prepared environment where materials are organized by subject area, is accessible to children, and is appropriately sized
- Freedom, within limits
- A trained teacher experienced in observing a child's characteristics, tendencies, innate talents, and abilities

Montessori education involves free activity within a "prepared environment", meaning an educational environment tailored to basic human characteristics, to the specific characteristics of children at different ages, and to the individual personalities of each child. The function of the environment is to help and allow the child to develop independence in all areas according to their inner psychological directives. In addition to offering access to the Montessori materials appropriate to the age of the children, the environment should exhibit the following characteristics:

- An arrangement that facilitates movement and activity
- Beauty and harmony, cleanliness of environment
- Construction in proportion to the child and their needs

Montessori education:

is based on a model of Human development. This educational style operates abiding by two beliefs: that psychological self-construction in children and developing adults occurs through environmental interactions and that children (especially under the age of six) have an innate path of psychological development.[Based on her observations, Montessori believed that children who are at liberty to choose and act freely within an environment prepared according to her model would act spontaneously for optimal development.

Although a range of practices exists under the "Montessori" name, the Association Montessori International (AMI) and the American Montessori Society (AMS) cite these elements as essential.

Mixed-age classrooms: classrooms for children ages 2+½ or 3 to 6 years old are by far the most common, but 0–3, 6–9, 9–12, 12–15, and 15–18-year-old classrooms exist as well

Student choice of activity from within a prescribed range of options

Uninterrupted blocks of work time, ideally three hours long

A constructivist or "discovery" model, in which students learn concepts from working with materials rather than by direct instruction

Specialized educational materials are often made out of natural, aesthetic materials such as wood, rather than plastic

A thoughtfully prepared environment where materials are organized by subject area, is accessible to children, and is appropriately sized

Freedom, within limits

A trained teacher experienced in observing a child's characteristics, tendencies, innate talents, and abilities

Montessori education involves free activity within a "prepared environment", meaning an educational environment tailored to basic human characteristics, to the specific characteristics of children at different ages, and to the individual personalities of each child. The function of the environment is to help and allow the child to develop independence in all areas according to their inner psychological directives. In addition to offering access to the Montessori materials appropriate to the age of the children, the environment should exhibit the following characteristics as-

An arrangement that facilitates movement and activity

Beauty and harmony, cleanliness of environment

Construction in proportion to the child and their needs

Reservation to Depress community in India

Reservation was a known concept in India for a very long period. Let's know the history of reservations in India.

Reservation was there at the time when the Britishers ruled India.

It is generally thought of as **who decides reservation in India**. Originally, William Hunter and Jyotirao Phule in 1882 conceived the idea of a caste-based reservation system. When the Hunter Commission was established in 1882, Mahatma Jyotirao Phule urged that all citizens have free, mandatory education and government employment. **William Hunter and Jyotirao Phule** in 1882 originally conceived the idea of caste-based reservation system.

In 1902, a notification established 50% of service reservations for economically disadvantaged people in the state of Kolhapur. This was India's first notification establishing a reservation for the benefit of the country's underprivileged.

Reservation was instituted in 1908 in support of the castes and communities that participated in the administration under British rule.

The Morley Minto Reforms, also known as the Government of India Act of 1909, contained provisions made in 1909.

The Government of India Act of 1919 introduced provisions for reservation in 1919.

A GO issued by the Madras Presidency in 1921 allocated 44% of reservations to non-Brahmins, 16% to Muslims, 16% to Anglo-Indian Christians, and 8% to Scheduled Castes.

The reservation system that exists today, in its true sense, was introduced in 1933 when British Prime-Minister Ramsay Macdonald presented the **'Communal Award'.**

The Government of India Act 1935 included provisions for the reservation in 1935.

The award made provision for **separate electorates** for Muslims, Sikhs, Indian Christians, Anglo-Indians, Europeans and the Dalits.

After long negotiations, Gandhi and Ambedkar signed the **'Poona Pact',** where it was decided that there would be a single Hindu electorate with certain reservations in it.

The **Communal Award** was created by the British prime minister Ramsay MacDonald on 16 August 1932. Also known as the MacDonald Award, it was announced after the Round Table Conference (1930–32) and extended the separate electorate to depressed Classes (now known as the Scheduled Caste) and other minorities.[1] The separate electorate was introduced in Indian Councils Act 1909 for Muslims and extended to Sikhs, Indian Christians, Anglo-Indians and Europeans by Government of India Act 1919.

The separate electorate was now available to the Muslims, Sikhs, Indian Christians, Anglo-Indians, Europeans and Depressed Classes (now known as the Scheduled Caste) etc. The principle of weightage was also applied. Sir Samuel Hoare asked for clarification of the ninth and last paragraph that applied directly to the Depressed Classes. The Award favored the minorities over the Hindus causing consternation and eliciting anger from Gandhi. From the fastness of Yervada Jail he made contact with the Cabinet in London declaring in September 1932 an open fast until death.

The reason behind introduction of Communal Award was that Ramsay MacDonald considered himself as 'a friend of the Indians' and thus wanted to resolve the issues in India. The Communal

Quota systems favoring certain castes and other communities existed before independence in several areas of British India. Demands for various forms of positive discrimination had been made, for example, in 1882 and 1891. Rajarshi Shahu, the Maharaja of the princely state of Kolhapur, introduced reservation in favor of non-Brahmin and backward classes, much of which came into effect in 1902. He provided free education to everyone and opened several hostels to make it easier for them to receive it.

He also tried to ensure that people thus educated were suitably employed, and he appealed both for a class-free India and the abolition of untouchability. His 1902 measures created 50 percent reservation for backward communities. In 1918, at the behest of several non-Brahmin organizations criticizing Brahmin domination of administration, the Mysore Raja Nalvadi Krishnaraja Wadiyar created a committee to implement reservations for non-Brahmins in government jobs and education over the opposition of his Diwan M. Viswesvaraya, who resigned in protest. On 16 September 1921, the first Justice Party government passed the first Communal Government Order (G. O. # 613), thereby becoming the first elected body *in Indian* legislative history to legislate reservations, which have since become standard across the country.

The British Raj introduced elements of reservation in the Government of India Act of 1909 and there were many other measures put in place prior to independence. A significant one emerged from the Round Table Conference of June 1932, when the Prime Minister of Britain, Ramsay MacDonald, proposed the Communal Award, according to which separate representation was to be provided for Muslims, Sikhs, Indian Christians, Anglo-Indians, and Europeans. The depressed classes, roughly corresponding to the STs and SCs, were assigned a number of seats to be filled by election from constituencies in which only they could vote, although they could also vote in other seats. The proposal was controversial: Mahatma Gandhi fasted in protest against it but many among the depressed classes, including B. R. Ambedkar, favored it. After negotiations, Gandhi reached an agreement with Ambedkar to have a single Hindu electorate, with Dalits having seats reserved within it. Electorates for other religions, such as Islam and Sikhism, remained separate. This became known as the Poona Pact.

Award was announced after the failure of the Second of the Round Table Conferences (India). The Award attracted severe criticism from Mahatma Gandhi.

The Award was controversial as it was believed by some to have been brought in by the British to create social divide among the Hindus. Gandhi feared that it would disintegrate Hindu society. However, the Communal Award was supported by many among the minority communities, most notably B. R. Ambedkar. According to Ambedkar, Gandhi was ready to award separate electorates to Muslims and Sikhs. But Gandhi was reluctant to give separate electorates to scheduled castes. He was afraid of division inside Congress and Hindu society due to separate scheduled caste representations. But Ambedkar insisted *on a* separate electorate for scheduled *castes*.

Akali Dal, the representative body of the Sikhs, was also highly critical of the Award since only 19% was reserved to the Sikhs in Punjab, as opposed to the 51% reservation for the Muslims and 30% for the Hindus. Gandhi concurred with the revival of Swaraj which became policy in May 1934 on ratification by the All-India Congress Committee. The Government reluctantly agreed to lift the ban on Congress. In return they received anxious support from the Muslim League still smarting from Gandhi's majoritarianism. After lengthy negotiations, Gandhi reached an agreement with Ambedkar to have a single Hindu electorate, with scheduled castes having seats reserved within it. The Poona Pact rejected any further advancement for the Depressed, yet satisfied electorates for other religions like Muslims, Sikhs, Indian Christians, Anglo-Indians, Europeans that remained separate.

During the parliamentary debates on the Government of India bill the Untouchables gained a notable champion in a Conservative MP, A.V.Goodman. He stressed their poverty should be ameliorated by greater representation in the provincial assemblies. But while Muslim League remained ambivalent to the Communal Award its ratification by the Central Assembly remained a priority.

Present Scenario of Modernization and Atomization of Industrial and Mega Business:

The European Industrial revolution *gave way to* Mega industrial organization and when *electrification was done* then Enter and Night *began* a part of life to *develop* industrial organization. When Electronic system *development is done* then it *comes* to Atomization through Computer system *whereas* Semi-Automatic mechanical system with cam system and hydraulic system or integrated system came at medical system. When Duel technology or multiple integrated technology *development is done* and then robotic and remote controlling *systems* implement through sensor by computer *programmable* system. Driverless vehicle become use in military operation and arms amination system started atomization and mega industrial organization started in Defiance sector, and other production system as food processing, machinery production, Automobile production and railways transportation and flexible technology system as mega organization making mass production in minimum time with minimum labours and with accuracy but management system made corporate to sealing as marketing management mainly. Same system Flowing to Asian and African countries through technology transfer and European Originated countries become developed *as the same* rots flowing as they also European native peoples.

Present Scenario of Political Business

Political Business executing in Democracy but it *remained a different* type *in the Bourgeois* Hydride Political system. In Bourgeois hybrids political Business there are remaining different Wings as

- Spiritual Business Organization: e.g. Ramdev Baba organization Patanjali, *Asaram* Bapu Organization, *Ram Rahim* Organization Dara Sachcha, Nirmal Bala organization, Rampal organization, Computer baba organization, Bulldogger Baba organization, Narmada Baba organization, Beggarware Dham organization, etc.
- Conflict creation organization: e.g. RSS, VHP
- IT shell organization (Shooting Video Audio and poster editing Organization, three-dimension lager Image virtual meeting Teleprompt dialog, etc. done)
- Rioting and Mob Lynching Organization: e.g. Bjorndal, Hindu Mashaba.
- Messenger Media Organization and agent anchor: e.g. Messenger media Ajtak, Zee News messenger Agent Anchor: Rubika Lyakat, Anjana Om Kashyap, Annaba Goswami, Amish Devgan etc.
- Dummy or Duplicate Rental Speech readers: e.g. Dummy duplicate of Noranda Modi
- Film Shooting organization: e.g. *makeup* and Photo shooting too advertising as Acting remain basic criteria of Narendra Modi.
- Illegal Funding Organization: Capitalist Business Holder e.g. Ambani, Adani organization, etc. cheating too eating that government fund and organization transfer and financial cheating through loan section, commission paid,

national property making self-property and loan with interest & taxes relief that cheating with nation and society.

General Activity of Bourgeois political Business:

- Economy drains to self-account or economy transfer to particular personality on commission
- Divide too ruling to executing Riots, Conflict
- Hypocrisy that enjoyment and entertainment life like as Mughal royal to acquiring hug money by cheating
- Conspiracy that *embraces* governmental money use for self-purpose and political purposes.
- Hybrid regime Electoral Autocracy-Nazi- Racism-Fascism
- Cheating with Nation and Society as acting *to the cheating* system as flak nationalist.
- Making *fools of* innocent common peoples by Mythical story or flash statement or propagandas.
- Conflict *created* Pre-Islamic Aryan *versus* Islamic Aryan as both groups invaded India and migrated *from the Central* Asia Region.

Reality and Spiritual Myth in Society

- Lord Hanuman And their groups remained Vannar peoples a branch group of Jat a Indo-European Groups and even today vannar caste executing in South India and Sree Lanka but Myth create that Lord Hanuman made as Monkey face and tail added as Lack of Old Sanskrit knowledges
- Viman *means* Vayu ka man that means speed of Air but when Aeroplan given name as Viman in Indian language peoples of India confuse that Ravenna used Aeroplan but actually Ravenna used *a Chariot that was operated* by Five horses.

- Shyla or Shila *means a series* of small *mountains* and shatu *means* connectivity but *Myth is used as a floating* Bridge.
- Mountain climbing by Lord Hanuman with Lord Rama and Laxman myth *made* Lord Hanuman able to *fly*.
- Hindu means Land of Hind that means European branch group that hind peoples group migrated to Asian part Hindu Kush. Indu as diversion form of Hindu which also means Mountainous peoples. If you read mythology of Ancient North European than it seen that two main groups remained in ruling but Vanir Group defeated who migrated in different locality. Sindy/ Sindi, Parisian Arabian also European originated. Brahmin or brahman are European originated whereas Kshatriya are Eurasian that means European mixed with *Mongols* originated. In Indus civilization god and goddess have similarity with gods or *goddess* of ancient Celtic European community. Saxon or old language as well as Lithuanian language have most similarity with Sanskrit. Kalasha, Nuri, Aryan valley peoples, Balti, Kashmiri Hindu peoples genetically European. Vannar caste remain in south India who are Indo-European.
- In Norse, Celtic or Slavic Mythology indicated Black gods and *goddesses* which Indicated that African peoples ruled in Ancient European *fields* and later when defeated than *abolished* due to either killing or migration.
- Dravidian language match with Mediterranean that indicated Dravidian peoples migrated from Africa mainly but it has evidence that Mauri language match with Santhal that Australasian peoples migrated to India at primitive boating age that about 60000 years ago. That Dravidian are mixed peoples of Afro- Australasian. Hence *Mara, the goddess* of Slavic black *group, has a* match *with the Kali goddess, a Dravidian* goddess.

- Siva/ Shiva/ Siwa means Light of God that *also means* moon and Lingaa means stone and symbols but North *Indians* misused the meaning of Lingaa. Joti Lingaa called to Shiva Stone.

- Jatayu, Garur, Simbha, Kakara, Kakra, Varaho etc. are branch groups of Jut/Jat community who migrated from northern European *parts, mainly* Jutland, or Baltic region. At ancient *times it was also* habitual to use *a mask,* but Misguided to common peoples as Sami *humans* that some part made *animals*.

- Human leaders or *guides* or *rulers are given* identity by name first and then landmark, rivers, mountains and cosmological bodies name given on the rulers or guide for identity. Rulers or *Guides who are now* given status as Gods or *goddesses*. Spiritual *businessmen misguide* society and mind turn to cosmology bodies when god or goddess or epic revision given by Religious text reader or Spiritual businessman.

- Nag, Voraho, Gurur, Vannar are branch groups of Jat/ Jut Clint but animal *figures* made to *them* in Arts and Sculpture and Spiritual Business executing by flash statement.

- In *Mahabharata* mention Ulupi at central Indian *Nagvanshi* but Narendra Modi misguided that he added Ulupi remained from Nagaland. Nagvanshi of central India are Jat Clint whereas peoples of Nagaland are Chinese Burmese.

Historical Misguide and misinformation

- Vikromadita who is not started Vikram Samvat and Chandra Gupta- II and *Vikramaditya* were different personality Vikrom Sambat is meaning Victory Declaration which done by Satavanshi king when Sakha of West India ruler defeated in 56 BC as old Saka Era transformed to Vikrom Sambat and later when recapture

Saka community than new Saka era started again. Chandra Gupta ruled in 3rd century AD as capital city of *Patliputra Magadha Kingdom* that old Morja dynasty part which had not any linkage with Ujjain. In Ujjain king Vikromadita had scholler Kalidas, Barahomihir who remained in 5th Century AD. But misguided and Misinformation given as three events assimilated

- Meaning "Who Discover of Sea root of India?" do not *translate* in Hindi properly but misguided and said Who Discover India only and controversy creating that *India remained* before Vasco Dagama when came to India. It is reality that Indian Spices *were* directly trading to European countries in Greek ruled from *Alexander* to Pre-Islamic *rule in* Central Asia. But when Central *Asia was captured* by Islamic community and converted to Islamic *faith,* indirect trading was done through Turkey by Islamic Ruler *at heavy* cost. Then South West European decided that through sea root it *was a requirement* to *reach* India as Indian traders *traded to the South* West part of Africa. Hence by helping of Indian trader to made communication by Portugal personality Vasco Dagama at South West African *coastal* area and reach to India that called discovered sea *route* of India

- Indian National Army (INA) called As Azad Hind Froze that force of Azad Hind Nation foundation done by Subash Chandra Bose Where Raj Bihari Bose was founder of INA but BJP RSS misguide that *founder as* Subhas Chandra Bose. Actually, Arrested Indian Army by Japan Royal Army in Second World War given Instruction that fight against British Ruler who ruled at India and Raj Bihari Bose remained Commander deputed by Japan Government and Later the INA hand over to Subash Chandra Bose. Andaman Some parts, Singapore, some parts of Burma and some part of Nagaland captured by Japan Army in Second World War hand over to Subash Chandra Bose by Japan which called as Azad Hindi and that nation recognized by Japan Royal Government. INA fight again British with helping of Japan Royal Forces and hence Subash Chandra Bose sent to Taiwan which also captured by Japan forces from British but in !8 August in Aeroplan Crushing Died and Subash Chanda Death Body identified by his wife and his body cemented at Japan.

India Cum Under Bourgeois Rule

- Myth used to *be brainwashed* by BJP- RSS joint Venture leadership.
- Spiritual leaders or Spiritual Businessman or organizations integrity with BJP-RSS who *brainwash* as *agents* of BJP- RSS.
- *Capitalists Ambani* Adani and some other commission paid to BJP-RSS and alliances and get profit as undue advantages as loan section, loan relief, Taxation relief, national property or fun capturing on recommendation of BJP-RSS leadership.
- Enjoying and entertainment done by BJP-RSS leaders, Spiritual Businessman, Capitalist Ambani, Adani and quickly *becoming the richest* personality.
- Every Essential Commodity rate *becomes* thrice higher or more, Each and every stage of common people's life locomotion there have heavy taxation paying which maximum newly *implemented* by BJP-RSS joint venture ruling.
- Poor become poorest and rich become richest by policy made Autocratic Nazi system where carders of BJP-RSS mainly use for brainwashing and enforce through hooligan or mob lynching, etc. Through audio Video misinformation and misguide done in What app link and IT shell as well as Messengers Media agent Anchors using for *advertising* and *brainwashing common* peoples to *make* blind supporters as making *fools eat* and

enjoying entertainment life where nationality *remains* flak and cheating *remained the main* activity.

Ancient Politics and Myth

Ramayana mythic story:

Politicians mainly BJP- RSS leaders apply spiritual alliance political business who used to myth as Lord Hanuman intentionally made monkey as well as added tail behind him and face made *like monkey* to showing supper monkey. Actually, Vannar *groups* are *Indo-European sub* Jut branch groups *who are now* rehabilitated in south India and *Sri* Lanka. Vannar group neither remain tail nor face remain like as Monkey but due to done insult to south Indian they made honorable Lord Hanuman as monkey. Natural small mountain series *called man* made which remain secret ways of roots to enter Lanka that Island *nowadays* called Rameswaram as geographical structure similar as per description as Hill *block* island and Lord *Shiva* Temple indicated. *Nearby remains* Ramnath Puram meaning vigorous battle with Lord Rama. Actual Ajodhya mean Ajoy Doha the city name given on the name of grand father of Lord Rama which parts captured by grandfather of Lord Rama and as per Ramayana description it remained northern side toward Himalaya that remained as Dowers' of Himalaya that is actually located at Nepal that now a day as village of Ayodyanagar tehsil situated at Nepal but a cow of Vkramadiyta decided *Ayodhya* of Uttar *Pradesh* which actual named Sakata in 5th century AD.

Mahabharat

Ulapi remain Nagvanshi but BJP RSS leaders explain that she remained Chinese Burmese Naga land female *whereas* Nagvanshi are ruled at north India and Central India and on their name Nagore district, Nagda, Nagpur, Choto Nagpur locality given on their surname and they are actually Indo- European group of peoples. Nanda Nagore, Dave Nagore are two branch *groups* of Nagvanshi language and script of ancient India but it is character to misguide and misinformation given by BJP-RSS leaders that is their *genetic* heredity.

Bhagavad Gita:

Bhaga means powerful Vat means Kingdom or landmark. Bhagavat is a text of powerful rulers and the common people's respect for them. Bhavoti means ash of a powerful ruler's death body and Bharat means who worships Fire which means for power gain ancient people worshiping fire after fire discovery. Gita means poems *whereas Bhagavad* Gita means poems of powerful *rulers*.

Background of Present India/ Bharat:

There have to be a central body as United India Federation as per history Barats was mention only North-Western India in Rig Veda period on the base of Bharatas Tribal region and in Mahabharat only Kurukshetra region called as Bharata as indicated Vagarious Warrior field. If we analyze the Vedic period where there was the Janapada and the Mahajanapada there was not any nation or kingdom as Bharat and Kuru Kingdom divided into Kuru and Indraprastha only and thereafter beetles hold on to a story called Mahabharata which means Great Warrior field. On the other hand Turkish and Afghan Islamic ruled locality called Hindustan and mainly that locality which remained under Ibrahim Lodi ruling area. But the Mugal who remained actually Uzbek that they captured Hindustan from Ibrahim Lodi and expanded up to Bengal in East and Karnataka and Andra Prades in South. Hence Both names Bharat and Hindustan should not be considered the whole Nation. Present scenario India is an Ex British Colony which was constructed under British rule where Democracy was implemented by the British in 1920 and Fully given independence in 1947. From the beginning Islamic leaders wanted to ruling whole British India under islamic rule whereas Indian Peninsula remain as Northern Sikh ruled, west and central Marathi Ruled, Northern and Eastern Islamic Ruled as

Hinduistan, Southern Hindu Ruled as Vijayanagaram, Rajasthan part remain as tax pay rulers of Mughal Indirect ruled which later become tax payee ruler of British. British ruling started at South India and when France ruling started to South India then Eastern India Kolkata became spot to ruling area where Fort William build up by East India British Company by legal permission of England Royalism and later due to objection beetle hold at Plashi and Bengal, Biher, Orisha become under British ruled called Bengal presidency. Thereafter whole india came under British ruled either direct ruled or Indirect rule as tax payee agent rulers association working as political parties or union and later democracy introduced by British in 1920 and due to ego of islamic leaders Pakistan formed in 1947 where Islam League win continued in central and provincial election in British India till 1946.

Bharat Basha actually Sanskrit meaning "The Flow of Warrior " that when executing battle by bow and arrow they execute war or battle.

Bharat Matta means Warrior Goddess and it is History of Independence that image drawn protrad by Abanindra Nath Tagor to compare goddess Durga / Chandrika who is considered as Goddess Laxmi also . Hence the lion is used as a pet of Bharat Mata, an imaginary goddess created as MotherLand.

Bharat Mata is a work painted by the Indian painter <u>Abanindranath Tagore</u> in 1905. However, the painting was first painted by <u>Bankim Chandra Chatterjee</u> in the 1870s. The work depicts a saffron-clad woman, dressed like a <u>sadhvi</u>, holding a book, sheaves of paddy, a piece of white cloth, and a <u>rudraksha</u> garland (mala) in her four hands. The painting was the first illustrated depiction of the concept and was painted with Swadesh ideals during the larger <u>Indian Independence movement</u>. Bharat Mata as <u>Mahadevi</u> or Yagani. Mahadevi (<u>Sanskrit</u>: महादेवी, also referred to as Adi Parashakti, Adi Shakti, Yogani and Abhaya Shakti, is the supreme goddess in the <u>Shaktism</u> sect of <u>Hinduism</u>.

India required Democratic Consulate Confederation System

BJP-RSS joint venture executing Hindiana that is new form of Aryan racism that called Hindi racism and hence discrimination partiality *insulation* done with *Non-Hindi* peoples that basically it is with North-eastern peoples and South Indian as South India language are Afro-Australasian language whereas North Eastern language are Mongolian-Australasian. Now identity of Non-Hindi peoples targets to *abolish* demolishing as well as Hindi culture enforcement done forcefully. The Western Indian peoples *are an Indo-Iranian* branch of Indo-European peoples and hence Script and dialects remain *similar* with Hindi as Arabian Persian originated language reformed at Islamic period of India at Medieval political era. Hence there required to form equality and right to speech freedom Indian Union Federal system required reform as Democratic Consulate Confederation system. Islamic and Hindu conflicts are actually Ancient Aryan *versus* Arabian Non-Formal Aryan contradiction whereas genetically both groups are same. It *required* to *dilute* the mythical conception and required to increase scientific reality conception *to* both Aryans groups only. In North India conflict among Pre-Islamic Aryan *versus* Islamic Aryan form as an Agenda of political groups but Hindi racism and Brahmin Racism form *by depressing* Tribal as well as caste and Non-Hindi peoples of North- Eastern and Southern peoples of India. Hence it required to implement Democratic Consulate Confederation systems as-

Union of India required to two Zonal Autonomous Confederation Council as-

- Hindustan Autonomous Zonal council with two regional *councils required as* Western Region and North Central Region. It is the zone where Hindi *is the Zonal* Official language.
- Liberal Bharat Autonomous Zonal Council with two regional *councils* required as North Eastern region and Southern Region. It is the zone where English *is the official Zonal* language.

Democratic confederalism (Kurdish: Konfederalîzma demokratîk), also known as Kurdish communalism or Apoism, is a political concept theorized by Kurdistan Workers Party (PKK) leader Abdullah Ocalan about a system of democratic self-organization with the features of a confederation based on the principles of autonomy, direct democracy, political ecology, feminism, multiculturalism, self-defense, self-governance and elements of a cooperative economy.[5][6][7] Influenced by social ecology, libertarian municipalism, Middle Eastern history and general state theory, Ocalan presents the concept as a political solution to Kurdish national aspirations, as well as other fundamental problems in countries in the region deeply rooted in class society, and as a route to freedom and democratization for people around the world.

Although the liberation struggle of the PKK was originally guided by the prospect of creating a Kurdish nation state on a Marxist–Leninist basis, Ocalan became disillusioned with the nation-state model and state socialism. Influenced by ideas from Western thinkers such as the anarchist and social ecologist Mr. Murray Bookchin, Ocalan reformulated the political objectives of the Kurdish liberation movement, abandoning the old statist and centralizing socialist project for a radical and renewed proposal for democratic-libertarian socialism that no longer aims at building an independent state separate from Turkey, but at establishing an autonomous, democratic and decentralized entity based on the ideas of democratic confederacies.

Rejecting both the authoritarianism and bureaucratism of state socialism and the predation of capitalism, seen by Ocalan as most responsible for the economic inequalities, sexism and environmental destruction in the world, democratic confederacies defends a "type of organization or administration can be called non-state political administration or stateless democracy", which would provide the framework for the autonomous organization of "every community, confessional group, gender specific collective and/or minority ethnic group, among other" It is a model of participatory democracy[18] built on the self-government of local communities and the organization of open councils, town councils, local parliaments, and larger congresses, where citizens are the agents of self-government, allowing individuals and communities to exercise a real influence over their common environment and activities. Inspired by the struggle of women in the PKK, democratic confederacies have feminism as one of its central pillars. Seeing patriarchy as "an ideological product of the national state and power" no less dangerous than capitalism, Ocalan advocates a new vision of society in order to dismantle the institutional and psychological relations of power currently established in capitalist societies and to ensure that women have a vital and equal role to that of men at all levels of organization and decision-making. Other key principles of democratic confederalism are environmentalism, multiculturalism (religious, political, ethnic and cultural), individual freedoms (such as those of expression, choice and information), self-defense, and a sharing economy where control of economic resources does not belong to the state, but to society. Although it presents itself as a model opposed to the nation-state, democratic confederalism admits the possibility, under specific circumstances, of peaceful coexistence between both, as long as there is no intervention by the state in the central issues of self-government or attempts at cultural assimilation. Although it was theorized initially as a new social and ideological basis for the Kurdish liberation movement, democratic confederalism is now presented as an anti-nationalist, multi-ethnic and internationalist movement.

The general lines of democratic confederalism were presented in March 2005, through a declaration "to the Kurdish people and the international community" and, in later years, the concept was further developed in other publications, such as the four volumes of the Manifesto of Democratic Civilization. Shortly after being released, the declaration was immediately adopted by the PKK, which organized clandestine assemblies in

Turkey, Syria and Iraq, which resulted in the creation of the Kurdistan Communities Union (Koma Civakên Kurdistan, KCK). The first chance to implement it came during the Syrian Civil War, when the Democratic Union Party (Partiya Yekîtiya Demokrat, PYD) declared the autonomy of three cantons in Syrian Kurdistan that eventually grew into the Autonomous Administration of North and East Syria).[l]

Federalism is a combined and compound mode of government that combines a general government (the central or "federal" government) with regional governments (provincial, state, cantonal, territorial, or other subunit governments) in a single political system, dividing the powers between the two. Federalism in the modern era was first adopted in the unions of states during the Old Swiss Confederacy.

Federalism differs from confederalism, in which the general level of government is subordinate to the regional level, and from devolution within a unitary state, in which the regional level of government is subordinate to the general level. It represents the central form in the pathway of regional integration or separation, bounded on the less integrated side by confederalism and on the more integrated side by devolution within a unitary state.

The terms federation and confederation refer to similar – yet very different – concepts. In a confederation, states come together creating a loose (often temporary) union for matters of political, economic or administrative convenience. Within a confederation, member states maintain their sovereignty and often appoint a weak central authority to speed up bureaucratic matters. Conversely, states or provinces that join a federation, agree to give up part of their powers and to answer to the central government, which has the power to enforce laws and regulations. In both cases, we are talking about a union of countries, states or provinces, but members of the confederation maintain a large degree of autonomy and independence – and can (almost) freely leave the union when they decide to do so –

while members of a federation are bound to respect the authority of the central government and maintain limited powers.

A federation is a political system in which individual states come together under the umbrella of a central authority. The decision of entering a federation of state can be voluntary, but in most cases, it is the result of a long historic process or the transformation of a confederation (i.e. temporary and voluntary agreement) into a federation. The balance of power between the constituents and the central government is laid out in a written constitution. Provinces and states members of a federation do not entirely lose their power, and can enjoy a certain degree of independence. Individual states can maintain separate laws, traditions and habits, but the central government has authority over:

- Defense and security matters;
- Foreign policy;
- International relations and diplomacy;
- Decision to start or end a war;
- National currency; and
- Military.

A confederation is a system of governance, in which the constituents (states or provinces) come together for political, economic, security or administrative reasons. Entering a confederation is entirely voluntary and depends on the government of every individual state – or on the local authority in the case of provinces. Once entered the confederation, the constituents maintain their sovereignty and their powers (almost entirely), and there is no superior, unified, central government. Depending on the structure of the confederation, there might be a weak central body, appointed by all constituents, created to speed up bureaucratic processes and facilitate communication. In a confederation there is no:

- Unitary budget;

- Common military;
- Common foreign policy strategy;
- Common diplomatic representatives; and
- Common legal system.

Confederalism is a system of organization in which there is a union of states with each member state retaining some independent control over both internal and external affairs. For international purposes there are separate states rather than just one state.

This can be contrasted with a federation, in which there is a union of states with some internal control but external affairs are controlled by a central government, in which the states are represented in a unified manner

The European Union is a type of confederation. It operates common economic policies, there are common laws that enable a single economic market with open internal borders, a common currency but each member also has control over many internal affairs. So, the EU doesn't have exclusive powers over taxation, defiance and foreign affairs. Laws must be transcribed sometimes into national laws by their own parliaments, and decisions by member states require special majorities – with blocking minorities accounted for. Furthermore, treaty amendment requires ratification by all member states before coming into force.

Therefore, academic observers have claimed that the EU would be a fully-fledged federation, but remains a confederation due to the Member States' exclusive power to amend or change the constitutive treaties of the EU, and the EU lacks a real 'tax and spend' capacity as fiscal power is retained by the member states.

For quite a while now, there have been debates in Belgium about the form its state ought to take. According to Article 1 of the Constitution, Belgium "is a federal State composed of Communities and Regions". Many analyses have shown, however, that there are a few so-called "confederal features" to the state system as well. Various political parties, moreover, are calling – or have called – for Belgium to be transformed in the next round of state reforms into a true confederation. But what do the parties hope to achieve through this appeal? Do they use the term "confederalism" in the sense in which it is used in comparative state law? Or are they thinking of something else, a confederalism "Belgian style"? If the latter, what exactly does that consist of? This contribution seeks to bring some conceptual clarity into the debate. The classic theory of confederalism, about which there is widespread consensus among lawyers, is taken as the golden thread. Confederalism is, according to that theory, a relationship between states that agree, in a treaty, to form a confederation in order to work together in a number of different areas. This confederation is not itself a state, but does have its own institutions that represent the participating states. It has a limited number of powers assigned to it in the treaty. In principle such a treaty can also be terminated. In this article, three historical examples of confederation (the United States, Switzerland and Germany) are considered, as well as the few confederations that still exist today. Contemporary Belgium is not one of them. Rather, Belgium today exhibits all the characteristics of a federal state. It is true that the bipartite nature of the country, which is made up chiefly of Flemish and French-speaking citizens, and the mechanisms available to protect the French-speaking minority within the federal institutions (an 'alarm bell' and special majority provisions in Parliament, parity in the cabinet), mean that the decision-making process in Parliament often resembles a negotiation between the representatives of two political communities. To qualify a state system as confederal, however, this is not sufficient. The plans for a future "confederal" Belgium being put forward by the political parties cover a multitude of meanings. They may refer either to a deepening of the current form of federalism (e.g. by allocating most of the powers to the constitutive states or by no longer assigning residual powers to the federal state), or to a form of confederalism in which the constitutive states enjoy the so called "Kompetenz-Kompetenz", and assign various competences to the confederation by means of a treaty. For the sake of clarity in the democratic debate, this contribution calls for greater conceptual orthodoxy.

Dravida Nadu is the name of a proposed sovereign state demanded by the Justice Party led by the founder of the self-respect movement, E.V. Ramasamy Periyar, and the Dravida Munnetra Kazhagam (DMK) led by C. N. Annadurai for the speakers of the Dravidian languages in South India.

Initially, the demand of Dravida Nadu proponents was limited to Tamil-speaking regions, but it was later expanded to include other Indian states with a majority of Dravidian-speakers (Andhra Pradesh, Telangana, Kerala and Karnataka). Some of the proponents also included parts of Ceylon (Sri Lanka),[2] Orissa and Maharashtra. Other names for the proposed sovereign state included "South India", "Deccan Federation" and "Dakshinapath".

The movement for Dravida Nadu was at its height from the 1940s to 1960s, but due to fears of Tamil hegemony, it failed to find any support outside Tamil Nadu. The States Reorganisation Act 1956, which created linguistic States, weakened the demand further. In 1960, the DMK leaders decided to withdraw their demand for a Dravida Nadu from the party programme at a meeting held in the absence of Annadurai. In 1963, the Government of India led by Jawaharlal Nehru, declared secession as an illegal act. As a consequence, Annadurai abandoned the "claim" for Dravida Nadu – now geographically limited to modern Tamil Nadu – completely in 1963.

The concept of Dravida Nadu had its root in the anti-Brahminism movement in Tamil Nadu, whose aim was to end the Brahmin dominance in the Tamil society and government. The early demands of this movement were social equality, and greater power, and control. However, over time, it came to include a separatist movement, demanding a sovereign state for the Tamil people. The major political party backing this movement was the Justice Party, which came to power in the Madras Presidency in 1921.

Since the late 19th century, the anti-Brahmin Tamil leaders had stated that the non-Brahmin Tamils were the original inhabitants of the Tamil-speaking region. The Brahmins, on the other hand, were described not only as oppressors, but even as a foreign power, on par with the British colonial rulers.

The prominent Tamil leader, E. V. Ramasamy (popularly known as "Periyar") stated that the Tamil society was free of any societal divisions before the arrival of Brahmins, whom he described as "Aryan invaders". Ramasamy was an atheist, and considered Indian nationalism as "an atavistic desire to endow the Hindu past on a more durable and contemporary basis". Ramasamy notably remarked that upon seeing a Brahmin and a snake, he would encourage people to attack the Brahmin.

The proponents of Dravida Nadu fabricated elaborate historical anthropologies to support their theory that the Dravidian-speaking areas once had a great non-Brahmin polity and civilization, which had been destroyed by the Aryan conquest and Brahmin hegemony. This led to an idealization of the ancient Tamil society before its contact with the "Aryan race", and led to a surge in Tamil nationalism. Ramasamy expounded the Hindu epic Ramayana as a disguised historical account of how the Aryans subjugated the Tamils ruled by Ravana. Some of the Dravidians also posed Saivism as an indigenous, even non-Hindu religion.

The Indian National Congress, a majority of whose leaders were Brahmins, came to be identified as a Brahmin party. Ramasamy, who had joined Congress in 1919, became disillusioned with what he considered as the Brahmanic leadership of the party. The link between Brahmins and Congress became a target of the growing Tamil nationalism.

In 1925, E.V. Ramasamy launched the Self-respect movement, and by 1930, he was formulating the most radical "anti-Aryanism". The rapport between the Justice Party and the Self-Respect movement of E.V. Ramasamy (who joined the party in 1935) strengthened the anti-Brahmin sentiment. In 1937–38, Hindi and Hindustani were introduced as new subjects in the schools, when C. Rajagopalachari of Congress became the Chief Minister of Madras Presidency. This led to widespread protests in the Tamil-speaking region, which had a strong independent linguistic identity. Ramasamy saw the Congress imposition of Hindi in government schools as further proof of an Aryan conspiracy.

In 1949, Annadurai and other leaders split up and established Dravida Munnetra Kazhagam. Annadurai was initially more radical than Ramasamy in his demand for a separate Dravida Nadu. In highlighting the demand for Dravida Nadu, the economics of exploitation by the Hindi-speaking, Aryan, Brahminical North was elaborated upon. It was contended that Dravida Nadu had been transformed into a virtual marketplace for north Indian products. And, thus, Annadurai explained that to change this situation, a separate Dravida Nadu must be demanded. Throughout the 1940s, E.V.Ramasamy spoke along the lines of a trifurcation of India, that is dividing the existing geographical region into Dravida Nadu, Muslim India (Pakistan), and Aryan Land (Hindustan). In public meetings that he addressed between March and June 1940, he projected the three-nation doctrine as the only solution which could end the political impasse in the country.

In 1950, E.V.Ramasamy stated that Dravida Nadu, if it comes into being, will be a friendly and helpful state to India. When the political power in Tamil Nadu shifted to the non-Brahmin K. Kamaraj in the 1950s, EVR's DK supported the Congress ministry. In the late 1950s and early 1960s, the Dravida Nadu proponents changed their demand for an independent Dravida Nadu to an independent Tamil Nadu, as they did not receive any support from the non-Tamil Dravidian-speaking states. Ramasamy changed the banner in his magazine Viduthalai from "Dravida Nadu for Dravidians" to "Tamil Nadu for Tamils".

The reorganization of the Indian states along linguistic lines through the States Reorganisation Act of 1956 weakened the separatist movement. In June–July 1956, the founder of Kazhagam, E. V. Ramaswamy, declared that he had given up the goal of Dravidistan.

However, by this time, DMK had taken over from DK as the main bearer of the separatist theme. Unlike Khalistan and other separatist movements in the Republic of India, DMK never considered violence as a serious option to achieve a separate Dravida Nadu.

DMK's slogan of Dravida Nadu found no support in any state of India other than Tamil Nadu. The non-Tamil Dravidian speakers perceived the ambitions of the Tamil politicians as hegemonic, ultimately leading to the failure of the Dravida Nadu concept. C. Rajagopalachari, the former Chief Minister of Madras State and a Tamil Brahmin, stated that the DMK plea for Dravida Nadu should not be taken seriously.

Total Central Eastern Region, North Eastern Region, Southern Region Suffering same type of Problem and they missing their identity due to the New Form of Indo-Iranian (Aryan/ Arian) Race that is Hindiana. Enter the Eastern Zone required to form as United Liberal Bharat and rest to form as Hindustan as it is their main identity.

Resolution of World Political Crisis

Valdemar Putin, the member of the United Party of Russian Federation, continued to help terrorist groups around the world and opposed the Liberal Society as it is the history of Russia. In First World War it seen that Russia participated for their own interest to executing agency ruling to different countries and they're after *socialist communist* movement hold on and political dictatorship executing by which in maximum Europeans and Asian countries either assimilated as to formed USSR or supported to political parties competitors or opposition leaders by which *socialist* political dictatorship executing to several nation. Quin *turned* over to China Federation on *help from* Russia and that *became a threat of the world* when by joint venture helping to Islamic conservative Terrorist groups of different Islamic *nations* and terrorist activity spread up *around the world*.

Worldly *thought is required* to *develop* and implement unity in diversity. *The Social* Consulate Confederation and Council system give *the right* path to *development, world* peace and harmony. Live and let live freely *is the aim* of our life and it *requires* the path creation *around the world* by Collaboration and cooperation system to *execute* world peace and harmony. *It is the only* path *to be done* through social *globalization, liberal* social system as manmade and social consulate confederation liberalism only.

By joint venture of Liberal groups of *nations attracted* to Russia and divided to several parts and trans Siberia *must be required* to *make an independent* nation which previously remained under Mongolian *rule* which *was captured* by Rus at Tsar ruled. Actual Rus remained European parts of Rus which extended by captured different Europeans and Asian parts and formed Russia and in 1921 assimilated others nation due to *socialist* movement to formed political dictatorship which called as USSR and later demolish USSR in 1991 and when target to formed as Independent commonwealth but not remained success but Russian federation form by several Autonomous region and Republican assimilation too form Russian Federation Security Council.

Consulate Cooperation Confederation Council

The system required to form equality and minimization of partiality, criticism and avoided racism, fascism, Nazi and hybrid Regimes. When Religious and capitalist make *alliances with political* leaders, Capitalist, Spiritual leaders jointly *steal* national *funds* and hence land mafia, oil mafia, national fund mafia become powerful. As now a days Capitalist Ambani, Adani and some alliance of Narendra Modi and Amit Shah are build up policy that through black hand loan sections and land and national organization transfer name on minimum rate and then loan with tax and interest relief taken as donating to BJP- RSS party fund that national fund, land and property theft by back door that hack government formed. As anti-Nationalist and Antisocial conflict created where rapist getting respects, hooligan remained safe as hippish, mob lynching done through carder of BJP named Hindu mahasava, Bajrang dal and others.

Consulate Cooperation Confederation Council system is by the peoples and for the peoples that liberal system of three phase three stage system where *people's* voting *to be done* for national bill pass which to be justified by expert team and there remain corporate autonomous *bodies* as judiciary, Electoral. Jointly state federal security, central military, border security formed as Security council. The governmental bodies remained as Central, Zonal, Regional, State, Divisions, District, Sector, Urban, Village stages only. Electronic card system required to implement voting through Pin system application.

For Example India is required to divide into two zones as (1) Eastern Zone as Non-Hindi and (2) Western Zone that is Hindi and Allied nearest to Hindi language zone. The Eastern Zone has to be the North Eastern Region, Eastern Central Region and Southern Region. Western Zone should remain the North Western region and North Central Region. Eastern Zone has to be Autonomous Confederation council as United Liberal Bharat Republican and Western Zone Autonomous Confederation as Hindustan Republican.

Zonal Autonomous confederation republicans and Central Cooperation Confederation Council have to form a Security council to make international military regulation for defiance whereas home security should be controlled by alliance of Zonal with regional Security Council. Police security to be used by the state federal governmental system. Jurisdiction also to be reform as well as Bureaucratic administrative distribution should be like as Decentralized Corporate system through Judidiction Council and Bureaucratic Council system remained as Central, Zonal, Regional, State, Divisions, District, Sector, Urban, Village stages only.

For Example India required to divided into four Zones as-

1. *Eastern Zone As East Indian Autonomous Consulate Confederation which has to be two Regions as North-Eastern Region and East-Central Region.*
2. *Southern Zone as Dravidian Autonomous Consulate Confederation which has to be two regions as South Region and South-Central Region.*
3. *Western Zone As West Liberal Autonomous Consulate Confederation which has to be two regions as North-Western Region and South-Western Region.*
4. *Central Zone as Hindustan Autonomous Consulate Confederation which has to be two regionsNorthern region and Central Region.*

On the other hand there have to possibility to formed as Two Autonomous Republicans as -

1. *Hindustan Republican Confederation is to be formed by the Hindi and Allied Hindi Zone where Hindi remained as Official Language and there have to be two regions as Pour Hindi Region as Central belt and Semi-Hindi Region of Western Belt.*
2. *Eastern Indian Alliance Republican Confederation which is Non-Hindi Zone where English remains as official language and three Regions remain as North Eastern Regions, East-Central Region and South Dravidian Region.*

Another Example are as-

1. *Canada which have two zone as English language zone and France language Zone and there have formed discrimination and partiality and hence Canada require to form two autonomous confederation as-*

    (a) English Consulate Confederation and

    (b) Fancies Consulate Confederation

2. *United Kingdom that Great Britain as Central Formed as British Consulate Central Federation that under which remained Four confederations as -*

    (a) England Confederation Republican
    (b) British Ireland Confederation Republican
    (c) Schotland Confederation Republican and
    (d) Wales Confederation Republican

-: End: -

www.ingramcontent.com/pod-product-compliance
Lightning Source LLC
LaVergne TN
LVHW091613070526
838199LV00044B/779